W9-AUK-662

POISONED LOVE

CAITLIN ROTHER

PINNACLE BOOKS
Kensington Publishing Corp.
http://www.kensingtonbooks.com

"A true-crime thriller that will keep you on the edge of your seat. This first-time author has done a brilliant job of capturing the inner workings of a female killer . . . someone who uses her cunning ways to commit murder."

—Aphrodite Jones, *New York Times* best-selling crime author

"Caitlin Rother has written a gripping and chilling book. A tawdry and twisted story of sex and drugs, deception and murder. And here's the scariest part—it's all true."

—Tom Murray, producer for *Pretty Poison*, Court TV's documentary on the Rossum case

"Absorbing and impeccably researched, *Poisoned Love* is classic California noir, a story of passion and betrayal and death, with a beautiful, scheming adulteress at the center of the web."

—John Taylor, author of *The Count and The Confession: A True Mystery.*

"*Poisoned Love* chillingly illustrates how Kristin Rossum and others refused to accept responsibility for their behavior and choices. Caitlin Rother paints a portrait of the culture that raised Kristin, hired her, was lured by her beauty, and now must share in the dire consequences."

—Kevin Barry, producer for *The Kristin Rossum Story* on Oprah Winfrey's Oxygen Network.

"*Poisoned Love* is a concise and riveting account of one of the most challenging but fascinating investigations of my police career. Reading Rother's book brought back the many exhausting hours, effort, and stress I lived and breathed for close to two years in bringing this case to trial. Time's passage sometimes changes a person's convictions. *Poisoned Love* reaffirms my belief that justice was served."

—Laurie Agnew, San Diego Police Department homicide detective

CAST OF CHARACTERS

ROSSUM FAMILY
Kristin Rossum, oldest child
Ralph Rossum, father
Constance Rossum, mother
Brent Rossum, middle child
Pierce Rossum, youngest child

DE VILLERS FAMILY
Greg T. de Villers, oldest brother and Kristin's husband
Jerome T. de Villers, middle brother
Bertrand T. de Villers, youngest brother
Yves T. de Villers, father
Marie T. de Villers, mother

SAN DIEGO POLICE DEPARTMENT
Detective Laurie Agnew, lead detective on the case
Sergeant Howard Williams, Agnew's boss
Detective Jimmy Valle
Detective Felix Zavala
Detective Lynn Rydalch
Detective George "Randy" Alldredge

UCSD CAMPUS POLICE
Detective Sergeant Bob Jones
Officer Edward "Scott" Garcia
Officer Bill MacIntyre
Officer Karen Scofield

PROSECUTION TEAM
Deputy District Attorney Dan Goldstein
Deputy District Attorney Dave Hendren
Frank Eaton, investigator
Meredith Dent, paralegal
District Attorney Paul Pfingst

DEFENSE ATTORNEYS
Deputy Public Defender Alex Loebig, Kristin's criminal
attorney
Deputy Public Defender Vic Eriksen, Kristin's criminal
attorney
Michael Pancer, private attorney
Gretchen von Helms, fill-in attorney for Pancer

JUDGES
Superior Court Judge John Thompson, criminal trial judge
Superior Court Judge John S. Meyer, civil trial judge

REGIONAL COMPUTER FORENSIC LABORATORY
Bob Petrachek, examiner

MEDICAL EXAMINER'S OFFICE
Dr. Brian Blackbourne, chief medical examiner
Lloyd Amborn, office administrator
Michael Robertson, Kristin's married lover and boss in
toxicology lab
Donald "Russ" Lowe, toxicologist, did drug audits
Angie Wagner, investigator on Greg's case
Frank Barnhart, Kristin's friend and mentor, later changed
jobs to sheriff's crime lab
Cathy Hamm, toxicologist
Ray Gary, toxicologist
Dr. Harry Bonnell, pathologist
Bob Sutton, manager of autopsy exam room

KRISTIN'S FRIENDS/ADVOCATES
Melissa Prager, high school friend
Chris Elliott, friend
Rick Hogrefe, head of TriLink Biotechnologies
Kelly Christianson, Kristin's lab manager at TriLink
Claire Becker, Kristin's coworker at TriLink
Jessica Vanella, Kristin's coworker at TriLink
Kathy Vanella, Jessica's mother, took Kristin in before trial

GREG'S FRIENDS/ADVOCATES
Bill Leger, high school friend
Aaron Wallo, high school friend
Christian Colantoni, high school friend
Stefan Gruenwald, his boss at Orbigen
Terry Huang, office manager at Orbigen

MICHAEL'S ASSOCIATES
Nicole Robertson, Michael's wife
Dan Anderson, supervising toxicologist in Los Angeles
County coroner's office
Chuck Goldberg, Michael's criminal attorney

ATTORNEYS FOR APPEAL
Lynda Romero, Kristin's criminal appellate attorney
Deputy Attorney General Niki Shaffer, state's appellate
attorney

ATTORNEYS IN CIVIL CASE
Craig McClellan, de Villers family's attorney
John Gomez, de Villers family's attorney
Cindy Lane, de Villers family's attorney
Michael Gardiner, Michael Robertson's attorney
Walter Tribbey, Kristin's attorney
Deborah McCarthy, attorney for San Diego County

Chapter 1

It was a Monday morning, November 6, 2000, when Stefan Gruenwald pulled up to the building his small biotech company shared with three others. He was surprised to see that his licensing manager wasn't at his desk, making calls.

Typically, Greg de Villers had already started his day by the time his boss arrived. He was a dependable guy. Meticulous, diligent, and a team player to boot. Gruenwald had known Greg since he'd hired him several years earlier at another biotech company. After Gruenwald left to start his own business, he lured Greg away to work for him.

Greg was one of only eight employees at Orbigen, so it didn't take long for Gruenwald to poke his head in each office to ask if anyone had seen Greg that morning. They hadn't. Greg was rarely late, and when he was, he always called to let Gruenwald know. He'd never missed a day of work without calling.

Gruenwald wondered if Greg was having car problems. Maybe he'd broken down somewhere. Greg had no cell phone, so around 10:10 A.M., Gruenwald called the apartment in the San Diego neighborhood of University City, where Greg lived with Kristin Rossum, his pretty, petite, blond wife of seventeen months. He let it ring for a while. But no one picked up.

Although Greg tended not to socialize with his coworkers after hours, he did drink a Coke or a beer with them at the occasional TGIF gatherings, and Gruenwald had worked with him long enough to feel that he knew Greg pretty well. Greg had good manners and was liked by his colleagues, who thought he was a nice guy and a bit of a health nut. He'd gone on a fishing trip with them to Mexico once but said he was anxious to get home to Kristin rather than go out for drinks on the way back. She, his two brothers, and the small circle of close friends he'd made over the years were the people with whom he liked to spend his spare time.

Greg wasn't the kind of outgoing guy who got noticed in a crowd for his strong personality. He was more of an easygoing, middle-of-the-road kind of guy, a little on the shy side around new people and somewhat soft-spoken. Kristin, on the other hand, had more of an allure, especially when it came to men. Greg really seemed to be in love with her, always rushing home to eat one of her special dinners and watch a video. The only time Gruenwald had seen Greg stay late at the office was the week in early October, when Kristin went to a conference in Milwaukee. Kristin worked as a toxicologist at the San Diego County Medical Examiner's Office, where she conducted tests to determine what drugs may have caused suspicious or sudden deaths.

Gruenwald met Kristin at a company Christmas party before she and Greg were married in June 1999, and they'd all gone out for drinks afterwards. She seemed nice. A little flirtatious, but funny, outgoing, and very intelligent. She and Greg seemed to get along well, and they looked good together. Recently, Greg had asked Gruenwald to keep an ear out for a new job for Kristin. He'd also talked about having Orbigen help him go to law school so he could become a patent attorney for the company. In a year or two, once

Orbigen got off the ground, Gruenwald told him, "We can definitely do that."

When Greg still hadn't shown up by eleven o'clock, office manager Terry Huang was getting concerned as well. Nearly three hours late without calling—it was so unlike Greg. Huang tried reaching him at his apartment around 11:15 but got no answer. It just rang and rang. Huang and Gruenwald shared their unease a few hours later and tried calling Greg again from Huang's office. Still no response.

By this point, Gruenwald was worried enough to wonder whether he should go over there. Greg lived only ten minutes away. But he got lost in his work and never made it out of the office.

By 5 P.M., Gruenwald figured Greg must've had a family emergency. The previous week, he'd worked a half day on Thursday so he could deal with a family problem, and he left a little early on Friday to meet up with his in-laws. Maybe the problem had gotten out of hand. Greg also hadn't been feeling well the week before. The previous Monday morning, he came to the office feeling crummy and told a coworker that he'd thrown up after drinking only a couple of beers that weekend. Not to mention he seemed unusually agitated all week. Especially on Friday.

At 5:40 P.M., Huang and Gruenwald huddled together and tried calling Greg again on the speakerphone. There was still no answer. They were quite befuddled.

Huang tried once more around 7 P.M., just before leaving the office, and this time Kristin picked up. He asked to speak to Greg, but Kristin said he was sleeping. Huang asked if everything was all right, because Greg hadn't come to work that day. Kristin said she'd phoned Orbigen that morning and left a message saying Greg wasn't feeling well and wouldn't be coming in. Didn't they get it? She apologized if no one received the message. Kristin thanked him for calling and hung up.

The call left Huang feeling uneasy. He sensed a strange edge to Kristin's voice. She seemed unresponsive, like she wanted to get off the phone. He wondered why she wouldn't let him talk to Greg. Why, if Greg was home all day, didn't he pick up the phone? And why didn't anyone at Orbigen get the message Kristin said she left?

Gruenwald called Greg's apartment once more as well, around 9:30 P.M. A frazzled Kristin answered on the first ring. She was crying, and he could hardly understand her.

"Greg isn't feeling well, and the ambulance is here. I really can't talk," she said. "I'll call you back."

Gruenwald waited until 1 A.M. to hear back from her. Still troubled, he finally gave up and went to bed.

Paramedic Sean Jordan and his assistant, April Butler, had just finished a quick dinner at Rubio's, a fish taco restaurant, when they got a call at 9:23 P.M.: young male down, not breathing and no pulse. They were only a mile or two from the address on Regents Road. With the ambulance siren blaring and red lights flashing, they sped down Torrey Pines Road and arrived three minutes later.

The University of California, San Diego (UCSD) had purchased the La Jolla Del Sol complex about a year earlier as off-campus housing, so the 911 call went first to the campus police dispatch center.

"My husband is not breathing," Kristin told the dispatcher.

The UCSD dispatcher transferred Kristin to the city of San Diego's fire-medical dispatcher, who stayed on the phone with her until the paramedics were inside her apartment. The Del Sol security guard was also alerted about the 911 call, so he'd already opened the gate for Jordan and Butler by the time they pulled up to the red-tiled driveway.

Balconies with gray railings lined the mocha-colored buildings of Del Sol, which blended into the sea of residential towers in north University City, a densely populated neighborhood of college students and young professionals who worked at UCSD or the biotech, high-tech, and finance companies nearby. The area, dubbed "the Golden Triangle" because it was contained by three intersecting freeways, had grown up first around the university and then, during the late 1970s, around University Towne Center, a shopping mall. Apartment or condo complexes sprang up and filled up, followed by office and medical buildings, restaurants, bars, and gyms, until virtually every lot was developed. Many of the local professors, doctors, lawyers, and real estate developers lived a couple of miles to the west in the older and more affluent coastal community of La Jolla.

Jordan and Butler carried their gear up the stairs to the second-floor apartment, where they found Kristin standing in the living room, crying and talking to the dispatcher on a cordless phone. She motioned them to the bedroom, where Greg was lying on the floor, flat on his back and framed by an unmade queen-size bed to the left, a chest of three long drawers to the right, and a taller six-drawer bureau above his head. His slim, six-foot, 160-pound body was dressed in pajama bottoms and a T-shirt. His skin was pale, and his lips were blue around the edges. Red rose petals were scattered on the carpet around his upper torso, with a single stem and stamen lying between his head, the bureau, and a princess phone. Jordan started setting up next to Greg's left arm. Butler tripped over the comforter as she squeezed into position between Greg's head and the bureau, setting aside an unframed wedding photo of the couple, which had been propped up against the base of the bureau, as if someone had positioned it just so.

Greg looked a little nervous in the photo. He smiled for the camera with a quiet contentment, all dressed up in his tuxedo and striped cravat, his dark brown hair slicked back and his blue eyes shining. Kristin looked radiant, her shiny blond locks pulled up under a white-flowered tiara and a veil trailing down her back. She wore a string of pearls with her white dress, which had short lace sleeves that covered her shoulders, and she held a bouquet of pink and white flowers tied with bows of ribbon. They both seemed so very happy as Greg declared his supreme devotion to her in front of their friends and family.

In all the commotion, the wedding photo got moved to the top of the chest on Greg's right side, next to a blue plastic cup of clear, odorless liquid that looked like water. An open bottle of aspirin that contained about a quarter of its original two hundred tablets sat atop the bureau behind Butler. And a yellow cup, also containing clear, odorless liquid, rested on a nightstand on the opposite side of the bed.

Several campus police officers arrived just before paramedic Joe Preciado rode up on a fire engine and joined Butler and Jordan in trying to resuscitate Greg. Apart from the fact that their twenty-six-year-old patient looked too young and healthy to have a heart attack from natural causes, something else seemed odd to Preciado. Initially, he thought the red blotches on the beige carpet were smudges of wet blood. But when he kneeled down on Greg's right side, the smudges moved. He was dumbfounded. What were red rose petals doing all over the floor?

It was a scene right out of that movie *American Beauty*, where Kevin Spacey is lying on his back in bed, fantasizing in a dreamlike state, and red rose petals slowly float down from the ceiling and cover his body.

Jordan checked for a pulse but found none. Greg felt warm to the touch, as if he'd recently taken his last breath. Jordan took a quick scan of the bedroom, looking for clues to explain what Greg might have taken. But he saw no prescription pill vials, no syringes, no sign of illegal drug use, nothing that looked out of place, and no suicide note. He and Preciado asked Kristin if her husband had any medical problems or was taking any medications.

"Not that I know of," she told them, though at one point she brought out a bottle of Vicodin from the bathroom.

Greg's pupils were fixed and dilated, but Jordan was determined to make every effort to bring him back. Jordan intubated Greg, then Butler hooked up the breathing bag and rhythmically squeezed air into his lungs. The heart monitor registered a flat line. With Greg's heart refusing to pump blood through his veins, Preciado tried but found it virtually impossible to get a needle into Greg's right arm. Jordan had more luck with the other arm, though he had to try a couple times before he got the needle in.

Jordan tried everything in his drug box that might get Greg's heart beating again. Atropine. Epinephrine. A pure sugar substance usually given to diabetics. And finally, 2 mg of Narcan, which reverses the effects of opiates, just in case Greg had overdosed on one. But nothing worked.

Jordan rolled Greg's body over to slide him onto a backboard for transport to the nearest hospital. That was when he saw the purple marks of lividity on Greg's back and buttocks, a sign that the heart had ceased to beat and gravity was causing blood to pool in areas closest to the ground. There were no rose petals under his body.

At 10:03 P.M., Jordan and Butler carried their patient down the stairs to their ambulance and drove him to Scripps Memorial Hospital La Jolla, about four minutes away. One of the campus police officers followed, with Kristin in his cruiser. The emergency room doctor tried again to revive Greg, but he was gone. Greg was officially declared dead at 10:19 P.M., six days before his twenty-seventh birthday.

* * *

Kristin called her boss, a handsome, thirty-one-year-old Australian toxicologist, as soon as she got to the hospital and asked him to join her there. Two minutes later, she called her parents, crying. Her father answered the phone.

"Daddy, Greg stopped breathing," she said. "I'm so scared."

Ralph Rossum said he would meet her at the hospital as quickly as he could, handed the phone to his wife, Constance, and ran out to the car. Kristin spoke briefly to her mother, explaining that Greg was in intensive care.

Kristin's boss, Michael Robertson, arrived at the hospital about fifteen minutes later. While they were in the waiting area together, he put his arm around her, comforted her, and held her hand. The nurses thought he seemed like a very supportive supervisor.

Kristin was still crying, but she was able to answer the ER nurse's questions about Greg's medical history and what drugs he might have taken. Kristin said he might have used some old prescriptions she'd purchased in Tijuana five years earlier, when she'd been trying to get off crystal methamphetamine. Then, the nurse told her the bad news. They'd tried again to resuscitate her husband, but they couldn't get him back.

Kristin's mother got a call at 10:49 P.M. from Michael, who introduced himself as Kristin's boss, and they talked for about ten minutes. He said Kristin was cold standing there in her pajamas, and he wondered what to do. Constance thanked him and suggested he drive Kristin back to the apartment. Kristin's father was on his way down to meet her at the hospital, but he would figure out where to go.

After allowing the news of Greg's death to settle in, a social worker approached Kristin about tissue donation. Greg had decided to join Kristin as an organ and tissue donor about two weeks earlier, when he'd renewed his driver's license, but because his heart had already stopped, his organs couldn't be harvested. However, some of his skin could be used to help burn victims; his corneas, veins, and heart valves could be transplanted into needy recipients; and some of his bones could be saved as well. At 11:30 P.M., Kristin signed the necessary paperwork and then headed home with her boss.

Earlier that night, Constance phoned Greg's mother, Marie, to tell her Greg was being taken to the emergency room after having a bad reaction to cough syrup and some other medication.

Marie called the hospital to see if she could learn more. But since Marie was home alone, the nurse said she'd have to call her back. Marie immediately called Jerome, the oldest of Greg's younger brothers, with the upsetting news.

Jerome tried calling Scripps himself, but he, too, was home alone, so the nurse told him to go to his mother's and call back from there. Why wouldn't she just tell him what was going on? Jerome drove to Marie's condo in Thousand Oaks and called Constance to see if he could get some better information. She didn't know anything more and promised that Ralph would call them from the hospital with any new developments.

But Jerome couldn't wait for that. He wanted to know what happened, and he couldn't understand why no one would tell him. He called the hospital again, and this time the nurse asked if the sheriff's deputy had arrived. "No," he said, so she put him on hold to talk to the deputy, who was coming to deliver the bad news in person. Marie, who was sitting by the window, saw a Ventura County sheriff's cruiser pull up outside. The nurse got back on the line with Jerome, but he was so insistent that she went ahead and told him that Greg had "expired" before the deputy made it to the front door.

Jerome couldn't believe it. How was this possible? He'd

spoken to his brother only a few days earlier. Greg had
called while Jerome was watching a DVD on Alaska, and he
was too tired to talk, so he put Greg off and promised to call
him back. Unfortunately, he never got around to it.

Marie was beside herself. A chronic smoker and an asthmatic since childhood, she'd had part of a lung removed, and
now she was sobbing so hard she could barely breathe. Jerome
was upset and he was scared. He didn't want to lose his
mother, too. Now the oldest of Marie's sons, Jerome tried to
comfort her while he called his other brother, Bertrand, and
told him to meet them at their mother's in Thousand Oaks.
Bertrand, who lived about forty-five minutes south, near the
University of California, Los Angeles, started crying and
said he'd come as soon as he could. He was so emotional that
his roommate decided to take the wheel and drive Bertrand to
his mother's.

When they arrived around 11 P.M., Marie and Jerome
were still waiting for more definitive answers. But they never
came. So, the family spent the night together, wracked with
grief and confusion, asking each other questions and trying,
unsuccessfully, to make sense of it all.

Jerome figured that now was the time to tell Marie that
Kristin—the only one of her sons' girlfriends she'd ever really
accepted—was a former methamphetamine user. But when
Jerome raised the question of whether Kristin might have
had something to do with Greg's death, Bertrand said he was
talking crazy. Marie, who loved Kristin like a daughter,
wouldn't hear of it. There had to be a rational explanation.

UCSD Detective Sergeant Bob Jones met Kristin and
Michael on the landing in front of her apartment when they
returned from the hospital around 11:45 P.M. It was understood that Michael should stay outside while Jones picked
up the interview with Kristin where his officers had left off.

Sitting at the dining-room table, Jones asked Kristin to tell him what happened.

She told Jones that she and Greg had been fighting all weekend. It started on Thursday, she said, when she announced that she was moving out. They'd had dinner with her parents on Friday, spent Saturday night together, and then, on Sunday night, Greg, still upset, had taken some of her old prescriptions to help him sleep. He'd been sleeping all day on Monday, in fact. Her lab was only fifteen minutes away, so she came home a number of times to check on him. Each time she'd found him breathing—a little loudly at times—but otherwise he seemed fine.

Kristin said they'd had some soup together around lunchtime, and that's when he told her he'd taken some of her old oxycodone and clonazepam. Oxycodone is a narcotic painkiller similar to Vicodin. Clonazepam, a sedative and also a narcotic, is classified as a date rape drug.

She told Jones she'd run some errands after work and then came home to take a long bath and a shower. She was about to get into bed sometime around nine o'clock, when she leaned over to kiss Greg. His forehead was cold, and he wasn't breathing, so she called 911. The dispatcher told her to pull Greg off the bed and onto the floor, so that he was flat on his back and she could start doing CPR. Kristin wasn't sure she'd be strong enough to get him off the bed by herself, but the dispatcher insisted. She pulled back the covers so she could turn him sideways, and that's when she saw the rose petals all over his chest and their wedding photo under his pillow.

Jones asked her about the shredded letter he'd found in a plastic ziplock bag on the dining-room table. Kristin said Greg found it on Thursday and got angry, so she put it through the shredder, but he'd been trying to piece it back together with tape. Jones took the letter as evidence, along with a note in Kristin's handwriting that one of his officers found in the kitchen. Signed with a heart and Kristin's first initial, it said: "Hi, sleepy. Hope you feel better. I'm out to get a wedding gift," and told him there were leftovers in the fridge. Jones didn't take Kristin's diary, which an officer found lying on the coffee table.

Ralph Rossum arrived at the apartment around midnight, after stopping first at the hospital, where the social worker notified him of Greg's death. He joined his daughter and Jones at the dining-room table.

Angie Wagner, an investigator colleague of Kristin's at the Medical Examiner's Office, showed up around 1 A.M. By then, Kristin was sitting on the couch in the living room. Wagner didn't know her very well. In fact, she hadn't even known Kristin was married. Wagner asked Kristin her own series of questions for her report.

After all the interviews were over, Michael left, and Ralph helped his daughter into his car to start the difficult drive back to Claremont. Kristin's hair was a mess, her face was puffy, and her eyes were swollen from crying all night.

"I've lost my Greggy," she told him. "I've lost my best friend."

It was about 1:40 A.M. The investigators saw no reason to disbelieve Kristin's story. There were no broken doorjambs and no sign of a struggle. They left the apartment, thinking it was probably a suicide.

Stefan Gruenwald arrived at Orbigen on Tuesday around 9:45 A.M. and scanned the parking lot for Greg's car. It wasn't there, so he headed inside, intending to call Greg's apartment first thing. But before Gruenwald even got to his desk, his assistant told him there was a phone call for him in his office.

"Who is it?" he asked.

"I don't know—a Mike Robertson," she said. "It's about Greg."

Michael Robertson introduced himself as Kristin's boss and told Gruenwald that something had happened to Greg. He gave Gruenwald the Rossums' phone number in Claremont and asked him to call them right away. Michael said he couldn't answer any questions and deferred to the Rossums.

Gruenwald called the number and got Constance Rossum. She said Greg had passed away the night before.

"What happened?" he asked, in disbelief.

Constance said Greg had experienced flu-like symptoms over the weekend, so he started taking cough syrup with some other drugs on Saturday and continued on Sunday. He must have had an allergic reaction, she said.

That sounded odd to Gruenwald, who'd earned a medical degree and a Ph.D. back in Frankfurt, Germany, and had spent some time doing forensics work. If someone was going to have an allergic reaction, he thought, it would develop right away, not two days later. He didn't say anything to Constance at the time, but he thought the story sounded suspicious. Gruenwald called back a few hours later so he could talk to Kristin directly.

"I can't believe what happened," he said. "He was such a good person."

Kristin was crying. She agreed and said she couldn't believe it, either. But from there, he said, the story changed. This time Kristin described Greg's death as more of an overdose, perhaps an accidental one.

An overdose? Gruenwald had never seen Greg drunk, let alone under the influence of any drugs. He wouldn't even go near the lab at Orbigen, which was used mostly for cancer research. Gruenwald had once asked Greg to help clean out the storage room, where they kept hundreds of containers of chemicals, but he refused, saying he didn't want to touch them. Greg was much more comfortable with the business side of things. So, for Gruenwald, the idea of Greg dying from a drug overdose, even accidentally, just didn't ring true.

Jerome de Villers felt the same way. Greg wasn't the kind of guy to do or take too much of anything, and now he was dead. It just didn't make sense. His head was jumbled with questions: Where did Greg get the medication that killed him? Did Kristin give it to him? Did Kristin have drugs in the apartment? Were they were doing drugs together and something went wrong?

He dismissed the last scenario because he remembered it wasn't that long ago that Greg wouldn't even take the anti-histamines Marie offered him for his stuffy nose. Jerome, an insurance investigator, was determined to find out from Kristin—and whomever else he had to ask—exactly what happened to his brother and why.

Chapter 2

Kristin Margrethe Rossum, the eldest child of two driven and accomplished Midwestern parents, was raised with the pressures to perform and to succeed, almost from the very start. At an early age, they instilled in her the importance of image and appearances, which no doubt contributed to the perfectionism she described in her diary years later.

"It was always obvious to me that I was expected to do well in school," she wrote. "I wanted to make my parents proud of me. I wanted to be the best in everything I did. I wanted to be perfect. For the most part, I excelled at everything I tried."

But this sense of self-confidence was vulnerable to other forces at work in her psyche. At times, she wrote, she found herself "torn between sound, logical ideas and unreasonable, unattainable ideals. It's an interesting internal conflict."

That conflict was perpetuated by a persistent inner voice that criticized the way she looked in the mirror. She thought her legs and arms were strong and she had an attractive face. But her butt was rounder than she liked, her inner thighs were a little too flabby, her stomach wasn't flat enough, and her arms could be more toned. "At 5 feet, 2 ¼ inches tall," she wrote, she was "vertically challenged. OK, SHORT!!!"

"I continue to feel dissatisfied with my body, because I don't think it's perfect," she wrote. But, she added, "I guess that my belief is that it is within my power to control the shape of my body. Therefore, if I am dissatisfied with my body, it is only the result of my own failings."

It's possible that this drive to be perfect grew so overwhelming at times that her only relief came from getting high. One friend said Kristin's addictive relationship with methamphetamine may have been the only part of her life that Kristin saw as her own, separate from the parents who had such a strong influence on her. And people high on meth don't think or act rationally.

Kristin came into the world on October 25, 1976, in Memphis, Tennessee, where her father was a political science professor and her mother was a marketing researcher. Kristin's brother Brent was born in nearby Germantown about three years later, and Pierce, the youngest, about four years after that.

As Kristin and her brothers were growing up, they moved around the country as their parents' careers progressed. Sometimes, Kristin said, her mother "would hold down the fort" when her father had to leave town for a professional opportunity elsewhere.

When Kristin was four or five, the Rossums moved to Wilmette, a suburb on the north shore of Chicago, where she saw a lot of her extended family. She and her mother would take the train into the city to watch a performance of *The Nutcracker* or go Christmas shopping at Marshall Field's.

The focus on her outward appearance started when she was very young. When she was four, her parents arranged for Kristin to have a commercial head shot taken. The photographer sat her at the piano, laid one of her little hands on the keys, and told her to turn and smile. Her straight, shoulder-length blond hair was pulled back with a barrette, and she wore a tent dress with a tiny white collar and embroidered flowers that covered her legs. She was three feet three inches tall, weighed thirty-four pounds, and wore a size 4 to 4T dress.

In a head shot taken two years later, in December 1982, she'd grown in confidence and dress size. This time her big, hypnotic green eyes stared straight into the camera. She was simply beguiling.

On the back of the photo, along with her particulars, she was featured in five different poses, illustrating her versatility and ability to switch from mood to mood and from one outfit to another. She was goofy in one, serious or playful in the others, wearing a dark leotard and white tights, a sailor suit, or a button-up shirt with a sweater tied around her neck, clutching a handful of daises or holding a balloon on a string. In one shot, she feigned surprise as she pretended to read one of the *Madeline* children's books, glasses perched on her head, her mouth and eyes agape.

The pretty, towheaded girl worked as a model for Marshall Field's, Sears, McDonald's, and Montgomery Ward. She was a natural. She wore a standard size 6X dress, and the camera loved her.

Kristin gave up modeling for ballet the following year, when the family moved to Bethesda, Maryland, and her father took a job as a deputy director of the Bureau of Justice Statistics at the U.S. Department of Justice. He worked for the Bureau—the national repository for crime statistics collected by government and law enforcement agencies—in 1983 and 1984, during the Reagan administration.

Six-year-old Kristin began training at the Maryland Youth Ballet Academy, where she proved to be quite a talented little dancer. She was chosen for a walk-on role as a page in the Joffrey Ballet's performance of *Romeo and Juliet,* reveling in the honor of being backstage at the Kennedy Center in Washington, D.C. Years later she wrote in her diary that the powerful Prokofiev score touched her to the core and remained one of her favorites.

"There is so much passion in his notes," she wrote.

Around that time, she also began to discover a love for science. And the academic pressures soon began to mount.

Ralph Rossum relocated to Claremont, California, in 1984, when he was granted tenure as a faculty member at Claremont McKenna College. He stayed for one semester, then spent some time working on a grant in Washington, D.C., where his wife, Constance, was a marketing manager for the Marriott Corporation. By June 1985, the family had reunited in Claremont, a small enclave of primarily white, highly educated residents. This community would serve as the family's base in the years to come.

The fourteen-square-mile city is located about thirty miles east of downtown Los Angeles. In 2000 it had a population of 34,000 and a median income of about $70,000. Known for its tree-lined streets and small-town feel, Claremont generally houses about five thousand students and professors associated with the eight institutions of higher learning in the area. Of those, seven are within the city's limits and are collectively its largest employer: Claremont McKenna College, Pomona College, Pitzer College, Scripps College, Harvey Mudd College, Claremont Graduate University, and the Claremont School of Theology. Azusa Pacific University, a small evangelical Christian university where Constance Rossum was director of nonprofit graduate programs and a professor of marketing and management, is ten miles away.

One resident once likened Claremont to the community depicted in the movie *Pleasantville*, where residents live a 1950s lifestyle in black and white until two modern teenagers introduce art, literature, sex, independent thought, and a symbolic sense of color to a town previously unaware that life existed beyond its boundaries.

"People feel reasonably safe here," said Lieutenant Stan Van Horn, who headed the Claremont Police Department's detective bureau in 2004.

Van Horn said the city's crime rate was pretty low, averaging one homicide every four or five years, which left police officers with plenty of time to deal with low-level crimes like vandalism and high school kids partying on weekends. His department's philosophy on crime fighting was as follows: "If you can take care of the small stuff, it doesn't develop into larger problems."

Kristin's parents passed their work ethic onto their children and drew them into the academic world early on.

In the summer of 1988, Kristin posed with her professor father for the cover of Claremont McKenna's campus magazine, *Profile*. With their heads together and her arms wrapped around his neck, they looked happy, almost serene. But unlike his daughter, Ralph did not grow up around parents with such academic drive, let alone the money to pay for it.

Raised on a small dairy farm in Alexandria, Minnesota, Ralph was the only member of his extended family to graduate from college. His father's education ended with the eighth grade, and his mother's with high school. Since his parents weren't able to pay his tuition, he had to qualify for scholarships and work to make up the difference. In 1968, he graduated *summa cum laude* from Concordia College, a four-year liberal arts institution in Minnesota associated with the Evangelical Lutheran Church in America.

The first academic job listed on his ten-page curriculum vitae is instructor of behavioral sciences in the City Colleges of Chicago's Department of Police Academy Services, where he started working in 1970. He earned his master's degree from the University of Chicago in 1971, married Constance in 1972, and by 1973 had obtained his Ph.D. Over the course of his career, he held high-ranking academic and administrative positions in California, Louisiana, Iowa, Illinois, Virginia, and Tennessee.

In 2004 Ralph was still a professor of political philosophy and American constitutionalism at Claremont McKenna, where he also served as director of its Rose Institute of State and Local Government.

Ralph appears to have taken the academic community's motto—"publish or perish"—to heart. In 2004, his curriculum vitae included seven books he wrote or coauthored, as well as dozens of articles and book chapters. A number of his writings focus on the jurisprudence of Antonin Scalia, a conservative Republican on the U.S. Supreme Court and a Reagan appointee. Ralph team-taught a class with Scalia at the University of Aix-Marseille III Law School in Aix-en-Provence, France.

Constance, who was raised in Indiana, was no slouch herself. She studied radio and television journalism as an undergraduate and journalism again in graduate school at Indiana University in Bloomington. She earned a master's degree in management from Claremont Graduate University, where she went on to earn her Ph.D. in education and management.

With her background, Constance was able to straddle the worlds of academia and business, starting her own consulting firm, Management Directives, in 1991, after working twenty years in advertising, marketing/management, and consumer research for major companies, such as Procter & Gamble, United Airlines, McDonald's, and the Marriott Corporation. She has taught at various public and private colleges, including Azusa Pacific University; the University of California, Riverside; and California State University at San Bernardino. She also has been involved with a New York–based group called the Leader to Leader Institute, which helps nonprofit groups perform effectively. She and her husband have coauthored books and articles on topics such as constitutional law.

By the time Kristin was nine or ten, she was taking her dance classes seriously. As the years went on, she split her after-school time between ballet and homework, earning straight A's.

Her bent toward perfectionism also influenced her dancing. She wrote in her diary years later that at twelve or thirteen, she began to feel "hypercritical" of her abilities, her technique, and her own physical limitations. "I wanted so badly to be the best—the prima ballerina," she wrote. "The girls with high arches, long legs, and a flexible back . . . [They] had physical traits I so desperately wanted."

She'd just turned fourteen and was a freshman in high school when her talents had progressed enough to land her a coveted role in *The Nutcracker* with the Forum Dance Ensemble in neighboring Orange County. She was supposed to be an understudy, but when the star ballerina got sick, Kristin ended up with the role of the Sugar Plum Fairy, dancing with a professional cavalier from the Houston Ballet.

Her father drove her to and from rehearsals in Anaheim every afternoon, a thirty-two-mile drive each way. Kristin sensed that Ralph got a little frustrated when the hours-long sessions ran late, as they often did, but he remained supportive of her efforts. He felt a deep pride when he watched her dance. She had such a passion for it.

Kristin was popular at Claremont High School, where her dancing skills were well known among her classmates. Her fellow students thought Kristin, who always seemed to be smiling, had a sweet nature. She was the model student.

As a freshman, Kristin briefly dated a junior named Chris

Elliott, the son of family friends who used to baby-sit her little brothers while Kristin was at ballet practice. Chris's father also taught at Claremont McKenna. The two teenagers first met when Kristin was thirteen and Chris was seventeen. Chris was impressed that Kristin was such a high achiever, dancing even when she had a 102-degree fever and focusing so intensely on her ballet rather than just hanging out after school. All her friends were "bunheads," as her mother called them—dancers who wore their hair up in a bun.

In 1991 Kristin auditioned for a spot in a prestigious summer program with the Boston Ballet. She got it and spent the summer back east.

That fall, Ralph took a job as president of Hampden-Sydney College, a private liberal arts school in southern Virginia. Kristin enrolled at an Episcopalian boarding school for girls about sixty miles away so she could dance with a troupe in Richmond. She and Chris wrote letters to each other while she was away. She took a bad fall that year, when a fellow dancer dropped her. She tore several ligaments and had to wear an ankle cast for nearly two months. She reinjured her leg a few months later, and by the time she healed, she'd lost the calluses on her toes that allowed her to go *en pointe*. She also developed a stress fracture that wouldn't heal. She grew frustrated and quit.

Kristin began experimenting with drugs and alcohol around that time—mostly beer and marijuana, though she didn't much care for pot because "it didn't do anything." She also developed a fondness for cigarettes and would turn to them again later in life when under stress.

Her father remembered Kristin leaving Claremont as a girl in 1991 and returning from Virginia as a woman, just before the start of her junior year in 1992.

Ralph returned to Claremont McKenna to teach constitutional law, and Constance transferred within Marriott to a job as director of marketing. The family was happy and healthy, and everything seemed to be going along swimmingly.

"Frankly, we thought we were blessed with three lovely children," Constance said.

Although ballerinas typically are self-conscious about their bodies, Kristin, who usually weighed between 100 and 110 pounds, took this concern to a new level, often taking laxatives and diet pills to make her small frame look even smaller.

"For some reason, she thought she was fat," Constance said. "I don't understand that."

After Kristin stopped dancing, Constance noticed a sadness in her daughter that she didn't recognize.

"She just didn't seem like our Kristin," she said. "I thought it was the sixteen-year-old teenage angst. . . . Her grades were still very good."

Kristin's brothers also started noticing that something was different. She was exhibiting strange behavior and staying up late at night. One day they found a pipe and a small mirror in the house and showed them to Constance. Naïve and unaware that these items were drug paraphernalia, Constance had no clue what her daughter was up to.

Kristin had always excelled in school, so when she began turning in her homework late, her parents felt something must be wrong. When they asked what was going on, she told them everything was fine. She'd do better next time. Ralph encouraged Constance to give their daughter some space. Surely, her behavior would improve. But it didn't. It got worse, and her parents grew increasingly anxious.

Kristin's parents made a point of getting to know their children's friends. What they didn't know was that Kristin had forged a new relationship she knew her parents would never condone, a relationship with crystal methamphetamine.

Kristin's close friend since the third grade had moved to

England. So Kristin filled the void with a new set of friends, a more social group that liked to party. Before the big Homecoming game, a girlfriend pulled out a bindle of white powder while they were sitting in a car in the parking lot. The girl said it was speed and drew them some lines. Kristin inhaled the powder and felt a burning sensation. After the burn came a rush. She felt revved up. Positively euphoric.

She knew the stuff was illegal, but she liked it so much that she wanted to do it again. Only crystal meth wasn't a very socially acceptable drug. Their other friends gave them flack about using it, and her girlfriend didn't make a habit of it, so Kristin decided to pursue a buy on her own.

Two weeks later, Kristin approached the dealer who'd sold the meth to her friend. It was easy. She bought some, and little by little, she began using it more frequently, smoking it, and always alone. Soon, Kristin was spending less time with her friends. She lost a few pounds, and her grades began to suffer. She couldn't focus as easily on her schoolwork, and during her second semester, her usual A's fell to B's.

The first family crisis Kristin caused occurred in early 1993, after Ralph and Constance went on an anniversary cruise in the Caribbean. The Rossums asked some adult friends to check on the children during the day, but they left Kristin in charge overnight. They also left Kristin some money for pizza or any emergency. Instead, she used it to buy drugs. She threw a surprise birthday party for Pierce on St. Patrick's Day, but word leaked out at the high school that Kristin was having "a rager." Older kids started showing up. Seniors and football players. With beer.

"It kind of got out of control for a little bit," Kristin admitted later, saying she didn't remember whether she'd used meth that night, but it was possible. Kristin let a group of girlfriends stay over, and sometime during the same week, Kristin's dealer came by with some friends.

A couple of weeks after her parents returned from their

cruise, they discovered that some credit cards, personal checks, and a video camera were missing. On March 21, they called the police and reported a burglary. Constance also found a suspicious package of white powder in the mailbox. When she asked Kristin about it, her daughter said she had no idea where it came from, so Constance turned it over to the police. The lies were starting to pile up, and Kristin's parents began to think the worst: Their daughter was using drugs.

Kristin knew she had a problem. She felt tired and worn out, but she couldn't stop using. In the beginning, she'd smoked crystal because it made her feel so good. But it had become a necessity. She needed it just to feel like herself.

Methamphetamine is classified as a psychostimulant, just like amphetamine and cocaine. Methamphetamine and cocaine are structurally quite different, but both result in an accumulation of dopamine, the neurotransmitter that produces an unnatural level of euphoria in the brain. While cocaine is quickly metabolized by the body, methamphetamine stays in the system twelve times longer, and so it creates more lasting effects. Meth can produce a high that lasts eight to twenty-four hours, compared to a rush of twenty to thirty minutes with cocaine. Even in small doses, meth can decrease the appetite and keep people awake for hours. High doses can raise the body temperature to dangerous levels and cause convulsions.

On the street, methamphetamine has many names, including speed, meth, crank, ice, crystal, and glass. It can be inhaled, smoked, snorted, or injected. Chronic users can have episodes of violent behavior, anxiety, confusion, insomnia, hallucinations, delusions, and paranoia that can result in homicidal and suicidal thoughts. Psychosis can persist for months or years after a person stops using the drug. Experts say the continued use of the drug also tends to heighten the desire for sexual gratification and prompts users to seek increasingly high levels of sexual stimulation.

* * *

On March 30, 1993, around 7 P.M., Kristin said she had to go to the library to study for a class. Her parents, who'd been making calls to try to figure out what happened to their credit cards and checks, decided they needed to settle a few things with Kristin before she went anywhere.

Kristin decided otherwise and tried to leave. Ralph told her he wanted to look in her backpack, but she refused. Ralph tugged the pack away from her and unzipped it. He pulled out a white box and demanded to know what was in it. Kristin said it was a present for her mother. But when Ralph opened the box, he found a glass pipe, a plastic pen casing, and some razor blades inside. He demanded to know how she could have lied to him like this. She had betrayed his trust.

Ralph became enraged and started yelling as he hit her repeatedly on the upper arm, hard enough to leave a bruise. Then he grabbed one of her sandals off her bedroom floor and hit her on the butt with it. Constance yelled at him to stop, but she did nothing to pull him away. At some point, Constance slapped Kristin in the face.

Kristin ran into the kitchen, picked up a knife, and tried to cut her wrists with it until Ralph wrestled it out of her hands. She turned and ran back upstairs, where she locked herself in the bathroom and made superficial cuts in her wrists with a razor blade.

"I'm worthless," she cried through the door. "You'd be better off without me."

Because the cuts weren't deep, Constance and Ralph determined she didn't need medical treatment.

Sometime in the next few days, Kristin showed the bruise on her arm to a couple of girls at school and told them her parents had "beaten on her" during an argument. She started banging on the lockers and talking about committing suicide.

The two girls, concerned about Kristin's recent odd behavior, went to the office to talk to a counselor, Leopoldina
Abreu, a Cuban mother and grandmother to whom the high
school yearbook staff dedicated their 1993 edition. School
officials immediately reported a potential case of child abuse
to the Los Angeles County Department of Children and
Family Services and to the Claremont Police Department.

Larry Horowitz, a police officer who was working on a
master's degree in social work at the time, got the call around
lunchtime on April 2, while he was out on patrol. When he
arrived at the high school, Kristin and her two girlfriends
were sitting outside the office of Barbara Salyer, the dean of
discipline, waiting for him. Horowitz went into Salyer's office and closed the door. Given the bruise and Kristin's lack
of disciplinary problems, Salyer was concerned her story
might be true. Horowitz called the girls in one at a time and
interviewed them.

The first girl told him that she and her friend had grown
very worried about Kristin because her behavior had changed
so much over the past week. So they talked to their counselor about it, and she decided to bring Kristin in for some
help.

Kristin's parents didn't like the two girls, one of them told
Horowitz. Describing Constance as "very curt" with them,
she said that Constance wouldn't "allow Kristin to talk with
us or do anything with us. They don't seem like very friendly
people."

Horowitz sent the two girlfriends on their way and spent
the next forty-five minutes talking to Kristin. She seemed
flat, numb, and depressed. She wouldn't look him in the eye,
and he had a hard time establishing a rapport with her. To
him, all of these indicators pointed to a problem at home. He
spent a few minutes asking for basic information, such as
which grade she was in and where she lived, before proceeding to the hard questions.

Kristin told him that she had confided in her girlfriends, but she said, "I guess they wanted me to get into trouble, so they went to Mrs. Abreu and told her what was going on. I was brought into the office, but I didn't want to bring up family matters with the school."

This was the first time her father had hit her, she said. Most of the problems with her parents stemmed from their complaining about her friends. But this time, she said, it went further than usual, and her mother called her "worthless" and "a slut." She said she didn't want to see her parents get into trouble over their fight; she thought they could work the whole thing out over spring break.

Horowitz examined her arm and wrote in his notes that she had "pronounced bruising to the upper arm." He took photos of the area but decided the injury wasn't serious. He did notice, however, that she had fresh wounds on her knuckles—apparently from punching the lockers—and appeared to have picked at sores on the back of her hands. He figured drugs were involved.

She told him she felt safe going home because things had already improved.

"My dad even welcomed me back into the family on Thursday night," Kristin told him.

Horowitz told Kristin to inform her parents about their conversation and to warn them he'd be calling that night to set up an interview. Back at the station, he followed police procedures by notifying the child abuse hotline of the incident and preparing a written report of suspected child abuse.

Around six o'clock, Kristin called to clarify her story. She said the bruise on her arm was really caused by her dad grabbing her as she tried to leave the house, not from hitting her as she'd said before. Horowitz thought she was backtracking to minimize what had happened, posturing to protect her parents.

When he called the Rossum house at 7:15 P.M., he told Constance that he was investigating a reported case of child abuse and made an appointment to meet with her and Ralph at home around 8 the next morning.

The Rossums lived in a white, two-story house at the end of a cul-de-sac on Weatherford Court, a short, quiet street with well-kept lawns and flowerbeds. In 2004 the house had red rose bushes growing in the front yard.

Horowitz talked with Constance and Ralph for about an hour in the family room off the kitchen, while Kristin stayed in her bedroom. He found the Rossums to be quite cooperative. After their anniversary cruise, Constance told him, she and Ralph learned that Kristin was using drugs, smoking cigarettes, and having parties for friends who stole checks and credit cards. The incident happened when they tried to confront her about all of this.

"Ralph got mad and did hit her in the arm," Constance said. "I admit that I slapped her in the face, but she tried to hit me first."

Constance explained how Kristin tried to cut her wrists, first with a knife and then with razor blades, but that she had made only superficial cuts, so they didn't take her to see a doctor.

"I was afraid of what would happen if we took her to the hospital," she told Horowitz. "We don't know who to go to or what to do."

Then it was Ralph's turn. He said he found it unusual that Kristin had asked to use the car to go to the library because her driving privileges had been suspended due to "her actions while we were gone." It was also unusual, he said, for her to carry a backpack. When he found the drug paraphernalia inside, he said, he began tugging on her arm, demanding to know the truth.

"I admit that I took my open hand and struck her three or

four times on the upper arm," he told Horowitz. "She told me what had been going on and apologized. Kristin was visibly upset and started talking about killing herself."

After things had settled down later that evening, Ralph told him, they all agreed to work on the situation.

"I realize that there's a lot going on and that we need some help," Ralph said.

Horowitz saw a few discrepancies in the stories he'd heard. For one, Ralph said he hit Kristin with an open hand, while Kristin claimed it was a closed fist. Still, Horowitz didn't see any basis for the child-abuse claim.

After the ordeal, Constance and Ralph took Kristin in for a full physical. They told the doctor about finding the glass pipe, and he gave her a good talking-to about using drugs. Then, life in the Rossum household seemed to calm down for a while.

"We thought we had the problem licked at that point," Ralph said.

Like all the other seniors at Claremont High, Kristin went to a photo studio for her senior yearbook portrait. The boys posed in tuxedo shirts and bow ties, and the girls wore black, V-necked formal dresses. Kristin's photo showed no sign of drug use. She seemed healthy, wearing a string of pearls, her hair long and very blond. She looked attractive and comfortable with herself, just like the model she was trained to be. Kristin also sang with the A Cappella Singers Choir that year, posing for the yearbook with the other students in a long dark dress, the pearls, and some tasteful makeup.

But that fall, her parents began to notice the unwelcome reminders of her troubled past: she was picking at her hands again, she was losing weight, and her grades weren't as good. They definitely knew something was wrong when they saw that she was doing poorly in calculus. Kristin had always been so good at math.

It's typical for parents to feel sad, frustrated, helpless, and angry when they can't fix their child's drug problem, and the Rossums appeared to follow the norm.

"All this beauty and talent and wasting it all on people who were unworthy of her," Ralph later recalled thinking.

This would become a sad refrain throughout Kristin's life.

On January 14, 1994, Kristin came home from school around 3 P.M., acting erratically. Constance suspected her daughter was using methamphetamine again and felt compelled to confront Kristin about it. But that only escalated the situation.

Kristin started to touch her tank top protectively, so Constance asked if she had drugs on her. Kristin became defensive and tried to run away. Constance grabbed her, reached into her shirt, and pulled a glass pipe out of her bra. She was horrified. She didn't know what else to do but call the police and report that her daughter was under the influence of drugs. She'd hoped they were done with this mess.

Because Officer Horowitz had dealt with the Rossum family before, he took the call. When he arrived at the house on Weatherford Court, Constance seemed to be at her wit's end as she handed him the pipe. She also handed him a few other things she'd found in Kristin's belongings—some Ex-Lax, a small mirror, and some razor blades.

"Kristin has had a drug problem for the past several years," she told him. "The episodes with her friends using the credit cards and the checks and taking the car have caused us to realize how extensive her involvement was. We have tried doctors and therapy, but nothing so far has worked. This incident is the last straw, and something needs to be done about this."

After talking with a distraught Constance, the officer went upstairs, where the door to Kristin's room was ajar. Kristin was inside, sobbing, her nose running and her eyes red from crying. He asked what was going on, but she didn't answer him. The floor of the room was covered with papers and clothes strewn about. She was fidgety and obviously distressed, unable to complete a sentence or express a clear thought.

He did a quick physical examination, shining a penlight into her eyes, which did nothing to shrink her dilated pupils. She seemed dry-mouthed, and her pulse was going at a rate of 118 beats a minute. He asked if she'd smoked speed before going to school.

Yes, Kristin admitted, she'd gotten some drugs and the pipe from a boy the night before at Claremont High, where she'd gone to watch a performance of the musical *Oklahoma*.

"He owed me some money, so he paid me back with the drugs and pipe," she told Horowitz.

Kristin said she'd smoked at the high school that night and again the next morning in her bedroom before going to school. She took the pipe and the remainder of the drugs with her to school and brought them home again. She told him she used the drugs to help her study and with "other activities."

Horowitz placed Kristin under arrest for possession of paraphernalia and for being under the influence of a controlled substance. He snapped handcuffs on her wrists, read her her rights, and took her away in his squad car. He got the feeling that Kristin's family was more concerned about the image problem her drug addiction caused than about the drug problem itself.

At the city jail, the seventeen-year-old was fingerprinted, booked, photographed and ordered to produce a urine sample. A marked contrast to the pretty pictures Kristin took as a child model, her first booking photo shows her with her eyes closed, grimacing and crying.

Since Kristin was still a minor, Horowitz had a choice of moving her to Juvenile Hall within six hours of the arrest or releasing her to her parents. He chose the latter. Kristin was placed in a holding cell for about two hours until her parents came to get her.

Generally, he explained later, juveniles are released to a parent or guardian unless they are habitual offenders or have committed a violent crime. He was unable to explain why nothing ever came of the arrest, saying that county probation officials had jurisdiction over her case. Perhaps, he said, it fell through the cracks because she was so close to turning eighteen. At the time, he'd hoped that the court would compel her to attend a drug rehab program and get some help.

"She had every resource and ability through her family to get through life . . . but again, methamphetamine is a very, very pernicious drug, and you don't lose the taste once you cross that line," he said.

This time the Rossums decided to try something different. What Kristin needed, they concluded, was a change of environment. Surely, it would help to get her away from her drug friends at Claremont High. So, they had her graduate early and enrolled her at the University of Redlands, about thirty miles from home. She took only two courses her first semester there, but getting mumps and chicken pox didn't help.

Since Ralph was teaching a course at Redlands that semester, he drove her door to door so he could monitor her comings and goings. The two of them coordinated a Monday-Wednesday-Friday schedule and tried to rebuild their tattered relationship in the car driving to and from school each day. It worked. They soon recaptured the rapport they'd had when Ralph drove her to ballet rehearsal in Anaheim. At night, after school, the two of them attended twelve-step family-group therapy meetings in Chino, a city southeast of Claremont, where no one knew them.

* * *

Kristin dated Chris Elliott for a couple of months in 1994, before he went off to Johns Hopkins University. To him, she seemed to be trying to figure out what made *her* happy, not her parents. Elliott didn't think Kristin was that interested in him romantically, but he never had the impression that she was doing drugs.

"She seemed like an incredibly motivated person, very disciplined," he said.

For their final date, they went surfing together at Dana Point Sands. Elliott was still a beginner, but he was hoping this would strengthen the bond between them. Unfortunately, his plan went awry. Nothing seemed to go right.

First, the waves were much bigger than he expected. He offered to help Kristin, but that only seemed to insult her because she was so athletic. Meanwhile, the waves kept getting bigger. They paddled out, trying to get beyond them. Kristin tried to catch one particularly large wave, but it crashed over her. All but her feet disappeared into the wall of water, her board shooting into the monster and out again. She seemed upset and embarrassed by the experience.

"I felt really bad about it," Elliott said.

After surfing, Elliott thought they could try roller-blading so Kristin could regain her self-esteem. At one point, they stopped skating, and for no apparent reason, she fell. On the way back to the car, she fell again. From there, they went to a party, and when the date was over, they didn't speak to each other for two years.

That summer the sores on Kristin's hands and face healed. Ralph saw no other signs that the drugs were back, and he thought she was over the worst of it. She was spending time with friends he and Constance liked, and they thought it would be good for her to live in the dorms the fall semester.

They didn't sense anything unusual when they saw their daughter at Thanksgiving. In fact, they didn't know anything was wrong until Kristin disappeared one day in December 1994.

Chapter 3

Kristin was nowhere to be found the day her mother and two brothers came to pick her up from the University of Redlands for Christmas vacation. There was no note in her dorm room and no clue as to her whereabouts. Only a ringing phone.

Constance Rossum picked it up.

"This is Patrick," the man said. "Is Kristin there?"

Constance felt a surge of anger as she recognized the name of her daughter's drug dealer.

"I know who you are, and I know what you've done. Now stop it," Constance snapped and hung up.

All she wanted was for these predators to stop trying to persuade Kristin to buy crystal methamphetamine. Then, maybe Kristin could have a chance to get her life back on track, the family could return to its normal routine, and the nightmare of the past two years would end.

It was December 17, 1994. And that nightmare was far from over.

* * *

Kristin's boyfriend, Teddy Maya, also came to the dorm that day to pick her up. When he found her room empty, he figured she'd already left with her parents.

It had been a regular routine that fall semester for him to make the drive from UCLA, where he was going to school, to Redlands on weekends. He would collect Kristin from her dorm, they would go out on a date, and he would drop her at her parents' home in Claremont afterward.

They'd been dating since the summer, when they got re-acquainted through Kristin's friend Melissa Prager, whose parents knew the Rossums. She was dating a friend of Maya's. Kristin's parents liked Maya and Prager, and thought they were good influences on their daughter.

But Maya's stepmother, Karen Greenbaum-Maya, a psychologist in Claremont, wasn't so sure about Kristin. For one thing, Maya's stepmother didn't like the way Kristin always asked Maya to drive her places. Greenbaum-Maya held her tongue until Kristin asked Maya to shuttle her around while he was still heavily medicated from having his wisdom teeth removed.

"That finally got through to him," she said. ". . . I really didn't care for her calling on Teddy for everything. Even if you're eighteen, that's really just not a good relationship."

She also didn't like the fact that Kristin's parents allowed Maya to transport her to and from school on weekends, which she saw as a parental duty.

Greenbaum-Maya repeatedly asked her stepson to bring Kristin by the house. The couple did stop by one Friday evening for a few minutes to pick up a jacket for Maya, but that didn't allow for any meaningful conversation.

Greenbaum-Maya watched her stepson agonize over whether to wear a jacket or tie to Thanksgiving dinner at the Rossums', where propriety seemed to be the order of the day. Apparently, Kristin had expressed concern that he might not dress up enough for the occasion.

"That seemed odd to me," Greenbaum-Maya said.

Finally, Greenbaum-Maya, his parents, and Kristin all had breakfast together one Sunday. Greenbaum-Maya tried to get to know Kristin, but she didn't open up much.

"She wasn't going to let anything out," Greenbaum-Maya said. "She wasn't going to show us or tell us anything. She was guarded, and I couldn't help but notice."

The day after Maya's failed attempt to pick up Kristin for Christmas vacation, Ralph Rossum called the house and Greenbaum-Maya answered the phone. Ralph demanded to know where his daughter was.

"I don't know," Greenbaum-Maya said. "We thought you or your wife had picked her up yesterday."

Ralph's voice softened, saying they, too, had gone to get her, but she wasn't there. "We thought maybe—" he said, his voice trailing off.

Greenbaum-Maya didn't much like Ralph's tone and didn't think she or her stepson had done anything to deserve it. But when Ralph asked if she would call him if she heard anything, she said yes.

Kristin left the Redlands campus that morning because she couldn't face Teddy Maya or her mother. There would be hell to pay once her parents learned that she'd started smoking meth again. Plus, with an embarrassingly low grade point average of 1.67, Kristin had received a notice that she was on academic probation.

She'd gotten away from her druggie friends that spring, after her parents enrolled her at Redlands. She'd stayed clean over the summer, often double-dating with Melissa Prager and her boyfriend.

Kristin was pleased to have her parents' approval again, and they, in turn, were thrilled to have their old Kristin back.

So thrilled, they let her move into the dorm at Redlands, where she decided to take a full load of courses that fall. After struggling with a meth addiction since her junior year, it felt great to be drug free.

But that didn't last long. Kristin ran into a student who'd been in her calculus class the previous semester and, unbeknownst to her, was a fellow meth user. The friend offered her some at a party, and she took it. The problem was, it left her wanting more. So, she started using again. Gradually at first, once a week, then maybe every few days. She figured she could handle smoking just enough to help her study harder, to earn the good grades she used to get, so she could please her parents and feel good about herself again. But the cravings grew stronger, and things began to snowball.

By midsemester, Kristin was using every day. As Christmas vacation approached, she knew she couldn't let her parents see her like this again. They would be so disappointed. She knew it would upset them, but she decided she'd better go before her mother came to pick her up.

Kristin decided to go visit a male friend in Hemet. On Christmas Eve, her parents received a call from a family in Newport, telling them she was okay. Then, on Christmas night, she called Teddy Maya from a motel in Redlands and asked him to join her.

Kristin looked bad, nothing like her usual attractive self, and she seemed edgy after not sleeping in who knows how long. The next morning, Maya got out of the shower and found she'd emptied his wallet and left. Again, not even a note to say where she'd gone.

Kristin felt she still needed more time to get her act together. So she boarded an Amtrak train and got off at the end of the line in downtown San Diego. She transferred to the slow-rolling red trolley and continued south.

At the first trolley stop in Chula Vista, there was a Motel

6 to the east, and beyond it, across the parking lot, a Best Western. To the west, with the Pacific Ocean as a backdrop, was a Good Nite Inn. It's unclear which motel she chose, but with only $200 in her pocket, Kristin likely rented the cheapest room she could find.

But, after smoking some meth that morning, she was in no mood to sit around the room. She'd heard that Tijuana, the first town across the border into Mexico, was a fun place for college students to party. And, since she'd just turned eighteen, she could drink legally—all night if she wanted to. So she hopped back on the trolley and took it to San Ysidro, the last stop on the U.S. side of the border. She followed the signs to the pedestrian crossing and joined the throng of people walking over the bridge, their noses stinging from the fumes that emanated from the long lines of stop-and-go traffic heading into Mexico. It would be only a few minutes before she could lose herself in another country, another culture, another reality.

Greg de Villers, his brothers Jerome and Bertrand, and Aaron Wallo were walking across the bridge that same evening. Their trip to "TJ" was intended to be a rite of passage for Bertrand, who came down with Wallo from Palm Springs to visit. At fourteen, Bertrand had never been drunk before.

Night had fallen by the time the de Villers crew was walking along the dirty sidewalk leading to the intertwining metal bars that made up the first of two turnstiles at the border crossing. A loud clanking sounded repeatedly as a stream of tourists and Mexican day laborers pushed through the worn gate.

Kristin was walking sideways near the turnstile when she bumped into Greg. She dropped her brown leather jacket, and they both went to pick it up, which sparked a conversation. Since Kristin was alone, she was happy to tag along with his group, and Greg was happy to have her. She thought Greg seemed like a really nice guy, and it was obvious that he was attracted to her. They walked along the dimly lit sidewalk, past a long mural caked with the same dark layer of car-exhaust dust that seems to cover much of Tijuana.

They passed the money exchange booth as they approached the second turnstile and the bright yellow taxi sign, its edges lined with the same tiny blinking lights found on strip-club marquees. As soon as they pushed through the turnstile, they were surrounded by taxi drivers offering to take them into the city. They got into one of the cabs and asked to be dropped off at the most popular tourist destination, a street called *Avenida Revolución,* which is lined with bars and dance clubs. The taxi driver drove fast, which was a little nerve-wracking given that there were no seat belts in his car.

For some Americans, Tijuana is a place to stock up on prescription drugs, which are far cheaper and easier to obtain without a prescription than in the United States. It's as easy as walking into a pharmacy and asking the clerk behind the counter for a drug of choice. The clerks don't ask for a prescription, nor do they tell buyers that purchasing medications without one could get them arrested at the border. Kristin would take advantage of this opportunity in the years to come, buying muscle relaxants, diet pills, and other drugs.

For students or young members of the U.S. military stationed in San Diego, Tijuana is more of an escape destination, where they can act crazier than is acceptable back home. In essence, Tijuana is a bombardment of the senses. Everything is bright, loud, aggressive, and sometimes a little surreal. The neon lights flash across buildings so rapidly a person can almost hear them, making him feel as if he were starring in his own cartoon.

As tourists walk down *Avenida Revolución,* they are accosted every few feet by vendors whose arms are covered with hanging necklaces. Barefoot children with grimy faces thrust out empty paper cups, begging for money. Or they sell small, individually wrapped packets of chewing gum squares, eight for $1. Mothers with two or three toddlers in tow sell handwoven bracelets or crepe-paper flowers in brilliant colors. Men sitting on benches call out "something else," code words for drugs.

Over the years, the stores that line *Avenida Revolución* have offered little variation in the goods they sell: hand-carved onyx chess sets, velvet paintings, ceramic pots, figurines, leather wallets and belts, pocket knives, and white cotton dresses with floral embroidery.

Outside the nightclubs, clusters of young men hand out free drink tickets, trying to entice passersby to enter their steep black stairwells. "This is the place," they say. "Come inside."

The de Villers crew strolled along *Avenida Revolución* and went into several of these bars that night, at least one of which had a second-floor balcony overlooking the street. They ordered tequila shots and beers, while the bass beat of the dance music pounded the night air, and smoke machines belched out streams of gray fog. It soon became clear that Greg and Kristin were together.

Sometime between midnight and 2 A.M., the group walked back over the pedestrian bridge to San Ysidro and their car. Greg invited Kristin to stay with him and his crew at the two-bedroom apartment he shared with Jerome and a roommate in the La Jolla Del Sol complex. Kristin felt safe with Greg. She sensed no permanence in the situation, and she didn't want to go back to an empty motel room. So she accepted his offer.

Greg and Kristin shared the same bed, and they had sex. There was no mention of Teddy Maya. Greg was smitten, and it appeared to be mutual.

"Greg wasn't the type to bring women home for one-night stands," said Chris Wren, Greg's roommate.

The next morning, Bertrand woke up on the couch with a plastic trash bin next to him in case he got sick. The whole crew got up late and went out for something to eat before Bertrand and Wallo drove back to Palm Springs.

Then Greg asked Wren to move out of the bedroom they shared and into the other bedroom with Jerome. Kristin was going to stay for a while.

Kristin's parents checked in with her teachers and learned that she'd missed her finals. When she hadn't turned up by the day after Christmas, they filed a missing person's report with the campus police. They also contacted the Claremont Police Department.

George Dynes, a Claremont police officer, wrote in his report that Maya had seen Kristin on the morning of December 26. She had a 104-degree fever and "was depressed and suicidal." Ralph Rossum told Dynes that his daughter might "try and hurt or kill herself."

"The parents are worried about the safety of their eighteen-year-old daughter. According to people that the parents have contacted, their daughter has been very depressed lately," Dynes wrote.

Dynes also filled out another form, recording the Rossums' report of a "voluntary missing adult." He put Kristin in the "at risk" category, stating she was "depressed and suicidal," with a destination unknown. He described her as being five feet two inches, 105 pounds, with green eyes and chin-length blond hair, wearing a brown leather jacket.

Constance feared that Kristin might have fallen prey to foul play. She and Ralph were both devastated by the cold fact that their daughter likely had relapsed. When Kristin was on drugs, she became self-destructive. And this time, they had no idea where she'd gone or what she was doing.

A couple of times in the weeks after Kristin ran away, Constance answered the phone and heard a mewing on the other end of the line. She figured it was Kristin making those quiet sobbing sounds, but her daughter wouldn't say anything. She would just hang up. She knew she'd ruined her family's Christmas.

In early January, Kristin sent her parents a letter saying she was very sorry for running away like she did. The letter had no return address or phone number but carried a San Diego postmark. Soon afterwards, Kristin called her parents.

"Thank God you're safe," Constance told her.

Kristin said she'd been staying with some nice people in San Diego. She hadn't wanted to call until she was ready to prove that she was serious about getting herself together. If the family wanted to see her, she wanted to come home for a visit.

"Mom, I have three jobs. I'm starting to turn my life around," she said.

Her parents were thrilled to hear that Kristin was okay and that she was trying to get better. Borrowing Greg's car, she drove up to Claremont on a Sunday to see her family and to collect some belongings.

"There was a little bit of the prodigal son kind of feeling," Ralph recalled later.

Over a tearful but happy reunion lunch, Kristin shared how she'd driven up in the car that her friend Greg de Villers loaned her. Seemingly clearheaded, she told them that she was teaching ballet classes and working at a pasta restaurant and that she had also landed a third job, at California Pizza Kitchen. It seemed important to her that they believe she'd turned the corner. They were happy to buy in and got her the uniform she needed for the pizza place. They also managed to squeeze a church service into her visit.

Constance and Ralph were eager to meet Greg, so they arranged to come down to San Diego in a few weeks. Greg wanted to take them all out to lunch.

They met in a parking lot in the Gaslamp District in downtown San Diego, an area lined with bars and restaurants that are teeming with people on weekend nights. Greg was wearing sunglasses and a suede jacket.

When he took off his glasses, Constance noticed that he had kind eyes. Ralph thought he was charming and good-looking.

"I thought Kristin had met a really good person," Ralph said.

Kristin spoke with Teddy Maya at one point in January about her sudden disappearance, telling him she'd been kidnapped at gunpoint and driven around Mexico in the trunk of a car.

About a month after the Rossums' lunch with Greg, Kristin told her parents she was renting a van and moving in with a young female coworker from the pizza restaurant. In reality, however, she was still living with Greg.

The Rossums eventually figured this out. As devout Episcopalians, Constance and Ralph disapproved of premarital sex. But at the same time, they were relieved. Kristin seemed to be in such good hands with Greg, who obviously had her best interests at heart. And if he could do what they couldn't—get her off drugs—then so be it. Her previous lifestyle was certainly worse than this.

To them, Greg was their "saving angel."

Meanwhile, back in the La Jolla Del Sol apartment, it wasn't long before tensions began to rise. Not only was Jerome being forced to share his bedroom, but the rent was still being divided only three ways. He also wasn't thrilled when Greg started letting Kristin drive to work in the car that he and Greg had been sharing.

To make matters worse, some of Greg's jewelry—a gold ring with the family crest and a gold necklace—went missing from the bathroom, and Greg blamed Jerome's friends for taking it. Jerome said it was more likely Kristin. But Greg didn't want to believe it.

Jerome called Christian MacLean, a friend of theirs from high school, and expressed his frustration.

"There's this girl staying with us," Jerome told him. "She's weird."

After meeting her, MacLean came to agree. He noticed Kristin didn't really connect with the people around her. To him, she seemed like a nerdy, serious bookworm who didn't really get the joke.

"She's just kind of off," he said.

Chris Wren felt that Kristin was kind of quirky, which in his mind wasn't necessarily a bad trait, at least in most people. But in her, he saw something else, something he didn't recognize or understand. She acted erratically, swinging from one extreme emotion to the next. One afternoon he walked into the apartment and found her alone with a strange man. Kristin didn't introduce them.

About a week after Greg's jewelry disappeared, Wren discovered that some of his personal checks were missing. Greg admitted that Kristin had taken them. He also said he'd torn them up so she couldn't use them.

"You can't use someone else's checks, anyway," Kristin said later, trying to dismiss the act and claim she wasn't intending to use them to buy drugs.

When Greg found a glass tube containing a whitish yellow substance in Kristin's jacket pocket, he showed it to Wren and asked if he'd ever seen anything like it. No, Wren said, he hadn't. But it certainly helped explain Kristin's nervousness and what Jerome described as her "twidgety" behavior. She was smoking drugs, and it sure wasn't marijuana.

Jerome wanted her out of the apartment, but Greg wouldn't listen. Kristin was going through some rough times, he said. She was trying to stop using drugs, and he was trying to help her do it. He'd fallen in love and he'd fallen hard.

Other than Kristin's problem, drugs weren't a part of Greg's life. He didn't drink much alcohol or do recreational drugs. His friends couldn't even remember him using over-the-counter cold remedies. Greg made it clear he didn't like Jerome smoking pot and told him he'd have more motivation if he didn't. Greg also didn't approve of the couple of marijuana plants that Jerome and Wren tried unsuccessfully to grow in the apartment as an experiment.

Greg and Jerome had always been close, but things had become strained between them since Kristin arrived. Jerome was doing laundry in the apartment one day and put his clothes in the dryer before he went out. When he came back, he found his clothes—still damp—heaped on top of the dryer and Greg's clothes tumbling inside. Jerome was so angry, he and Greg started fighting over the insult. The two brothers had always roughhoused and wrestled, pinning each other and putting the other in a headlock or a choke hold. Only this time, things got so rough that Jerome thought they might really hurt each other. Luckily, Wren came home and broke them apart.

Kristin never really confided in Jerome, but she did feel comfortable talking with Wren. She told him she'd run away from home because things weren't going well with her parents, and she admitted to having a problem with crystal meth.

"She was looking for acceptance, and when you have a problem, you need to talk about it," Wren said.

Two or three months after she'd moved in, the roommates decided to have a party. Kristin sat on Wren's lap as the guests began to arrive. At one point, she told Wren she felt she was meant to be with him, not Greg, and started to cry.

Ralph and Constance took Greg and Kristin to dinner one night and expressed their concern that neither of them was back in school, informing them that education was important for their futures. Since he'd stopped taking courses at UCSD, Greg had been supporting himself by working at Rush Legal, where he'd also helped Kristin get a job, but it didn't provide health benefits. Kristin decided to enroll at San Diego State University (SDSU) in the fall, and Greg planned to return to UCSD.

Constance filled out Kristin's SDSU application for her, purposely omitting her two lousy quarters at Redlands, even though the form required a listing of all previous coursework. She thought her daughter should have a fresh start, and that was that.

When the lease to Greg's apartment ran out in June 1995, Wren moved to Solana Beach. He still played tennis with Greg and came by the apartment, but they saw less and less of each other. Wren had always admired Greg for believing that if things weren't going well, he could turn them around. He figured it was Greg's optimism that made him want to help Kristin. And perhaps a little gullibility as well.

"That's what made him honest," Wren said.

Jerome moved out that summer, too. He'd been studying chemistry at UCSD, but he decided to transfer to the University of California, Santa Barbara, which offered better economics courses. His girlfriend and another good friend were also thinking of transferring there, so he was guaranteed a roommate.

Wren and Jerome kept wondering when Greg was going to wake up and see Kristin for what she really was.

* * *

That summer Greg told Kristin's father that he wanted to marry her. But Ralph told Greg he needed to finish college first, so Greg and Kristin settled on getting informally engaged. As much as the Rossums didn't approve of the couple's living arrangement, they decided to acknowledge the situation and allowed them to move into another apartment together.

"Kristin loved Greg, and we wanted to help them both to the extent that we could," Constance recalled.

So, they agreed to pay the rent. They also bought furniture for the couple and a white 1990 Toyota Cressida for Kristin. They were proud of both young people and so pleased that Kristin seemed like her old self again that they happily paid for her tuition, books, clothes, and car insurance. They even threw in a little extra spending money.

Constance took Greg aside and made him promise to tell them if he saw any signs that Kristin was back on drugs. He told her not to worry; he knew what to do. His father was a doctor.

By all accounts, the couple seemed giddy with love, sitting close on the couch and holding hands all the time. Marie, Greg's mother, described them as lovebirds.

That summer Kristin went with her family for a vacation in the south of France. Every day she would wait by the phone for Greg to call at a prearranged time, and he would follow through, no matter where he was.

Greg waited as best he could to formally propose marriage. Then, on October 25, 1996, he couldn't wait any longer. The two of them were driving down to Puerto Nuevo, Mexico, to celebrate Kristin's twentieth birthday with dinner at Lobster Village. As they were driving down the toll road, Kristin opened the glove compartment to store the toll ticket and thought she saw a jewelry box. She was right. After dinner Greg opened the compartment, pulled out an engagement ring, and popped the question. She said yes.

The next day, Kristin drove to her parents' house in Claremont to show off the ring. The Rossums were happy—cautiously happy—and said they hoped it would be a long engagement.

Chapter 4

Greg, like Kristin, came from a well educated, suburban family. Although their childhoods and teenage years were quite different, experiences in their formative years groomed them to come together as a codependent couple, with strengths and needs that complemented each other.

Greg's family life trained him early and often to be a protector, an adviser, and a caretaker. As the oldest son in a single-parent household, Greg shouldered the responsibility for the welfare of his two brothers and their mother, whose respiratory problems put her in the hospital starting when they were in elementary school. It is not uncommon for children of parents who are chronically ill or addicted to drugs or alcohol to end up in a romantic relationship with a substance abuser.

Through all of this, Greg somehow learned how to stay positive, or at least to maintain the appearance that everything was fine. And if it wasn't, then he'd do his damnedest to make it better.

When Greg met Kristin in late 1994, she was eighteen and addicted to crystal meth. At twenty-one, with little experience in the girlfriend department, Greg was determined to be her savior and get her off drugs. His efforts were successful. Their troubles developed in the next few years, as Kristin increasingly wanted her independence. In turn, Greg displayed the typical behavior of someone involved with an addict—he tried to control and protect Kristin and their relationship, even more so when he saw signs that she'd relapsed. The knowledge that she was having an affair and that their marriage was falling apart—especially after living through his parents' acrimonious divorce—undoubtedly fueled the dynamic.

Gregory Bernard Paul Yvon Tremolet de Villers was the first of three American sons born to Yves and Marie-France Tremolet de Villers. Greg and his brothers grew up in Southern California, across the globe from France, their parents' native country. But because their mother always felt more comfortable speaking in her native tongue, all three were fluent in it.

Marie-France was born in 1943 in Gaillac, a small town near the Pyrenees. When she was a child, her mother would spread hot vapor rub on her chest to help her asthmatic breathing. Her father's military career exposed her and her younger sister, Marie-Paul, at an early age to African cultures in Algeria, Morocco, the Ivory Coast, and the Congo. Marie-France was in her twenties, working as a physical therapist, when she met Yves in Mende, a town in the south of France, where her parents had settled. Yves, who was eight years her senior, worked in a hospital there.

Yves lost his father when he was eleven, so his mother raised him and his sisters with the help of two uncles, both members of the French Parliament. When their town of Montpellier was bombed during World War II, Yves' family hid in a vaulted basement across the street from their home, biting on pieces of wood to keep their mouths open and prevent their eardrums from rupturing. The next morning they learned that thousands had died in the night. Yves saw people gunned down in the street and was awakened one night at 2 A.M. by the Gestapo, who were looking for one of his uncles.

Ambitious and intelligent, Yves started medical school in Montpellier in 1953. He also studied medicine at a university in Marseilles. He trained in surgery and anesthesiology and also interned at a hospital in Nice.

Yves and Marie moved to the Chicago area in 1970 so he could continue his medical studies, and they were married there in 1972. Greg was born the following year, on November 12. Yves did a residency in hand surgery at Northwestern University, one in general surgery at Michael Reese Hospital, and one in plastic surgery at the University of Illinois, where he also taught classes. In 1974 he opened a surgical practice in Monte Carlo, which is in the tiny country of Monaco, on the Mediterranean Sea near the French and Italian borders. A resort area, Monte Carlo has a population of about thirty-two thousand, is a vacation spot for the rich, and is known for its casinos and for being home to the late Grace Kelly after she married its chief of state, Prince Rainier III.

In 1975, two years and three days after Greg was born, Marie gave birth to Jerome Henri Vincent Louis Tremolet de Villers, continuing the tradition of naming their sons after three relatives. The family soon moved to Westlake Village in California, a community that straddles Ventura and Los Angeles Counties. They bought a modest condominium there that December, and Yves opened a second plastic surgery practice, this time with a partner in the neighboring city of Thousand Oaks, a mostly white, family-oriented city of about 117,000 people in Ventura County.

The third de Villers son, Charles Bertrand Jean Francois, who went by Bertrand, or Bert to his friends, was born on March 10, 1979, in a hospital across the street from the family's condo.

Over the years, Yves would travel back and forth between his dual practices in Thousand Oaks and Monte Carlo. Yves worked as a surgeon at L'Hospital Complex Princess Grace. Back in California, Bertrand remembered that Yves did some work on Walt Disney to fix a broken nose, and that he brought home a Mickey Mouse watch as a token of appreciation.

But pure medicine was never enough for Yves, who had a very active mind. He went on to coauthor a textbook titled *Body Sculpturing by Lipoplasty* in 1989. A student for life, he also received a master's degree in business administration, finance, and marketing from the University of Southern Europe in Monaco in 1998.

Two months after Bertrand was born, the family moved to a more upscale neighborhood a couple of miles away, where Yves and Marie bought a two-story house on Silver Springs Drive. Lined with tall, thin conifers, an olive tree, jasmine, and rose bushes, the house looked onto a soccer field that was part of a K-8 school that Greg and Jerome attended across the street. With a pool and a hot tub in the backyard, this was suburbia at its best.

But before long, Yves and Marie's marriage went sour. Greg and Jerome were rousted out of bed by doors slamming or Yves yelling at their mother. They would climb to the top of the stairs outside the master bedroom, trying to figure out what the ruckus was about. It scared them and made them cry to hear their parents fight.

Yves filed papers to dissolve the union on September 2, 1981, when Bertrand was two and Greg almost eight.

A month later Yves filed papers asking the court to stop Marie from selling their community property and to award him custody of the boys. Upon returning from Europe, he claimed, he discovered that Marie had sold their 1973 Volkswagen and a "very expensive gun" without his consent. Given his wife's "emotional state," he was worried that she'd run off with the boys to their house in Monte Carlo.

"I feel I am qualified to make the statement, as I am a

medical doctor," he wrote. He also asked the court to restrain Marie's "personal conduct," so she would not be allowed to "contact, molest, attack, strike, threaten, sexually assault, batter, telephone or otherwise disturb" his peace.

Marie filed her own set of divorce papers on October 1, asking for the same restraint on Yves's conduct.

Each parent gave a dramatically different version of the events that contributed to the split. But one thing was obvious to any neutral party: Even though Yves moved back into the house for a time, the high drama reflected in four years of divorce filings must have created an emotionally volatile environment for Greg and his brothers, one in which money was always an issue. Each parent went through several attorneys.

In Marie's initial filing, she asked the court to award her custody of the boys, along with $1,500 in child support and $4,000 in alimony, monthly. She asked that Yves, who wasn't living at home at the time, be forced to stay at least one hundred yards away from her.

"In the past, respondent has on many occasions beat me with a closed fist, and police reports have been made," Marie's signed petition stated. "After he beat me up, respondent sent me to a doctor for treatment, and I had black-and-blue marks all over. I am afraid of him, and he has stated he will break my teeth and mouth and will make me an ugly person."

Years later Marie would testify that Yves never hit her. Yves also denied hitting her, saying those allegations were "a fabricated maneuver" by her attorney and that Marie may have signed the divorce papers without reading them carefully. California bar association records show that Marie's attorney, Saul Nadel, had one disciplinary action against him—his law license was temporarily suspended in 1990—but the charges remain confidential. He died in 1998.

Although the boys don't remember ever seeing Yves hit

their mother, they said Marie told them she'd been scared of his behavior and recounted stories of him throwing over chairs and breaking down a locked door she was hiding behind.

The judge granted a mutual restraining order to Marie and Yves, but less than a month later, Marie complained that her husband had already violated it.

"[Yves] is annoying me, and he has removed various wires from my car so that I could not use the car," her filing read. "I called on my neighbors for help, and they replaced the removed wires so that I could take my son to the doctor." She said Yves had not paid "sufficient monies" for the family's living expenses, such as the boys' tuition and other necessary household bills.

Yves and his attorney responded by asking the court to order Marie to undergo a mental examination. The judge approved the request.

Marie "has been treated for a substantial period of time by certain psychiatrists for mental conditions," Yves's attorney wrote, saying Yves told him Marie "suffers from substantial delusions and other mental diseases." Her emotional state, he wrote, was relevant because it related to her ability to hold a job and care for the boys properly. He said Marie, who had been employed at a local hospital, "terminated said employment due to an alleged mental condition."

Marie's attorney responded by filing a petition to subpoena two years of Yves's personal and business tax records. Yves's attorney followed up with a proposal for a family living arrangement, complete with photos and a floor plan, giving Yves the master suite upstairs and Marie the smaller downstairs bedroom. The couple wouldn't eat meals at the same time, and Yves would buy his own food, do his own laundry and cooking, and take out the trash. Marie would pay for a new phone for herself and the boys.

On February 12, 1982, the American Savings and Loan Association filed a legal notice that Yves and Marie had defaulted on their mortgage and that their house could be sold if they didn't pay up within three months. A few weeks later, Marie's attorney wrote the judge to complain that Yves had evicted her from the master bedroom and relegated her to the "maid's room" downstairs. She, too, submitted photos and a floor plan, asking for exclusive use of the house.

The judge ruled that Yves should move into the downstairs bedroom. If Yves violated any part of the order, the judge warned, he'd have to leave the house. Yves was ordered to pay $500 in alimony and $900 for child support each month, and the children would no longer attend private school. Yves was also ordered to pay Marie's $2,750 in attorneys' fees. When Yves failed to pay those fees, her attorney had to get a court order to garnishee Yves's bank account.

On August 29, Yves asked the court to free him from having to pay the mortgage on the family home and to force Marie to consult with him on the boys' education. He said he couldn't pay child support or alimony as ordered because his practice was $206,900 in debt and the family home was in foreclosure. He said he'd fallen, breaking one arm and the other wrist, which had prevented him from working for several months.

Meanwhile, Marie and the boys had to move in with a woman she worked with at a nearby hospital. For a time, the four of them had to share one bunk bed.

Marie's attorney renewed the judgment against Yves on September 28 to try to collect the rest of his fees. The next day Yves tried to modify his alimony and support order and asked for joint custody of the boys, with the right to be consulted on their education and religious training. He also complained that since his bank account was garnisheed, he could no longer access his own safety deposit box, which contained documents he needed to drive and operate his medical practice in Monaco.

In November the judge ruled that a sheriff's deputy could

watch Yves remove his citizenship papers from the box, but no stock certificates, automobile pink slips, insurance policies, or personal property with "tangible value."

On March 15, 1983, Yves filed papers contending that his income had fallen to zero. Two weeks later, he sought sole custody of the boys, saying Marie was trying to take them back to France to live with her mother without telling him. He claimed Marie either prevented him from visiting the boys or harassed him so much she made visits virtually impossible. She had even yelled threats at him at his office in front of patients and staff, saying she would "do anything she can to 'hurt' me."

A few weeks later, the judge ordered a new child visitation schedule for Yves, telling Marie she needed to give Yves any new phone numbers or addresses. He prohibited both parents from making derogatory remarks about the other in front of the children. Marie couldn't take them to France until the summer break, he said, and she had to bring them back in time for the fall term.

After that order, the divorce dispute shifted to how community property and assets from Yves's medical practices should be divided.

In October Yves complained to the judge that he'd tried several times to visit his children since April but was still being refused access. Marie had also taken the children out of school in Ventura County, he said, and enrolled them at a school in Riverside County. Marie had, in fact, moved with the boys to an apartment complex in Palm Springs that year. By this time, Greg was about ten.

On November 8, Marie's divorce attorney filed papers to remove himself from the case against Yves, saying he feared it was endangering his life and his children's. He'd received an anonymous threatening call four days earlier. Then, a package from an unknown company was delivered to his home, and he had to call in the bomb squad to investigate. After getting numerous disturbing phone calls at his house, he had to change the number.

The divorce case finally got to a nonjury trial on January 10, 1984. The judge awarded joint legal custody of the boys to Yves and Marie, and full physical custody to Marie. Yves could visit the children during July and August and on alternating weekends and holidays. He would pay $500 a month in alimony and $900 in child support, as well as $900 in outstanding bills for the boys' private schools. He was to pay about $11,500 in debts and attorneys fees for Marie and was awarded all assets and debts from his medical practices and all personal debts he shared with Marie. He also got to keep his "over and under Franchi hunting gun."

The divorce became final on August 6, 1985.

Bertrand and Jerome didn't recall their childhoods being all that clouded by the divorce battle, at least not so much that they would discuss it with someone outside the family.

Bertrand remembered that they never had enough money after the split, but he chose to focus more on the positive outcome: The brothers learned early how to amuse themselves. They always played outside, doing something athletic, like riding dirt bikes, hiking, or thrashing around in the swimming pool at their apartment complex. They also learned how to be creative. They built forts out of palm fronds, waged dirt-clod wars, made up their own games, and built a BMX bike-racing course with jumps and ramps.

The brothers often played together, at least until Greg started working odd jobs and then was employed at a drugstore to help their mother support the family. Greg was sixteen or seventeen when he got a job at Longs Drugs, where Jerome joined him a year later, after working at another pharmacy. In the coming years, the two brothers would stay in close touch with their coworkers, Aaron Wallo and Bill Leger.

Leger, whose father was the store manager, was over at the de Villerses' apartment most weekends, playing tennis or hiking.

The de Villers boys never had allowances, so they'd have to ask their mother to give them money when they wanted something, and she would decide if they could afford it on a case-by-case basis. Greg and Jerome had to pay for their own orthodontia.

The brothers never understood why Marie had to struggle so much. They saw how much easier life was for other kids whose fathers were plastic surgeons, and they wondered why their father couldn't help out more, especially when he had a practice in Monte Carlo, a playground for those with a glitzy lifestyle.

Yves and Marie always watched the evening news, and as the boys got older, their parents encouraged them to participate in dinner discussions about current events or whatever they were learning in school.

Marie taught the boys table manners: Don't come to the table without a shirt, fork on the left, knife on the right, and sit up straight. Marie made her own salad dressing, shepherd's pie, and ham and cheese sandwiches, which sound so much more sophisticated when called by their French names— Purée Parmanchiez and Croque Monsieur. She also taught Bertrand to cook, and he often started dinner when she had to work two jobs to make ends meet.

With the boys at soccer or tennis practice and with Marie and Greg working late, the family might not have sat down to dinner until 9:30 P.M. But they always ate together. It was just something they did, and it helped keep the family together.

"We are a team," Marie would tell her sons. "Everybody has a role to play. If you want to win the game, everybody has to keep his position and to play the game. But don't forget, I am the captain."

Marie was a strong woman with a deep sense of pride, and once she'd made up her mind, it was difficult to change. But she could also be gentle. Her children were the primary focus of her life.

Jerome and Bertrand recalled their parents staying in regular contact but admitted those days seemed a bit blurry in their minds. They remembered spending summers alone with their father soon after the split, saying that in later years, Marie would come along, too. When Yves still had his practice in Thousand Oaks, they would summer there and hang out at the YMCA or go to the beach while Yves was at work.

Sometimes Yves would rent a cabin for two or three weeks at Mammoth Lakes or take them camping there, a summer trip that gradually became a family tradition.

One summer Yves took the boys to a dude ranch in Wyoming for two weeks. There they learned how to lasso a goat and do other rodeo tricks. Greg made a leather belt with his name on it. And he and Jerome got to go horseback riding, but Bertrand had to stay behind because he was too little.

During the rest of the year, Yves visited the boys in Palm Springs some weekends and over the holidays. They would go hiking together, and he'd take them to church on Sunday.

Marie worked in various clothing boutiques and then high-end department stores in Palm Springs, selling clothes and helping to put on fashion shows. Later she studied massage therapy, and after Bertrand went off to university, she moved into a town house Yves was renting in Thousand Oaks. Eventually, she opened her own massage business, called Somacare, at the Hyatt Westlake Plaza hotel.

The boys grew up knowing that Yves was supposed to pay child support and alimony. They also remembered that the checks often didn't come on time, which made it difficult for Marie to make rent. Sometimes, they said, Yves would buy things for the family instead.

Asked recently about the financial situation back then, Yves claimed he gave Marie "more money than [he] was required to" and never had to be reminded to do so by those enforcing the custody arrangement. "I did struggle, for obvious reasons, but I worked very hard," he said.

Nonetheless, Marie had to ask friends to help out her family. In a January 1984 divorce filing, she listed debts including $18,400 in personal loans from friends for living expenses, $2,500 in unpaid rent, $1,280 in medical expenses, and $9,500 in attorneys' fees.

The boys attended a number of different schools, some of them private and run by the Catholic Church, but scholarships weren't always available. All three brothers attended the four-year public Palm Springs High School, where Jerome and Bertrand played on the tennis team.

Marie was strict but understanding, and she used her own unique disciplinary techniques. She stopped letting the boys stay the night with friends once they became teenagers. And when they did go out, Marie would tell them to call in. She'd ask for the phone number, then she'd call them back to make sure they were where they claimed.

Greg, being the eldest, got his own room. His brothers looked up to him as a fix-it guy and arbiter of sibling spats. Interested in the mechanics of things, Greg would take his bicycle apart, surround himself with its pieces, then put it back together. He also felt very comfortable with computers.

Jerome and Greg were close, though they competed with each other on many levels. As they got older, Greg was more shy and less experienced than Jerome in the ways of meeting girls, so he relied on his younger brother's expertise. One day, when Jerome was fifteen and Greg was seventeen, they went to the mall together and discussed the best technique.

Greg had seen his brother at work. "You give them the eye," Greg noted. It was a private joke between them for years to come.

Greg wasn't a great student like Bertrand, but he managed to keep a decent grade point average in high school, even when he was working at Longs. After graduating from high school in 1991, he spent two years at the College of the Desert, a community college in Palm Desert, apparently because it was cheaper than a four-year college. He earned enough credits for an associate's degree, though there is no record he applied for one.

In 1992 and 1993, Greg and Jerome went to stay with their father in Monaco for the summer. Bertrand and Marie came over and joined them later. Both years, Greg got an internship there at the International Atomic Energy Agency Marine Environment Laboratory, where he used his computer skills to analyze data related to marine radioactivity and pollution levels in the Mediterranean Sea.

As his sons got older, Yves wasn't around as much, but when he was, the boys increasingly felt he overexerted his role as an authority figure. Yves could be a very sweet man, but he seemed elusive to his sons.

"It's hard to know who he is exactly," Jerome said. "He's a real smart guy. He likes having his own space."

Yves was very particular about his belongings. When the boys were young and he came back from a trip, he would know if one of them had moved something in his room. He kept a detailed journal, recording everything from expenditures to details of conversations. Jerome adopted these practices and employed them years later as he investigated Greg's death. Bertrand, who later went on to pursue a Ph.D. in physical chemistry, believed he inherited his father's academic drive.

* * *

After Greg returned from Monaco in the fall of 1993, he started classes at the University of California, San Diego, where his grades were less than stellar.

During his first quarter, he earned an F in organic chemistry, a D in a European Renaissance humanities class, and a C in physics, which gave him a D grade point average for the quarter. The next quarter, he did slightly better, raising his average to a C by earning a B+ in an introduction to acting class. In the spring of 1994, he continued to struggle with organic chemistry and physics.

Jerome joined him at UCSD that fall, and they shared a two-bedroom apartment in the La Jolla Del Sol complex with a third roommate, Chris Wren.

Greg and his father did not get along, and over the years, their relationship grew progressively stormier, until Greg and he became estranged.

Yves had a way of causing mental turmoil, which made communication with his sons difficult, so Greg—and sometimes Jerome—felt it was easier to live independently with little or no contact with him. Yves said he believed the conflict between him and Greg developed "because he was too young for the kind of responsibilities his mother gave him and the resentment she could not completely hide."

But others saw it differently, saying that Greg resented Yves for not helping their mother more financially. Then, later, when Greg said he couldn't afford to pay for college and wanted to take a break, Yves told him to stay in school and assured him that he would cover the costs, but the money never came. Yves denied this version of events but did not elaborate.

Memories differ on the breaking point for Greg and his father. Jerome remembered it coming during a family trip to Mammoth, when Greg left abruptly and returned to San Diego. Yves remembered that Greg left abruptly one year because he wanted to go home to try to make money selling vitamins, a job Yves didn't think was worthy of him, but he said that wasn't the breaking point for him and his son. He did not elaborate.

Greg withdrew from classes at UCSD partway through the quarter in October 1994 and started working at Rush Legal Services. The firm offered an array of copying, researching, process serving, notary, delivery, and other services.

Greg returned to classes at UCSD in the fall of 1995, about nine months after meeting Kristin. By the following summer, he was able to focus his energies on just one organic chemistry course, and his grades began to improve. He earned a B+ in that course, and by the winter quarter of 1997, he was earning all A's and B's. In his last quarter before graduating in 1997, he brought his grade point average up to a 3.85 even while taking biomedicine/cancer and developmental neurobiology.

After Bertrand graduated high school in 1997, he came to San Diego for the summer. He lived in Solana Beach, a small coastal town just north of San Diego, where he learned to surf with his brothers. Greg got Bertrand a job at Rush Legal, delivering subpoenas for the firm in the northern part of the county. Later that summer, Bertrand was transferred to the downtown office where Greg worked. He left to start classes at UCLA that fall.

"I always felt a strong tie to my brothers," Bertrand said. "We were always there for each other."

The brothers remained close, even when they lived apart. Jerome transferred to the University of California, Santa Barbara, in 1995, and after graduation, he worked as a hotel valet until he could decide what to do next. Greg called him almost every day, encouraging Jerome to do more with his life.

"More than my parents, he was there to help me out, and

I remember he had a real influence on me," Jerome said. "Greg could always figure something out."

Before staying out late drinking, for example, Jerome would stop and think about what he was doing, not wanting to worry Greg.

"In a sense, he helped keep me in check without really saying anything," Jerome said. "I wouldn't want him to be disappointed. I just thought he had it together."

In between visits, the brothers stayed in touch by phone. But like most young men, their conversations didn't delve much into the personal realm. Mostly, they discussed movies or the fishing, camping, hiking, or snowboard trips they took together on a regular basis. Intimate feelings and relationship issues just didn't come up.

Chapter 5

One activity that Greg and Kristin both viewed as important was spending time with family. As their relationship progressed, their two families began to integrate.

The couple often spent time with Marie de Villers or went on camping, hiking, or skiing trips with Jerome, Bertrand, and the occasional friend Greg had known since high school. In turn, Kristin frequently took Greg to her parents' house, where he would play video games with her youngest brother, Pierce, or hit the golf course with Pierce and her other brother, Brent, followed by dinner with her parents.

When Bertrand was still in high school, he started playing soccer more seriously and joined a traveling squad that competed regionally with teams such as Claremont's. He even played for a while on Brent's team in Claremont. At practice one afternoon during his senior year, he remembers Brent mentioning that his sister was dating Bertrand's brother. Bertrand, who never felt like he fit in with all the rich kids on that team, didn't play on it for long, so he and Brent never got that close.

The Rossums invited Greg and Marie to their house for

Thanksgiving dinner, and in subsequent years, Greg's brothers came, too. Everyone seemed to get along well. Ralph and Constance thought it would be good for Greg if they could reunite him with his estranged father. But Greg wasn't interested.

Once she got clean, Kristin was able to focus on her schoolwork. And it paid off.

She started off slowly, taking only two courses her first semester at SDSU, in the fall of 1995, while she continued to work with Greg at Rush Legal. On her application to the Medical Examiner's Office two years later, she stretched the time she'd worked at Rush, claiming she'd started in June 1994 and worked as assistant office manager through December 1995.

Kristin earned a B+ in probability and an A in the principles of physics that semester. By the spring of 1996, she was taking a full load, earning an A in chemistry, an A- in philosophy, a B+ in biology, and a B- in physics. That summer she took two more courses, getting an A in calculus and an A- in oral communication.

Kristin impressed her chemistry professors at SDSU as being one of their best and brightest. Professor Dale Chatfield, chairman of the Chemistry Department, had Kristin in several of his classes.

"She excelled at everything she did," he recalled. "She was really a perfectionist, as far as I can tell."

When she worked in groups of three, he noticed that she "took over and told everyone else what to do," which he attributed to her higher level of experience. Nonetheless, he noted, she still got along well with the other students. She was meticulous and thorough.

Kristin studied forensics, which included such topics as how to identify mysterious white powders at crime scenes.

This was not an uncommon sight at crime scenes in San Diego County at the time, when the region was known as the meth capital of the world.

In forensics classes, Chatfield explained, "You're trying to recreate any evidence you can from the scene of a crime. So you go into a place. You collect fingerprints. You collect dust. Sherlock Holmes business."

Kristin was also in Professor Bill Tong's chemistry lab.

"She was one of the best students we've ever seen," said Tong, who served as a mentor to Kristin.

From the fall of 1996 until she finished her coursework about three years later, Kristin earned almost all A's or A-'s. When she was awarded her bachelor's degree with a distinction in chemistry on December 29, 1999, her transcript showed a cumulative grade point average of 3.83. That average would have been lower if the Redlands coursework had been included as required. An average of 3.8 is required to graduate *summa cum laude* from SDSU.

Greg's academic performance at UCSD wasn't nearly as good as Kristin's. When he graduated with a degree in biology in 1997, his overall grade point average was 2.47. The Rossums didn't attend Greg's graduation, but they took him and Kristin out to dinner to celebrate.

In the weeks after the ceremony, Greg spent hours on the phone talking with the Rossums about his career options. The Rossums saw themselves as surrogate parents to Greg, and they bought him his first business suit.

It is unclear when, but Greg returned to work at the legal services company, which changed its name from Rush Legal to XL, until he got a lab assistant position at a pharmaceutical drug research firm, Biophysica, Inc. Greg told Constance that he found the lab environment boring and smelly. He wanted to work outdoors. Constance told him to follow his heart, so Greg applied for a position with the California Department of Fish and Game in the summer of 1997. Five months later, he received a notice that he failed the qualify-ing exam.

In August 1998, Greg was hired by BD Pharmingen, a company with four hundred employees. Tina Jones, the human relations executive who gave him the job, later described him as "an extremely nice young man. . . . He had a very bright future ahead of him."

Greg started as an administrative assistant to Stefan Gruenwald, the vice president of research and development. Greg was so driven, intelligent, and organized, he exceeded all of Gruenwald's expectations. He was promoted to a posi-tion where he issued licenses for medical research products the company developed and sold.

Greg was also well liked by his coworkers, who saw him as an even-tempered, low-key, and friendly guy.

"This was a very well-thought-out, well-balanced, got-it-together type of a fellow," said one colleague, Eldon Horn.

When Gruenwald left Pharmingen to form Orbigen, he and Greg stayed in touch by phone and e-mail.

In June 1997, Kristin answered an ad at SDSU for a stu-dent worker in the county Medical Examiner's Office's toxi-cology lab.

Kristin interviewed with Frank Barnhart, the supervising toxicologist. He'd started working there twenty-nine years earlier, doing urine drug screens, and inched his way up the ladder to help run the lab. Barnhart had testified in court many times to validate his lab's test results and was some-what of a meth expert. But since the office didn't run any type of background check on applicants, he had no reason to ask Kristin about her drug history. If he had known about it, he said later, he never would have hired her.

That's because forensic toxicologists' jobs revolve around

drugs, including those that cause death, alone or in combination, and are difficult to detect. While Kristin worked at the Medical Examiner's Office, the lab's shelves were filled with bottles and vials known as drug standards, which were purchased in a synthetic form for testing purposes. She and the other employees also had access to illegal street drugs and paraphernalia that Medical Examiner's investigators impounded from death scenes to help identify the cause of death.

The investigators often collected prescription drug vials and bags of unidentified white powder, which, in San Diego, generally turned out to be methamphetamine or cocaine. They also removed glass pipes, straws, syringes, and any other medications that family members said they didn't need anymore. Unidentified white powder wasn't tested, but if the cause of death was later determined to be a methamphetamine or cocaine overdose, a toxicologist could call up the case number on a computer to see what was impounded.

Investigators placed the impounded items in evidence envelopes, which were dropped through a slot in a locked box back at the office. When the box got too full, someone could have theoretically reached into the open slot and pulled out an envelope.

But the easiest point of access came when the contents of the box were emptied into a large plastic bag and then moved to the toxicology lab's Balance Room, which was left open during the day. The room was locked at night, but all the toxicologists knew where the keys were kept, and the office had no electronic system to monitor employees' comings and goings. Eventually, the envelopes were transferred to lockers, from which the controlled narcotics were removed and sent to the Sheriff's Department to be destroyed.

Barnhart was impressed by Kristin's resume and transcript from SDSU, which showed she had not only taken many chemistry classes, but had done very well in them. He recommended she be hired, and she got the job. Of all the interns Barnhart had worked with over the years, Kristin turned out to be his favorite.

"In that twenty-nine years, we had some incredibly talented people, but Kristin was the best," he said. "She stood out in terms of her ability to understand what you needed."

He became a mentor to her and considered her a close friend, nicknaming her "Lil Bandit" because she did her work so well and so fast.

By 1999 Barnhart wasn't happy working at the Medical Examiner's Office. He'd felt compelled to express his disapproval to Dr. Brian Blackbourne, the chief medical examiner, for hiring Blackbourne's girlfriend as the office operations manager, and Barnhart felt his remarks ended up costing him a promotion to head up the lab. After Blackbourne appointed someone else, Barnhart grew even more frustrated because the new guy kept asking him how to do things.

Barnhart finally decided he needed to leave, so he took a cut in pay to become a criminologist at the San Diego County Sheriff's Department's crime lab that March.

He and Kristin stayed in touch by e-mail, and a couple of months later, he asked her to come meet some of his new colleagues. He'd always been so impressed with her work that he urged his new colleagues to try to find her a job.

At the time, the only job position available was a nonpaying internship, so Kristin filled out a citizen volunteer application. The form, which she submitted on September 13, 1999, asked if she had ever used drugs, what type, and how many times. She wrote that she'd used methamphetamine thirty to forty times, most recently in May 1995, and cocaine and marijuana twice each. She checked "yes," that she'd been arrested, jailed, or charged with, convicted of or pleaded guilty to a crime.

She also checked "yes," that she'd been fired or asked to

resign. "I was let go from employment at California Pizza Kitchen because of bill discrepancies and mistakes," she wrote. "I was using drugs at the time, which influenced my performance."

During an interview in the personnel office on October 6, Kristin was told that her application had been denied because of her admitted drug use. She didn't say anything to Barnhart until he called and asked if she'd heard anything.

"Frank," he later recalled her saying, "I have got to tell you, I just told them that I used methamphetamine a couple times when I was in high school, and that did it."

Barnhart was shocked. He had no idea. He couldn't believe she never said anything before they went through the application process. He felt embarrassed that he had to tell his supervisor and colleagues she'd failed the background check. He also felt as though she'd betrayed their friendship a little. But true friends stick together through the good and the bad, and he decided not to give up on Kristin. If she'd used drugs only a couple of times and it was so many years ago, he thought, she might still qualify for an entry-level criminalist position. So some months later, he suggested that Kristin apply for one. He offered to look at the application—before she submitted it, this time—so she brought it over to his house with Greg in tow.

To him, Greg seemed like a really nice kid, but overly protective of Kristin—so much so that it made Barnhart uncomfortable. They all started off in the living room, watching some TV, then Barnhart took Kristin into his home office. They weren't gone for more than a couple of minutes when Greg joined them. Barnhart didn't understand why Greg was so worried about leaving Kristin alone with him.

This time she scored a ninety-five on her application. Later Barnhart said she must not have disclosed her previous drug use on that form or she wouldn't have scored so high.

She didn't get that job, either. The supervisor of controlled substances, who reviewed the application, told him he found out why she'd failed the original background check and decided that the Sheriff's Department wouldn't be an appropriate environment for her.

Even though the Sheriff's Department and the Medical Examiner's Office were sister county agencies, the sheriff's staff didn't share any of this information with Kristin's superiors.

Kristin and her high school friend Melissa Prager grew apart once they went away to college, but they became friends again after Kristin moved to San Diego and enrolled at SDSU. Prager, who came home from college in Ohio during the summer, spent weekends with her parents at their house in Encinitas, a small coastal city just north of San Diego. Prager tried to get together with Kristin while she was in the area.

The problem was that she never got to see Kristin alone. The first time she came over to visit Kristin at the apartment, Greg wouldn't make eye contact with Prager. She thought he seemed standoffish and not very interested in her, but he simply wouldn't leave the room. She wondered if he felt threatened by their friendship. Prager also found him too possessive and controlling of her friend, who had always seemed so strong-willed and independent. Prager recalled that when she asked Kristin to meet for lunch, Kristin would say things like, "Greg and I, um, think it would be better if you came to the house."

Kristin described Greg as some sort of "savior" and said she was happy he was "keeping her on track." Prager often wondered why Kristin had done drugs but had never gotten a good explanation.

"I've never been able to talk to her about it," she said later.

Back when they were in high school together, Prager wondered if Kristin was doing drugs, because she wouldn't eat anything at dinner, she'd breathe heavily, she looked nervous, and something in her voice sounded "really fake." But when Prager asked Kristin if she was doing drugs, she said no.

Since Kristin's parents were such a strong influence in her life, Prager said, perhaps Kristin did drugs to have "something of her own," a part of her life in which she wasn't trying to please them or anyone else.

"Her parents put a lot of academic pressure on her, a lot of pressure in general," she said.

When it came time to get married, Prager thought Kristin was succumbing to a different kind of pressure, and this time it was coming from Greg. It was as if she felt obligated to Greg because he'd helped her get off drugs. Prager thought Kristin loved him, felt loved by him, and had convinced herself that she should marry him. But she never got the impression that Kristin was *in love* with Greg. Prager thought Kristin was also motivated by a sense that her parents viewed proceeding with the wedding as the right thing to do.

"They completely inserted themselves" into Kristin's life, she said.

Kristin asked Prager to be her maid of honor, but Prager felt uncomfortable about accepting the offer.

"I was hesitant to be in it because I wasn't that supportive of it," she said.

When Prager found out that her brother was getting married in Israel in early July, she told Kristin she couldn't attend her wedding and was going to her brother's instead.

Apparently, Kristin wasn't too sure about her marriage plans, either, because she kept saying she wasn't certain the wedding was going to happen.

* * *

Jan Genovese, who was a Chemistry Department secretary at SDSU while Kristin was a student there, got to know her after she was honored for being the Most Outstanding Chemistry Student in 1998. Kristin would come into the office, and the two of them would chat. Kristin made quite an impression on Genovese.

"She was so magnetic, especially to men," Genovese said. "There weren't a lot of beautiful chemistry students."

Genovese thought Kristin played to her professors a bit, presenting herself in the best way possible for advancement. But, at the same time, Kristin seemed extremely needy.

In May 1999, Genovese ran into Kristin and a male student in the hallway, as she often did. The student, who lived near Kristin and Greg, had gotten to know Kristin in class and was about to graduate. He was a tall, athletic, premed student with chiseled features, nice parents, and a good background, just Kristin's type.

That day in the hallway, Kristin announced she was getting married. Her comment caught Genovese by surprise, but apparently not as much as the student. An expression of shock crossed his face. Genovese got the impression that Kristin was, frankly, bored by the prospect of marriage.

"What?" Genovese asked in disbelief. "You're getting married?"

The male student remained silent. As they watched Kristin walk away, Genovese recalled him saying, "Well, she's sure hot to trot for someone who's engaged."

Genovese and the student had become friendly over the years, so she felt comfortable telling him what she thought. Kristin seemed so ambivalent that Genovese thought she would call off the wedding. Genovese also thought that Kristin and the student would continue the close relationship that was apparent to her whenever she saw them together.

"You could do worse," she told him.

But the student dismissed the idea. He told her he didn't want to have anything to do with Kristin. He was going to medical school, he told Genovese, and he wasn't going to let a flirtatious girl derail him.

Genovese didn't get the sense that Kristin loved Greg. As Kristin walked away from her down the hall that day, Genovese remembered thinking, " I don't even know her."

The Rossums wanted an outdoor June ceremony for their daughter. They also wanted to invite a hundred people. Greg didn't like the idea of wearing a suit and tie in the summer sun, and he really didn't want a big wedding.

Kristin had her own reservations about the wedding, but they were more emotional in nature. She told her mother she couldn't decide whether Greg was the right man for her. He'd helped her so much over the years, getting her off drugs and supporting her as she put her life together, so she felt obligated to him. She even loved him. But she wasn't sure she felt as deeply passionate about him as she was supposed to. Kristin told her that Greg wanted to be with her all the time. He didn't seem to want her to have her own friends.

"Mom, I've made mistakes in my life, and I want to make sure I don't make another one," Constance recalled Kristin saying. "I want to make sure they're the right reasons. Every time I look at him, he reminds me of my past."

Constance suggested that both of them needed to develop their own sense of self, so they could continue to grow as individuals. She also said that wedding jitters were common.

"Remember," she told Kristin, "you've been talking about getting married since you were eighteen."

A year or so later, Kristin wrote in her diary that she thought she had "valid points and a deep-rooted reservation," but she didn't listen to the "inner voice" that told her to run away. Instead, she decided it was too late to break her commitment to Greg. She wished her mother had been more understanding and supportive, insistent, in fact, that they put off—or even call off—the wedding. If her own daughter didn't want to go through with her wedding, Kristin wrote, she "would take her hand and drive her away to safety. I certainly wouldn't imply that she had poor timing, and I wouldn't ever give the idea that it is a tragedy that my planning and hard work was all put to waste."

Finally, a couple of weeks before the wedding, Kristin called her mother and said she'd decided to go through with it. But the drama didn't end there.

In the days before the ceremony, Constance said, Greg almost called off the wedding when he found out his father had been invited and had already flown in from Monte Carlo. Constance said she apologized to Greg for not being more sensitive to his feelings about his father.

The Rossums and Marie had invited Yves de Villers to the wedding after meeting with him for an introductory lunch during Lent. They were hoping to arrange a reconciliation between Greg and his father, at the very least for the sake of their future grandchildren. Greg was not pleased when he found out about the lunch, complaining that his mother and in-laws had gone behind his back.

Yves arrived a couple of days before the wedding and went with Marie to order a rented tuxedo. Greg got upset when he heard that Yves was in town. He hadn't seen his father in quite some time, and he didn't want that kind of distraction at his wedding. He wanted it to be a day of celebration. So he called Jerome and told him as much.

"I don't want him messing anything up," Greg said.

Jerome passed that sentiment on to their father.

The day of the rehearsal dinner, Bertrand and Yves ran

some errands in Thousand Oaks and picked up the tuxedo that had been altered to fit Yves. Yves wanted to reestablish contact with Greg, but he was torn as to whether this was the best time to do so, especially given what Jerome had just told him. Yves said he forgot something back at the house, but Bertrand said they didn't have time to go back because they were late. So, Yves asked to be let out of the car to take a walk. Ultimately, he decided not to attend.

June 5 was the perfect sunny day for a wedding, albeit a little humid. Because of the good weather, the ceremony was held under the larger of two gazebos in the olive tree–lined courtyard of the Padua Hills Theatre, an historic Spanish Colonial building nestled in the Mt. San Antonio foothills of northern Claremont.

As the guests assembled to watch Greg and Kristin exchange vows, a little blond girl handed out white roses to the women, while a string quartet performed a selection of Bach pieces.

Ralph walked his daughter up the aisle as she carried a bouquet of flowers that, from the photos, look like roses. She was beaming, as if she felt she'd made the right decision.

Because Kristin had no bridesmaids or maid of honor, Greg had two best men, his brother Jerome and Kristin's brother Brent. Bertrand was the only groomsman.

The minister delivered a ceremony that was peppered with religious references as he spoke to the couple under the gazebo, with family and friends looking on from folding chairs.

"Marriage is not to be entered into unadvisedly or lightly, but reverently, deliberately, and in accordance with the purposes for which it was instituted by God," the minister said.

He asked Kristin and Greg the usual questions, starting with the bride: "Kristin, will you have this man to be your husband, to live together in the covenant of marriage? Will you love him, comfort him, honor and keep him in sickness and in health and, forsaking all others, be faithful to him as long as you both shall live?"

"I will," Kristin said sweetly, making a vow that would echo with irony in a matter of months. Greg made the same promise, repeating the words softly and with meaning. Then the minister led the guests in prayer and guided the couple through their final vows.

After the ceremony, the guests moved inside to the intimate dining room, which had once been used for dinner theater. There, amid the tables on the hardwood dance floor, Ralph welcomed Greg to the family. He noted that this was an international event that Marie's sister, Marie-Paul, had come all the way from France to attend. The Rossums' relatives, he noted, had flooded in from all over: Michigan, Indiana, Illinois, Texas, Arizona, Utah, California, and Minnesota.

Jerome gave an awkward but heartfelt speech, eliciting laughter as he admitted that marriage was almost a foreign concept to him, so much so that he was shocked when Greg called him one day at his dorm and told him he'd asked Kristin to marry him.

"My brother has never hesitated on this marriage, and I'm just really proud of him," he said. "I know relationships are a lot of hard work. It takes patience, just a lot of compromise."

Greg had told him and showed him that "the rewards were all worth it. So, I guess," he said, pausing to raise his glass, "Cheers."

Brent Rossum made a short toast, making way for his father to stand up once more to share his feelings of pride about his daughter. He'd felt it while watching her physically conquer the role of the sugar plum fairy to such beautiful music, dancing with a professional in *The Nutcracker* all those years ago. A few weeks earlier, she was inducted into Phi Beta Kappa at SDSU. And with her marriage on this glorious sunny day, he said, she'd done it again.

Ralph said he also was proud of his new son-in-law and his expanded family, wishing the couple "a life of love, happiness, health, and success."

Greg, the only one to take the floor and make a toast without a drink in his hand, introduced his mother and his aunt, then thanked Constance and Ralph for making the day, including the weather, so perfect.

"Kristin is the most wonderful person I've ever met," he said. "She's incredible in so many ways, in everything she does. She's a perfectionist. She's so intelligent. She's so kind and caring and sharing."

Greg's closing words came slowly, his voice thick with emotion. "I just can't wait to spend the rest of my life with her."

Finally, Bertrand, who'd had a bit too much champagne, gave the final touching toast featured on the homemade wedding video.

"Kristin is a beautiful woman inside and out, and I couldn't think of a better person to have with my brother. I'm so proud to have you as a sister now and to have an extension of our family here in the United States. It's wonderful."

Bertrand, turning to Greg, teased his older brother about the deep and sincere feelings he had for Kristin, admitting that when he and Jerome ribbed Greg about the relationship, it was only out of love.

"Sometimes we just think we're losing you," he said. "I can only hope that I'm so in love with a girl like you are when I get married, because it's really beautiful, and I can tell you're totally infatuated. As much as we give you a hard time about it, we really think it's beautiful. . . . I don't know if you understand how well you complement each other. No one's perfect individually, but, Greg, you do such a good job of bringing out the best in Kristin, and she does a wonderful job [of doing the same with you]. . . . May God bless your relationship forever and ever."

Chapter 6

During the next six months, Greg and Kristin seemed happy. As a wedding gift, Greg's family paid for them to honeymoon at Whistler-Blackcomb Mountains, a vacation area north of Vancouver. The newlyweds started talking about having children.

"Mom, I'm going off birth control," Constance recalled Kristin telling her, "and what happens will happen."

Greg had already come up with a name for the baby if they had a girl: Isabelle. Constance suggested Marie Isabelle, after Greg's mother.

But the marital bliss didn't last long.

In January 2000, Kristin started complaining to Constance during their phone conversations and shopping trips that Greg was getting more clingy and controlling, and that she felt like a bird in a cage. Kristin wrote in her diary about one such shopping excursion in La Jolla, where she and Constance engaged in some heart-to-heart "mother-daughter bonding." She wrote that she never felt very close to her mother, but she was trying to get closer. It was a very emotional afternoon.

One night, when her parents came down to San Diego to

visit, Kristin showed up alone, saying she'd left Greg home in bed because he wasn't feeling well.

"He seemed . . . not robust," Constance said, "though he'd never really been robust."

At one point, Constance said, Greg wondered if he might have chronic fatigue syndrome. However, he never mentioned any such thing to his own family, who thought he was quite healthy.

None of the negative sentiments Kristin confided to Constance showed up in the e-mails she regularly exchanged with Greg. Oftentimes, Greg would make a suggestion and ask her what she wanted to do for lunch, dinner, or the weekend. He didn't dictate what they were doing. In turn, she would often ask him to make decisions for them.

On January 14, 2000, for example, she told him she'd picked up her transcript from SDSU and was excited to learn she was graduating *summa cum laude* with distinction in chemistry. She suggested going out for a celebratory beer or renting some movies, but asked him to choose their activities for the evening. She ended with, "Let me know the plans. Love you with all my heart, Wifey."

It was apparent from the e-mails that Greg liked to spend his spare time with her and to plan different activities for them. And it appeared to be mutual. Kristin seemed to be trying hard to please him as well.

"I'm going to go to the grocery store this afternoon. Any requests?" she wrote on February 22. ". . . Your wish is my command."

Kristin made lunches and tins of biscotti for Greg to take to work, often checking with him about what he wanted to eat for dinner and offering him a choice of entrees. She obviously liked to cook them nice meals, anything from salmon to stir-fried chicken, sun-dried tomato cream pasta with steamed artichokes, shrimp, pork tenderloin, or steak.

Frequently, they'd discuss renting a video or two to watch the same night. *American Beauty* was one of Kristin's favorites, and she'd seen it three or four times. Greg liked basic guy movies, but he also enjoyed more thoughtful films, such as *A River Runs Through it, Legends of the Fall,* or *Shakespeare in Love.*

The e-mails they exchanged rarely had sexual overtones, although Kristin and Greg often said "I love you" and gave each other pet names like "Mr. Big," "Sweetie," "Dolling," "Gregie," "Wifey, "Bunny Kristin," and "Kristinie."

But, in general, the gist of most of their messages was pretty mundane. They discussed emptying the dishwasher, dropping off the rent check, getting the car fixed, or planning a trip to visit the in-laws. The only notable exception was a series of quick notes that Kristin started on February 2, sending Greg a "giant, wet, slobbery kiss" and telling him she loved him. Greg said he didn't usually like those wet kisses, but by e-mail, it wasn't that bad. Kristin offered a "soft, tender, gentle" kiss instead, and Greg said he especially liked those kinds of kisses.

Like best friends, they shared their good news with each other and celebrated one another's successes. While Kristin was waiting to hear whether she'd get a permanent job as a county toxicologist, she explored other career options, including the Navy's engineering officer program. But on March 1, Kristin got her dream job. She sent an e-mail to Greg—written in capital letters with two lines of exclamation points—to tell him how excited she was to get a job offer as a permanent toxicologist at the Medical Examiner's Office.

"Yippee for me!" Kristin wrote.

"See, you are the best!" Greg replied.

A letter from Lloyd Amborn said her new job would offi-

cially start March 17, as long as she passed a law enforcement background investigation and a medical screening. The
starting annual salary was $32,448, with a 3 percent raise
scheduled to go into effect in July. If county officials ever
did that background check, they wouldn't have had access to
her arrest in 1994 because she was under eighteen when it
happened.

On May 22, when Greg was winding down at Pharmingen,
Kristin wished him a good day in his last week before starting his new job at Orbigen.

"I'm so proud of you," she wrote.

Many of Greg's e-mails supported Constance's claim that
he was not in the best of health. He repeatedly mentioned
feeling tired and sluggish, having a hard time getting out of
bed, and being plagued by headaches.

"I hope my head is not pounding by the end of the day,
though! Still feeling achy and sore in my muscles! I just need
to get more rest," he wrote on April 24.

Greg's ailments continued throughout the summer. "I did
not feel well this morning," he wrote Kristin on the morning
of July 7. "Feeling a little dizzy with a bad headache and also
just feeling sick. It was something that seemed to hit me
yesterday evening."

Nonetheless, Greg usually tried to rally after work so he
could go with Kristin to swing dance lessons or yoga class or
to watch her take a ballet class.

At the same time Kristin was sending her husband these
e-mails, she was also corresponding with other men.

Joe Rizzo had worked with Kristin at the Medical Examiner's Office as an accounting clerk while he was attending
law school but then moved to the East Coast to work for a
law firm.

"I really can't wait to see you, too," he e-mailed Kristin on June 18, 1999, just two weeks after her wedding. He was coming to town that August and promised to call when he had a firm arrival date. "I was really worried you didn't love me anymore."

In mid-December, he wished her a Merry Christmas. "I miss you terribly and think of you all the time," he wrote. "I am truly sorry we have grown apart over this time."

By the spring of 2000, the tone of the e-mails had grown more urgent. Rizzo contacted Kristin on March 27, starting off a volley of increasingly intimate messages.

"Oh my God!" she replied. "I've been thinking about you so much lately. . . . So when are you going to be visiting? Miss you terribly."

Rizzo must have taken Kristin's welcoming reception to heart, because he invited her on an all-expenses-paid weekend in New York. "I am going to be all alone, and I thought immediately of you," he wrote.

Kristin said such a trip might be hard to explain to her husband, "but, hey, a girl can dream, can't she?"

Rizzo urged her to make it happen. "I don't want to just imagine anymore," he wrote.

Kristin seemed open to the idea, saying they'd have to give it "some serious consideration."

Rizzo explained in some detail how he was getting physically excited at the prospect of seeing her again. "Those old feelings are back," he said.

Dan Dewall, whom she'd met in a plant physiology class at SDSU, sent her several e-mails at the lab. One invited her to meet at "that park" around noon. Another recounted the contents of an e-mail he'd sent after they'd last seen each other, which he thought might have gotten lost in cyberspace: "I like you a lot, etc., etc., etc. . . . I promise that the next time you tell me you are tired, I will slow the pace and hold you a while so you can rest."

* * *

In early March, a handsome, athletic Australian toxicologist named Michael Robertson started working as the lab's unofficial manager, a title that would become official once his work visa issues were resolved. There was an immediate attraction between Kristin and her soon-to-be boss, a married man in his early thirties who came with a Ph.D. and an impressive resume.

She later wrote in her diary that she'd had a teenage fantasy about falling in love at first sight, knowing immediately that she'd found "the one." Well, she wrote, she wasn't sure if that's what had happened, but when she and Michael made eye contact, "My legs got weak and my tummy was full of butterflies."

Michael, who went by Mic or Robbo, had been offered the job of lab manager on December 1, 1999, but his visa issues were taking so long to resolve that he and Lloyd Amborn, the office administrator, negotiated a deal whereby Michael could start in early March as a "visitor." That way, he could get familiar with how they did things in the lab until he could legally take over. In the meantime, Donald "Russ" Lowe continued as acting lab manager. Michael didn't officially assume the position until June 12.

Michael had been a forensic toxicologist at National Medical Services (NMS) in Pennsylvania since April 1996, performing, supervising, and certifying toxicology test results that were going to be used in court. He also testified as an expert witness.

He testified, for example, in a highly publicized case involving several teenage boys who were charged with fatally drugging fifteen-year-old Samantha Reid of Lansing, Michigan, by putting gamma hydroxybutyrate—the date-rape drug known on the street as GHB, Liquid X, or Liquid Ecstasy—in her Mountain Dew. Reid's death on January 17, 1999, led to the passage of the Hillory J. Farias and Samantha Reid Date-Rape Drug Prohibition Act of 2000, which added GHB to the list of drugs that are unlawful to manufacture, distribute, or dispense unless authorized by the federal government.

Michael started at NMS as a postdoctoral fellow and trainee, using the High Pressure Liquid Chromatograph, or HPLC, machine for toxicology testing. He also taught classes at Thomas Jefferson University in Philadelphia. He got the job at NMS after his teacher, Olaf Drummer, called the company head, Dr. Fredric Rieders, to recommend him for an internship. Rieders, who was originally from Austria, found the Australian toxicologist to be "a very bright young man" and hired him. Michael, Rieders said later, turned out to be "a great pleasure to work with."

Michael had earned his doctorate in forensic medicine at Monash University in Melbourne in 1996, where he studied pharmacology and biochemistry on a graduate scholarship. From 1991 to 1996, he worked as a part-time scientist at the Victorian Institute of Forensic Medicine in Melbourne, an agency with functions similar to an American coroner's or medical examiner's office, earning an annual stipend of $10,000.

His would-be employees in San Diego were impressed by his qualifications and experience. When he applied to San Diego in 1999, his resume listed fifteen published articles. The subjects ranged from the forensic investigation of drug-related fatal traffic accidents to the concentration of benzodiazepines, a class of drugs commonly known as tranquilizers, in the liquid surrounding the eyeball, the vitreous humor, which can be key in identifying toxic substances in the body.

Michael also had given a number of presentations at conferences in the United States, Europe, and Australia on topics such as date-rape drugs and how drugs can change in structure and concentration after a person dies. Clonazepam, one of the drugs found in Greg's body, is a benzodiazepine and is classified as a date-rape drug.

Employees, such as Cathy Hamm, who had worked in the toxicology lab for more than fifteen years, were hopeful he would make some changes to improve the operation.

Michael seemed friendly, calling his new coworkers "mate." He wasn't a tall man, but he had a solid build and a nice smile. He quickly developed a schedule, outlining a division of work for getting things done in a more organized fashion.

"Initially, we were excited," Hamm said. "He was pretty aggressive, presenting studies, like a mentor."

But within a month of his arrival, the whole working environment had changed. When Kristin started her permanent job as a toxicologist in March 2000, it just so happened that the only open desk available was right in front of Michael's office. The top half of his office door was made of glass, so the other lab workers could see what was going on inside, even if the door was closed.

It wasn't long before Michael was spending what seemed like an inordinate amount of time in Kristin's workspace near the HPLC machine, and she in his office. Although Hamm noticed that Michael and Kristin shared the habit of standing too close to other people, the two of them stood even closer to each other.

"When two people are attracted to each other, you can't hide it," Hamm said.

Hamm and the other toxicologists found their working environment more and more uncomfortable. Plus, there seemed to be some favoritism going on.

"It was just the way that they looked at each other," she said.

The toxicologists who had worked there for years started to talk. Michael was going to be their boss as soon as his visa issues were resolved, and the close relationship between him and Kristin was already breeding resentment. It seemed that most of his attention was focused on her and whatever projects she was working on.

Kristin wrote in her diary that she never imagined she would develop such deep feelings for a married man, especially so soon after she'd gotten married herself, but it was out of her control. She wasn't getting what she needed emotionally from Greg, and Michael felt the same way about his relationship with his wife, Nicole.

Kristin and Michael quickly developed a close bond of friendship, sharing their feelings, their frustrations, and their dreams with each other. They soon realized they were kindred spirits, both in marriages with partners who did not share their values, beliefs, goals, or interests. She and Michael, she wrote, were "inspired by art and love reading, [and] we share a passion for music." They also realized they had something else in common that was very dear to Kristin: They were both "die-hard romantics."

"We just shared so many philosophies on what it means to have a good life; what is important in life; basic, fundamental ideals," Kristin wrote as she traced back her feelings months later. She described Michael as "witty, charming, intelligent, and handsome," saying she admired him and was inspired by him and his professional accomplishments. He made her feel thrilled to go to work.

"I realized that I really loved him and was truly in love with him," she wrote.

And the feeling was mutual.

Michael already had a history of extramarital flirtations, at least one of which led to an affair. When he first started working in San Diego, a woman from Pennsylvania frequently used to call the lab. He would speak to her in low tones so no one else could hear. She and Michael communicated by e-mail at least through March 2000.

The woman sent Michael an e-mail on March 17, saying she wished she had more photos of the two of them. She wrote that she could look at photos of him all day and wished she could hang one up at work, but then everyone would know about them. She said she'd even take one to work on a Saturday so she could look at it, but she never worked alone. She added that she would try to call him from work one morning when no one else was around, because the weekends were rough when she couldn't talk to him. It drove her crazy, particularly if she was at home without enough to do.

"Am I pathetic or what," she wrote. "You probably think I'm crazy and obsessed."

On March 27, she sent Michael another e-mail, thanking him for writing her every day while she was in the hospital, even when she wasn't there to receive his notes. She had just reread all of his recent e-mails and realized she'd missed a "get well" card from him.

"Some days I don't know which is worse, the pain in my side from the operation or the pain in my heart from missing you so much," she wrote.

Michael told some of his friends about his extramarital activities, but others knew nothing about them and thought he was happily married.

Dan Anderson, a fellow toxicologist at the Los Angeles County Department of Coroner, fell into the latter group. He and Michael were both members of the Society of Forensic Toxicologists (SOFT), an organization formed in 1970 for the "express purpose of promoting understanding and goodwill" among professionals in their shared field. The two men first met in 1996 at a SOFT conference in Denver.

"We drummed around a little bit in Denver, and we became friends," Anderson said. "He was a really nice guy."

While Anderson and Michael were on a bus, Michael told him how he'd met the love of his life in Australia—his wife, Nicole—who came with him to the United States. Anderson got the feeling that they were married after only a few months of knowing each other. Nicole worked as an auditor of medical research.

The two men met up at another five-day SOFT conference in October 1999. This one was held at a resort in Puerto Rico, so both of their wives came along and made it a vacation. Cocktails were expensive, so Anderson and his wife invited a bunch of friends, including Michael and Nicole, to party in their room. They bought a blender, a few cases of beer, and fixings for banana daiquiris at Wal-Mart, filled their bathtub with ice and spent most of the time partying. They would lie by the pool or play volleyball during the day and go out to restaurants at night, piling far too many people into their rental car.

Anderson thought that Nicole, whom he described as about five-feet-five-inches and sandy blond, was a pretty girl with a bubbly personality. She and Michael were affectionate with each other and seemed happy together, although Michael did confide in Anderson that she was very insecure and constantly needed reaffirmation of his feelings for her.

While they were in Puerto Rico, Michael told Anderson he was getting ready to leave Pennsylvania and was hopeful after interviewing for a job in San Diego.

The next month Anderson attended a California Association of Toxicologists (CAT) conference at a hotel on Shelter Island in San Diego. He saw an attractive blond girl working at the registration table and asked a colleague who she was. He was told that she was Kristin Rossum, a student worker at the local Medical Examiner's Office who was helping out toxicologists Russ Lowe and Cathy Hamm, the conference hosts.

Anderson gave a talk that afternoon titled "Basic Drugs: Extractions, Methods and New Drugs." The day's agenda also included a presentation on services offered by the poison control system.

Anderson didn't actually meet Kristin until the state toxicologists' conference in May 2000, which was held at the Holiday Inn in North Hollywood. Kristin came with Michael, her new boss, who gave a talk on the pharmacology of rave drugs entitled "Why all the RAVE?"

During his presentation, Michael described the history, street names, effects, and chemical makeup of drugs such as ecstasy, methamphetamine, mushrooms, LSD, GHB, ketamine, also known as Special K, and the date-rape drugs Rohypnol and clonazepam.

He said methamphetamine was first made in 1919 from amphetamine and was currently available for the treatment of obesity. It was used in World War II by the military to keep the soldiers alert in the United States, Japan, and Germany. Hitler was reported to be a meth abuser.

In 1997, he said, 4.4 percent of high school seniors had used crystal meth, compared to 2.7 percent in 1990. He said the drug caused symptoms such as dilated pupils, constriction of blood vessels, hypothermia, and hot and clammy skin.

Anderson hosted the conference. And because he knew that Michael was temporarily working without pay at his new job, Anderson invited Michael a month or two in advance to share a hotel room. Initially, Michael had accepted, but when Anderson saw him the first day, Michael said he didn't need the room after all.

That night a group of toxicologists went to dinner at Universal CityWalk, near Universal Studios in Hollywood. Anderson sat between Kristin and Michael at the bar but didn't notice anything going on. Later that night, two female colleagues told Anderson they noticed an obvious attraction between Kristin and Michael. They saw her flirting and giving him the eye.

Anderson was in denial about it at first and didn't put it all together until later. "I think they were sleeping together at that conference," he said.

Based on e-mails that Michael sent right after the conference to a friend in Australia and shortly thereafter to Kristin, Anderson appeared to be correct.

On Tuesday, May 9, Michael wrote to a female friend asking for advice. Yes, he said, he knew he was married, but he'd met a woman in the lab who'd swept him off his feet, calling it "déjà vu again."

"She, too, is married, and the feelings between us are mutual, both very confused and both trying hard to find a solution," he wrote.

Despite Nicole's mood swings and emotional issues, he told her, he'd thought he was happy with his wife. But then he met Kristin, who seemed much more compatible, and it "all just kind of happened." They shared values, she liked the outdoors, and she even said she'd be willing to move to Australia with him. Now that he'd met Kristin, he wrote, he'd lost his "deep feelings for Nicole" and wasn't sure if he could ever get them back. He was having a hard time pretending that everything was fine at home and wanted to talk to Nicole about it, but he knew she'd be tremendously upset.

Three days later, Michael used his personal e-mail account to send Kristin a short note and some photos of his sister's wedding.

"Thinking of you and missing you already," he wrote.

By the following week, he and Kristin were professing their eternal love for each other.

"I want nothing more than to give my all to you," Michael wrote her on May 16. "My life, my love, my world."

"I'll be thinking of you and all that the future has to offer," Kristin wrote Michael on May 18. "I can't wait for it to begin."

That same day, Kristin wrote an e-mail to her brother Brent, expressing regret that she hadn't called off the wedding and that she'd let their parents convince her she was just having "cold feet."

"Mom and Dad encouraged me to go through with it and . . . they had invested so much time and money into the event by then, I guess I felt that I didn't really have a choice," she wrote. "Well, here I am a year later, and looking back, I wish I hadn't gone through with it."

As she weighed the good and the bad aspects of staying with Greg, she said, it all boiled down to not wanting to disappoint her family. "And that is not a very good reason for staying married," she wrote. Feeling "so torn apart inside," Kristin asked Brent for his feedback. There was more to tell, she said, but that would come later. She never mentioned that she'd started an affair with her boss.

Brent wrote back, offering his complete love and support for whatever decision she would ultimately make. He said he didn't think she should stay with Greg just to avoid disappointing their parents.

"Sure, no one wants this to happen, but if you are not happy, which is all that matters in this case, then it is justified," he wrote.

He also underscored how proud their parents were of her, constantly bragging about her accomplishments.

"They want what is best for you and will no doubt act accordingly," he wrote.

Kristin told Brent how much she appreciated his support

and thanked him for listening to her troubles. "Now I'm stuck with the heavy realization that I married the wrong person," she wrote.

A couple of days after Kristin and Greg's first anniversary on June 5, Brent checked in with his sister by e-mail. He apologized for not calling but said he didn't feel comfortable wishing them a happy anniversary after what she'd told him.

Kristin wrote back and said she was "hanging in there." She'd made a nice candlelight dinner for her and Greg and bought him a few gifts. "He didn't even bring home a card," she wrote. "But that's okay, I guess, because he was sick."

Kristin wrote Brent again on August 9, letting him know that she'd discussed her marital problems with their parents over the weekend and they were very supportive. "I wish I knew what to do," she wrote.

A week later Kristin received a confirmation by e-mail that she'd used her Visa card to pay $60 for a two-month subscription to an apartment rental service.

After the CAT conference in May, Michael and Kristin continued to express their feelings for each other in a consistent stream of greeting cards, letters, and e-mails, developing their own shorthand language for the powerful emotions they were experiencing. Both said they'd never felt this way about anyone else, repeatedly using dramatic words like always, forever, destiny, fate, adoration, and passion. They constantly talked about getting married to each other, having children, and growing old together.

They often left the office for lunch, and on at least one occasion, came back with wet hair. One day they were gone for ninety minutes, and Kristin was seen eating lunch in the coffee room after she got back.

On Friday, May 19, Kristin took Michael to the SDSU

Chemistry Department picnic. She thanked him in an e-mail later that afternoon and said she wished she were better at articulating her feelings for him.

The following Tuesday morning, Michael e-mailed Kristin to thank her for "dropping by," apparently at his apartment. He said he'd intended to make her a cup of tea, but "one thing led to another. . . ."

The next morning he e-mailed Kristin to tell her he loved her. "I'll tell you more slowly at lunch," he wrote.

The aftermath of their lovemaking must have been quite obvious to their coworkers, because Lloyd Amborn confronted Michael about "their conduct" that Thursday. Amborn said the other toxicologists were complaining that Michael was having an inappropriate relationship with their newest and youngest colleague. Michael denied that anything was going on, then e-mailed Kristin right after the meeting to warn her that Amborn planned to call her in that afternoon. Amborn, he wrote, had noticed the two of them "being a little too close" and told him that such behavior needed to stop.

"I need a 'Hi, it's all going to be okay' kinda hug, but I guess that would be inappropriate, hey?" Michael wrote.

He also suggested that Kristin delete all his e-mails after reading them.

"Any snoop can check your 'inbox' while you're out if no one is around, and my e-mails to you may not be well received," he wrote.

After their respective meetings with Amborn, they stopped going to lunch together in the same car. But their coworkers still noticed that they were gone at the same time, often leaving and returning within five minutes of each other.

The two lovers could not and would not stay away from each other during the week. Over the weekend, though, they had to.

On Sunday, May 21, Michael wrote her a note from the

nearby Ralph's supermarket, where he often stopped at the computer café to send her weekend notes on his way to play Australian football.

"At 9 A.M., my missing you has been officially upgraded to 'intensely,' soon to move to 'unbearably,' " he wrote, fantasizing about the time they could be together on a Sunday morning so he could tell her in person.

He wrote her again from Ralph's the following Sunday afternoon at 2:30. Kristin was graduating that day, right about that time, and he wanted to let her know he was thinking of her.

"Dear Adrenalin," he called her, explaining that the nickname stemmed from the physical sensations she caused in him. He told her he wished he could be there to "cheer from the back row. I'm cheering on the inside."

Most of Kristin's coworkers, including Michael, met Greg for the first and only time at a going-away party for a colleague at the 94th Aero Squadron restaurant in Kearny Mesa that spring.

Throughout the summer, Michael and Kristin met after work at a place just blocks from each of their apartments in University City. They dubbed their meeting place "the Willows" for the trees that grew where Regents Road dead-ended near a path at Rose Canyon. It was a secret spot, where Kristin once instructed her beau to "bring your biggest muscles." They would meet there for a walk, a talk, and who knows what else. They also met a number of times during the lunch hour for what they referred to as a "quickie breakie," apparently at Michael's apartment.

Kristin initiated a secret game of treasure hunt in the office, where they left hidden gifts for each other, then sent directions by e-mail to find them.

On June 12, Michael e-mailed Kristin to thank her for the card she'd hidden in his office. It reminded him of a game his grandparents played throughout their marriage of more than fifty years, in between stealing kisses, flirting, holding hands, and finishing each other's sentences. Their game, he explained, consisted of taking turns scribbling the word "shmily" in unexpected places for the other one to find—in the steam on the bathroom mirror, in the ashes in the fireplace, in the sugar and flour containers, and in the dew on the windows overlooking the patio, where his grandmother fed them "warm homemade pudding with blue food coloring." Once, his grandmother even managed to write the word on the last sheet of a roll of toilet paper. After she developed breast cancer, his grandfather continued to display affection for his one true love by painting her bedroom yellow and taking her to church until she was too weak to get out of bed. He played the game until the very end, writing "shmily" on the pink ribbons of her funeral bouquet.

> "Although I couldn't begin to fathom the depth of their love," Michael wrote, "I had been privileged to witness its unmatched beauty.
> S-See
> H-How
> M-Much
> I-I
> L-Love
> Y-You."

On June 14, Michael directed Kristin to look under his desk for a box with a folded newspaper and a sheet of paper on top.

"Remove the sheet of paper (I need it) and remove the newspaper. The contents are just for you just because!" Michael wrote.

Kristin replied, "It seems as if you know me so well and

can anticipate my feelings without fail. . . . Everything I ever imagined in a lifelong companion, husband, best friend is present in you."

On June 20, Dr. Blackbourne asked Michael to meet with him and a police detective, Terry Torgeson, about a case the Medical Examiner's Office had handled five years earlier. The office had determined the cause of death to be Versed, a sedative in the benzodiazepine family, but Torgeson had recently gotten a tip that fentanyl was the true cause of the woman's death. So, another investigation was conducted. Michael sent the woman's blood samples to National Medical Services, his former employer, and it came back positive for Versed *and* a significant amount of fentanyl. The Medical Examiner's Office had missed the fentanyl because its toxicology lab didn't test for it.

Even while Kristin was engulfed by emotion for Michael, she also seemed to need the same level of affection from Greg. She continued to tell her husband she loved him and seemed to get frustrated and upset when he pulled away. At the same time, she was also trying to please Michael, constantly reminding him that he was the most important person in her life.

On June 5, her first wedding anniversary with Greg, she sent Michael a hug and kiss through cyberspace. "I LOVE YOU!!!" she wrote. "See you in my dreams."

In an e-mail on June 20, Kristin wrote to Greg, "What? No 'I love you'??? You must be busy."

Greg apologized by e-mail nine minutes later and told her the words she wanted to hear.

On June 26, Kristin e-mailed Greg to tell him that Michael had an extra ticket to the Natalie Merchant concert for the following night. She said his wife ended up not being able to go and suggested he take a coworker. She said they had a raffle, and she won. She'd like to go if he didn't mind.

"Let me know what you think so that he can give it to the runner-up if you don't want me to go, okay?" she wrote.

There was no such raffle.

That same day Michael and Kristin had lunch together. After lunch he asked Kristin if she was up for submitting a paper to the Society of Forensic Toxicologists and presenting it at a conference in Milwaukee in October. He'd been sending her copies of e-mails he'd sent to a toxicologist from SOFT, discussing the possibility of presenting a strychnine case the San Diego lab had worked on. He'd finally gotten the go-ahead.

It was a huge career opportunity for Kristin, and Michael wanted to help her with it. Later that day, before they both left the office to go home to their respective spouses, he e-mailed her to say how beautiful she looked reading at her desk.

Kristin obviously felt torn and confused by her two relationships. The next day she messaged Greg twice, trying to connect with him. She said he looked "really tired" that morning, and she was wondering how he was feeling. "I guess you must be pretty busy," she wrote. "You never seem to have time to respond to my e-mails."

She tried messaging him again the day after that, first thing. "I'm sorry that I haven't been able to make you happier," she wrote. "I feel so lousy and empty inside, very alone." She said she missed him and had for a long time. They should use an upcoming trip to Mammoth "as a chance to escape and re-connect," she said, and asked him what he thought of her idea.

He agreed, asking her what time she'd gotten to the lab. Apparently, they'd had an emotional conversation that morning, and she'd left the apartment upset. She replied that she stopped at Starbucks on her way to work, taking time to let the tears pass and to compose herself. She asked how he was feeling, but he didn't answer. Two hours later, her tone grew more insistent. She found it difficult to concentrate at work with so much on her mind. Why wasn't he answering her?

"Are we going to be alright? I miss our closeness. I miss you," she wrote, urging him to respond.

"I'm okay, I guess," he replied finally, saying they could talk when they got home.

Kristin e-mailed him again that afternoon, telling him she loved him and that she hoped he'd enjoyed his lunch. She said she was thinking of him, signing off by using her pet nickname "Wifey."

The couple did go on the de Villers brothers' annual summer camping trip to Mammoth over the Fourth of July holiday. Jerome's girlfriend, Jacinta Jarrell, known as J.J., went along, too. Greg's brothers thought Kristin seemed more needy than usual on that trip. Jerome and Greg went off hiking for two and a half hours, and when they came back, the brothers said Kristin was upset and crying because he'd been gone for so long.

Meanwhile, back in San Diego, Michael was having a difficult time dealing with the thought of Kristin vacationing with Greg. It was most difficult at night, when he wondered what she was doing, what she was thinking. So, he wrote her e-mails every day to tell her that she was on his mind. He reread the notes she'd written to him, perfumed with her scent, and replayed memories of their time together. He missed her like crazy and was counting the days until her return.

On July 4, she'd been gone for five days and just as many long nights. He was rereading some of her e-mails, trying to warm his heart, when the phone rang. It was Kristin. Her call raised his spirits so much that he wrote to her about it after-wards: "A well-tuned orchestra playing a waltz could never sound so wonderful, the voice that induces the growth of a smile, the feelings of love, of warmth, and of so many" other feelings he couldn't even describe.

Greg found one of Michael's love letters in the apartment in June or July. Furious, he made Kristin give him Michael's home phone number and called him around 9 or 10 that night.

Michael and Nicole were in bed when the phone rang. Michael picked it up, but Nicole could hear Greg shouting into the receiver. Michael's face went gray, and he took the phone into the next room.

"Stay the hell away from my wife," Greg told him.

Michael had told Nicole that he was attracted to someone in the office. But even after the phone call, Michael told her the same story that Kristin told Greg: The two of them were having an emotional relationship, but they weren't physi-cally involved.

However, the e-mails the two lovers exchanged reflected a connection that was all encompassing.

"You are my love, my perfect match, the one I see beside me at the altar, at home, holding my children, waking beside me in the morning, and kissing good night," Michael wrote on July 23.

Later that summer, Kristin told student worker Tom Horn she wasn't happy in her marriage and wasn't sure her hus-band was the right man for her. She asked Horn if he knew of any apartments available in Mission Hills, but she said nothing about having an affair with their boss.

For the first time ever, Greg told his brothers that he and Kristin were going to have to back out of plans to go to Mammoth over Labor Day. They didn't have the money for it. Greg apologized to nonfamily members that he and Kristin had to cancel at the last minute because of their work schedules. He was working at a start-up company, he explained, and it was a bad time to take time off. Kristin also had a work project that needed her full attention through September.

In August or September, Greg's high school friend Bill Leger came to San Diego with his fiancée and went to the zoo with his parents. They invited Kristin and Greg to come along, and the two couples made plans to get together over Thanksgiving for a ski trip to Tahoe. Sometime after that, Leger and Greg talked on the phone about the ski trip, and Greg told him he was thinking about buying a house. The lease for their apartment was about to expire, and it was the last one that the university would renew since he wasn't a UCSD student anymore. By the end of the year, he told Leger, he and Kristin should be completely out of debt.

Kristin saw her friend Melissa Prager once in March 2000 and several times over the summer. The March rendezvous was at Miracles Café in Encinitas, where Prager was excited to spend some alone time with her friend for the first time since she'd met Greg. But Greg showed up, too.

Finally, in August, Kristin came alone. She and Prager had dinner in La Jolla and watched the sunset together, and Kristin said she'd been taking ballet lessons again. She seemed more relaxed, clearheaded, and healthy than Prager had ever seen her. Kristin glowed as she talked about this guy she'd met at work. Michael was her boss, she said, and he appreciated and respected her for her mind, her beauty, and her true spirit.

"She was definitely in love with him," Prager said. "You could see it in her eyes."

Kristin told Prager that she wanted to tell Greg about the affair but didn't know how to break it to him. Their relationship was so fragile. Kristin said she was terrified that Greg would get depressed and upset if she tried to talk to him about her feelings, but she knew she had to.

Kristin said she and Michael were both confused about what to do with their respective marriages, but she was thinking she should go to counseling with Greg or spend some time away from him so she could decide whether she ultimately wanted to stay married.

Sometime after Prager moved to the Bay Area in September, Kristin called to say that she'd told Greg about the affair, but he wanted her to stay and try to work things out.

As always, Prager encouraged Kristin to follow her heart. "I could never understand why she didn't want to get a divorce," she said.

Kristin asked if the studio at the Pragers' house in Encinitas was available. Prager said Kristin also asked if she would consider moving down to San Diego so they could share an apartment together.

On September 21, Kristin took a trip to Tijuana, where she saw Dr. Victor M. Martinez. He wrote her a prescription in Spanish for Somacid, a muscle relaxant that many American doctors won't prescribe because it can be addictive. He also wrote her a prescription for a drug called Asenlix in Mexico and Clobenzorex in the United States, a diet pill that metabolizes like amphetamine, or speed. The drug literature says it's not intended for people with drug or alcohol addictions.

Kristin later admitted that by taking the diet pills, she had gone into relapse. "Relapse" is a therapeutic term that encompasses the problems, thoughts, and actions that lead recovering addicts to begin taking their drug of choice again. This combination of factors works in a chain reaction, similar to a line of dominos falling, one at a time, until the last one knocks the addict down.

The week before Kristin and Michael left for the October SOFT conference, they each submitted travel request and expense forms to the office administrator, Lloyd Amborn, with the estimated cost of their trip. Amborn said nothing of their plans to leave San Diego on Saturday, September 30, two days before the conference started, and to return from Milwaukee on Saturday, October 7, the day after it ended. Each made a notation that personal time would be included in the trip.

Sometime before the trip, Amborn confronted Michael about the rumored affair for the third time, and Michael continued to deny it. So, Amborn approved the expense forms for meals, separate hotel rooms for Kristin and Michael, airline tickets, a shuttle, and registration, which cost taxpayers a total of $2,691. It's unclear whether Amborn knew until afterwards that the two of them planned to stay at the Inn Towne Hotel, a different hotel from the one hosting the conference, the Hyatt Regency.

On September 22, Kristin e-mailed her old friend, Frank Barnhart, at the sheriff's crime lab. She told him how busy it had been over at the "house of death" and asked if he still intended to attend the conference. She told him that she and Michael were going to arrive on Saturday, and that she was scheduled to give a fifteen-minute presentation on a strychnine death case the following Friday.

"I'm petrified, but I'll get over it," she wrote, signing the note with the nickname he'd given her, "Lil Bandit."

Barnhart could not believe that the county was paying to send her to an out-of-town conference. In the twenty-nine years he worked there, he couldn't think of a single time they'd paid for him to do that. He teased her about that over the phone, so she e-mailed him to ask if he still loved her. Yes, he wrote back, he did. Barnhart didn't understand why Kristin was going to Milwaukee on Saturday, since the conference wouldn't really get going until late Sunday or early Monday morning.

That same day Greg e-mailed Kristin with some suggestions on how to use computer graphics to help illustrate the chemical structure of strychnine for her presentation. He seemed eager to help make it easier for her since she'd worked so hard on it. A week later—the day before she was to leave on her trip—Greg e-mailed her with an 800 number she could use to call home while she was away. He wished her luck on her "practice talk" and asked her to call and let him know how it went.

Before Michael left for the trip, he and Nicole decided to separate. On October 5, Nicole wrote him a letter to mark the start of their separation, which began the day he left for the SOFT conference. Assuming that he'd be feeling a similar sense of loss, she told him she knew what he'd be going through during his week away.

After speaking with his sister the previous week, she told him she now understood that he had modeled their marriage on his parents' and his behavior on his father's. As Nicole saw it, their marriage would be destroyed if he did not come to terms with a few things. Just like his father, Michael seemed unable to commit to his wife. He didn't know how to be in love over the long term because he was always chasing "the spark of falling in love." And he didn't know how to be loyal except to people who fed his self-esteem, such as "the needy women in the background."

Nicole said she didn't feel he was being manipulative or nasty, it was just learned behavior, and bad behavior at that.

But if he didn't deal with these issues, they would haunt him forever. The separation would be difficult for both of them, she said, but she was hopeful their relationship could survive.

Chapter 7

Dan Anderson arrived at the conference on Sunday and was warned by another toxicologist in the bar that Michael and Nicole were having problems, that Michael was sleeping with someone else, and that he was going to leave Nicole. Anderson couldn't believe it. He'd thought Nicole and Michael were so happy. He also didn't think Michael was the kind of guy to cheat on his wife.

"Little did I know him," he said later.

Because of this unsettling news, Anderson hoped to avoid Michael as much as possible that week. He didn't want to have anything to do with the affair. Nonetheless, Anderson ended up going to the workshop on benzodiazepines that Michael was giving with four other toxicologists on Monday afternoon.

Meanwhile, Anderson was all set to give his presentation on GHB. An article on fentanyl patches, which he'd coauthored and presented at the 1999 SOFT conference in Puerto Rico, had just been published in that month's issue of the *Journal of Analytical Toxicology* and was being distributed at the Milwaukee SOFT conference. Entitled "Duragesic® Transdermal

Patch: Postmortem Tissue Distribution of Fentanyl in 25 Cases," the article analyzed twenty-five deaths, including three suicides, investigated by his toxicology lab in Los Angeles.

Fentanyl, a short-acting narcotic painkiller about one hundred times more powerful than morphine, is in the same opiate family as heroin, morphine, and Demerol. Fentanyl acts on the central nervous system and, in excessive doses, can render users unconscious and can cause seizures, comas, severe breathing problems, nausea, and vomiting. Unavailable to the general public, the fast-acting opiate is often injected as an anesthetic during surgery or for short procedures where the patient needs to be out for only a brief time, such as wisdom teeth removal or endoscopies. The drug is so fast-acting that people who have purposely or accidentally overdosed on it have been found with syringes in their arms, in their hands, or lying next to their bodies. In October 2002, one hundred and seventeen people were killed when Russian security police used the drug in a gaseous form to end a hostage standoff in a Moscow theater, where Chechen rebels were holding eight hundred hostages.

The fentanyl skin patch, similar to the nicotine patch for people trying to quit smoking, is most often used to treat chronic pain in cancer patients. Another form of administration is the berry-flavored lollipop, used for flare-ups in cancer pain and also as a sedative for children who are about to undergo surgery.

The SOFT welcome reception was held Tuesday night at the Milwaukee Public Museum, a natural history museum with bones and dinosaur artifacts on display.

Barnhart saw Kristin talking to Richard Shaw, who used to be his boss in San Diego when the Medical Examiner's Office was called the Coroner's Office. Barnhart came over, and Shaw noted that Kristin was very popular—all the men were gathering around to talk to her. Barnhart, joking that it wouldn't do them any good, reached down to grab her left hand and said, "Because she's married."

But when he pulled up her hand, he saw that she wasn't wearing a wedding ring. He asked Kristin where it was, and she said she'd left it back at the hotel room. Shaw could tell something was going on, but Barnhart didn't want to see it. She was his friend.

Kristin and Michael were together that night, but it wasn't obvious to anyone who didn't know that they were a couple. Michael came up to Anderson after they'd both had something to eat. He said he wanted to tell Anderson personally that his relationship with Nicole was on the rocks and that he was seeing Kristin. Anderson thought Michael was crazy for jeopardizing his position by getting involved with a subordinate, and he told him so. He also made it clear that he didn't approve of the affair. Then the two parted ways.

Within five minutes, Kristin approached Anderson and said she and Michael both valued his opinion. She wanted his approval for the relationship. Anderson asked if she was planning to leave her husband, and she said yes. Anderson told Kristin that both of their spouses should be told about the affair, because he didn't think it was fair to them otherwise. Kristin started tearing up. The more emotional she got, the more uncomfortable Anderson became. He told her he didn't want to continue the conversation and started walking away. But Kristin wouldn't let it go. She followed him around the atrium, crying and saying, "I value you as a toxicologist." Anderson, who couldn't understand how that was relevant, couldn't get away fast enough. He felt that Kristin was making a scene, and he was embarrassed.

The next night was an informal gathering known as the Elmer Gordon Forum, which the organization holds at every conference. It generally consists of about one hundred toxicologists, including bigwigs and pioneers who started in the field half a century ago, sitting in a circle and discussing problems in the workplace. Kristin and Michael walked in late to the meeting. During a lull in the conversation, the discussion leader made a special point of introducing Kristin to the big-name toxicologists as a new, up-and-coming toxicologist. This irritated Anderson and some of his colleagues, who'd never gotten any such introductions so early in their careers.

Friday came, and it was time for Kristin to give her talk in the small ballroom, which was attended by a couple hundred people. She was extremely nervous, so much so that her voice fluctuated with anxiety. She even called attention to it during her presentation. Titled "Death by Strychnine—A Case for Postmortem Redistribution," Kristin's presentation covered the investigation of a recent death in San Diego caused by the well-known poison. In addition to listing her name, the abstract for her talk credited Michael and another lab coworker, Glenn Holt.

The dead man, the abstract said, was thirty-one and had a long history of depression. He was found in a hotel room with a suicide note, some over-the-counter medications, and a container of Quick Action Gopher Mix, in which strychnine was the active ingredient. Also found were two plastic bottles of Coke, some rum, and two plastic cups containing moist unidentified seeds. More seedlike material was found in the deceased's stomach. The death investigation showed that strychnine in the seeds had caused his death.

According to the abstract, the case demonstrated that "strychnine concentrations in blood following ingestion vary depending on site of collection. In this case, the variation is most likely due to ongoing postmortem diffusion from the gastric contents into the central blood vessel." In other words, after he died, the strychnine in his stomach seeped into his blood, causing a variation in the levels measured in different parts of his body.

To Anderson, it was obvious that Kristin hadn't written the paper, nor, he thought, could she have fully understood what she was saying given her experience level. Anderson felt sure that Michael had written the paper for her. Her talk was the culmination of one long, annoying week for him.

Anderson and Barnhart independently said they remembered Fredric Rieders, Michael's former boss, laying into Kristin after her presentation, questioning her and pointing out a number of flaws. Anderson said Rieders essentially insinuated what he, too, had been thinking—that Michael had been the true author of the talk.

Four years later, the eighty-two-year-old Rieders said he did not attend Kristin's talk. But Anderson said he was certain Rieders did because he remembered thinking that Rieders seemed to be attacking Kristin and, in effect, Michael, because he'd left Rieders's company. Anderson said Michael tried to come to Kristin's aid and deflect some of Rieders's questions after Kristin kept repeating, "I don't know" and started to cry.

Everyone in the audience knew that Kristin was new to the organization and that this was her first talk. Rieders's attack was so brutal, Anderson recalled, that it was a topic of conversation at the farewell lunch afterward. As irritated with her as he was, Anderson said he wouldn't have wished such a barrage of criticism on his worst enemy.

That night Kristin and Michael went out to dinner. As they were walking through the lobby, Barnhart saw them and thought they looked awfully comfortable together. Like a couple. He was disturbed by the thought.

The next day Barnhart gave Kristin and Michael a ride to the airport. Kristin rode in the front seat and Michael in the back. Once they reached the airport, Barnhart and the couple went their separate ways.

* * *

After Kristin returned from her trip, she and Greg got into an argument about some pills Kristin was taking. On Monday morning, October 9, Kristin sent an angry e-mail to Greg, listing the color, shape, name, and purpose of three prescription drugs.

One, she said, was a muscle relaxant for cramps called diazepam, the generic name for Valium. Another, she said, was called zolpidem, a "hypnotic" for the flight home. And the third, she said, was called Seroquel, an antipsychotic antidepressant she was taking to help with the "severe anxiety" stemming from their relationship.

"You've hurt me beyond repair," she wrote. "I wish that I had been able to talk to you about more. But your reaction always scares me off. You make me feel so uncomfortable, so alone. It's a very unhappy place to be. I don't know what to do."

On the weekend of October 14, Greg and Kristin drove to Palm Springs for the wedding of Aaron Wallo, one of Greg's high school friends, who was with him the night he met Kristin. Greg seemed determined to help make his new company successful; it had been on his mind a lot lately. But he was happy to be hanging out with some of his closest buddies. And despite their tight finances, Greg bought Kristin a pair of sunglasses and some perfume.

At the reception, Kristin and Greg posed for a photo. She leaned her head toward his so that their temples touched, and both of them smiled wide. She wore a dark blue sleeveless cocktail dress with a string of pearls; he, a white dress shirt and a black tie with tiny white polka dots. To their friends and Greg's brothers, they seemed like they always did, a happy couple who had been together for a long time.

On Saturday night after the wedding, a group of friends went over to the house of Greg's high school friend, Christian

Colantoni, where Greg and Kristin were staying, to hang out and watch a video of the black comedy, *Office Space*. In one scene, one of the characters tries to commit suicide by drinking alcohol and asphyxiating himself with carbon monoxide in the car in his garage, but his wife interrupts him before he finishes. He backs the car into the street, and another car rams into him. Despite being in a wheelchair with multiple broken bones, he ends up happier than he was before, thanks to a hefty legal settlement.

The scene led to a debate among Greg's friends about the best way to die. One guy, who worked as an emergency medical technician, joked that the movie portrayed the best way. Kristin disagreed, saying that a certain combination of drugs could cause a completely painless death, without side effects. The two of them seemed eager to prove they were the most knowledgeable about medications. The discussion struck Colantoni as odd.

On Sunday Colantoni and his wife had lunch and played nine holes of golf with Kristin and Greg before they drove back to San Diego. Colantoni said he was anxious about his bar exam results. If he passed, he and Greg decided they would go to Las Vegas to celebrate. Kristin said she wanted to come, too.

On October 17, Greg forwarded an e-mail invitation to Kristin from some friends and asked if she wanted to go to their Halloween housewarming party in Clairemont, a neighborhood just south of, and across the freeway from, University City. Kristin said it sounded like fun. Greg suggested they go out and look for costumes after work on October 24, four days before the party. On the night of the party, they posed for photos, Greg with a big grin on his face and his finger on a blender. He wore a black-and-white striped inmate costume, complete with a matching striped cap.

A week later Greg bought Kristin a dozen or so red roses for her twenty-fourth birthday.

In an e-mail on the afternoon of Halloween, Kristin offered to make a special dinner of teriyaki pork tenderloin or filet mignon with herbed red potatoes that night. They seemed to be getting along well. "BOO! Did I scare you? I hope you've had a spooky Halloween so far," she wrote.

The next day, Greg e-mailed Kristin that he'd made reservations for their birthday dinner with Kristin's parents at the Prado in Balboa Park for Friday at 7 P.M. He thought it would be nice if they could sit inside, but if she wanted to sit outside, he would change it. She thanked him for making the arrangements and agreed that sitting inside was best.

On Thursday, November 2, Kristin e-mailed Greg to say she tried to call him at home and at work but kept missing him. She asked if he'd rather go out to eat for lunch that day and thanked him for getting up early to have breakfast with her. Greg agreed to go out to lunch as long as it was someplace "not too expensive," so they went back and forth, trying to decide where to go. They settled on an authentic Italian submarine sandwich at Mimo's, a deli in Little Italy, even though it was a bit of a drive for both of them. After he left for lunch, Greg called Terry Huang, the office manager at Orbigen, to say he needed to take the rest of the afternoon off to deal with a "family issue."

On Friday, November 3, Greg told Gruenwald how mad he was at the guy he'd recommended be hired as a fund-raising consultant because the guy hadn't done the work he was supposed to do for Orbigen. Gruenwald noticed that Greg was acting unusually hyperactive and angry that day.

"He used to be my friend, and he screwed me over," Gruenwald recalled Greg telling him.

That night after work, Greg and Kristin went to Vons and bought all the fixings for gin martinis before they went out to dinner at the Prado. Constance and Ralph arrived late because traffic was bad, so they were only able to take a couple of quick sips before they had to head downtown. They ate dinner and then walked around the Gaslamp District so Kristin and Greg could show the Rossums the Friday night scene.

On the previous Thursday, October 26, someone sat at the iMac computer Greg brought home from Orbigen and searched the Internet, using key words such as "speed," "crank," "meth," and "amphetamines."

Four days later, someone sat at the same computer and searched for a job as a translator, foreign language teacher, and bilingual tutor in New York, Atlanta, San Francisco, Beverly Hills, Oklahoma City, Costa Mesa, Los Angeles, and Minneapolis.

On the following Saturday, November 4, between 11:15 A.M. and 12:05 P.M., someone used the computer to do a Google search for facilities in San Diego that screened blood and urine for drugs, including LabCorp Patient Service Centers. Other Internet searches were done on how to make opium and crystal meth using household chemicals, to access the Mayo Clinic's medical reference library on various prescription drugs, and to check the weather report for Mammoth. Some of the same drug sites were visited by someone using Kristin's computer at work, which required a password to log on.

Then, on December 30, around 6 P.M., someone sitting at the new Compaq computer in Kristin's apartment, which Greg had purchased sometime in October, did a search for information on the Narconon drug addiction treatment program, developed by William Benitez, an inmate at Arizona State Prison, who drew inspiration from the writings of L. Ron Hubbard, founder of the Church of Scientology. The person also searched the site for Narcotics Anonymous.

* * *

Kristin came into the Medical Examiner's Office on Sunday morning, November 5, to update her resume. She made a quick call home around 9:23 A.M. and then called Woody's Smoke Shop, a head shop in Normal Heights that sells all kinds of smoking paraphernalia, around 9:30 A.M. She dialed her apartment again at 10:04 A.M.

Around 3:30 that afternoon, Bertrand called Greg from Marie's condo in Thousand Oaks. Bertrand was having trouble setting up an e-mail account for Marie and asked Greg for his help. They talked for about half an hour. Greg said he was tired and had been "just kind of hanging around the house" all day. He said he and Kristin had been drinking gin the night before, and he wasn't used to it. They talked about going snowboarding for Greg's birthday, and Greg said he would make the arrangements. As an alternative, they also talked about Greg driving up to Ventura County for a family dinner the following weekend.

Michael had noticed a change in Kristin's behavior of late, so he came into work on Sunday, November 5, and decided to go through her desk. He found a bindle of white powder that looked like meth, which he flushed down the toilet. He felt physically sick, angry, and disappointed. Why hadn't she told him she was using methamphetamine again?

Cathy Hamm came in at midday and saw Michael going through cabinets in the lab. He looked disheveled, as if he hadn't shaved in a couple of days. She asked how he was doing and told him he looked like he was "bach-ing it," meaning he was living like a bachelor.

Michael was short with her. He said he was cleaning up, tossing stuff away. But she saw no pile of items that he might have gathered to throw away.

She told him she'd come in to get ready for a lab meeting by setting up the equipment she was going to use. He said he'd help her.

After they set it up, he said, "Now are you happy?"

"I want to try it out," she said.

Michael turned on the machine and it worked.

"Now are you happy?" he asked again.

The two of them got ready to go together, but Hamm left first, leaving Michael behind in the lab.

Michael spoke to Nicole for about half an hour just before 5 P.M., then again for twelve minutes around 8:20 P.M.

Chapter 8

On Monday morning, November 6, Kristin made a quick series of calls from the cordless phone in the kitchen to Armando Garcia in Tijuana: two at 7:16, one at 7:17, and one at 7:33.

Then, at 7:42 A.M., Kristin called in sick for Greg. But for reasons that would be debated later in court, she left a message on Greg's own voice mail at Orbigen. She later said she figured someone else would hear the message because Greg shared a phone number with Chris Gruenwald, the owner's son.

"Yes, hi, this is, um, Kristin, Greg's wife, calling," her message said. "He's not feeling well at all today, so he's most likely going to be taking the whole day. He's sleeping right now, but I just wanted to let you know. Hopefully, someone else will get this message and um, that it will [not] be a problem. Okay, thank you. Bye."

Kristin got to work later than usual, between 8:00 and 8:30 A.M. She looked tired and upset, as if she hadn't slept. Her coworkers saw her go into Michael's office and close the door right after the morning meeting that he typically attended, which ended around 9 A.M. She was in his office for at least half an hour, and they could see through the glass pane in the door that she was crying.

After that, Kristin left the lab and went back and forth several times to her apartment to check on Greg. Just after noon, maintenance manager Herman Schledwitz saw Kristin drive into the La Jolla Del Sol parking lot a little faster than he liked to see in a residential area. In fact, she almost hit another car as she parked in front of the office. He knew it was she because he'd helped her jump-start that white Toyota. He saw her jump out and run toward her apartment.

Kristin called the Medical Examiner's Office on her cell phone—her second call ever on that phone—at 12:20 P.M. A little while later, she returned to the lab for a bit, still looking upset. She met with Michael again and then left for the day around 2:30 P.M. Michael took off shortly thereafter to meet Kristin somewhere outside the office, where they'd arranged to talk in private.

Around 2:45 P.M., Donna Tabor, the Del Sol's marketing director, came out of her office and saw Kristin's white Toyota parked askew in the space next to hers. When she came back from lunch between 4:00 and 4:30, Kristin's car was gone.

At 9:22 P.M., Kristin called 911. She told the dispatcher that her twenty-six-year-old husband was in bed—cold, unconscious, and not breathing. The dispatcher told Kristin to pull him off the bed and onto the floor, flat on his back. Kristin couldn't even respond to some of the dispatcher's instructions, she was sobbing so hard.

"Is there anybody there to help you?" the dispatcher asked.

"No," Kristin said. "I'm by myself."

The dispatcher told her to kneel by her husband, tilt his head back, put her ear next to his mouth, and see if she could feel or hear any breathing, or see his chest rise. Kristin said he wasn't breathing, so the dispatcher started telling her how to do CPR, alternating mouth-to-mouth breathing and compressions on his chest. The dispatcher had to repeat herself several times through Kristin's sobs.

"What I want you to do is put the heel of your hand on the breastbone in the center of his chest, right between his nipples," the dispatcher said.

"Okay," Kristin said, sobbing.

"Put your other hand on top of that hand. . . . Are you doing that?"

"Yes," Kristin said.

The dispatcher told her to push down firmly, pump fifteen times, and count out loud. "Go ahead and do it."

"9, 10, 11 . . . ," Kristin counted.

After leading Kristin through the steps of CPR—pumping, counting, and breathing—the dispatcher told Kristin that the paramedics were outside the building but instructed her to keep pumping and breathing for Greg. Kristin continued to cry as she counted aloud.

"Okay, two more breaths," the dispatcher said. "You're doing fine. . . . Are they inside?"

"No," Kristin said, wailing. "They're here. They're inside."

The dispatcher asked if they'd taken over or if Kristin was going to continue.

"They're with him now," Kristin replied.

"Okay. Are they doing CPR?"

"Not yet," Kristin said.

When the dispatcher heard the paramedics trying to talk to Kristin in the background, she told Kristin to hang up.

UCSD officers Bill MacIntyre, Karen Scofield, and Edward "Scott" Garcia arrived at the Regents Road apartment at 9:27 P.M., along with the fire engine. The paramedics had already begun CPR on Greg by then, so the officers started looking around the apartment.

They found a nearly empty bottle of prescription cough medicine, dated February 6, 1999, in the bathroom, but no other drug containers. On the dining-room table, they found a shredded letter that was partially taped together and stuck in a ziplock bag, a note Kristin wrote to Greg that she was going shopping for her cousin's wedding present, some apartment rental ads from the newspaper, and a listing of some mental health counselors. The officers saw no evidence of a struggle and no suicide note.

Garcia thumbed through a three-ring binder he found on the coffee table, hoping to find a suicide note, but soon realized it was Kristin's journal. He later summarized its contents in his report: "Rossum felt her marriage was a mistake, she'd gotten married too young, she's self-conscious about her looks, wants to separate from Greg."

Garcia questioned Kristin about what had been going on with her husband. She told him she and Greg had been discussing a separation on Saturday and Sunday. She said Greg told her "I can't live without you," but he wouldn't discuss it further. Then he'd taken some pills "to sleep," she said.

After the paramedics had given up on trying to resuscitate Greg and carried him out on a backboard to the ambulance, Garcia took Kristin to the hospital in the backseat of his cruiser. She cried the whole way. Once she got to the hospital, Garcia heard her calling a friend on her cell phone. Her boss arrived about fifteen or twenty minutes later, and Garcia saw them standing close, whispering. Garcia left and returned to the apartment.

UCSD Detective Sergeant Bob Jones was asleep when he got a call at 10:22 P.M. He usually went to bed early so that he could get up at 4:30 A.M. and into work by 6 A.M., bypassing the commuter traffic between his home in Escondido and the station on the La Jolla campus.

He was told that an hour earlier, three of his officers had responded to a medical aid call for a man who had stopped breathing at the La Jolla Del Sol apartments. Jones was told the man had possibly committed suicide.

Jones spent the next few minutes waking himself up, then he called back to arrange a four-way conference call with Garcia at the hospital; MacIntyre, who'd stayed behind at the apartment; and the dispatcher. After nailing down who'd seen what, Jones got into his car and headed for the Regents Road complex. He arrived at 11:25 P.M.

Garcia and MacIntyre showed him around the apartment, while Scofield stayed outside on the front landing. The fewer people inside the apartment, the better. While looking for drug vials, MacIntyre found a plastic syringe cap on the floor, next to the bed, under the comforter. Jones put on some rubber gloves and took everything out of two small white trash receptacles that his officers had moved into the living room. He found nothing of interest in them.

Jones interviewed Kristin after she returned from the hospital around 11:45 P.M., listening closely for inconsistencies with what she'd told his officers earlier that evening. She was visibly shaking, sometimes incoherent, and crying. It was hard to understand what she was saying. When her father arrived around midnight, she jumped up to hug him.

That morning, Kristin told Jones, Greg didn't feel well so she called in sick for him. She left for work at the Medical Examiner's Office and arrived around 8 A.M. Later that morning, she called Greg several times, but there was no answer. So she drove home around 10:30 to check on him and found him asleep. She returned to work fifteen minutes later. She came home again for lunch around 12:30, woke Greg up, and saw him eat "a little soup." Over lunch, she said, he told her he'd taken some of her old oxycodone and clonazepam to sleep, but she didn't know when or how much. She said she thought the drug vials had been thrown out, but Greg must've saved the pills somehow. Greg returned to bed, and she went back to work around 1 P.M.

Kristin said she came home again between 5:00 and 5:30, found Greg sleeping, and gave him a kiss. He was warm and breathing. She ate some leftovers for dinner and left around six o'clock to shop for a wedding gift for her cousin at the University Towne Center, a shopping mall nearby. She then went by the lab to turn off a machine she'd left on earlier that day and stopped to get some gas. She returned home around 8 P.M., saw Greg sleeping and heard him breathing, then took a long bath and a shower, dried herself off, and got ready for bed.

She said it was about 9:20 when she walked over to the bed. Greg's head was sticking out from the covers, with the blanket all the way up to his face. She went to give him a kiss and realized he wasn't breathing and his face was cold. She immediately called 911. When the dispatcher told her to put Greg on the floor, she said, she pulled back the blanket and saw rose petals over his chest. They fell to the floor when she pulled him off the bed.

Jones was surprised by how different Kristin looked compared to the healthy and attractive young woman in the wedding photos that were displayed around the apartment. She seemed distraught, but as he listened to her story, he saw no immediate reason to disbelieve her. Her emotions seemed sincere. Plus, since the paramedics took the body, he figured they must've thought they had a chance to revive him. If Greg had been dead for a while, he thought they would've left his body on the bedroom floor.

In his twenty years with the campus police department at UCSD, Jones had investigated dozens of deaths, and about half of them were determined to be suicides. The most common method that suicidal students chose was to jump off a building. He'd also seen several cases involving students who shot themselves in the head, two who drove off a cliff, two who hung themselves, and one who lit himself on fire. Another died of carbon monoxide poisoning, and another from sliced wrists.

In Jones's experience, there were only four ways a person could die: murder, suicide, accidental death, or natural death. And in domestic violence cases, he found there were always three sides to every story. Her story, his story, and the truth, somewhere in the middle.

His department was not qualified or equipped to investigate homicides and had an agreement with the San Diego Police Department (SDPD) to pass those cases along. However, Jones had never been faced with that necessity before.

Jones and his officers took Kristin's "Hi, sleepy" note, the shredded letter, the list of mental health counselors, and the apartment listings as evidence. Kristin told the officers that the shredded letter was one an "old boyfriend wrote," and that Greg had been trying to tape it back together.

Angie Wagner, the investigator from the Medical Examiner's Office, got a call at 10:41 P.M. from Scripps Memorial Hospital, saying they had a sudden and unexpected death. Michael Robertson called the office on his cell phone at 11:04 P.M. and 11:27 P.M., and spoke at least one of those times to Wagner, letting her know that the man who died was Kristin's husband. The only other investigator on duty already had a death call pending, and it would have been hours before she could respond, so Wagner said she'd handle Greg's case. The Medical Examiner's staff considered it a professional courtesy not to keep a coworker waiting when a relative died.

Wagner arrived at the hospital around 11:45 P.M., only minutes after Kristin and Michael had left. She pulled back the sheet that covered Greg's body and did her examination, noting that he was wearing boxer shorts and a T-shirt that had been cut during the resuscitation efforts. She saw no obvious trauma or sign of foul play. Because Kristin worked at the Medical Examiner's Office, Wagner secured Greg's body bag with a red, tamper-resistant seal. The red tag meant that no one was allowed to open the bag in the absence of the pathologist assigned to the case.

After finishing at the hospital, Wagner went to Kristin's apartment around 1:00 A.M. and saw Michael standing at the base of the stairs leading to it.

As Wagner examined the bedroom, she noted that the bedding had been rolled down to the foot of the mattress and that there were numerous rose petals, along with a stem and sepals, on the carpet but not in the bed. They felt moist so she could tell they were fresh. Because she'd been told that Greg probably died of an overdose, she was looking for clues to help identify whatever he'd taken. She took note of a quarter-full bottle of aspirin on the nightstand and two plastic cups of a clear liquid that looked and smelled like water.

She explored the drawers and cupboards, looked behind the mattress and under the pillows, but found no drug vials or containers. Wagner collected a nearly empty and uncapped bottle of prescription cough syrup, which contained a generic form of Vicodin, from the bathroom counter as evidence. She didn't go out on the balcony, so she didn't notice the two trash cans out there.

After Jones was done with his interview, Wagner asked Kristin her own questions as they sat on the couch in the living room. Either Wagner's investigative report was more detailed than that of the campus police, or Kristin told her a more in-depth account of the past few days.

Kristin told Wagner that she and Greg "enjoyed an evening together" in their apartment on Saturday, consuming several gin and tonics. Greg got drunk, she said, threw up several times throughout the night, but "appeared to be in good spirits and complaint free for the majority" of the next day. On

Sunday evening, the couple got into a "heated verbal marital dispute" and discussed a separation again. She said Greg told her he "couldn't live without" her and appeared withdrawn and depressed.

The timeline Kristin gave Wagner for Monday was pretty similar to what she told the campus police, although this time she said she came home around noon and that Greg was awake and joined her at the kitchen table for lunch, appearing "somnolent, with a mild slurring of his speech." She also added that the clonazepam and oxycodone he told her he'd taken were originally prescribed to her five years earlier, and that Greg returned to bed, saying he would "sleep off their effects." This time, she said, she returned from doing errands at 8:15, checked on Greg, and then took a forty-five-minute bath. When Wagner asked her about the rose petals, Kristin said she had no idea where they came from. She said Greg had given her two dozen red roses for her birthday, twelve days earlier, but she'd thrown out the last few the night before. No, she said, Greg had never attempted or talked about suicide.

Wagner left the apartment thinking that Greg had killed himself. In her report, she wrote that the rose petals were fresh, but their origin "remains undetermined."

Jones left the apartment before Ralph and Kristin, but he decided not to go home. Something wasn't adding up for him. So he went back to the station around 1:30 A.M., reviewed his notes, listened to the 911 tape, and started working up his report.

A number of questions were gnawing at him.

Kristin met the paramedics in the living room, holding a cordless phone whose cradle was in the kitchen, not the bedroom. Why would she go into the kitchen to pick up that phone when there was a princess phone on the floor right next to the bed? The rose petals were another unusual factor. He'd never seen rose petals at a suicide scene before. Also, if Greg had taken pills, why were there no empty containers?

Finally, Kristin said she'd taken a long bath and a shower, yet the stopper was sitting on the ledge above the bathtub. The stopper was the kind that screwed in and pushed down to keep the water in, so why would she have unscrewed it all the way out after taking a bath? If she'd taken only a shower, and no bath, that would have sliced about forty-five minutes out of her timeline. And since Greg's body showed signs of lividity, he had to have been dead for some time before Kristin called 911. Why hadn't she called sooner?

Chapter 9

Jones was still at the station, mulling over these questions, when the sun rose on Tuesday morning, November 7. It was Election Day, and the presidential race between Democrat Al Gore and Republican George W. Bush would be decided.

Jones called paramedic Sean Jordan first thing, around 7:15 A.M., and asked if he could estimate how long Greg had been down when he and the other paramedics arrived. Jordan said the body was warm, but Greg was "way gone." Jones couldn't remember later if he asked Jordan why the paramedics had taken Greg's body to the hospital if they knew there was no real chance of reviving him.

About fifteen minutes later, Jones called Ralph Rossum at his home in Claremont and got his permission to tape their conversation. He asked Ralph if he'd learned anything on the ride home with Kristin that would shed some light on what happened.

Ralph, who'd barely gotten any sleep, stuttered and stammered his way through the conversation. He later would say that he felt rushed because he had to take his son to school.

He told Jones that he, Constance, Kristin, and Greg had spent a "very pleasant evening" Friday night, celebrating Kristin and Greg's birthdays, which were only a couple of weeks apart. He said they had a nice meal at the Prado in Balboa Park, then walked around the grounds, and talked about Thanksgiving. Kristin and Greg didn't think they were going to be able to join the Rossums because they had plans to meet friends in Las Vegas. Ralph also mentioned that Greg and Kristin had had an argument over the weekend and that Greg had taken it hard.

Greg "was down and apparently used some of his medicine that had been apparently, uh, to, uh, to Kristin's knowledge, long since, uh, disposed of," he told Jones, clarifying that he meant "the pharmacy bottles were themselves disposed of." Greg, he said, had taken the drugs to "deal with the, uh, uh, depression and apparently took [some] maybe Sunday night. Um, she had called in to work on Monday morning that, uh, he wasn't coming."

Ralph explained that Kristin thought someone else would check Greg's line for the message. He repeated essentially the same timeline Kristin had given Jones the night before, but with one notable addition.

"They had this, uh, argument and, uh, whether Greg was, um, aware of, um, the amount or he was, was taking or the potency of this or who knows, uh, uh, whether was accidental or, or intentional, she doesn't have the, the slightest clue," he said.

After they'd finished their brief conversation, Jones spoke to Kristin. He asked how she was, then had her go over some details again, such as where the rose petals came from. A red flag went up for him when she began her response with "to be honest with you," followed by the claim that she saw the petals for the first time when she pulled back the bedcovers. Kristin gave Jones permission to reenter her apartment so he could take another look around.

Jones and one of his investigators arrived there within the

hour, this time with a video camera. They recorded the contents of each room, even though some items had been moved and others removed.

Jones looked closely at the fitted bed sheet and saw some horizontal red streaks across the middle of the bed, about a foot from the edge. They seemed to be the result of a swiping motion.

Then, trying to corroborate Kristin's claim that she'd had some soup with Greg at lunchtime, he went out on the balcony and started digging through one of the two thirty-gallon trash bins. The can was right there, near the top of the heap, so he stopped digging.

At 8:24 A.M., Constance called Orbigen to notify them of Greg's death. She dialed the same number Kristin had used to call in sick for Greg and got his voice mail again.

"This message is for Chris Gruenwald," she said, referring to Stefan Gruenwald's son. "Uh, Chris, this is Kristin de Villers's mother. Uh, and we have very sad news. Greg died last night. He had a reaction to, uh, some medication he was taking, and Kristin is with us now in Claremont."

She left her home phone number and asked him to give her a call.

Four vials of Greg's blood, drawn in the Emergency Room the night before, were collected that morning from the hospital by James Buckley, a Medical Examiner's investigator. Buckley hand-delivered them to the morgue and put them in a refrigerator in the autopsy exam room.

At 6:30 A.M., toxicologist Jim Fogacci called Frank Barnhart over at the sheriff's crime lab to tell him what happened. Fogacci asked Barnhart to call him back on his cell phone so he could talk more freely outside, away from prying ears.

Dr. Harry Bonnell, the deputy chief medical examiner, also spoke with Barnhart and faxed him Angie Wagner's investigative report. As the pathologist on the case, Bonnell had already given the go-ahead on the organ and tissue donation. He examined Greg's body before it was wheeled next door to the organ and tissue bank, which was attached to the Medical Examiner's Office. Bonnell had a photo taken of the large bruise he noticed on Greg's right arm.

At the morning meeting in which the division heads typically went over the cases they'd be handling that day, Michael summarized the investigative report on Greg's death, describing it as an apparent suicide. It was unusual for Michael to present a case, and some of his coworkers thought he seemed a little out of sorts. The group's general consensus was that an autopsy was warranted since Greg was young and died so suddenly.

Following office policy for autopsies of employees' relatives, Bonnell was planning to do Greg's at UCSD Medical Center to avoid any conflict of interest. But later that morning, Bonnell learned that his boss, Dr. Brian Blackbourne, the chief medical examiner, was coming in on his day off to do the procedure. Kristin had specially requested that Blackbourne handle it, and he had agreed.

After the meeting, Michael called his staff into his office and told them that Kristin's husband had passed away. The toxicologists took the news with disbelief.

"What do you mean, he passed away?" one of them asked.

"It looks like it might be a suicide," Michael replied, explaining that drugs may have been involved.

After the meeting, toxicologists Cathy Hamm and Ray Gary were discussing the situation, and in light of Kristin and Michael's affair, the suggestion of foul play came up.

"What do you think?" Gary asked.

Hamm initially dismissed the idea. But when Hamm called

her defense attorney friend to tell her the news, the first thing out of her friend's mouth was, "Do you think she killed him?"

Lloyd Amborn learned about Greg's death at 8:15 A.M., when he arrived at the Medical Examiner's Office after voting. As the office administrator, he spoke to Blackbourne from home, and they agreed that the autopsy should be done at UCSD. They also decided that the toxicology testing should be done by a private lab. Barnhart called and offered to handle the tests that Blackbourne ordered based on Kristin's suicide story: a blood alcohol level and a general screening for drugs of abuse, clonazepam, and aspirin.

When Amborn told Michael about the decision to have a private lab do the toxicology testing, a momentary look of shock crossed Michael's face, but it passed. Michael said he understood why that was appropriate in this case.

Amborn also told Michael not to let anyone touch the stomach contents, blood, or tissue specimens, which would be stored in the refrigerator for the next thirty-six hours, until they could be sent out for toxicology testing. Barnhart had Wednesday off and couldn't take them at the sheriff's crime lab until Thursday. Michael was familiar with the sheriff's crime lab because he'd gone over there after the SOFT conference to discuss the idea of merging the Medical Examiner's and sheriff's toxicology operations, a move he thought could be mutually beneficial.

Around 11 A.M., Michael e-mailed a thank-you to Angie Wagner for hopping on the case the night before. "I'm sure Kristin appreciated you expediting things and helping her out," he wrote.

Michael called Barnhart at 11:14 A.M. and tried to tell him which drugs the toxicology tests should be looking for, such as strychnine and cyanide. He also said he wanted to be notified of the results.

But Barnhart said he was going to follow protocol. Blackbourne had already ordered the tests he thought were necessary, he told Michael, and Barnhart would give the results straight to Blackbourne. If the chief medical examiner chose to show them to Michael, that was his business. Michael didn't push the issue.

The two of them briefly discussed how Kristin was handling things. Michael said she was pretty broken up and was staying with her parents.

Greg's heart, corneas, and some of his bones, joints, and skin from his back and legs had already been harvested by the time Blackbourne started his seventy-minute autopsy at 3:30 P.M. He found half an ounce of "soft white material" and 3 ⅓ ounces of bloody fluid in Greg's stomach. He found heavy congestion in his lungs and 550 milliliters of urine in his bladder, which meant that Greg hadn't gotten out of bed to urinate in quite some time.

The bruise near his right elbow measured 2 ½ by 2 inches and had a needle mark in the middle of it. Inside, Blackbourne could see that the artery had been punctured. Twice. He noted one other puncture wound on the right arm from the intravenous line and two needle marks on the left elbow. Blackbourne also noted that Greg hadn't shaved in three or four days.

Later that day, Michael went to the autopsy room and asked Bob Sutton, who was in charge of that area, if he would show him Greg's stomach contents. Michael looked at the cup and remarked that the contents were red, as if they contained cough syrup.

*   *   *

The de Villers family got up early and drove to the Rossums' house in Claremont that morning, arriving around 9:00. They noticed that Kristin looked very skinny and had scabs on her face. No one had gotten much sleep, but the two families sat down and talked about making arrangements for Greg's body and a memorial service. Everyone was on edge.

Kristin said she wanted to cremate Greg's body in the next few days. Marie cried as they discussed it, though she seemed to think cremation was a nice idea. Marie said Yves was coming to town and might want to see the body, but Kristin said she didn't want to delay the cremation. Jerome thought that was weird. He sensed that Kristin wasn't telling them everything.

Outside, in the courtyard, Jerome tried to get more information from Kristin about what happened the night before. Kristin told him that Greg had been upset because she "wouldn't stop seeing a past relationship" and that he must have taken some medication.

Jerome kept asking, "What do you mean?" trying to get her to be more specific. But when he pressed her for details, Kristin would start crying. She never mentioned anything about the rose petals.

Finally, her mother came and took her into the house, away from Jerome's probing. Jerome felt that Kristin and her mother were doing whatever they could to escape the conflict brewing between him and Kristin. Jerome went back inside and was talking to his mother when Constance came over to them. She said she couldn't believe that Greg would kill himself out of anger. Jerome was so upset by her remark that he walked out the front door and closed it behind him. Hard.

At one point, Brent, Bertrand, and Kristin were talking about whether Kristin should return to her apartment. She wanted to go back that day. Brent offered to stay with her, but Kristin refused.

"Why don't you stay with your friend Mike?" Brent asked Kristin.

"Oh no," she said. "That would be inappropriate. He's my boss."

Later, in the car, Bertrand told Jerome and Marie about the conversation. Jerome couldn't understand why Kristin would want to rush back to sleep in the same bed in which her husband had just died. And her reaction to Brent's suggestion about staying with her boss—what was that all about? Jerome said he was going to drive down to San Diego the next morning and start trying to get some answers.

Doug Frost, who worked at the San Diego Tissue Bank, called Kristin at 9:00 that night and asked her a list of forty-six questions about Greg's social, medical, and drug history. He was doing this after the bones and tissues were harvested, to ensure they were healthy before they were implanted into another human being. Opiate use, for example, precludes tissue donation because it's a high-risk behavior associated with contracting HIV or hepatitis.

Frost asked whether Greg had ever used non-prescribed drugs or other substances, such as cocaine, heroin, crystal meth, marijuana, steroids, or inhalants. Kristin said yes, marijuana. How much? Very little, she said. How many times? Three or four, she said.

Did Greg drink alcohol? Yes, she said, beer. How often did he drink? Two to three times a week. Did Greg take any medications on a regular basis? No, Kristin said. Had he injected drugs for a nonmedical reason in the past five years or had sex with anyone who had in the past twelve months? No. Was there anything else she thought he should know from a medical or behavioral standpoint about the death? No.

* * *

Kristin had talked to Melissa Prager about coming up to the Bay Area for a visit around her birthday. When Kristin called her on November 8, Prager was expecting to hear about arrival and departure times for the trip.

"Greg is gone," Kristin said.

At first, Prager didn't understand. "Where'd he go?" she asked.

"No, he's not with us anymore," Kristin said.

"What happened?"

Kristin started bawling. Prager couldn't understand half of what she was saying, but she got the gist of it: Greg had taken some "old medication" and died. Kristin felt traumatized. When the 911 dispatcher told her to put him on the floor to start CPR, she had to hold his lifeless body in her hands. Kristin said she didn't know whether Greg had taken the pills on purpose. Prager couldn't believe what she was hearing.

On Wednesday Jerome left his apartment in Thousand Oaks around 5:30 or 6 A.M. As he was driving south, he called his and Greg's old roommate, Chris Wren, who had moved to Huntington Beach, to tell him Greg had died. Jerome said he was going down to San Diego to try to get to the bottom of what happened, and Wren asked if he could come along. Maybe he could help ask questions. So Jerome picked him up on the way.

As they were entering the city limits around 8 A.M., Jerome called the San Diego Police Department and asked to speak to a detective about his brother's death. They put him through to Detective Laurie Agnew, and she agreed to see him. He and Wren arrived at the station about half an hour later, and Agnew met with them in the lobby for twenty to thirty minutes. As Jerome relayed his concerns and suspicions, she took notes and said she would check out what he was saying. The two of them probably spoke half a dozen more times that day as each of them proceeded with their own independent investigations.

Jerome and Wren tried to look at Greg's medical records at Scripps Memorial Hospital, but the staff wouldn't release them. Jerome called Agnew to see if she could help, and she told him the autopsy was done at UCSD Medical Center. But when he and Wren went there to pick up a copy of the autopsy report, they were told autopsies weren't performed there.

Blocked at every turn, Jerome called Agnew again for help. She suggested he talk to Dr. Brian Blackbourne at the Medical Examiner's Office. Perhaps he could provide better information. So Jerome and Wren drove to the office in Kearny Mesa, where Blackbourne met with them in the conference room. Jerome, suspicious of the doctor's true allegiances, secretly taped their conversation.

Blackbourne told them he'd done a quick autopsy and thought Greg had died of an overdose. He said he found some amorphous white substance in Greg's stomach, and his esophagus was very irritated. Jerome asked if the irritation could've been caused by drinking alcohol. Blackbourne said no, it was something more corrosive. He also said that the paramedic who'd stuck a needle into Greg's arm had punctured an artery—it must've been the paramedic's first day on the job.

Jerome asked if Kristin had a boss named Mike or Michael, and Blackbourne confirmed that she did.

After that, Jerome and Wren went to Orbigen, where Greg's coworkers said they were just as shocked by the news. Greg had seemed in such good spirits. Stefan Gruenwald recounted that Greg had come in the previous Monday and told a coworker that he'd only had a beer or two over the weekend but felt hung over. Gruenwald said they'd since become suspicious of that comment and wondered if Greg had been given drugs the week before he died. Like Jerome, none of them could see Greg committing suicide.

Laurie Agnew had been a police officer for twenty-two years, first in patrol, then in community relations, juvenile investigations, street crimes, domestic violence, and special investigations. She'd spent the last four years as a relief detective in the homicide unit but had only been working full time there for two months. Her team was third in the rotation, which meant it was their turn to answer the phones that morning. Since the detective who handled suspicious deaths also wasn't there, Agnew took Jerome's call.

Jerome's voice sounded emotional and distraught as he spoke in rapid-fire sentences, jumping from one topic to the next. His brother died two days ago, he said. They were saying it was a suicide. He didn't think it was. His brother's wife was a toxicologist for the county, and he thought she was having an affair. Her office was handling the death, and he thought that was a conflict of interest. He wanted an independent autopsy. Kristin was trying to rush a cremation. He wanted to come down and talk to a homicide detective.

Agnew didn't realize that Jerome was calling from a cell phone, heading southbound on the freeway, so she told him she would talk to him the next time he was in San Diego. She was surprised when he and Chris Wren arrived at the station about half an hour later.

As Agnew talked with them in the lobby, she thought that Jerome was acting very hyper, almost over the edge, so she wasn't sure how credible his information would turn out to be. He wasn't clear on many of the details she needed—the spellings of names, whether his sister-in-law had taken his brother's last name, that sort of thing. In her experience, suicides were usually pretty straightforward, and it was not uncommon for relatives to be in denial about it. But she said she'd certainly look into the matter.

She spent most of the day on the phone, first trying to figure out which agency was handling Greg's death, and second, where the body was. There seemed to be some confusion among the various offices she called. Because Greg was the spouse of a county toxicologist, his death wasn't being handled in the usual manner.

Even though Greg and Kristin's apartment was in the city of San Diego, Agnew's department had no death report. When she called the Medical Examiner's Office, they couldn't find any record of an autopsy scheduled for someone named Greg de Villers. The head investigator, Cal Vine, called her back and told her that the autopsy had been done the day before at UCSD Medical Center. But when Agnew called the hospital, the staff couldn't find a record of the autopsy being done there. Agnew later learned that since Greg wasn't a patient at UCSD, his name wasn't entered into the hospital's computer.

Meanwhile, unbeknownst to them, Kristin called North County Cremation Service, a funeral home in San Marcos, at 3:36 that afternoon to make arrangements for Greg's body. Kristin stopped in the next day to sign an authorization and pay for the service with her Visa card. But the cremation didn't go forward as Kristin had planned.

Once Agnew figured out that the autopsy had been done and Greg's body was back at the Medical Examiner's Office, Agnew asked her boss, Sergeant Howard Williams, if they could put a hold on the body. Williams called Blackbourne to make a verbal request, promising to send a written one within a few days. Blackbourne agreed.

That same morning, Amborn learned that Michael had looked at the biological specimens in the refrigerator, going against Amborn's explicit instructions not to touch them. When Amborn confronted him about it, Michael said he'd committed to Kristin's family that he would keep them informed. Amborn, a former navy captain, was irritated that Michael had disobeyed a direct order. He told Michael that his actions were inappropriate.

While Jerome and Agnew were conducting their own separate investigations, the UCSD Police Department got a break in the case. At 1:35 P.M., one of Jones's investigators got a call from Russ Lowe, who'd been the acting chief toxicologist at the Medical Examiner's Office before Michael arrived from Pennsylvania. Lowe said he thought it was important for the investigators to know that Michael and Kristin were having an affair.

Of the choices listed on Jones's report for the means of death—suicide, or equivocal death—he and Officer Garcia had decided on the latter. But when Jones heard about Lowe's call, he talked it over with his assistant chief, and they decided it was time to call in the SDPD homicide unit.

Neither Kristin nor Michael had mentioned any such relationship—not that adulterous coworkers would readily admit to an affair—but Jones thought it certainly created a motive for homicide. He communicated his feelings to a homicide detective and suggested that the city's department take over the investigation.

By the end of November 8, Agnew and her boss had reached the same independent conclusion. But since they still didn't know whether they were looking at a suicide, accidental death, or homicide, they decided to open a "special death" investigation. Agnew didn't do that officially until the next morning, when she entered the details into the computer under case #00-071646.

On Thursday morning Bertrand picked up his father at Los Angeles International Airport. They met up with Jerome in Huntington Beach, where he'd stayed the night at Chris Wren's house, and the three of them drove down to San Diego. Their first stop was Kristin's apartment.

Yves asked her to sign a permission slip allowing Scripps Memorial Hospital to release his son's medical report to him. She signed it, and they took it to the hospital to pick up Greg's records. They found it interesting that Kristin had told the medical staff she'd purchased oxycodone and clonazepam in Mexico to help her come down from methamphetamine in the past. The day before in Claremont, Jerome remembered her mentioning only oxycodone and Vicodin as drugs Greg might have taken.

Their next stop was the Medical Examiner's Office. They showed Greg's medical report to Blackbourne, who said the page about Kristin's methamphetamine use had not shown up in the report that his investigator, Angie Wagner, had filed. Jerome wondered whether she was involved in some kind of cover-up.

Asked again about Michael Robertson, Blackbourne told them Michael's coworkers had suspected he was having an affair with Kristin, but when confronted, he denied the allegation. After hearing Jerome's concerns the day before, Blackbourne said he'd reexamined the puncture wounds on Greg's arm and taken a new tissue sample from that area.

Jerome asked whether he was aware that Kristin was a former methamphetamine user. Blackbourne said no. Jerome also asked whether he drug-tested his employees. Again, the answer was no.

Jerome remembered Kristin pointing Blackbourne out to him at Greg's college graduation ceremony and saying that Blackbourne might help her get a job at the Medical Examiner's

Office. At this point, Jerome was seeing conspiracies every-where and wondered whether Blackbourne might be in-volved in Greg's death. Maybe he, too, was having an affair with Kristin.

Blackbourne still wouldn't say which drug he thought Greg had taken. That information would have to wait until the toxicology tests came back. Jerome emphasized that he didn't believe his brother had committed suicide.

Next, the de Villers family went back to Orbigen, where Greg's coworkers had been doing their own investigation, on Greg's computer. They had gone through his e-mails and re-traced his steps on the Internet browser to see which sites he'd visited and what if any other clues they might find. They did find what they thought was a significant e-mail from Kristin, which she'd sent to Greg on October 9, detailing three different prescription drugs she was taking. That was the first they learned that Greg's relationship had been in trouble.

Around 9 A.M., Jones got a call from Jerome, who told him he questioned the suicide story and thought an indepen-dent autopsy should be conducted because the Medical Examiner's Office had a conflict of interest. Jones told him he'd already talked with the San Diego Police Department about investigating Greg's death as a possible homicide.

Jones talked to Detective Laurie Agnew at 10:40 A.M. and learned she'd officially opened the investigation, then called Jerome a couple of hours later to give him the news. Jones took all the evidence he'd collected, his report, and the crime scene video to the police station downtown that afternoon and handed them all over to Agnew and her boss.

* * *

Every day since Greg had died, Stefan Gruenwald became more and more convinced that something wasn't right. First he was told Greg had died from an allergic or adverse reaction to some cough medicine or other drug. Then it became an overdose or accident. And now Gruenwald was being told that it was a suicide, that Greg's organs and tissues had been donated, and that his remains were going to be cremated.

With eighteen months' experience working in forensic medicine, Gruenwald felt strongly that the police ought to hear his concerns. So he and Greg's former coworkers decided to write the San Diego Police Department a letter that day.

They wrote that they'd never seen any symptoms of suicidal behavior in Greg and asked to speak with a homicide detective. "He has been a very hardworking, happy, ambitious, and extremely optimistic person that always looked into the future and had many goals for himself to accomplish in the following years," they wrote.

On Thursday evening Jerome told his father and brother that he wanted to talk to Kristin again. Yves cautioned that it would be better if his sons, given how upset they were, spoke with Kristin one at a time. They were acting like bulldogs, he said, and they'd never get anything out of her that way. So Bertrand volunteered to go up to the apartment alone and tell Kristin that Yves and Jerome had gone to get coffee.

Bertrand knocked on the door, and Kristin answered. Michael was there and stood up as Kristin introduced him as her boss. The two men shook hands. Bertrand was surprised and confused about why Michael was in her apartment at night. He started to get scared when Michael disappeared into the kitchen and started opening drawers, as if he were looking for something. Bertrand left rather abruptly, saying he was going downstairs to see whether Jerome and Yves had come back yet. Bertrand was pale when he got back in the car and told his brother and father what happened.

Jerome was so upset and eager to confront Kristin and Michael about what was going on that it took twenty minutes to calm him down. But by the time Jerome and Bertrand went back upstairs, Michael had gone. Jerome noticed that Kristin had dumped Greg's Nike sandals and some of his clothes into the trash can on the balcony. Greg's body was barely cold, and Kristin was already throwing out his personal belongings?

He and Bertrand told Kristin they weren't trying to confront her or to blame anybody. They just wanted to make better sense out of things. Meanwhile, unbeknownst to Bertrand or Kristin, Jerome had slipped a small tape recorder into his jacket pocket, and it was running.

"It's hard for me to believe that my brother committed suicide," Jerome said.

"I don't think he did," Kristin said. "I think it was accidental. I don't know if he had a reaction to something. Maybe he's allergic to a drug. Maybe, maybe he just—Jerome, I don't know. I know we don't know, and we won't know until the [toxicology] results are back. I'm just as confused as you."

Jerome explained that he couldn't sleep, thinking about it all. Kristin asked him to recognize that she was feeling pain and loss, too.

"I can certainly understand your confusion and frustration," she said, "because, whereas my parents, my family, knew about our problems and Greg. He didn't talk to you about it."

No, he didn't, Jerome said. All he knew was that Greg loved her very much. Jerome asked Kristin to walk him through the days before Greg died, starting with Thursday night. He also reminded her of their conversation a few days earlier when she said Greg had been upset because she hadn't stopped seeing "the past relationship." But she cut him off and changed course. Given her history, she said, Greg thought her job was a bad influence and unhealthy for her.

"Since my problem, I've been very interested, especially in the psychosis of meth and similar drugs," she said. "And when I bring it up at home, Greg didn't like that . . . thought that the job was a bad environment. He thought that I was pushing him away, and he thought that I was taking drugs, and it hurt so badly. I told him that I wanted a separation. That's it. And he gave me an ultimatum: Kristin, you either quit your work or I tell your work about your drug history."

Jerome said that didn't sound like something Greg would say. "There's got to be a reason he didn't want you to work there if he's threatening you," he said. "What about these conventions?"

Kristin acknowledged that she'd gone to a conference in Milwaukee with her lab supervisor, Michael Robertson.

"The guy who was here earlier?" Bertrand asked.

"Yeah, he was dropping off a paycheck," she said. "He's a good guy."

Jerome asked if she was having some kind of emotional relationship, not necessarily sexual, but something that would make Greg upset. Yes, Kristin said, she'd had an emotional relationship with Michael and she'd told Greg about it, but she'd also told him that it was over and that she and Michael were "just good friends." Greg believed her.

"Does Greg ever take any type of aspirin?" Jerome asked.

No, Kristin said. When he got sick, he often couldn't sleep, so she'd tried to give him some cough syrup, but he'd "stopped taking [it] because it didn't work anymore. Or Vicodin, but he didn't like Vicodin because it upset his stomach."

Bertrand said Greg didn't seem "like the type of guy" to take Vicodin, and Jerome wanted to know why they even had it in the house. Kristin said Greg got a prescription for it when his wisdom teeth were removed and another one for when he had a cough or a cold. She said he also would "take Nyquil when he was home sick to knock himself out. Most people do that."

"I just know Greg doesn't do drugs," Jerome said.

Kristin told Jerome he was right, that Greg didn't normally take aspirin or a lot of other drugs. It was unlike him.

Bertrand tried to reduce some of the anxiety in the room. "I know. That's why we're trying to ask you," he said. ". . . I know it's hard for us; it's hard for you."

"It is," Kristin said. "It's so hard for me because I feel partial responsibility because I got him so upset. I miss him, and I love him, and I didn't appreciate what I had. I am so lost right now, and I am hurting so badly. I'm trying to understand, just like you, but I crushed him. I devastated him. He thought he lost me. I was looking at apartments."

Kristin's mind was going all over the place, and Jerome wanted to get her back on track. Why had Greg taken half a day off work on Thursday? To talk, Kristin said. Jerome wanted to know more.

"I came home, and I made him lunch, and, um, he became very, very aggressive and accusatory towards me, saying, 'You're doing drugs. I know you're doing drugs,' " she said. "He searched my purse, and he started searching me, and he found an old letter. It was from Michael."

Kristin said she shredded the letter. She knew it wasn't a nice thing for Greg to see. From the tone of the letter, it was obvious that Michael was falling for her. Bertrand asked why she would bring home a letter like that.

"Because it is not something that you keep at work," Kristin said.

"Weren't you afraid that Greg might find it?" Bertrand asked.

Jerome was getting frustrated. Didn't she understand why

they thought it was strange that Michael was writing her love letters? Especially when she told them that Michael had come by just to drop off her paycheck?

"There's other emotions going on here, Kristin," Jerome said.

"No, there aren't," Kristin snapped. "He dropped off the check and—"

Jerome cut her off. "For you to tell me, real defensive, he just came here to drop off the check—there's something else here going on," he said.

Kristin insisted that Michael was just a good friend. He, too, felt responsible for hurting Greg. Jerome countered that guys didn't feel bad about that kind of thing.

"Well, maybe he's a good BS-er," she said, "but he does feel emotions."

Jerome asked if Michael was in a relationship. Yes, Kristin said, he was married. That's why they decided that what they were doing was wrong and that they should work on their marriages. Bertrand asked if she and Michael were hoping to have a relationship.

"No, no. I was, I am very fond of him," Kristin replied.

Jerome said he thought it was weird that Michael was in her apartment three nights after her husband had died there. Kristin said she didn't have any friends in San Diego outside of work who weren't Greg's friends, too. She was at the hospital, she told him, "scared out of my mind, not knowing what to do." She'd called her parents, and her father said he'd be there as soon as he could, but in the meantime she had no one else to turn to. So she called Michael.

"This is just so scary," she said. "This has taken over all parts of my life. I have nothing left. The career that I loved, the husband that was wonderful. . . . I made mistakes, I did. I regret that our last days together were spent arguing. I regret that I decided to freakin' take a long bath and then read a political poll [for the next day's election] before going in and going to bed. Otherwise, he might have been okay. . . . Don't make me bear more than is mine. I don't know either why he did this."

Jerome came back to the affair, asking why Greg was so upset if it had truly ended. How did he even know about it? Kristin said she'd told him. She'd sat him down and told him how unhappy she was, that she'd met someone else who made her happy. They drank a lot of wine, and they ended up arguing.

After that, she said, "he was literally in bed for two days. He didn't get up at all. Then, on Monday, he went to work, came home at five, had chips and salsa and a beer, and went to bed. He did the same thing the next day, too. Didn't talk to me at all."

She said they agreed to work on the relationship, and he was going to try to show her that it was the right thing for her, that she "was just looking for things that were fantasy."

Then she skipped to the Friday night before Greg died. "Friday night was fun. We were with my parents, and we were being friendly. It was a big night. He wanted things to look good for my parents."

Kristin's timeline ran one day into the next, and she told them about eating some steaks one of her brother's had sent her. They drank beer and wine, she recalled, and said things they shouldn't have.

"He got sick," she said. "And the next day [Sunday], we picked up where we left off."

Greg went to bed early, she said, and around 11:30 P.M., he got up with a headache and said he couldn't sleep. Then he went back to bed and snored for the rest of the night.

"On Monday morning," she said, "his speech was slurry. He sounded like he was drunk. . . . It was unusual. I didn't know till later that he had taken some pills."

"Did you ask him what he took?" Bertrand asked.

Greg told her he'd taken some clonazepam, Kristin said. But no, she didn't ask how many he'd taken, and he didn't volunteer that information.

"Didn't it scare you?" Bertrand asked.

"Of course, it did," she said. "So what did I do? I called in sick for him."

Jerome wanted to know if Greg asked her to call in for him. No, Kristin said, it was her decision. She thought he just needed to sleep.

Bertrand and Jerome tried to pin Kristin down on when she thought he'd taken the pills.

"You told me that Greg had thrown away these pills," Jerome said.

"He did," she said. "I saw him throw away the prescription bottle, and you always throw away the prescription bottle and the drugs in separate places."

Jerome wouldn't let up. "Kristin, you told me on Tuesday that 'Greg took all of them.' "

"All of them, yes, but that's not how many," she said. "He didn't say how many."

When she came back at noon, or maybe 11:30 A.M., she said, he got up, and his speech still sounded a little slurred so she asked him not to take any more pills. That's when he said, "There aren't any more."

"So, at that point, if he took more, I don't know what happened," she said.

She said she made him some soup, but he didn't eat much. He mostly pushed it around. He still seemed upset at her, so she went back to work. She said she shared her concerns about Greg with Michael, and the two of them left work around 3 P.M. to talk some more.

They stopped at the grocery store to pick up "some more soups and stuff," she said, then they parted ways, and she went home to check on Greg again around 5:00 or 5:15 P.M. He was lying on his back, still sleeping and snoring.

"There's no way," Jerome said. "You don't know for sure if he was sleeping? Did he say something?"

"Did he grunt?" Bertrand asked.

Greg did give her some sort of acknowledgment, she said. She was frustrated he wasn't more responsive but figured he was still mad at her. So she went back to work around 6:30 P.M. because she wasn't sure if she'd shut down her equipment properly.

When she got home, she took a bath and a shower. And when she got out, Greg was cold and not breathing.

"I called 911, hysterical, and turned on the light, and he was white, and I had to take him off the bed and onto the floor," she said. "[He was] dead weight, and I was struggling. I couldn't keep the phone in my ear, and he was flopping. Do you know what that's like? When you pull someone and they just clunk?"

No, Jerome said. He didn't.

"It's the worst experience ever, and you try to breathe life into a lifeless body," she said. "I looked at him, and he's the color that he is and I know . . . that's what they look like when they come in to work. That was the scariest thing I have ever witnessed. The paramedics came here and worked on him so much, and the officer is going to call me back with their names because I want to write them a letter. . . . His color was coming back, and they even detected a little heartbeat thing. I feel haunted by knowing that I was here the whole time."

Jerome said he couldn't relate to the pain of going through something like that.

"God, I miss my Greg, my husband," she said. " I go over in my head wondering, wishing I could've done more, wishing I knew it was like that. I didn't know. I didn't know."

The irony of the situation, she said, was that the pills were hers. He'd taken them away from her so she wouldn't use them. It was an unfortunate situation, she said, and it was unlike him to take pills, but he was depressed.

"Greg is a wonderful, wonderful person, but he does have a streak of both stubbornness and wanting to get back at people," she said. "Your father, for instance. He decided his life was better without him and that it would hurt his father that he was no longer in his life, and he told me that time and time again."

That was Greg's pride, Jerome said. "He didn't want to break first."

Kristin said Greg definitely had a problem dealing with his anger.

"I think he was trying to get back at me," she said.

Jerome said he still couldn't understand why Kristin would want to come right back to the apartment.

"I'm here because I'm visiting mortuaries, deciding where we're going to celebrate him. I'm here to feel like I'm kind of home, because I miss him and I'm surrounded by him here."

Jerome said it was all such a shock. He didn't know how to deal with it. Kristin said she was barely holding on and started crying. She said she wished she could share her pain with Greg's family, so they could grieve together.

"All I can think of is, my God, what did I think I was looking for in life. I had it. I miss him so much. I keep getting calls from everybody who loves him and worked with him, saying that they are so sorry, and what a good man he was, and he was such a great man."

"He just seemed happy to me," Jerome said.

He was happy, Kristin said, when he thought things were going well between them. "You hear people say things like, I couldn't live without you. You make me so happy. I don't want to be with anyone else but you because you make me happy."

Kristin said she hadn't dated anybody during college and wondered how she could've "been so fortunate to have met the right person under those circumstances. . . . But now I realize, you know what, it was fate that brought us together. He was sent to me. It wasn't fair for him or for me to be questioning things like this, and I wanted to find out before we were married for five years with two children. . . . I just needed a little space."

Jerome said he was still bothered by the same questions: Did she give him the drugs, and if not, how did he get them? Greg didn't take drugs, he said. None of this made any sense.

"I'm afraid that the death certificate is going to say suicide, and I don't want that, and that's why I'm doing my hardest to rule out any possibilities," he said. ". . . He was happy and paying off his debt. He was happy about work."

Kristin said their debts were always an emotional issue for Greg. For a long time he would bring up the subject every day, repeatedly. When they first got married, she was only working part time, and so she racked up even more bills. He was upset about his mother's money problems, too.

"He had a lot weighing down on him," she said.

After they'd finished talking, Jerome went into the bathroom for a few minutes. He saw cigarette ashes in the sink and around the toilet. He had no idea Kristin smoked.

"Wow," he thought. "I really don't know this girl."

He opened the medicine cabinet to see what other unknowns he might discover but found nothing of note. As he was leaving, Kristin tried to give him a hug, and he felt himself stiffen. He didn't want to hug her.

Dan Anderson came down to San Diego on Friday, November 10, to attend a CAT conference at the same Shelter Island hotel as the previous year's. Anderson hoped that

Michael's affair with Kristin had ended, and that he and his buddy could play a bit over the weekend.

When Anderson didn't see Michael there that morning, he asked his friend's coworkers where he was. Michael was coming later, they said, and you won't believe what happened: Kristin Rossum's husband is dead.

"You've got to be kidding me," Anderson said, shocked. "How?"

Suicide, they said. The first thing Anderson wondered was whether Kristin's husband killed himself over her affair with Michael.

Michael seemed in fairly normal spirits when he showed up that afternoon, although Anderson noticed that he talked on his cell phone quite a bit, away from everyone else. When the two of them finally chatted, neither one mentioned the affair.

Later that week, the de Villers family hired an attorney to file a petition in probate court, attempting to gain some control over the case. They asked the court to appoint Jerome as special administrator of his brother's body so that the organ and tissue specimens could be turned over to him, and he could hire an independent pathologist to perform a second autopsy.

Because Kristin worked at the Medical Examiner's Office and was having a "possible relationship" with her supervisor, the de Villers family told the court they didn't believe the county's autopsy results were trustworthy. "The family members do not believe the decedent committed suicide, but rather that Ms. Rossum may have poisoned him," their petition stated.

"Ms. Rossum has informed the family of her intention to have decedent's body cremated as soon as she has custody of the body. The immediate family members do not want the body to be cremated at the conclusion of the [San Diego Police Department] investigation."

A probate judge approved the petition on November 15, but after talking again with Blackbourne, Yves decided a second autopsy wouldn't be necessary.

Greg's old friend Bill Leger got a call from Kristin on Tuesday evening, November 7, to let him know that Greg had overdosed by taking some of her old prescription drugs. She sounded upset, like she was crying. It was tough to hear her through his own tears.

Kristin told him he was the second person she'd called. He said he'd come down to San Diego as soon as he could get on a plane, hoping to provide some comfort to the grieving widow of one of his closest friends.

Leger got to her apartment in the early evening that Friday, and they ordered a large pizza around eight o'clock. He ate two pieces, and Kristin, who looked withdrawn and a little distraught, barely made it through half a piece. Kristin informed Leger that she'd been to a conference with her boss. She'd had too much to drink one night while she was at the conference, she said, and she and Greg got into an argument over the phone. Greg was very jealous and was wondering why she'd gotten drunk at a professional conference with her boss.

Kristin also told Leger she was starting to have feelings for her boss, an announcement that didn't sit very well with him so soon after Greg's death. Michael had called, she said, and he might come over, if Leger didn't mind. Leger was hesitant but agreed that it would be okay.

Sometime around 10 P.M., Kristin said she was getting tired. She wanted to take a bath, be by herself, and go to bed.

Kristin seemed to be in better spirits and a little more energetic when Leger arrived with his parents around 8:00 or 9:00 the next morning. He opened the fridge to store the platters of food his mother made for Greg's memorial service on Sunday and noticed there was only one piece of pizza left in the fridge. That was odd, he thought, because he'd wrapped up six or seven before he'd left. Leger assumed that Michael must have come over, but he didn't ask.

After that, Leger and Kristin spoke only once more by phone. He didn't like the way she'd rushed him out of the apartment, and he could tell she was back on the meth. She'd made several trips to the bathroom, and when she came out, she was all jumpy and weird.

"Plus," Leger said, "telling me she had feelings for another guy four days after her husband died really bugged me."

The memorial service, held on Greg's birthday, November 12, was just for family. Yves de Villers read part of the Bible, and Ralph Rossum said a few words. Since there was still a hold on the body, the de Villers family had to leave without their son's ashes.

Greg's body wasn't released from the Medical Examiner's Office until December 4, so he wasn't cremated until December 8. Kristin picked up the ashes and gave them to her parents to keep. It wasn't until April that a friend of the de Villers family came to pick them up, along with Greg's other personal belongings, including a fishing pole and a high school yearbook. When his brothers went through the items, Jerome noticed that Greg's more expensive fishing and camping gear was not among them.

For many nights, Jerome spent hours lying awake in bed, his mind spinning with questions. When he finally could let go and drift off, Greg showed up in his dreams. One night Jerome dreamed that he and Greg were fighting at the grocery store.

"Why did you let Kristin do this to you?" Jerome asked him.

Once Greg's family finally got the ashes back from the Rossums, they planned to scatter them around Duck Lake at Mammoth, one of Greg's favorite places in the mountains, a special spot they'd discovered when the boys were growing up.

Chapter 10

About a week after Greg's death, toxicologist Cathy Hamm was using the phone in Michael's office one night after he'd left the lab. She was making arrangements to go to Joshua Tree, and Michael's phone was the only one in the lab where she could sit down and take notes. She grabbed a yellow notepad on his desk and was flipping through it to find a blank page when she came across a letter he'd written to Kristin. She couldn't believe what she was reading. She was so shocked, she started shaking inside. All this time she'd suspected the affair, and they had denied it. But here was proof. Validation.

Michael had written the letter on Thursday night, October 26, right after the Yankees won the World Series and about two weeks after he and Kristin had gone to the SOFT conference together. He was missing her.

He told her how much he loved her and felt loved, and how he was looking forward to the day he could display his affection more publicly. He laid out the details of how they'd met eight months earlier. Perhaps it was comforting to put them on paper as he sat at his desk, fantasizing about the day they would finally be together. But for Hamm, it only confirmed what she'd felt in her gut all along.

"You and I played out what some may call fate, others destiny," he wrote.

Even though they were both married, Michael said, he was still excited about the prospect of spending the rest of his life with her. He'd never felt this way about anyone before. Then he began to get maudlin. He told himself that she was "progressing," but now that he was "alone," it was getting harder and harder to wait for her to leave Greg.

"Now as I sit here, time slows down," he wrote. "The days pass and another night drags on and I tell myself it's okay, not many to go now. Then days become weeks and weeks months. . . ."

Michael said he felt himself building emotional barriers to protect himself and his pride, frustrated that their time together was spent with her watching the clock "for fear of letting Greg down." He felt most "vulnerable" at times like her birthday, when she was at Greg's side, not his. And now he was thinking about the holidays, and he was still unsure whether she would actually leave her husband by then.

Hamm immediately called her coworker, Ray Gary, to tell him about the letter, and he told her to make a copy of it. Then they tried to figure out what to do with it in light of Greg's death. Hamm called her defense attorney friend to ask for advice and was told to take it immediately to the police. Hamm agreed that the police should have the letter but decided to leave that uncomfortable task to another coworker.

Within a few weeks of the toxicology conference in San Diego, Dan Anderson got a call from an investigator who asked a bunch of questions about fentanyl and the paper that Anderson had published about fentanyl patches. The investigator had no clue that Anderson was a friend of Michael's or that he was going on some wrong information. He thought Anderson had presented the fentanyl paper at the SOFT conference in Milwaukee, when, in fact, it had been a year earlier in Puerto Rico. Anderson tried asking some of his own questions, but the investigator wouldn't disclose why he was calling. After he hung up, Anderson told his colleagues about the call and asked if they thought the death of Kristin Rossum's husband was related to fentanyl.

Anderson e-mailed Michael to tell him about the strange call and asked what was going on in San Diego concerning fentanyl. Michael wrote back, saying he didn't know.

Anderson received a subsequent call from yet another investigator, who also didn't know that Anderson was a friend of Michael's. The investigator asked whether it was typical for a toxicologist to keep articles on fentanyl in his office. Anderson said yes, in fact, he probably had twenty-five to thirty articles about the drug in his own desk. That's part of what forensic toxicologists do for a living, he said, they study drugs and how much can be fatal.

Anderson informed the investigator of his relationship with Michael, telling him that the toxicology community was very close-knit. At that point, Anderson said, the conversation became more of an interrogation, and Anderson began to worry that he might accidentally or unknowingly say something that would get his friend in trouble.

On November 9, Barnhart called Pacific Toxicology Laboratories in Woodland Hills, which had all the sophisticated testing equipment needed to figure out what killed Greg. Barnhart told the director, Michael Henson, that he wanted the lab to do some testing on a case because he knew the people involved and didn't feel comfortable doing it himself. Barnhart followed up with a letter, along with samples of Greg's stomach contents, urine, and blood. He also did a "quick and dirty" screening of his own to see what, if any, drugs might turn up, but found nothing. The equipment at the sheriff's crime lab wasn't sensitive enough.

About a week later, Barnhart got a call from Henson to say they got a few hits with the comprehensive urine screen, which tests for several hundred different compounds. They found fentanyl, along with clonazepam and oxycodone.

"Oh, shit," Barnhart said.

Barnhart had no idea where Greg would've gotten his hands on fentanyl. It wasn't the kind of drug you could just go out and buy on the street. A Schedule II narcotic regulated by the Drug Enforcement Agency, it was usually kept under lock and key in labs or hospitals, where it's known as a drug of abuse among medical staff because of the sense of euphoria it creates. Barnhart called Blackbourne to tell him the news.

Barnhart called Henson again to ask him to determine the amount of each drug in Greg's body, and Henson called back with those results on November 20. There was a lethal level of fentanyl, a high but still therapeutic dose of clonazepam, and a trace amount of oxycodone. Barnhart notified Blackbourne of the findings, which were written up in the lab's first official report on November 21.

The tests showed 53.5 nanograms per milliliter of fentanyl in blood taken from the leg during the autopsy and 57.3 nanograms per milliliter in blood from the heart. These compared with much lower levels in the blood taken earlier at Scripps Memorial Hospital. At that time the blood taken from the upper leg measured fentanyl at 11.22 nanograms per milliliter. No one knew what to make of results from a tissue sample Blackbourne took from Greg's bruised right arm, which showed 21.3 nanograms per gram.

Fentanyl differs from other drugs in the way it distributes in the body after a person dies. For example, the longer the stretch of time between death and the autopsy, when a blood sample is taken, the higher the fentanyl level will rise in the blood within the heart chamber as compared to an arm or a leg.

Michael tried to be Kristin's advocate, both socially and professionally, while she was on bereavement leave.

On November 17, he e-mailed Amborn to ask if he would give Kristin the option of taking an upcoming seminar on the HPLC machine, which she'd been looking forward to attending. He said he thought it would be good to help "take her mind off other issues." Amborn wrote back, saying he was unsure whether Kristin was in any kind of emotional state to benefit from such training, but he would reevaluate his decision when he returned from a week's vacation.

Kristin, like Michael, already knew how to use this machine, which tests for the presence of benzodiazepines, such as clonazepam.

That same day Michael also e-mailed all his toxicologists, asking them to pull together some paperwork so that Kristin could work on something from home. "This will relieve the burden on [you] and enable her to do something productive," he wrote.

A few days later, Michael organized a small get-together for Kristin after work. He invited Angie Wagner, the investigator who worked on Greg's case, and a few other people from the lab, to meet at the 94th Aero Squadron around 4:15 P.M. for a couple of hours. Kristin showed up about an hour into the gathering, looking shaken up and sad. She was nervous and fidgety and had sores on her hands and face.

On November 20, Jerome had returned from the mall to the town house his father rented in Thousand Oaks, where his mother lived, when Bertrand told him that Yves had just hung up with Dr. Blackbourne. Blackbourne, he said, called to tell them that fentanyl was the drug that killed Greg.

Jerome and Bertrand had never heard of fentanyl. Yves said it was used as an anesthetic during surgery and also by veterinarians to put animals to sleep. Yves was surprised, though. Even Blackbourne had mentioned that it was a rare drug.

The brothers sat with their parents at the dining-room table and brainstormed where the fentanyl might have come from and how it could have gotten into Greg's body. Jerome asked Yves why, if Greg had wanted to commit suicide, would he have used such an obscure drug? Why not something more common and available like strychnine, GHB, or some other drug he could've bought on the street? Could Greg have gotten the fentanyl from Orbigen?

Jerome and Bertrand looked up fentanyl in Yves's physicians' reference book, and Jerome stayed up late searching the Internet to learn more about it. Maybe Kristin had purchased the drug in Mexico, he thought, or maybe she'd taken it from work.

Jerome spoke with Blackbourne a couple weeks later and asked if the Medical Examiner's Office kept fentanyl. Blackbourne seemed hesitant to talk to Jerome about this, but he admitted that some drugs were missing from the lab. He wouldn't say which ones because he didn't want to jeopardize the ongoing police investigation.

Meanwhile, Marie kept telling Jerome to let the police handle the investigation. He would try to tell her what he'd learned, but she just didn't want to deal with it. So he confided in Bertrand, and he also e-mailed information to his father.

Marie couldn't understand why Jerome needed to get so involved in the police's business. Jerome needed to know everything right away. More, more, more. Why couldn't he be more patient?

Marie couldn't even fathom the idea that Kristin might have had something to do with Greg's death. She loved Kristin like a daughter. She was the first girl to come into the family, the wife of her oldest son. Kristin would call and give her recipes. She seemed like such a sweet girl.

Nonetheless, Marie wanted to know what happened to Greg. If he committed suicide, as painful and unbelievable as that thought might be, she wanted to understand how and why. She tried to call Kristin every day, just to check in and see how she was doing. She remembered the last time she saw Kristin and Greg together. It was on her birthday, September 2. They'd come up to visit and take her to a nice dinner. Kristin looked more womanly, and Marie had thought she might be pregnant. But she later learned that her maternal instinct was wrong.

After spending a week away in Sacramento on business, Detective Agnew came to work on November 22 and started catching up on the de Villers case. The toxicology results had come in, so she and her team met with Blackbourne to go over the findings of Greg's autopsy and his opinion on the cause of death.

Agnew recalled Blackbourne telling them that based on the amount of urine in Greg's bladder and the bronchial pneumonia in his lungs, he was probably in a coma for at least six to twelve hours. He said Greg had clonazepam, oxycodone, and fentanyl in his body, but only the fentanyl dose was lethal. The clonazepam, a date-rape drug, could have rendered him comatose, he said, and that's probably when the fentanyl was administered.

Agnew had never heard of fentanyl, so Blackbourne gave her and her team a quick lesson. It was one hundred times stronger than morphine, he said, and between 2 and 4 nanograms per milliliter was considered a lethal dose. It was a fast-acting drug whose effects lasted only a short time.

The detectives asked if Greg, while under the influence of these drugs, could've gotten out of bed, thrown away any containers or whatever was used to administer the drugs, and get back into bed. Blackbourne said no.

Blackbourne told them he thought Greg couldn't have lived all day with such a large amount of fentanyl in his system, but he was going to send the blood samples to a buddy at the Ventura County Medical Examiner's Office to get another opinion. Blackbourne's buddy concurred.

With the knowledge that Greg died from a hefty dose of fentanyl—a drug Kristin never mentioned to anyone—Agnew and her team decided it was time to have the young toxicologist come down to the station for an interview. Agnew called her around noon and arranged for her to come in at 1:30 P.M. Thinking they would get a second interview, she and Detective Jimmy Valle decided they wouldn't bring up the fentanyl in their initial questioning.

When Kristin walked into the station, Agnew and Valle looked at each other knowingly. It was obvious from her appearance, particularly the sores on her face, that she was using meth. Kristin had already admitted to using meth in the past. Partway through the interview, Agnew scribbled a note on her pad to Valle, suggesting he ask Kristin whether she was using again.

Agnew, a tall blonde, started off the interview with the petite blonde by asking simple questions: Kristin's age, how long she'd been married to Greg, and why she was still using her maiden name. Kristin said she'd been in the process of changing it, but there was so much paperwork, she'd gotten a little overwhelmed.

Kristin's answers were rambling. She'd start and stop sentences, jumping from one subject to another. She was very fidgety, wiping her nose, scratching her shoulder, wadding and unwadding a tissue in her hands.

As she described first meeting Greg, her voice broke, and she put her hand to her face.

"He was my angel and I clung to him and he was the only person I knew and he helped me through [that period of] my life. And I needed him, and he really needed me, too."

After getting over her initial reservations about getting married, she said, she went through with the wedding but started questioning their relationship again six months later. Her mother suggested a separation, so she built up the courage to ask for one. She and Greg started arguing about it on Saturday, two days before he died.

But Greg couldn't handle such emotional discussions, she said, and he acted just as he had in the past. "He blows up, gets irate, and then sinks in and won't talk to me and goes and hides himself in, in our bed, lights off, won't talk to me, will not respond to me . . . [for several days before he can] deal with what's going on. So he did that. He turned in[ward], and I thought it was just normal."

Throughout the interview, Agnew forced Kristin to go into more and more detail about certain aspects of her story as the detective looked for discrepancies. On Kristin's first reference to Michael, she stumbled over how to identify him.

"I needed to talk to Michael, Dr. Robertson, about, um, some personal things. So, I left work early, and he also left early, and I, I spoke to him for about probably an hour and a half in the afternoon, before going home about five fifteen, five o'clock."

When she described finding Greg cold and not breathing that night, she broke down into a dramatic display of grief, her body racked with sobbing, her voice rising to a high pitch.

She put her head on the table, then wiped her eyes and blew her nose.

Agnew redirected the questions to Greg's family, which seemed to calm Kristin down. Describing Jerome as "the angry middle child," Kristin said they never got along, because she was scared of him. She described Yves as "a loose cannon" who was stubborn and had a volatile temper. The de Villerses were a strange family, she said. She never heard Greg tell his mother he loved her.

She described Greg as clingy, overly possessive, and unable to spend time away from her, saying he even tried to "put a guilt trip" on her for wanting to go to a professional conference in Milwaukee.

"He actually told me when I got back that he was upset because he didn't want me to go. . . . He wanted to hear me say that I wouldn't go for him," she said.

She said she and Greg talked about the separation again early Sunday evening. This time he cried, told her to go away, and went to bed. A couple of hours later, he got up and said he couldn't sleep. She asked if he was hungry. He said no and got "some water or something."

Kristin said Greg didn't tell her he'd taken anything until she came home for lunch the next morning around 11:30 or so, when he said "he had taken those little prescriptions of mine. I was so mad about that."

Kristin said Greg had taken something to help him sleep several times in the past—Vicodin from when he had his wisdom teeth out or "some of this cough syrup stuff," which had hydrocodone or oxycodone in it. But overall, he was not one to take drugs. That was more her problem, she said, but that was in the past.

"I ran away because I had a problem with drugs. So he met me, and he got me cleaned up. I got myself cleaned up. He was just there for me. . . . It's not in his normal behavior to [take drugs], but I do understand the need for escape."

Kristin explained that she'd gotten the oxycodone and clonazepam in Mexico more than five and a half years ago to try to help her get off methamphetamine.

"Greg was not amused at my logic in that," she said, laughing nervously.

Then, about five years ago, she said, he announced that he was getting rid of them, and she saw him throw away the containers.

"I said, 'Well, you do need to dispose of the drugs in a separate place,' and he said, 'Okay, I'll take care of it,' . . . but I guess he never did," she said.

Kristin said she was able to clean up her life, get back to school, and graduate with the highest honors in chemistry. When she got the toxicologist's job, she fell in love with it.

"It was something I was really close to—probably too close," she said.

Agnew asked if Kristin ever took oxycodone and clonazepam together. Kristin said no, she wouldn't recommend it. She didn't like oxycodone because it upset her stomach, but she'd taken some clonazepam for anxiety in her "attempts at self-medication."

Later in the interview, Agnew asked whether Kristin was surprised to find all those rose petals on Greg's body, and whether he was the type to make such a melodramatic gesture.

"I didn't even see them until I was on the phone with the paramedics," Kristin said. "They said, 'Okay pull him onto the floor.' I pull back the comforter, and I see a wedding picture just under the pillow and this rose torn to shreds and, um, I had always, it seems so selfish now that I was always wanting him to be more romantic and more emotional and tell me what he's feeling, and it made me mad, but I, I, I opened it and I saw the red and the petals and . . . his body just thumped and it hit hard. . . . He's never really done anything like that, but it seemed to me like he was just crying for help, saying, 'You know, I really do need you.' "

Next, Agnew asked Kristin about the shredded letter. Kristin laughed nervously again, saying she assumed they would keep what she was saying in confidence. She said she'd met someone at work who was in a similar marital situation, and they'd developed "a very close relationship."

Kristin said she told Greg in July that she'd developed feelings for this other man, but "it wasn't physical at all." Nonetheless, her announcement sent Greg to bed for a couple of days. He also called the man at home, furious. When Greg recovered, he said he would prove to her that the marriage was worth working on.

This close friend of hers had written her "a very sweet letter," she said, which Greg found the Thursday before he died.

"I had it at work, and I had brought it home," Kristin said, smiling at Agnew, "and I was reading it, to put in my keepsake box. You know how women are cheap and sentimental sometimes. I was reading it when he came home, and I couldn't refold it up in my pocket, and he basically wrestled me to the ground and read it. He was really upset. He got irate."

So, she said, she put the letter through a shredder they kept in the apartment, and that's when he gave her an ultimatum: "Either you quit your job," she said, pausing, "or I will inform him or them of your, um, drug history."

That ultimatum, she said, was the personal issue she and Michael talked about that Monday afternoon—what to do if Greg carried out his threat. Michael, she told Agnew, was her boss, the man she'd been seeing. And she'd opened up to him that day about her drug history.

Agnew asked how Michael responded. Kristin said he admired how she'd regained her life, and he was sorry she was in so much pain. He was very supportive and said it wouldn't affect his faith in her as a toxicologist.

"What did he say would happen if your husband had gone to your place of employment?" Agnew asked. "Would that have caused a problem?"

It would have made her uncomfortable if it affected everyone's impression of her, Kristin said, but "I don't think it would have caused me to lose my job."

Kristin said she knew Agnew would be in contact with the Medical Examiner's Office, and she would appreciate it if she "left some of this out."

Agnew asked if anyone at the office knew about her relationship with her boss. Kristin said Lloyd Amborn, a retired Navy captain who was their "administrative head honcho," confronted her and Michael over the summer, but they both denied the rumors that were going around the office. She said it was all "a null issue" now, though, because they'd only been meeting for coffee while they tried to sort out their respective marital issues.

Kristin told Agnew that Michael was separated from his wife and they were in counseling. She said she wanted to be there for him, to support him in whatever he decided to do, but Amborn had told Michael not to have any contact with Kristin for the moment.

A little more than halfway through the interview, Agnew excused herself and let Detective Valle take over. He picked up where Agnew left off, but he took the interview in a more confrontational direction, asking why Greg's family believed Kristin might have had something to do with Greg's death. Then he backed off a bit and assumed a more sympathetic tone, telling Kristin she shouldn't be so hard on herself about her attempted breakup with Greg.

"I know it's not my fault," Kristin said. "But, yes, I feel like a certain responsibility, especially when his family treats me that way."

They took a break so Kristin could go to the bathroom. Agnew rejoined the interview, and Valle explained they'd been talking about Jerome.

"He would rather believe some ludicrous conspiracy theory rather than his brother [killed himself]," Kristin said.

"What kind of conspiracy theory?" Agnew asked.

Kristin said Jerome thought someone might have entered the apartment while Kristin was taking a bath and drugged Greg.

Agnew showed Kristin the letter Hamm had found in Michael's office and told Kristin that someone had sent it to her. Kristin said she'd never seen it before. After scanning it, she said his other letters weren't so sappy.

"We were dreamers, I guess; it was a lovely romance," Kristin said. "It really was, and I, I don't know if or where it will lead."

Agnew decided to take a more blunt approach. "I don't know you, and I didn't know Greg," she said flatly. "I don't know Mike. I haven't talked to Mike. I don't know his wife. We have somebody that's dead, and we have two people that wanted out of the marriage, and we have somebody that wants somebody by the holidays."

Agnew continued to pound on Kristin with more specific questions, while Kristin grew increasingly defensive about her relationship with Michael.

"I love him," she said matter-of-factly. "I do; I love him. I, I love him. He's a very wonderful person. I, I love his character. I loved him as a person. He's—very dear to me."

"Okay, maybe you loved him enough that you guys just had to get rid of Greg," Agnew said.

"Maybe, through a separation," Kristin said, her brow creased with an expression of disbelief that Agnew could suggest such a thing. "That's disgusting. That's horrible."

"People do it," Agnew said.

"Not me," Kristin said. "This is, that's ludicrous. . . . He was such a sweet and good man."

"And he's dead," Agnew said.

"I know," Kristin said, raising her voice and crying. "I feel the responsibility for it, I really do, but I did not make him do what he did. I hurt him. Maybe I wasn't the best wife, but I'd never hurt him."

Kristin laid her head on the table, sobbing.

Later in the interview, Valle asked Kristin if she had access at work to all the drugs she'd been telling them about. They went over them one by one, and Kristin said, yes, she did. He also had her run through the procedures for logging in the drug standards and describe how the evidence envelopes were locked up.

Valle explained that he was asking her all these questions because there were rumors going around that she may have had something to do with Greg's death.

"I don't even know how to deal with that," Kristin said, shaking her head.

Kristin dismissed the rumored suggestion that she might have taken a drug from work and put it in Greg's food or drink.

"That is ridiculous," she said, rolling her eyes and looking away.

Valle asked if any of the drugs they'd been talking about came in a skin patch or in a form that could be injected intravenously.

"No, they're pills," she said.

"There was nothing at your home at the time that could've been taken with a needle or patches or anything else that had a hard and solid form?" he asked.

"I don't know," Kristin said, sounding frustrated and despairing.

Then Valle switched his attention to Kristin and her personal habits. "Look at me," he told her. "You don't have a drug habit at this time at all? Please don't lie to me."

Kristin took a deep breath. "I do," she said.

Her voice broke as she admitted she'd bought some meth on the street from an acquaintance and relapsed. She was working with a counselor and taking it day by day. She'd slipped up a couple of times but hadn't had any since the previous Saturday, four days earlier. She also admitted that she'd started using again two weeks before Greg's death.

"I was building up the courage to go through with this, and I, my escape," she said, stumbling over her words.

Kristin said she'd been spending about a hundred dollars at a time to buy drugs. She started out using a couple of times a day then trailed off to just sporadic use. In fact, she said, she was nervous when the investigators came to her apartment the night of Greg's death because she had some hidden in a kitchen drawer under a towel, and she was scared they were going to find it.

Valle asked if she'd ever given Greg any of her meth. "No," Kristin replied.

"Did you ever intentionally give [him] any of the other drugs that we've talked about?"

"No, of course not," she said.

Valle, who'd been out of the room during the earlier rose petal discussion, asked Kristin where they came from. The number of roses Greg bought her changed again, this time to eighteen. She said four of them lasted until the Friday night before he died, and she thought she threw them away Sunday night.

Valle asked if the petals she found on Greg looked like they were from the birthday batch.

"I don't know if they were from the same batch," she said, "but they were the same, I mean, it was a beautiful. . . ."

"The colors were the same?" Valle asked.

Yes, Kristin said, they were "beautiful red roses."

Kristin cried some more as the two detectives wound up

the interview. Agnew asked whether Greg had known that Kristin had relapsed.

"He confronted me and I denied it," Kristin said. He got very upset about it, she added. In fact, he threatened to tell her superiors, not just that she had a drug history, but that she was using again.

Finally, Valle said it would be helpful if they could read her journal, the one that was lying on the coffee table in the living room when the campus police arrived at her apartment the night Greg died.

"It's nothing that's going to be exposed to anybody at your workplace," he said.

Kristin agreed.

"The last thing we want to see is you go off into that kind of hell again, because you know what you went through to get away from [the meth]," Agnew said. ". . . But we do have to look at things."

Agnew walked Kristin out into the hallway and suggested for the second time that day that Kristin take a polygraph test. At the very least, Agnew told her, it could get the de Villers family off her back. Agnew could tell that it was finally starting to sink in with Kristin that the police were seriously looking at her as a suspect in her husband's death. Despite all the crying faces and sobbing noises Kristin had made, this was the first time Agnew saw actual tears in her eyes.

"You guys actually think I might have done this?" Kristin asked.

Now that they thought Kristin wasn't playacting, Valle became concerned about letting her drive home alone to get the diary in case she crashed her car. He and Agnew offered to drive her home in their police car, but she refused. So, Valle suggested that Agnew drive them both to the University City apartment in Kristin's white Toyota. Again, Kristin said no.

Kristin finally agreed to let Agnew ride with her in the Toyota, but said she had to drive because the car had some mechanical problems. Valle said he would follow behind in his unmarked vehicle, so he could bring Agnew and the diary back to the station. Agnew felt uncomfortable with the whole idea but went along because she was the junior partner.

For the first five or ten minutes, Kristin kept trying to talk to Agnew about the case, repeatedly asking why they would think she had something to do with Greg's death. Agnew tried to steer the conversation toward more neutral topics. With Kristin crying and so agitated, she was scared for their safety. She also knew that without a tape recorder running, whatever Kristin said would be virtually useless in court. When the ride was over, Agnew vowed never to take another one like it.

The cover of Kristin's diary was dark purple and decorated with an overlay of pale dried leaves. Agnew opened up the book to find that it was actually a small three-ring binder holding a short stack of lined pages that were filled with Kristin's handwriting.

The first entry was dated September 8. Many of the subsequent entries weren't dated, but they contained time references, such as "October is coming to a close."

Curiously, Kristin had written three separate entries dated November 7, the day after Greg died, and their content overlapped somewhat. Two of them were written as sorrowful letters to Greg, starting "My Dearest Gregie" and detailing how much she missed him. She could still hear his voice and see his blue eyes gazing at her lovingly. "I can feel your warm body wrapped around mine, lying like spoons," she wrote. "I keep expecting you to enter the front door at any minute, saying that it was just a terrible dream all along."

In the third entry dated November 7, she talked about

how Greg's death had helped underscore what was most important, pushing her to get out and explore her world and helping to rekindle her "appreciation and passion for life . . . I want to get out and get dirty—wander, investigate, and reflect. <u>Carpe Diem</u>!"

Two days after interviewing Kristin, Agnew and Valle went to the apartment Michael shared with Nicole to question him. The interview lasted about ninety minutes. Not knowing the details of Greg's death, Nicole had gone on a prearranged vacation with her sister to England and was due back later that day. Michael was there, getting the apartment ready for her.

Michael said Kristin came to work on Monday, November 6, "concerned about [Greg's] well-being."

He repeated the basic timeline Kristin had given to police, noting that he and his wife had gone to a counseling session after he spoke with Kristin that afternoon. After meeting Kristin at the hospital and going back with her to her apartment, he said, he talked to investigator Angie Wagner the next morning. She told him "this appeared to be a drug-related death of unknown identity."

Valle asked whether Kristin told him why Greg took the clonazepam and oxycodone. But as he continued to do throughout the interview, Michael didn't really answer the question directly. He suggested that Greg took the drugs because he was "trying to show her something," or to help him sleep, but "the effects on him suggest to me that he took more than just to get some sleep. It may have been related to the relationship issues."

But Valle said, "For an individual who says he can't live without her and to find him dead the next . . . day or two is one of two or three things. Either he committed suicide, accidentally overdosed, or someone just got tired of dealing with this individual."

Michael said he still wasn't clear whether this was "a scare tactic that went wrong." Based on what Kristin told him, he said, the couple had been having marital problems for several months, and about two or three weeks before he died, Kristin asked Greg for "some space, some separation."

Previously, Michael said, Kristin had tried to get Greg into counseling, but he didn't feel they needed help to deal with their issues.

"She had verbally communicated to me that she was concerned for his well-being, if she decided to separate," he said.

Michael said his "personal relationship" with Kristin began about a month after he started working at the Medical Examiner's Office. He quickly clarified that he meant the two of them were confidants, sharing personal information. Michael appeared to be very careful in his answers, saying as little as possible to the detectives, so Valle told him that Kristin had already disclosed the true nature of her relationship with him. Still, Michael continued to give measured responses.

Like Kristin, he initially talked about her drug problem as if it were in the past, though he eventually acknowledged that Greg had found a pipe in the apartment and suspected Kristin was using again. Kristin told Michael all about it on the afternoon of November 6, he said.

"My assumption is that perhaps she was . . . using [methamphetamine] again," Michael said.

"Being a close friend of Kristin, also in a relationship with Kristin, did she tell you that she was or wasn't?" Valle asked.

Michael stumbled as he answered. He asked her that question, and "she conceded that she had used recently in the past," he said, sighing. "Two or three weeks before his death, she had begun using again because of the . . . difficulty she was having with the relationship."

Michael said she told him she was getting the meth in the southern part of San Diego County, near the border. He said he was very upset and disappointed to hear that but didn't want to pry.

Valle, knowing full well that Greg died of a fentanyl overdose, discreetly tried to determine whether that information had been leaked to Michael or Kristin by one of their colleagues. But Michael insisted he knew nothing of the toxicology results. Michael said Kristin believed Greg's death was drug related, but she still wasn't sure what Greg might have taken. From reading the investigative report and talking to Kristin and Dr. Blackbourne, Michael said, his only conclusion was that Greg died of a combination of aspirin and possibly the prescription cough medicine found in the apartment.

Valle asked him repeatedly if Kristin was the reason that he and his wife had separated. But Michael kept insisting that he and Nicole weren't separated, that she was just away on vacation.

"We're still in counseling. We're still together," Michael said.

Valle asked if Michael and Kristin had discussed leaving their spouses for each other.

"I told Kristin that if my wife and I separate, then I would certainly look to pursue a relationship with her, if she was also separating," he said.

Valle asked Michael if he'd heard the rumors going around that Kristin may have had something to do with Greg's death. Yes, Michael said, and apparently unknowingly contradicted Kristin's claim that Lloyd Amborn had told him to stay away from Kristin. Michael said he'd initially told Amborn that rumors of his relationship with Kristin were untrue, but he'd since told the operations manager the "full story" so that he wouldn't find out "from other people."

"Did that include her recent involvement in drugs?" Valle asked.

"No, it didn't," Michael said. Asked why, Michael said he felt that information was unrelated to their relationship and was Kristin's private business. After Valle pushed harder, Michael conceded that Kristin's drug problem absolutely went to "the core of what we do and . . . someone that is a drug abuser or misuser is absolutely a problem to the lab." He said he made that clear to Kristin.

When Valle redirected his questions to the security of drugs kept in the lab, Michael acknowledged it was "a poor system."

"So, it's easy for anyone, not just Kristin and not just for you, but anybody to go in there, take drugs, take it out, and no one [would] ever know the difference," Valle asked, rhetorically. Michael had to agree.

Asked directly whether he and Kristin were ever sexually active, Michael said no. He admitted that he'd spent three or four nights at her place after Greg's death but said he hadn't had relations with her. "Simply comforting," he said.

Valle told Michael it was also rumored that he was somehow involved in Greg's death. "Has she ever asked you to get her any drugs?" he asked.

"No, she has not," Michael said.

"If she had asked, you would tell us?"

"I would," Michael said.

"Why? You'd get in trouble."

"This is of greater importance than me getting in trouble," Michael said.

Valle asked if it would surprise Michael to find out that Kristin did have something to do with her husband's death. Michael said yes, absolutely.

"I don't believe she . . . has the ability to do it, ability as in she's a sweet, caring, loving individual," Michael said. "And right up until his death, she was a sweet, caring, loving individual. Could she be fooling me? I guess."

Valle pointed out that she already had fooled him into

thinking she'd stayed clean and off drugs before she told him she was using again. Valle asked if it would surprise him that Kristin said Michael knew about her involvement in Greg's death. After stumbling and stuttering, Michael cleared his throat and said, "I'm not aware of anything that she has done."

The interview tape ran out shortly after this exchange, but Agnew later said that Michael finally let it slip that he had an apartment in Hillcrest. She said he didn't own up to being separated from Nicole until Agnew pressed the issue several times, telling him that Kristin said he'd left the Costa Verde apartment four or five weeks earlier. But even then, he still tried to cover his tracks. He said he and Nicole weren't legally separated and they didn't have an attorney, and that's what he thought Agnew was asking.

The next step was for Agnew to meet with Kristin a second time so she could confront her about the fentanyl. But when Agnew called her, Kristin said she'd been advised by her attorney not to say anything more.

After Kristin's interview with Agnew, she and her parents had retained attorney Michael Pancer, a well-known criminal defense lawyer in town. Pancer agreed to meet with Agnew but ended up telling her he saw no benefit to allowing Kristin to speak with detectives again.

"It was a calculated risk" not to confront Kristin during the first session about finding fentanyl in Greg's body, Agnew said. "It didn't pan out."

In the first few weeks after she got the case, Agnew went back and forth in her mind about whether Greg's death was a suicide or a homicide, and the confusion only continued as the investigation progressed. Kristin said it was a suicide, and Jerome said it wasn't. He-said she-said cases are never easy.

But this one proved to be unique and more challenging than most. An outside police agency had launched the investigation, gathered evidence from the crime scene, and initially thought Greg's death was a suicide, as did the Medical Examiner's Office. And although Agnew credited Jerome with helping to spur authorities to investigate further, he also made her job more difficult by repeatedly calling her, sometimes half a dozen times a day. It got to the point where she asked her sergeant, who normally dealt with victims' families, to handle some of Jerome's calls. It seemed that Jerome not only wanted the investigation to proceed, he wanted it to proceed in a timely manner. He also wasn't shy about telling her how and what he thought she should investigate. A couple of times she grew so frustrated with him, she had to tell him to "back off a little bit." This was a police investigation, and if she wasn't careful about keeping new or important findings under wraps, she was worried they might get back to Kristin and Michael—or the media—and ruin the investigation.

Sometimes, Agnew would get new information that convinced her she finally felt sure about what kind of death it was, but then, minutes later, she would find another piece of evidence that made her think the exact opposite. The last thing she wanted to do was put an innocent person behind bars for a crime he or she didn't commit.

Agnew was working long hours and often had to call a neighbor to feed her cat and two dogs. She also wasn't sleeping well. Typically, she was able to leave her work at the office, but this case followed her home. Even while she was jogging or bicycling, which usually helped to "clear out the cobwebs" in her head, the details coursed through her mind. And when she woke up in the morning, she felt as if her brain had been working all night to sort through the evidence in the case, as if she were trying to piece together a jigsaw puzzle.

So, to help her sift through and interpret the facts, she created a chart with two columns. One was for the evidence that supported suicide, the other homicide. Many mornings she and another detective on her team, Lynn Rydalch, would go into an office, close the door, and debate how certain information should be interpreted and into which column it should go. Rydalch played devil's advocate, so the discussions could get quite fiery, but never personal. Agnew continued to rely on Rydalch as a sounding board for the next year or so.

Take the letter from the Orbigen employees, for example. Yes, Gruenwald and his staff said Greg wasn't the type to commit suicide, but that was their opinion, not a fact. Sometimes the friends or relatives of someone who killed himself can't or don't want to accept reality. So Agnew ended up putting the letter in a third "nice to know, but it really doesn't get me anywhere" column.

Then there was the fact that police found no pill containers, no syringes, no fentanyl skin patches, and no foil packages the patches could have come in. Pills didn't have to be kept in a plastic vial. They could be stored in a bag or something else, like Kristin claimed. But since fentanyl didn't come in pill form, it had to be in some type of container, especially if it were in a liquid form. And if it were a liquid, there also should have been a syringe. That definitely went into the homicide column.

The rose petals were another piece of evidence that didn't fit with the suicide theory. None of the people Agnew interviewed said Greg was feminine or melodramatic. She asked Rydalch to name one straight man he knew who would make that kind of suicide gesture. She couldn't. Plus, the petals were scattered around Greg's body, not underneath him. Kristin said she'd found them under the covers, and when she moved him, they went everywhere. Yet none was found in the bed.

The shredded note, the diary, the wedding photo under the pillow, the rose petals, and other elements of the "suicide scene" all pointed Agnew toward homicide.

"It all was so hokey in my opinion," Agnew said. "Somebody who would go to this extent would leave a frigging letter."

On November 28, Detective Felix Zavala went to the Medical Examiner's Office and met with Amborn to discuss how drugs were used and stored there. Agnew and her team members had several subsequent meetings with the Medical Examiner's staff to learn more about the synthetic drug standards used in testing and the evidence envelopes of street drugs, white powder, and paraphernalia.

They learned that as a student worker, Kristin cleaned glassware and was taught to use some of the more complicated testing equipment. She also logged in the drug standards, which she used to do basic screenings of blood samples. In August 1997, for example, she logged in a new 100-milligram vial of amphetamine; in September, a 100-milligram vial of methamphetamine; and in October, a 10-milligram vial of fentanyl citrate.

The fentanyl vial was about 1 ½ inches tall, much larger than needed to hold 10-milligram of the powder and equivalent to a tiny portion of a packet of artificial sweetener. It was a teeny amount, but plenty potent to kill a person if it was dissolved in liquid and injected. At that time, the office didn't run tests for fentanyl, but the toxicologists bought the standard because they were hoping to set up a screening procedure sometime in the future. That procedure was never put into place while Kristin worked there.

By December, Agnew was sure she had a murder on her hands, but she thought it was going to be difficult, if not impossible, to prove in court. If she could just get the District

Attorney's Office to look at the case, she thought, she'd have done her job, and she could tell Jerome she'd taken it as far as she could.

Agnew and her boss gave a three-hour presentation to the chief and assistant chief of the DA's Family Protection Division. When the detectives asked if they thought they had enough to prosecute, the answer was yes.

The two division heads tried to brief Dan Goldstein, a deputy district attorney in that unit, but it was such an obscure and complicated story, chock-full of third-level hearsay, that Goldstein figured he'd better get it straight from the lead detective. So, within the next few days, Goldstein called Agnew, who came in with Rydalch and gave him the same presentation.

Goldstein, who'd worked as a paramedic for eleven years before becoming a lawyer, was the only one among them who'd ever heard of fentanyl. He felt in his gut that the evidence gathered so far pointed toward a staged suicide scene. The question was why Kristin would create such a scene. Goldstein found the case intriguing and thought it warranted a full investigation.

Sometime after Greg's death, possibly in late November, Kristin wrote Michael a letter on light blue parchment paper before she went to bed. She said she was trying to work through some of the "overwhelming" feelings that were running through her heart and mind.

She acknowledged that the past few weeks had been awful for both of them. They were lucky to have their love, their "only weapon" to help them through it.

"I have come out of this (so far) with a reaffirmation of self and a rededication to my own self-development, my own commitment to overcome my deamons [*sic*] for good," she wrote.

But amid all the turmoil, she said, she was coming to terms with what she needed to do. She promised to deal with her issues and strive to be the best person she could for him.

"You deserve nothing less," she wrote, especially when he'd stood by her even after her "repeated failings" and "a self-destructive act of my own." She was sorry for hurting him.

Knowing that he'd seen the "darkest corners of [her] soul" and still loved her unconditionally gave her strength and helped her look to the future—to their future together. Kristin believed that the recent events and emotions they'd shared would fortify their bond even further. She thanked him for his loyalty and for teaching her how to love so deeply. She hoped that over time their wounded relationship would heal, and she could regain his "absolute trust and confidence."

And, as if she couldn't say it enough, she told him again that she loved him.

"Truth and honesty will drive our lives," she wrote.

Right after Kristin's police interview, Agnew reported Kristin's admission that she was using drugs to upper management at the Medical Examiner's Office.

Amborn called Kristin in for a meeting on November 29. She seemed emotional and didn't look well. Initially, she'd been placed on bereavement leave, allowing her to work from home. But based on the ongoing drug audits and police investigation, Amborn decided it would be best to restrict her access to the office. So he switched her to administrative leave and asked her to turn in her keys so she couldn't go into the building unrestricted. At the request of the police, he also researched whether Kristin had her paychecks deposited directly into her checking account. She did.

Amborn placed Michael on administrative leave around the same time. On December 4, Amborn called Michael in for a meeting and, with Blackbourne and police detective Paul Torres in the room, told him he was fired. Amborn gave him a letter, making it official, but saying only that he'd failed to meet the requirements of the job he'd assumed on June 12, 2000.

"Your performance as a manager has not met an essential reporting expectation of this department's senior executives by your failure to inform us of a key personnel issue with serious operational implications," Amborn wrote. "Accordingly, you have lost sufficient confidence of your superiors such that you can no longer be effective as forensic toxicology laboratory manager." The key personnel issue, of course, was his failure to tell his superiors that Kristin was abusing illegal drugs.

Amborn told Kristin on December 1 that he wanted to review her job status. He met with her after Michael on December 4, with his secretary and Detective Torres present, and told her she was fired. She wore no makeup and looked even worse this time, drawn and as if she'd been crying. He gave her one letter that said her leave had been terminated and a second one that said she was being terminated for failing to meet the requirements of her twelve-month probationary period, which had started on March 10, 2000. But again, the real reason for Kristin's termination was her drug problem.

Word that the two toxicologists had been fired leaked out two days later. Television reporter Kevin Cox aired a story saying the two had left the Medical Examiner's Office, but county officials wouldn't confirm whether it had anything to do with the police investigation into Greg de Villers's death. County officials also wouldn't say whether Kristin and Michael had some sort of relationship outside the office.

Police, however, did confirm publicly for the first time that they'd opened a special investigation to look into whether Greg had, in fact, committed suicide. Kristin refused to be interviewed on camera for the story, but Cox quoted her as saying "the truth will come out."

Twelve days later, Cox did another story, giving more details about the case. Investigators had learned that Kristin was having an affair with her boss, he said, and none of Greg's coworkers believed he had committed suicide. Cox interviewed Stefan Gruenwald, who'd been doing some Internet research on Michael, and said the toxicologist was an expert on drugs that weren't easily detected in the body. Kristin declined to be interviewed once again.

Cathy Hamm found some interesting items when she cleaned out Kristin's and Michael's desks. In Kristin's bottom drawer, behind the hanging files, she found the bottle of Somacid muscle relaxants that Kristin had gotten in Mexico. In one of the files, she found two prescriptions written in Spanish, one for the Somacid and one for the Asenlix diet pills. She also found Armando Garcia's business card for Tijuana taxi service. When she pulled out the pencil tray from the top drawer, she found some dried reddish orange rose petals and a little note card from Michael, expressing his love.

In Michael's desk, she found Dan Anderson's case study on deaths involving fentanyl patches.

Goldstein became engrossed in the case fairly quickly. As soon as he heard the tape of Kristin's 911 call, he felt that something didn't ring true. Based on his experience as a paramedic, it sounded like Kristin was only pretending to try to resuscitate Greg. He saw no way that she could hold a cordless phone in the crook of her neck while pushing on

Greg's chest, breathing into his mouth, and counting into the phone for the dispatcher. The diary entries didn't ring true, either.

Later on, as Kristin's, Greg's, and Michael's e-mails trickled in, he cross-checked them against the diary entries and each other. He eventually concluded that the entries were fabricated, written for others to read, specifically Greg. Goldstein saw the diary as a prosecutorial gold mine.

Goldstein was known for having a strong personality and exuding confidence. He was smart and dynamic in a courtroom, but he could get a little myopic. Sometimes, he would call Agnew in the morning and go off on whatever topic held his attention at that moment. Agnew liked to lighten the mood by stopping him and saying, "Hi, Dan, good morning. How are you?"

One of San Diego's top prosecutors, Goldstein was already working two other cases when he got this one. For him, weekend relaxation was an oxymoron. But Goldstein didn't mind. He was on a victory streak. He'd handled—and won—more high-profile cases during the 1990s than virtually anyone else in the District Attorney's Office.

In April 1996, he persuaded a jury to send away the bodybuilding wife of Mr. California, bodybuilding champion Raymond McNeil. Sally McNeil, a former Marine, got a sentence of nineteen years to life for the fatal Valentine's Day shooting of her husband, who'd been about to leave her.

After three trials in a two-year period ending in 1998, Goldstein won the conviction of Ivan and Veronica Gonzales, California's first husband and wife to be sent to death row, for torturing and fatally scalding their four-year-old niece in a bathtub. Both of them were methamphetamine addicts.

In June 1999, Goldstein prosecuted a child-care operator who was accused of shaking a toddler to death because he'd refused to come to her to get his diaper changed. She got a life sentence.

In November 2000, he won a case against a businessman accused of bludgeoning his wife to death with a fireplace poker to collect pension and life insurance benefits. The county Medical Examiner's office said the woman died after she was hit at least twenty times in the head and twenty more times elsewhere on her body with a heavy, blunt object.

One of the cases he was working simultaneously with Kristin's was also based on circumstantial evidence. James Dailey was accused of killing his estranged wife because she was divorcing him. Goldstein won a conviction against him in August 2001—without a body or a murder weapon—and Dailey got twenty-five years to life.

A national television audience got a chance to watch Goldstein's prosecutorial skills during the Dailey trial, which was featured on NBC's courtroom reality show *Crime and Punishment* in June 2002.

The prosecutor said he was initially opposed to having cameras follow him around, but once he got into presenting his case, he didn't even notice they were there. Putting cameras in the courtroom served an important educational purpose for the public, he said, and it let the evidence speak for itself.

"I thought it was a great process," Goldstein told *The San Diego Union-Tribune*. "The public gets to see what prosecutors really do and that it's an honorable profession. They'll see that it takes a lot of hard work and dedication to convict these people accused of some of the most serious crimes in our society."

In the early months of the Rossum investigation, Agnew found Goldstein's medical background invaluable to the case they were building together. He knew what items paramedics might bring on a call, for example. So when they were following up on a point in Jones's report, where he said an officer had seen but not collected a syringe cap on the floor of Kristin's apartment, Goldstein knew to ask the paramedics which color-capped syringes they'd used that night. Goldstein was able to determine that one of the paramedics had dropped it, rather than trying to chase down a false, time-consuming lead that it may have been Kristin's.

"Having Dan on board really made the case," Agnew said.

Goldstein felt the same level of respect for Agnew. She was one of the best detectives he'd ever worked with. And because both were very aggressive and detail-oriented, their styles complemented each other. The tenacious prosecutor needed to feel like he had a complete grip on everything that happened before heading into trial.

"It was a really good marriage with us," Agnew said.

It was unusual to have a prosecutor assigned months before a homicide suspect was arrested, let alone a DA investigator as well. But the prosecution team saw this case as having the potential to be San Diego's most high-profile case ever. Agnew also thought the case was so complex that if she didn't brief Goldstein on the evidence from the beginning, he'd miss the important subtleties. Although Goldstein and his investigator, Frank Eaton, were also working the other two cases, the prosecutor still managed to deal with some aspect of the Rossum case every day, even when he was in trial.

Initially, Goldstein called Frank Barnhart to test his various theories and to help him understand the toxicology results. At the time Goldstein had no idea Barnhart was socializing with the prime suspect of his murder investigation, so he asked if Barnhart could identify any particular food or other substance in Greg's stomach contents. Barnhart said he didn't find anything but blood. Some of Barnhart's criminalist coworkers, who thought it inappropriate for him to be examining Greg's stomach contents, called in a tip to a local television station.

Then, one day, Goldstein got a call on his direct line from an FBI toxicologist. The man tried to assure him that Michael Robertson was a good guy and had nothing to do with Greg's death. Lights and sirens went off in Goldstein's head. Something definitely wasn't right.

To be safe, Goldstein decided to send a set of biological samples to a second lab to verify Pacific Toxicology's work and to make sure there were no false-positive results. Associated Pathology Laboratory in Las Vegas did the second round of testing and came back with high but different fentanyl levels.

When Goldstein finally learned about Barnhart's ties to Kristin, he feared that a cover-up was underway and that all the toxicology testing Barnhart had overseen could be tainted, or at least be vulnerable to that allegation. So, Goldstein had all the remaining biological samples impounded from the sheriff's crime lab and transferred to the Police Department so they could be sent out for yet another round of retesting. Because the American toxicology community was so closely tied, Goldstein decided to send out one last set of samples to a lab far, far away. He decided on a Medical Examiner's Office in the Canadian city of Edmonton, which found an even higher level of fentanyl in Greg's stomach contents than the Las Vegas lab.

By this point, Goldstein felt his investigation was being compromised by many of the agencies involved in the case. Certain people working in the Sheriff's Department, Medical Examiner's Office, and Police Department were leaking information, trying to protect themselves or unable to believe that Kristin was guilty. So, after receiving a tip that Greg's samples might have been switched with some others, Goldstein sent them out for DNA testing as well.

* * *

On December 28, Nicole e-mailed Michael to warn him that people back in Pennsylvania were gossiping about his situation.

"You may want to do some repair work," she wrote.

Nicole's message was retrieved by someone using the Compaq computer in Kristin's apartment.

The next day Michael e-mailed a friend of his in Australia, calling himself "the bastard" and letting the friend know he should send all e-mails to Michael's personal Hotmail account.

"Things here getting messier by the day," he wrote.

The friend wrote back on January 2, saying he'd talked to Nicole on New Year's and heard all about the "situation you managed to get yourself into this time." He offered to come to San Diego if Michael needed a buddy. But if Michael was coming back to Australia, he said, they should head off together for "a little medicinal port and a good dose of summer afternoon-evening sailing."

That message was retrieved from someone using Kristin's Compaq around 1 P.M. on January 2. Around 9 P.M. that same day, someone used the same computer to browse a Web page on different types of condoms. Kristin bought a pregnancy test from Vons on February 25 and a box of condoms on March 7.

Goldstein helped Agnew prepare the first search warrant, which she and her team planned to serve simultaneously at four locations in San Diego on the morning of January 4, 2001: Kristin's apartment on Regents Road in University City, Michael's apartment on Eighth Avenue in Hillcrest, the apartment he'd shared with Nicole on Costa Verde Boulevard in University City, and the Medical Examiner's Office in Kearny Mesa.

Agnew initially approached Judge Gale Kaneshiro to sign the search warrants and then seal them to prevent the media from screwing up their investigation with any more publicity about the evidence they sought. The television reports had been bad enough. She wanted her case to have integrity.

But Kaneshiro said she couldn't agree to seal the warrants and suggested that Agnew try one of her colleagues. So, Agnew walked down the hall and came to Judge John Thompson's courtroom. She didn't know Thompson or anything about him, but he agreed to sign and seal the warrants. He remained the judge who considered all her future warrant requests. By the time Agnew had finished, she'd obtained nine warrants, an unusually high number for a homicide case, which typically requires only one or two.

Goldstein was more familiar with Thompson's judicial talents.

"There's a lot of good judges on the bench, but John Thompson is probably one of the finest judges around," he said.

Chapter 11

Kristin's face registered shock as she opened her door to Detective Laurie Agnew and a group of police officers at 7 A.M. on January 4. Agnew handed her the search warrant and, as they walked into the living room, told her she could read it to her or Kristin could read it herself. Kristin chose the latter and sat down on the couch. Agnew stood next to her and did nothing until she'd finished.

Kristin was wearing a tank top and sweat pants. The apartment was messy. Clothes and papers were strewn about, there were dirty dishes in the kitchen, and the bathroom wasn't picked up. In a timid and nervous voice, Kristin asked to speak with Agnew alone in the bedroom. She seemed so fidgety that Agnew figured she'd probably been up all night, high on meth.

"I have something to tell you," Kristin said.

Agnew nodded. "Go ahead," she said.

"You're going to find something," Kristin said.

"What?"

"Paraphernalia."

"What kind?" Agnew asked.

"Meth," Kristin said.

Agnew asked if Kristin wanted to show her the stash or let the investigators find it during their search. Kristin agreed to show Agnew where it was, opened the top drawer of the chest next to the bed, and pointed to a small white box. Agnew opened it and found a plastic ziplock bag containing a disposable lighter, a glass pipe, and some white powder. Kristin sat on the bed and started to cry.

"Please don't do this to me," she said.

Kristin asked Agnew if she would get rid of the drugs or at least allow Kristin to get rid of them—flush them down the toilet or something. Agnew said no, she couldn't do that. That would be destroying evidence.

"Please don't do this to me," Kristin begged. "Please don't do this to me. Please don't do this to me."

Now that Agnew had proof Kristin had narcotics in the apartment, she asked Officer Dan Dierdorff to formally examine Kristin and evaluate her condition. During the search, he noticed that her mood fluctuated several times. She'd be sobbing, almost out of control, then stop, showing no emotion at all. Her resting heart rate was 103, which is ten to forty beats per minute faster than normal. Later, at the station, it rose to 133. Her pupils were so dilated they didn't even respond to a light shined in her eyes. She had bad breath, her lips were chapped, her cheeks were drawn, and she had sores on her face.

Meanwhile, Agnew began to search the rest of the apartment. She took some photos of the bathroom, specifically of the tub and shower area, following up on Jones's suspicions about the screw-in stopper. It was sitting in the same place as he'd noted, on a shelf above the bathtub. She noticed that it was covered with calcium buildup, but that none had been worn away along the threads. If Kristin had taken a bath as she'd claimed, Agnew figured some of the calcium buildup would have come loose when Kristin screwed the stopper into the drain.

Agnew found Greg's wallet in the bedroom and looked through its contents. Among other things, it contained his driver's license, credit cards, ATM card, and Ralph's club card. He'd written the address and phone number for Michael and Nicole's apartment on a little yellow sticky note, which was tucked inside. He apparently didn't know that Michael had moved into his own apartment in Hillcrest.

The wallet also contained an organ-donor card issued by the California Department of Motor Vehicles, which Greg had signed and dated on October 26, 2000. Kristin also signed the card as a witness to Greg's signature on the same date. He'd marked the box that read, "Donate my entire body," and listed Marie, Jerome, and Bertrand de Villers as next of kin.

Agnew pulled from a desk drawer a sixty-four-page academic paper, written by Frank Barnhart and dated January 28, 1999, called " Drugs of Abuse," which contained a section on the methamphetamine problem and related homicides in San Diego County. The paper, which drew information from a book by Randall Baselt, listed the most common behavioral and psychiatric symptoms exhibited by meth users: "violent behavior, repetitive activity, memory loss, paranoia, delusions of reference, auditory hallucination, and confusion or fright." Several studies, Barnhart wrote, have shown that people who have used methamphetamine don't actually have to be currently using the drug to exhibit methamphetamine psychosis or paranoia. In fact, it can show up years later. Barnhart reported that meth was detected in thirty-one of the one hundred fifty-five homicides, or 20 percent, that occurred in San Diego County in 1997.

Barnhart also made a brief mention of fentanyl. "Fentanyl analogues have a rapid onset (one to four minutes) and a short duration of action (approximately thirty to ninety minutes) which varies according to the particular drug. Because of the potency and quick onset, even a very small dose of fentanyl analog can lead to sudden death. The most common route of administration is by injection," he wrote, again quoting from Baselt's book.

A drug analog is a derivative of an actual drug and can be many times more potent. Such is the case for China White, the street name for the fentanyl analog, which is also called alpha-methylfentanyl.

The detective found another diary that Kristin kept in a drawer next to the computer in the bedroom. As in Kristin's first journal, Agnew found no mention of any drug use.

Kristin was arrested that morning for being under the influence of a narcotic and for possession of a narcotic, .36 grams of methamphetamine to be exact. She was taken to the police station downtown, where Dierdorff had her blood and urine tested. Then they took her to Las Colinas Detention Facility in Santee, the county's only jail for female inmates, where her parents bailed her out. When her test results came back, they were positive for methamphetamine and amphetamine.

Goldstein debated whether to file drug charges against her but ultimately decided it was better to keep her out of court and out of the media, so she could continue to do drugs, talk to potential witnesses, and incriminate herself further. Besides, charging her also would have required the search warrants to be unsealed. The last thing Goldstein and Agnew wanted to do was muck up a complex murder investigation over a measly misdemeanor.

While Agnew and her team were searching a dresser in Kristin's bedroom, Bob Petrachek, an examiner for the Regional Computer Forensics Laboratory (RCFL), showed up with a trainee to collect the remaining computer, a Compaq that had been sitting next to the desk where the iMac from Orbigen had been.

When Petrachek entered the apartment, he didn't even recognize Kristin. He saw a girl with stringy hair and a pale complexion sitting at the dining-room table with her head down, hugging her knees to her chest, and thought it was just some druggie. He walked right past her into the bedroom to do his job.

After taking the computer, Petrachek and his trainee went to the Medical Examiner's Office, where Petrachek met with Lloyd Amborn to figure out how their computer system worked so he could collect e-mails and search for evidence on Michael's and Kristin's computers. When he'd determined what he needed, he and the trainee disconnected the relevant hardware, including computers, disks, and hard drives, from Michael and Kristin's computers.

The RCFL bills itself as the first in the nation to work with the FBI to provide computer assistance to its county's law enforcement agencies. The lab aids in the investigation of activities related to terrorism, child pornography, violent crimes, theft or destruction of intellectual property, Internet crime, and fraud.

Although he worked in the RCFL offices, Petrachek, like other examiners there, was actually employed by another agency, which, in his case, was the California Highway Patrol. He'd worked for the highway patrol since 1986 and as an officer for the El Cajon Police Department for nine years before that. Along the way, he founded a company that designed and manufactured computer devices used by law enforcement.

By the time all was said and done in this case, Petrachek would have collected seventeen sources of electronic data, including two iMac computers, one from Kristin and Greg's apartment and one from Greg's office at Orbigen; two Compaq computers that had been in their apartment, one of which had been moved to Kristin's parents' house in Claremont; another computer Kristin bought some months later; Michael's laptop from work; e-mail backup tapes from the Medical Examiner's network server; and Kristin's Palm Pilot.

Before Petrachek could examine any of the electronic data he'd collected on these computers and components, he first had to make copies of the data so as not to disturb the original. That took a couple of months. Then, after searching through all the data, he organized the information into a form that could be digested by the prosecutors and then presented to each juror to examine. Since it wasn't realistic to try to read every file on these computers himself, Petrachek used key words and text strings with names of people or drugs specific to the case to find what the attorneys needed.

Petrachek sifted through a huge amount of electronic material to find such relevant information. All told, he searched through 137 gigabytes of information, including photos and graphics, which can take up a lot of space. In layman's terms, one typed character takes up one byte, and there are one billion bytes to one gigabyte. One CD-ROM holds about 650 megabytes, or 650 million bytes, of information. If all the information on a CD were printed out on paper, the stack would stand nearly as tall as the Washington Monument, which rises 550 feet over the nation's capitol.

For several months, this was the only case that Petrachek worked on. He'd get so engrossed that he could follow a thread of evidence for twelve hours, look up, and not even remember a coworker's name.

"It was a fascinating case," he said. "There was a great deal of significance to it."

At the same time that Agnew was searching Kristin's apartment, Detective Felix Zavala was doing the same thing at

Michael's Eighth Avenue studio apartment, and Detective
Jimmy Valle was examining the apartment Michael shared
with Nicole before they separated.

Nicole was not pleased to be woken up by police at 7
A.M., and neither was her sister, Claire, who was there visiting. While police searched her apartment, Valle interviewed
Nicole and tried to help her understand what was really going
on between Michael and Kristin and what a skewed version
of the relationship Michael had given her. When Nicole told
him that Michael said he'd gone to the conference in Milwaukee alone, for example, Valle said she might want to ask
Michael about that trip again. The officers seized Nicole's
diary and some pills.

Nicole told police she'd been beating herself up about the
demise of her marriage. Before they'd left Pennsylvania, she
and Michael had engaged in a one-time foursome with a
couple who lived in the same apartment complex. The other
woman and Michael initiated the liaison. Afterward, the
woman started having second thoughts about her relationship with her boyfriend and became more infatuated with
Michael. But when the woman talked to Michael about it, he
told her not to expect anything more from him and to go
ahead and marry her boyfriend. Michael and Nicole's move
to San Diego stemmed partly from a desire to get some distance from that situation. However, the woman and Michael
continued to stay in touch, and then she and her boyfriend
ended up moving to San Diego County. The court record includes a number of e-mails she and Michael exchanged that
mentioned getting together and also talked about his affair
with Kristin. The woman and her boyfriend lived in Encinitas,
where Michael and Nicole each stayed with them for a time.

The search of Michael's studio in Hillcrest, which is not
only San Diego's gay mecca but also has one of the city's

largest inventories of affordable apartments, lasted less than an hour. The officers seized a laptop computer and a black canvas briefcase labeled SOFT, a perk from the Milwaukee conference, which Michael kept in a closet. They also took his passport.

Inside the briefcase, the officers found a whole collection of mementos, cards, and letters that gave them a deeper and more personal insight into Kristin's relationship with her boss. Because Michael had written some of these cards and letters to Kristin, it appeared that he was holding them for her in case police searched her apartment.

Among the other items in the briefcase was a plastic box of little white scrolls of paper, each inscribed with a message, such as "I will be your servant for one day," "I will wash all of the dinner dishes," "I will make an ice cream sundae and feed it to you," and "I will wash your hair." It also contained an unopened box of Kamasutra love oils flavored with chocolate mint, cherry almond, raspberry kiss, and vanilla crème; a small bag labeled "French countryside seed mix"; and seven coupons, each redeemable for a romantic interlude—a stroll under the stars, a massage, breakfast in bed, a candlelight champagne bubble bath, a weekend getaway, or a favorite meal. Souvenirs from their Milwaukee trip, including airline ticket stubs, a business card from an Italian restaurant called Mimma's Café, and a photo of them sitting at a banquet table at the conference. A miniature hardcover book of love poems titled *The Kiss,* with a signed Christmas note from Kristin's brother Brent; a handful of candy Valentine's hearts, inscribed with "Husband & Wife," "Always and 4 Ever," "I Thee Wed," and "Mr. & Mrs"; four poetry books; and a sex manual titled *52 Invitations to Grrreat Sex.* Kristin had written a note in the sex manual that promised they would "enjoy a lifetime of passion" together.

Kristin also inscribed a note in each of the books of philosophical poetry by Max Ehrmann she'd given him. One of the notes was dated May 12, 2000, right after the CAT conference they'd attended in Los Angeles. In one of the undated notes, she explained that she'd been given that particular book, *Desiderata,* when she was a little girl. She wrote that it "illustrates what's important in life" and had "brought [her] comfort."

One of the cards Kristin gave Michael featured an elderly couple dancing barefoot on the beach. Inside, her handwritten message asked him to save her a dance in fifty years. "My dance card is filled with your name for the rest of my life," she wrote.

Michael gave Kristin a card with two small children dressed as adults, sitting on a bench and laughing. The little girl was holding a long-stemmed red rose. Inside, Michael wrote that he loved Kristin just the way she was.

"I will never ask you to do anything you don't want to do," Michael wrote in another card. "I will never need you to say anything you don't want to say."

Michael wrote a poem to Kristin on Hyatt Hotel notepaper, describing the color of her eyes, her skin, and her hair and the way her body moved, "with elegance, style and grace." If she would be a queen, he asked, "Can I be your King?" He signed the note "ELE," an abbreviation for "eye love ewe," a secret message they included in group e-mails to colleagues and each other as a private joke.

She wrote him back, also on a sheet of Hyatt Hotel stationery, thanking him for the poem. "I would love to be your queen. . . . Love, life, passion. You are everything. You are my King."

Roses were a running theme in their cards and gifts to each other, and Kristin made sure to share with Michael the common code for the emotional significance of roses by color: "Yellow for friendship, pink for love, red for passion, and white for purity," she wrote in one card.

Another card Michael sent Kristin contained dried yellow

rose petals, with a note sending her a "very warm hug. . . . As the days get tougher and the nights longer, our love, friendship, and support get stronger."

Zavala left Michael's neighborhood after he finished the search, but an undercover team of five detectives stayed behind, each parked along the block in his own car, to watch what Michael would do next. One detective was set up as a "scribe," to keep a log of events the other detectives dictated to him over the radio.

Around 9:52 A.M., about half an hour after the search, Detective George "Randy" Alldredge saw Michael come out of his apartment, look up and down the street, and go back inside. He came out again about ten minutes later and paced up and down the block as he talked on a cell phone, continuing to monitor activity on the street and perhaps trying to determine whether he was being watched. Then he went back into his apartment.

The next time he came out, he was holding a small white trash bag, which he placed in a dumpster at the side of the complex. He returned to his apartment and came out again to lift the lid on the left side of the dumpster. He pushed down some sort of tan paper object and put other trash on top of it.

Finally satisfied, Michael came out one more time with something in his hand that Alldredge couldn't make out, got into his car, and drove to Nicole's apartment in University City, a fifteen- or twenty-minute drive. Alldredge stayed behind to retrieve whatever Michael had tossed in the dumpster. He put on gloves, pulled out the white bag and a tan envelope, then caught up with the rest of his team at Nicole's. The bag and envelope contained cards and letters from Kristin, ripped into pieces.

Alldredge and his team followed Michael and Nicole as they drove to the Torrey Pines state beach in Michael's car. Alldredge could see from the couple's body language that they were fighting as they walked north up the beach, out of his sight. Alldredge started to worry after quite a bit of time had elapsed and they still hadn't come back, so he solicited the help of a lifeguard, who drove Alldredge in his jeep until he could see that the couple was just sitting and talking. Alldredge went back to his car to wait. Eventually, they walked back to the car, where Nicole beat Michael twice on the chest and slapped him twice in the face. Michael pushed her away.

Alldredge had to make a quick decision: Should he try to stop the assault or maintain the integrity of his undercover surveillance? He figured he'd better hang back, but he snapped some photos just in case. Eventually, Michael drove off in his car and left Nicole standing at the side of the road. Alldredge followed him, not knowing how Nicole was going to get home.

After reading Kristin's first diary, Agnew noticed that the new one contained entries that were written within the same time frame as the ones in the latter part of the first diary. Although many of them were undated, they were obviously written shortly after Greg's death.

Kristin had filled only the front fifteen pages of this journal, a dark blue book of lined pages, before the police seized it.

The diary started with an entry about going to church with her parents, where the reverend recounted a homily that seemed to speak directly to her. In the pages that followed, Kristin sounded increasingly like a victim of circumstance as she detailed how Greg's death had caused such sweeping devastation in her life. She described how alone and hurt she felt by the way Greg's family was treating her.

"Why do they reject me and vilify my image to all of our (or rather Greg's) friends?" she wrote. ". . . Everything is up in the air right now. I have suffered so much loss during the last month. My husband, my job, my career, my good name and reputation—practically everything."

People she thought were her friends were turning their backs on her and that hurt. "I don't know what horrible stories or vicious tales are being circulated through the rumor mill," she wrote. "All I know is that I've been shunned by virtually everyone. It is tremendously unfair and disheartening. . . . It is very surreal, like I'm stuck in a bad dream."

She also mentioned Michael by name for the first time, saying how much she loved him, "like I've never done and like I know I never will again. It is amazing. Words fail to do it justice. They can't begin to convey the emotions and the feelings that swell in my heart."

She described how she was struggling with the holidays and prayed the investigation would wrap up before the new year. "I know that I have done nothing wrong, but I'm terrified that if the detectives are determined enough, they may pursue it further and call it a homicide, and base their case on circumstantial evidence," she wrote. "I don't know if I could handle that. I think I'm fairly maxed out emotionally right now."

Agnew and Goldstein believed that the first diary was initially written for Greg's benefit and then left out for police to find as part of the elaborate suicide scene Kristin had concocted. She wrote in the second diary that she planned to use its pages to paint "a painfully true portrait of my spirit," but they thought that it, too, was actually intended for others to read.

On the morning of January 10, 2001, Valle and Agnew interviewed Michael for nearly two hours at the police station. His attorney, Chuck Goldberg, told the detectives that his client was doing the interview against his advice. Dan Goldstein, the prosecutor, was in another room, watching the interview on a closed-circuit television.

Michael spent a good portion of the interview explaining how drugs were stored in the lab and how he'd tried to tighten the lax controls and modernize the operation. Three years earlier, he said, Kristin created some forms to record how much of a vial, known as a drug standard, was used by a toxicologist and when.

Michael was the first one to bring up fentanyl as a drug that may have been involved in Greg's death, saying a colleague had contacted him about it. Later in the interview, he explained that the colleague was his friend Dan Anderson, who had been contacted by a detective.

Valle asked Michael what he could tell him about fentanyl and whether it was available at the lab.

"I have no knowledge of whether we had fentanyl," Michael said. "We did not do that analysis." He explained that such testing required specialized equipment, which the lab didn't have. He said he would've liked to start doing it in-house, though, because private testing was costly.

If the toxicology tests in Greg's case had been done in-house, Valle asked, did Michael think they would have detected the fentanyl?

Michael said no, at least not initially. But then, he said, they would have ordered more rounds of specific tests.

"Fentanyl isn't something that we commonly look for," he said. "It is something, however, that we wouldn't rule out if we didn't have anything else. So someone that knew the procedures would probably know that fentanyl would be found if nothing else was found."

Valle asked if Kristin would know that.

"Kristin is very young in the field," Michael said. "I don't know."

Valle asked Michael to go over the events of Monday, November 6, and his interaction with Kristin in more detail.

Michael said he'd suspected Kristin might be using methamphetamine again because he noticed she'd been taking a lot of breaks. So, on Sunday, November 5, he'd gone through her desk and found a bindle with a little white powder in it. He ran a quick test and found it was some sort of speed, so he planned to confront her the next morning.

The timeline he gave for Kristin's whereabouts and his interaction with her that Monday did not exactly jibe with what his coworkers, Kristin, and other witnesses described. However, he remembered meeting with her in his office for about half an hour in the morning and speaking with her on the phone during the lunch hour. He said he'd asked her to call in and let him know whether she was going to return to finish any tests she'd started. He also remembered seeing her back at the lab and meeting with her outside the office that afternoon. But he insisted his primary focus throughout the day was to discuss her meth use.

Michael said the two of them met on a "little grassy area not far from her house" around 4 P.M. for about an hour.

"I wanted to know how long she'd been using, all kinds of things, where did she get it from," Michael said.

He said Kristin was upset, scared, and embarrassed about his reaction to her drug use. But she was also concerned about Greg's welfare and said she needed to get home and check on him.

Michael said he met his wife in Mission Valley for a counseling session from 5:30 to 6:15 P.M. After that, they went to a restaurant nearby for dinner, then parted ways to go to their respective apartments. He was at home, asleep, when Kristin called around 10:15 P.M. from the hospital. He described her as "very gibberish in her chatting." He went to

Scripps and was shocked to find out, forty-five minutes later, that Greg was dead.

Valle redirected the interview back to drugs and told Michael that it appeared fentanyl might have killed Greg. Valle asked if Michael knew how fentanyl was commonly used.

"Fentanyl, by the general population, is often used as a patch," Michael said, tapping his upper arm to illustrate the typical placement. He wasn't aware of any oral form of the drug but said it could also be injected at a hospital.

Valle asked if there were any patches or injectable fentanyl stored in evidence envelopes collected at death scenes. Michael said he didn't remember, but syringes and needles were commonly collected.

Valle finally told Michael the whole truth, that investigators believed Greg died of a drug overdose and that fentanyl, clonazepam, and oxycodone were all found in his body. The fentanyl, he said, appeared to have been injected. Valle asked whether Michael would expect to see a syringe near Greg if he'd shot up with enough fentanyl to commit suicide. After hemming and hawing, Michael finally said yes.

"You'd expect probably a syringe puncture mark and perhaps a syringe somewhere around," he said.

"Exactly," Valle said, emphasizing that no such things were found. ". . . It appears that the dosage was extremely high. . . . No one believes that this guy would have time to make a sandwich, dispose of the paraphernalia, and then return to the site in which he was found."

"Right," Michael said.

"So it appears somebody had to have removed that evidence," Valle said.

"Uh huh," Michael said.

"Maybe somebody had to have injected him with the drug," Valle said.

In response to a series of rapid-fire questions by Valle,

Michael said he never entered Kristin's apartment until after Greg's death. In Greg's last days, he said, he never spoke to Greg, never took from the lab any syringes or the drugs found in Greg's body, and never saw Kristin with any of those drugs.

Valle asked Michael whether he'd ever seen Kristin with any methamphetamine. Michael said yes, at home, after Greg's death, she had a pipe and a small amount of meth.

"I told her to get rid of the stuff," Michael said, adding that she smashed the pipe and dumped the meth down the sink.

"Okay, so since you were not at her home at any time during that weekend . . . it couldn't be you that removed syringes or needles, is that correct?" Valle asked.

"That's correct," Michael said. "I wasn't there."

Valle asked Michael again about Kristin's understanding of their relationship and where it was going in the future.

"My question is, did Kristin believe once . . . she's rid of her husband, you've separated from your wife, which you eventually did, was it her thought that you and her were going to join up and become maybe one day husband and wife and live happily ever after?"

In the beginning, Michael said, they discussed what-ifs, but they decided to resolve their respective marital issues separately. Before Christmas, he said, Kristin probably thought they would end up living together, trying to see if the relationship would work, and if it didn't, that was okay, too.

But at the moment, he said, he was trying to "repair the damage" with his wife, some of which was caused by police feeding information to her. He said he thought Kristin believed that their relationship was "probably finished," and that he was going to try to work on his marriage.

Valle handed Michael some cards and letters that Kristin had written to him.

The detective asked if Michael knew where they'd gotten them. Michael was dumbstruck and mumbled something.

"They were recovered from the trash outside," Agnew said.

"Apparently, somebody had—" Valle said.

"Tore them up," Agnew said, cutting in.

"Really?" Michael said.

"Yeah," Valle said. " Do you know who tore them up and put them in your trash can?"

"Um, I, I tore them," Michael admitted.

"Why did you get rid of them that way?" Agnew asked.

"In all honesty, I didn't want them in the house," Michael said.

Valle asked if he'd talked with Kristin since the search. Michael said Kristin had called him from jail, asking if he could bail her out, but he said no. Then she had called him the day before this interview and asked if he would meet her for coffee. Again, he said no.

Valle asked if Michael had ended the relationship with Kristin. Yes, Michael said.

"I said, 'Look, we're not having any more contact,' " Michael said.

"Are you protecting her?" Valle asked.

"I'm not protecting her," Michael said.

Michael insisted that he would give the detectives incriminating evidence against Kristin if he had it. Valle asked why he would do that at this point.

"Because I've lost my job. I've lost my profession. I'm losing my wife. I want to get back with my wife. I don't want to be a part of this. . . . This isn't where I envisioned my life beginning in 2001—in the middle of a homicide investigation—and I want it over and done with," he said.

At the end of the interview, Valle asked if Michael would agree to take a polygraph test. Michael's attorney said that it was his client's decision, but that polygraphs were used as an interrogatory tool, not to determine the truth; and that he would continue to object to it as long as the police wouldn't allow him to be in the room with Michael.

"Okay, then, I have your answer," Valle said.

Among the cards and letters Michael ripped up was a three-page note that Kristin had written to him. It was undated but seemed to be written after Greg's death, while the two lovers were taking some sort of time-out. The letter reflected Kristin's typical flair for drama, though the tone was far more downbeat and apologetic than her usual missives.

Kristin talked repeatedly about the need to heal, to be honest, and to control her impulses, even admitting that she was suffering "physical withdrawals from last week." Things couldn't get much worse, she wrote. Saying she'd "never been faced with such complete devastation, chaos, and uncertainty," Kristin pleaded with Michael not to be upset with her or give up faith in what they had together. She wrote that she felt lonely and was having a hard time dealing with things all by herself, noting that "my family doesn't know the entire situation just yet," but she understood that Michael needed some time to "sort out" his life and his future.

After sharing her "demons" with him, she wrote, "I have been able to accept my own problem and own up to it by telling you of my failings. . . . I never have been able to do this in the past. I would deny, deny, deny, deny, even to myself." Still, she wrote, she didn't want to be a part of his future "because of a feeling of obligation or duty."

Based on questions the police started raising in November 2000, Amborn decided to conduct an audit of all drugs kept at the Medical Examiner's Office.

Once Agnew learned which drugs were found in Greg's

body, she met with Amborn once or twice and also talked to him by phone to outline more specifically what audit information she was looking for. She wanted to know, for example, if any drugs found in Greg's body or that Kristin used personally were missing from the office, either from the lab or the evidence envelopes. Since Kristin was in charge of logging in for drug standards, Agnew also wanted to know which ones had been logged in and out and when.

After Goldstein joined the investigation, he, too, wanted increasingly more specific information, so a series of audits, along with checks and rechecks, proved necessary. But by January, they at least knew the basics, that drugs related to the case—most importantly, fentanyl—were, in fact, missing. Goldstein saw no way Greg could have obtained the highly regulated narcotic that killed him. So the fact that it was missing from Kristin's lab completed the nexus that turned his gut feeling into a certainty: Kristin had stolen the fentanyl and used it to poison her husband.

But before Amborn could release any of the audit findings to the prosecution team, the county's attorneys wanted to see a warrant specifically asking for them. So, on January 22, Agnew served one up.

After watching Michael's second police interrogation, Goldstein waited a month or two for the transcript to be drafted and then compared it with the one from the first interview. He saw dramatic differences between the two statements and picked up on some new information, such as Michael's admission that he had gone through Kristin's desk the day before Greg's death and had found a bindle of meth. Previously, Michael had only admitted to knowing Kristin had a drug history. For Goldstein, that "rolling admission" pointed to Michael's guilt.

It also became clear that Michael had no alibi for his whereabouts between 3:00 and 5 P.M. the day Greg died, only his and Kristin's admissions that they were together, somewhere "near" the apartment. Given the autopsy results and the way fentanyl worked in the body, Goldstein suspected the two lovers were actually *in* the apartment that afternoon, administering the drug to Greg. After cross-checking Michael's police interviews with his e-mail exchanges with Kristin, Goldstein's suspicion that Michael had helped her kill Greg grew even stronger.

While Kristin was looking for a new job, she called Barnhart and asked if he'd be willing to write her a letter of recommendation based on her job performance at the Medical Examiner's Office. He knew she'd left the lab but didn't know why, so he agreed. When she came over to his house to pick up the letter, dated January 17, 2001, she looked strained and tired. She didn't mention that police had searched her apartment and arrested her.

Around that time, Kristin applied for a job at TriLink BioTechnologies, a company with about thirty employees that made synthetic DNA. Never mentioning that she'd been fired from her previous job, she was hired to run the company's HPLC machine, the same piece of equipment she'd operated before.

Kelly Christianson, one of the people who interviewed Kristin, was her supervisor in TriLink's Oligo group lab. She considered Kristin a quick learner and one of the best employees she'd ever had. Kristin was always on time, she got along well with everyone else, and she did whatever she was asked.

Kristin, who often went to happy hour with her coworkers, told them she left her last job because she needed a change. One day she mentioned to Christianson that she'd found it difficult to work at the county's toxicology lab because of someone "who came through the office." She didn't elaborate.

Kristin confided more intimate details to Claire Becker, another assistant chemist, who worked right next to her. The two of them ate lunch together, went out for dinner or drinks several times after work, and went together to a work-sponsored outing, where everyone played pool during business hours.

Kristin told Becker that she and Greg were very much in love when they were first married, but she came to realize that she loved him as more of a friend. She appreciated all his support in helping her get off drugs, but she wanted a more romantic relationship. Kristin told Becker that she'd found one with Michael, her boss at her old job, and that they began dating. She never mentioned that Michael was married. Kristin said she'd told Greg about her relationship with Michael, but he wanted to stay together and try to work things out. She, on the other hand, decided she wanted to get a divorce.

Kristin also told Becker that Greg committed suicide by overdosing on pills. After Greg died, she said, she started doing drugs again, drugs she bought in Tijuana. But she said she'd stopped using and was taking only Paxil, an anti-depressant.

She told Becker that her attorney had told her to stop seeing Michael, but she didn't want to stop. So when Michael came to her apartment for dinner or to spend the night, he parked a ways from her apartment so no one would see his car. Kristin said she wanted to have children with Michael and she had gone off birth control. If she got pregnant, that was okay with her and Michael.

Michael came to TriLink to take Kristin to lunch once or twice. He also went out with the company softball team after they played night games after work a couple of times. Kristin, Michael, and another coworker, Jessica Vanella, had dinner after a game. Kristin confided in Vanella that she'd run away from home when she was eighteen because her parents weren't supportive enough of her. She also told Vanella that

Michael was working on getting divorced and that the two of them were planning to be together.

Melissa Prager saw Kristin on a trip to San Diego in early 2001 and could not believe how much her friend had changed. She was all skin and bones and had black circles under her eyes. Kristin had looked so good and so healthy the last time Prager had seen her. It made her sad to see Kristin this way.

"What's going on?" Prager asked.

"Since Greg died, I totally had this relapse," Kristin told her.

She'd been suffering so much emotional pain, she said, and the de Villers family wouldn't mourn with her. Kristin said nothing about their accusations that she'd murdered Greg.

Kristin continued to see Frank Barnhart throughout the spring of 2001, while she was being investigated for murder. Barnhart later claimed they spoke only generally about the case because he didn't want to compromise the investigation. He also said she told him she had a relationship with Michael but didn't go into detail. She did make one comment that offended him, though, that Michael was the best thing to ever happen to the toxicology lab at the Medical Examiner's Office.

Barnhart and Kristin went to dinner at a Thai restaurant one evening near his house in Carmel Mountain Ranch. Another night the two of them went to a basketball game to watch the San Diego State Aztecs play at Cox Arena. Since Barnhart was good friends with Dr. Harry Bonnell the three of them sat together. Barnhart, who was sitting in front of Kristin and Bonnell, overheard them talking about the case. It made Barnhart uncomfortable, so at halftime he got up and walked upstairs. He bought two alumni sweatshirts, one for himself and one for Kristin. As he gave Kristin hers, he later recalled, he looked at her and Bonnell and asked them to stop talking about the case.

Kristin volunteered to keep Barnhart company in line one day at Qualcomm Stadium, where he was planning to buy San Diego Padres tickets through a lottery process. She showed up as promised, and after a couple of hours of waiting, he suggested that she go home, since they were his tickets. She said her family was in town and invited him to come to dinner with them at Fleming's, a high-end steakhouse in La Jolla. Barnhart agreed. During dinner Ralph and Constance thanked him for hiring Kristin and being her friend. As they were leaving the restaurant, Ralph thanked him again.

Barnhart cautioned him that he couldn't take sides.

"Ralph, do understand something," Barnhart recalled telling him. " If this thing goes to trial, I'm going to be a prosecution witness."

Ralph told him he was aware of that.

On April 2, toxicologist Christina Martinez was searching for a piece of equipment for the HPLC machine in some cabinets in the lab at the Medical Examiner's Office. She found a yellow box and expected to find a plastic cylindrical tube of guard columns for the HPLC machine inside. Instead, she found a glass tube, two inches long, with burnt residue on one end.

A day or two later, she found a white box in one of the cabinet drawers. Inside was an evidence envelope for case #377, rolled up with one end cut off. The envelope contained glass pipes, a small piece of foil, and some shards of broken glass that looked like they would form pipes if they were pieced together. The glass tube in the yellow box appeared to be one of five pipes listed as evidence collected at the death scene. Knowing the envelope wasn't where it was supposed to be, Martinez called her supervisor, Cathy Hamm, and showed the items to her.

The burnt residue in the pipe bowl from the yellow box tested positive for methamphetamine. But the clincher was that DNA matching the skin cells in Kristin's mouth was found at the other end of the pipe.

Chapter 12

In the coming months, Goldstein would issue hundreds of subpoenas for documents such as Kristin's phone, bank, and credit card records. Because the phone records listed numbers but no names, the prosecution team had to figure out which calls were potentially important, identify and then interview people who might know something, cross-check the records with the new information, then issue more subpoenas and do more interviews as leads emerged.

For example, they didn't know that Kristin had a cell phone until they discovered a purchase in her bank records. So, they went after her cell phone records and found what they thought was a significant call to Michael at 9:02 P.M. on Sunday, November 5, especially given that it was the first call she'd ever made on the phone after buying it on October 30. Goldstein came to suspect that Kristin called Michael to tell him about Greg's ultimatum and that they had to do something about it.

District Attorney Paul Pfingst gave Goldstein all the time and resources he needed to prosecute the high-profile case, which consumed the father of two even while he was playing basketball with friends or driving somewhere with his family. But that, Goldstein said, was as it should be.

By June 2001, Agnew and Goldstein felt they were getting close to making an arrest. But first, Agnew needed to put together affidavits to obtain search warrants for Kristin's new workplace and new apartment. She knew that Kristin had moved to Twenty-sixth Street in Golden Hill, a neighborhood of beautiful old houses, social service agencies, and some pretty low-end apartments, including Kristin's. However, Agnew didn't know where Kristin was working, and she wanted to search the two areas simultaneously. That way, Kristin wouldn't have time to hide or throw away important evidence.

On June 25, Agnew figured they were a week or two away from making an arrest, so she sent two detectives to camp out in front of Kristin's apartment and then follow her to work. They arrived around 5:30 or 6 A.M. in two unmarked cars, parked on the street, and waited for Kristin to emerge. The problem was, they were wearing suits, which, suffice it to say, did not blend into the neighborhood. And, to anyone who had been arrested, been followed home by an unmarked police car, or watched cop shows on television, their cars were identifiable as well. For whatever reason, Kristin figured out they were cops as she was leaving for work at 7 A.M. She took off in her white Toyota and lost both detectives on Interstate 5, a major freeway with an on-ramp a mile from her apartment.

When the two detectives returned to the office and told Agnew what had happened, she was not pleased. This changed everything.

That morning around 10:30, Becker saw Kristin looking very upset at her workstation. In fact, she looked panic-stricken. Becker followed her out of the lab and found her crying near the bathroom. Kristin told her she'd spoken to her attorney and learned she was going to be arrested later that day.

Kristin later said she'd thought it was safe to do some meth while her attorney, Michael Pancer, was away at a conference in Georgia, because he'd assured her she wouldn't be arrested while he was gone.

Back in the lab, Kristin gave Becker an envelope and a small stuffed kangaroo and asked her to hang onto them. Becker had previously noticed the kangaroo on Kristin's workbench. When she asked where it came from, Kristin said it was a gift from Michael. Becker would later say that she got the impression Kristin wanted her to hide the items for safekeeping.

After Kristin left TriLink that day, Becker looked inside the envelope and found some photos and a letter that Michael sent from Melbourne, Australia. In May, his attorney, Chuck Goldberg, had asked Goldstein if Michael could have his passport back so he could go home and be with his mother, who was dying of breast cancer.

"That's the last we ever saw of him," Goldstein recalled later.

Now that Kristin knew the police were watching her, Agnew was worried she might flee or destroy whatever incriminating evidence she might have in her apartment. So, Agnew called Goldstein, and they decided they had no choice but to arrest Kristin right away. It was time, he thought. Enough messing around.

Agnew got her search warrant materials together as quickly as she could and headed down to the courthouse.

"I expect to find evidence of communication between ROBERTSON and ROSSUM, which may show evidence of their relationship and/or planning of DE VILLERS' death,"

Agnew wrote in the affidavit. ". . . Additionally, I believe the presence in the premises of the drugs and drug paraphernalia . . . will provide evidence of the identity of persons responsible for the death of DE VILLERS. While it is common for suspects to discard evidence used in their crimes, it is also very common for them to retain items that may provide circumstantial evidence of their involvement. They do this because oversight is common, particularly when a suspect is working in haste to hide evidence."

Judge John Thompson signed the warrant but refused to approve the portion that allowed police to take yet another computer from Kristin. He told Agnew that if Kristin had purchased another one, Agnew would have to get a separate warrant to take it. In the meantime, Agnew sent a detective back to Kristin's apartment to prevent her or anyone else from going inside. By law, a detective could keep people out by saying he had probable cause that a crime had been committed and a search warrant was pending.

When Kristin got to TriLink that morning, she called her attorney. Goldstein had, in fact, told Pancer that he had no intention of arresting Kristin while Pancer was out of town. But that morning's events reconfigured the playing field. Attorney Gretchen von Helms, who was filling in for Pancer, left a number of messages for Agnew, saying she wanted to arrange for Kristin to turn herself in. But Agnew didn't get the messages until the next day because she was down at the courthouse. When von Helms couldn't reach Agnew, she tried calling Goldstein, but Kristin had already been arrested. That von Helms did not reach him before the arrest was of no consequence, Goldstein said, because he wouldn't have allowed Kristin to turn herself in, anyway.

When Kristin returned to her apartment around 3 P.M., she brought a private detective with her, perhaps, investigators thought, to help cleanse her apartment of incriminating evidence. Instead, Detective Felix Zavala arrested Kristin on suspicion of murdering her husband.

Zavala took her to police headquarters a couple of miles away, where she was tested for drugs. The results, which came back several weeks later, showed that she tested positive for methamphetamine and amphetamine.

Agnew's search warrant was signed and issued at 5:10 P.M. She took it straight to Kristin's apartment and saw that she'd been right: Kristin had bought another computer. But since the courts were closed by then, Agnew had to get another warrant approved by phone before she could take it.

Items seized during the search included a silver metal lighter labeled "Pocket Mega Torch," a device commonly used by meth users that was a step up from the plastic disposable lighters Kristin had been using. It was found in the outside pocket of Kristin's canvas briefcase, along with papers showing Michael's address and phone number at his parents' house in Melbourne. Agnew took Kristin's Palm Pilot, more cards and letters, and an address book, in which she found the Tijuana phone number for a man named Armando Garcia. She also found a third diary. In addition to the entries written in the book itself, a hardback titled "Meditation Journal," it also contained a number of entries on loose pages that were tucked inside.

Earlier that afternoon, Agnew had figured out that Kristin worked at TriLink and sent a detective to the lab. Within the next couple of days, Kristin's boss gave police two envelopes and the stuffed kangaroo. Both envelopes, one of which had been opened, contained greeting cards. Agnew got another search warrant on June 28 so she could open the sealed envelope right away. The cards were similar in tone and content: Michael loved Kristin, and he missed her.

* * *

Kristin was brought to Las Colinas in Santee, a quiet suburban city east of San Diego, at 3:30 P.M. The beige cinderblock building looks almost like a small public high school and is surrounded by tall conifers that drop pinecones on the grass in the winter.

Inside, Kristin was asked four questions by a nurse in a cagelike room with bars that separated her from the inmates: Are you injured/hurt or have you been in an accident within the last seventy-two hours? Do you have a major medical problem? Do you have an infectious disease? Are you feeling suicidal? If Kristin had answered yes to any of these questions, she would have been taken to a hospital.

Kristin stood on footprints made of tape so a sheriff's deputy could take her booking photo against the gray wall. Then, she was put into a room with wooden benches and two phones. State law required that inmates be allowed to make three phone calls.

According to jail officials, even if she were high on methamphetamine, Kristin wouldn't have been treated any differently than other inmates unless she became violent or seemed like she might hurt herself. Only then would she have been placed in a padded cell.

Next, she was strip-searched by a female deputy wearing rubber gloves, who was looking for drugs or weapons. During a search, female inmates are asked to take off their clothes so a deputy could search through their hair and look in their mouths, behind their ears, under their arms and breasts, and on the soles of their feet. Inmates are also asked to spread their legs, bend over, and cough twice to make sure nothing is hidden in the genital area, where women have been known to insert drugs wrapped in various materials. They are issued two pairs of socks, two pairs of panties, a pair of pants, a shirt, a sweater, a pair of slip-on shower sandals, a nightgown, and a thin white towel.

From there, Kristin's fingerprints were scanned and recorded by a machine that checks for outstanding warrants in the local, state, and federal criminal justice systems. The booking clerk took her address and phone, told her what crime she was being held on, and gave her her first court date—her arraignment. Because Kristin was charged with murder and the deputies knew her case would get media attention—"the whole rose petal thing," as one deputy put it—she was placed in the A-2 unit, where inmates are housed in single cells, each with a bunk bed. Hers was on a corner, #209.

"She was very polite and had good manners," said Corporal Erika Frierson. "She never disrespected the deputies. She was never a problem child at all."

Kristin's eight-by-ten-foot cell had a television mounted in a corner of the ceiling. The televison was encased in a cage, with a Plexiglass sheet covering the screen to protect it from anything an inmate might throw at it. A circular hole was cut out of the bottom, large enough for an inmate to stick her finger in to change the channel or turn off the power. Kristin had to climb up to the top bunk to reach the controls. Inmates don't get remotes.

Kristin's cell also had a metal toilet and a tall, very narrow double-paned window, where she could see out onto a cement patio area that had benches, three pay phones, and one stair-stepper exercise machine. She was allowed to use this "recreation yard" every other day. The other days she took showers. Her two pairs of prison-issued underwear were exchanged for clean ones twice a week, and her dark blue shirt and pants, which looked like medical scrubs, once a week.

The lieutenant in charge of the unit determined how long each woman got to use the yard during a twelve-hour shift based on how many requested it. Each day, inmate welfare officials provided the ten to twelve inmates on A-2 with one newspaper, and its pages were typically scattered about the patio by day's end. The deputies were supposed to read it first and cut out stories about a particular inmate for her own protection. Prisoners knew that if they harmed, did favors for, or forged friendships with high-profile inmates, it could bring them notoriety.

The inmates at Las Colinas were also known for trying to make friends with the occasional affluent prisoner so they could get free snacks from the commissary. Many passed the time playing checkers or cards, often making bets with each other for a commissary goodie. And when such a promise was broken, fights ensued, usually on a Tuesday, which was Commissary Day. In 2004, for example, the jailhouse store sold dandruff shampoo for $1.79, cold medicine for $2.10, pain reliever for $2.31, greeting cards for $1.16, phone cards for $10 and $20, and hot beef jerky for $1.21. After the phone cards, among the most expensive items were tennis shoes for $12.60, perfumed oil for $6.25, and sun block for $5.46.

When Kristin first got to A-2, she was more reclusive than the others and cried for a day or so, said Lieutenant Mike Barletta, who was in charge of the unit while she was there.

"She was probably a little more shocked by her place here," he said. "I don't think she became very acclimated to the jail."

He said Kristin generally didn't initiate conversations with other inmates through the walls or windows, though other inmates tried to console her, making remarks like, "It's not that bad" or "You'll make it."

While Kristin was on the patio, Barletta thought she seemed very hyper, dividing her time between talking on the phone, using the stair-stepper, and pacing back and forth. One thing Barletta found unusual was that she often became absorbed with her reflection in the windows, turning to the side and lifting her shirt to look at the shape and contour of her abdomen.

"We serve a very high carbohydrate diet, to the point

where they can't wear the clothes they were arrested in," he said.

Prisoners on A-2 have all their meals delivered to their cells in Styrofoam boxes, starting with breakfast at 6 A.M. On a given day, their first meal of the day might be cereal, milk, egg patties, salsa, pinto beans, flour tortillas, and sliced apple; lunch could be minestrone soup, saltines, turkey bologna sandwiches, sliced cheese, pickle chips, fruit jello salad, cake with icing, and fruit punch; and dinner might be Salisbury steak with brown gravy, scalloped potatoes, sliced carrots, cornbread with margarine, applesauce, gingerbread, and fruit punch.

Kristin smoked cigarettes on and off during her life, but the days when they allowed smoking anywhere in the jail—to pass the time, calm the nerves, or curb the appetite—were long gone.

The morning after Kristin's arrest, the story was all over the news, and her TriLink coworkers were abuzz, talking about what had happened. Becker took the items Kristin had given her and handed them over to Richard Hogrefe, the company president. He told Becker to be careful about what she said to the police detective and not to offer any unnecessary information. He was worried that it might reflect badly on TriLink and also might harm Kristin. Everyone at TriLink was shocked that the perky little blond chemist had been arrested for murder.

The *Union-Tribune* ran its first story on the case the next morning. The motive, gleaned when the search warrant was released some time later, was that Kristin was trying to stop Greg from carrying out his threat to report her affair and her renewed meth use to her superiors. In the first story, Lieutenant Ray Sigwalt said only that San Diego police were also looking at Michael as a possible suspect in Greg's death.

"The sheer nature of the death was suspicious," Sigwalt said. "There was no [suicide] note. Rose petals were sprinkled on his body in bed. Most men don't do those sorts of things. Subsequently, we found out the type of drug in his system, and we got suspicious. It was a controlled substance, illegal without a prescription."

The police and officials from the Medical Examiners' Office would say nothing more. And because of the pending investigation, all other relevant documents that would normally tell more of the story were sealed. But sources revealed to the *Union-Tribune* that the substance that killed Greg was fentanyl. They also revealed that Kristin had been fired from the Medical Examiner's Office in December because she had a drug problem, and Michael, her boss and lover, was fired the same day for violating county policy by not reporting his knowledge of Kristin's drug use to the upper management.

These juicy new tidbits sent the newspaper and local television stations off and running on one of the sexiest and most fascinating news stories to hit San Diego, a drug-addled love triangle that ended in death.

Kristin's former coworkers and professors expressed shock and skepticism that the bright young woman they knew could have done such a thing.

"It's a terrible feeling of incredulous disbelief. It's just one of those things you think won't happen to the person next to you," Hogrefe told the *Union-Tribune*. "Everybody fervently hopes and wishes there is an explanation."

At the same time, Greg's friends and coworkers said he was not the type to take his own life. They never saw him act depressed or use drugs. He was an ambitious, easygoing guy who was making plans for the future.

* * *

When Melissa Prager heard from her parents that Kristin had been arrested, she was simply baffled. Kristin had no reason to murder Greg, she thought, and the motive police were citing made no sense. Plus, she wondered, why would a highly intelligent person like Kristin choose poison as a murder weapon when it could so easily be traced back to her? It was far too obvious to be true.

Prager was convinced that Greg killed himself. She didn't know how exactly, but she thought he did it "because of the control he wanted to have over Kristin's life." Prager went to visit Kristin at Las Colinas, still convinced of her innocence. It was awful seeing Kristin in that cold place, on the other side of a pane of glass.

Kristin's third diary, like the second one seized by police, contained entries whose timing overlapped with its predecessor. The entries in the bound book were undated but referred to feelings that predated Greg's memorial service on November 12, 2000.

She repeated the credo of "*Carpe Diem*! Seize the day!" and described her need to separate herself from her life with Greg by removing his belongings from the apartment they shared. She wrote that she was unsure, however, whether "it would be considered disrespectful to Greg's memory" to remove his things before the service, which she saw as a "turning point" in her life.

"I intend to wait until Greg's memorial service is over before making any significant changes to 'our' home," she wrote. "But I think that after the service, I will begin to try to reclaim it as my home."

The earliest date on the loose pages that were tucked inside the book was November 28, 2000—about a week after her interview with police. The anger Kristin expressed there was even stronger than in the second journal. She'd been starting to feel a little better the previous week, she wrote, "Then, the rug was pulled right out from underneath me. Greg's death is being investigated as a HOMICIDE!! It's absolutely ludicrous. I am so angry that anybody could even imagine such a horrible idea."

In a six-page undated entry tucked into the diary, she wrote, "God, Greg, why did you do something so selfish and stupid? I don't know your intention. I believe in my heart that it was accidental. You were making me feel responsible for your life and well-being. . . . I'm sorry for all of the suffering I have caused so many people. But I didn't make him respond as he did."

The other entries reflected many of the same themes as in the previous journals, expressing a paradoxical mix of nostalgia and frustration about her time with Greg. She'd say how much she missed him, but then she'd launch into how frustrated she'd been with his inability or unwillingness to share his deepest feelings with his family and his refusal to take her marital unhappiness seriously.

"He told me that he thought I was 'just thinking too much.' Just relax and be happy," she wrote. "Well, I'm sorry, but happiness can't be forced, it comes from within your soul. It begins in your heart."

She described her love and passion for Michael, she reiterated her regret about not following her "gut instinct" to call off the wedding, and she expressed her infuriation at "being treated as if I was actually physically responsible for [Greg's] death," while she was still coming to terms with it emotionally.

Perhaps with unknowing foreshadowing, she wrote that she was worried the investigation would harm Michael, whom she called her mentor, and his future.

"He has achieved so much at such a young age; he has a

great deal to lose," she wrote. ". . . He is respected by some of the most reputable, famous people in tox. I would be so very crushed to see him lose all that he has achieved over me. He tells me that his career is less important than our relationship."

To Agnew, Kristin's diaries were different from those she'd seized in other homicide cases. Although they were riddled with expressions of blame, sorrow, and later, anger, Agnew thought they were "pretty much devoid of real emotions" and written for others to read.

"She envisions herself as what she thinks people will see her as," writing the entries such that "people will see her as something she's not," Goldstein said.

Goldstein and Agnew viewed Kristin and Michael as very intelligent, ambitious, and narcissistic people who shared the same motive in murdering Greg: Their jobs were a central part of their identities, their lives revolved around their careers, and they would do anything to protect them. If Greg carried out his ultimatum, Kristin's drug use and Michael's knowledge of it would be revealed, costing them their jobs, their careers, and because Michael's work visa was tied to his position in San Diego, each other. Ultimately, the two lovers did lose all of those things.

According to the *Diagnostic and Statistical Manual of Mental Disorders,* narcissistic personality disorder is characterized by an exaggerated sense of importance of one's experiences and feelings; ideas of perfection; a reluctance to accept blame or criticism; a lack of empathy; a grandiose sense of self-importance; feelings of entitlement; a preoccupation with fame, wealth, and achievement; a craving for admiration, attention, and praise; excessive emphasis on displaying beauty and power; the belief that one is special and

Marie-France T. de Villers shows off baby Bertrand to his brothers, Greg and Jerome, while their father, Yves, looks on.
(Photo courtesy of the de Villers family)

Kristin helps Greg celebrate his graduation from the University of California, San Diego in 1997.
(Photo courtesy of the de Villers family)

Kristin and Greg are married on June 5, 1999, at the historic Padua Hills Theatre in Claremont, California. *(Photo courtesy of Jacinta Jarrell)*

In 1997, Kristin was hired as a student worker in the toxicology lab at the San Diego County Medical Examiner's Office while she was attending San Diego State University. *(Author photo)*

Michael Robertson out with his buddies from his Australian football club, the San Diego Lions. *(Photo courtesy of Rob Liwanag)*

Kristin and Michael met after work at this spot, which they nicknamed "the Willows," on a dead-end street in the neighborhood of University City, where they lived within a mile of each other. *(Author photo)*

Michael gave Kristin these love note–IOUs, promising massages and dinners out. A coworker saw a box of them on her desk at the lab.
(Photo courtesy of John McCutchen)

Michael ripped up these cards he exchanged with Kristin and threw them in his trash after police searched his apartment on January 4, 2001. Police retrieved them, taped them back together, and used them to confront him during an interview a week later.
(Photo courtesy of John McCutchen)

Michael gave this card to Kristin with dried rose petals in it. Prosecutors used it as an exhibit during the trial to show the couple's fascination with roses.
(Photo courtesy of John McCutchen)

Police seized these candy hearts, along with cards, letters, a sex manual, and poetry books, when they searched Michael's apartment. (Photo courtesy of John McCutchen)

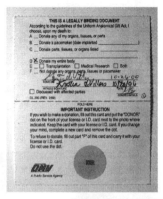

Kristin was a signed witness to Greg's becoming an organ donor when he renewed his driver's license about two weeks before he died. (Photo courtesy of John McCutchen)

Kristin Rossum and Greg de Villers attended a wedding and reception in Palm Springs for one of Greg's friends in October 2000, a few weeks before Greg died.
(Photo courtesy of Jacinta Jarrell)

Kristin and Greg lived in this gated apartment complex, owned by
UCSD, on Regents Road in University City. *(Author photo)*

This trial exhibit illustrates the layout of Greg and Kristin's
apartment. *(Photo courtesy of John McCutchen)*

This trio of crime scene photos shows the bed where Kristin said she found Greg, covered in rose petals with a wedding photo tucked under the pillow. Following the 911 dispatcher's instructions, she said she pulled him off the right side of the bed to the floor to do CPR. *(Photos courtesy of the UCSD Police Department and John McCutchen)*

UCSD campus police seized this shredded love letter in a Ziploc plastic bag from Kristin's dining room table the night Greg died. Kristin said Greg had been trying to piece it back together with tape. *(Image courtesy of the San Diego Police Department and John McCutchen)*

This crime scene photo shows one of two thirty-gallon trash cans on the apartment balcony that UCSD police did not fully search. Sergeant Bob Jones stopped looking once he found the soup can that corroborated part of Kristin's suicide story.
(Photo courtesy of the UCSD Police Department and John McCutchen)

Sgt. Jones returned to Kristin's apartment the morning after Greg's death to record a 10-minute videotape of the crime scene. This shot focuses on the red rose petals on the carpet next to the bed.
(Photo courtesy of the UCSD Police Department and John McCutchen)

UCSD police Sergeant Bob Jones in his office on the La Jolla campus. *(Author photo)*

Greg's brother, Jerome de Villers, is widely credited for dogging authorities to pursue his brother's death as a homicide, not a suicide. *(Author photo)*

Detective Laurie Agnew, a homicide detective with the San Diego Police Department, opened a special investigation and took over the case from the UCSD campus police three days after Greg's death. *(Author photo)*

Detective Agnew interviews a distraught Kristin on the afternoon of November 22, 2000, the only interview Kristin gave to police before she was arrested on June 25, 2001. *(Photo courtesy of the San Diego Police Department and John McCutchen)*

During the trial, prosecutors repeatedly showed Kristin's booking photo, taken when she was arrested on January 4, 2001 for being under the influence of methamphetamines and possession of the drug. *(Photo courtesy of John McCutchen)*

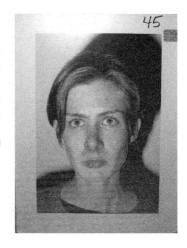

This bottle of Somacid, a muscle relaxant Kristin purchased in Tijuana, was found in her desk at the Medical Examiner's Office after she was fired on December 4, 2000 for using drugs. *(Photo courtesy of John McCutchen)*

This glass pipe was found in Kristin's apartment during the police search on January 4, 2001. *(Photo courtesy of John McCutchen)*

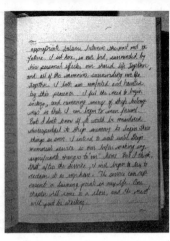

Kristin wrote in three different diaries which police collected during their investigation, including three separate entries for the day after Greg's death. Prosecutors said she wrote in the diaries as part of her staged suicide scheme, to be read first by her husband and later by police. *(Photo courtesy of John McCutchen)*

Michael gave two interviews to police, one on November 24, 2000, and this one on January 10, 2001, denying that he and Kristin were having a sexually intimate relationship. *(Photo courtesy of the San Diego Police Department and John McCutchen)*

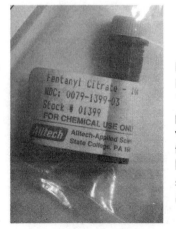

Drug audits at the Medical Examiner's Office found that this 10 mg vial of fentanyl, which was purchased for testing purposes, was empty. Fentanyl is the drug that killed Greg. The ME's office had not run any tests using the vial since it was purchased in 1997. *(Photo courtesy of John McCutchen)*

Kristin was coming down off methamphetamine, her face awash with emotion, during her arraignment July 2, 2001 on charges of first-degree murder with the "special circumstances" of using poison to kill her husband. *(Photo courtesy of* The San Diego Union-Tribune/ *Ernie Grafton)*

Deputy Public Defender Alex Loebig was Kristin's lead defense attorney. *(Photo courtesy of Joe Klein)*

Deputy Public Defender Vic Eriksen worked with Loebig to represent Kristin. *(Author photo)*

Deputy District Attorneys Dan Goldstein and Dave Hendren prosecuted Kristin's case. *(Photo courtesy of Joe Klein)*

Kristin, her brother Pierce *(left)*, father Ralph *(behind)* and mother Constance *(right)* walk out of the Las Colinas Detention Facility after she is released on $1.25 million bail on January 4, 2002, nine months before the trial. *(Photo courtesy of* The San Diego Union-Tribune/*John Gastaldo)*

Kristin is pursued by news cameras during the trial outside the courthouse in October 2002. Judge John Thompson wouldn't allow cameras in his courtroom. *(Photo courtesy of* The San Diego Union-Tribune/*Dan Trevan)*

On November 12, 2002, the day of the verdict and Greg's birthday, Kristin's parents and aunt, Marguerite Zandstra (behind), accompany her to the courtroom. *(Photo courtesy of* The San Diego Union-Tribune/*K.C. Alfred)*

Kristin is led to a sheriff's cruiser that will take her back to Las Colinas Detention Facility after the jury found her guilty. *(Photo courtesy of The San Diego Union-Tribune/K.C. Alfred)*

This cartoon by Pulitzer Prize winner Steve Breen was published in *The San Diego Union-Tribune*'s editorial pages the day after the verdict. *(Image courtesy of Steve Breen/Copley News Service)*

On December 12, 2002, Kristin is sentenced to life in prison without the possibility of parole. Here, sheriff's deputy Frank Cordle escorts her out of the courthouse to a vehicle that will return her to Las Colinas until she can be transferred to Chowchilla women's prison. *(Photo courtesy of The San Diego Union-Tribune/K.C. Alfred)*

unique and can only be understood by, or should associate with, other special or high-status people or institutions; a tendency to take advantage of others to achieve one's own ends; and arrogant, haughty behaviors or attitudes.

Chapter 13

Kristin was brought into court for her arraignment on July 2 on charges of first-degree murder with "special circumstances," those being that she used poison to kill her husband. Under California law, this made her eligible for the death penalty, which is delivered through a series of lethal injections.

With her short, dark blond hair tucked behind her ears, she wore her dark blue jailhouse suit and a wide, yellow plastic bracelet, marked with her name and inmate number, 01142131. Her eyes and nose were red and swollen from crying and coming down off meth. A look of terror flashed across her face as she walked in and took her place in front of Judge David Szumowski.

Her attorney, Michael Pancer, was still out of town, so Gretchen von Helms filled in for him again. The day before the arraignment, von Helms released a statement from Kristin's parents: "We love and support our daughter, Kristin. We know she's innocent of any wrongdoing. We grieve with the de Villerses for the loss of their son and our son-in-law, Greg, and we ask everyone to keep both families in their prayers."

During the hearing, Goldstein argued that Kristin was not entitled to bail because the offense with which she was charged "could be punishable by death." Police found no suicide note in the apartment, he said, and no sign of how the deadly fentanyl got into the body of Greg de Villers, a twenty-six-year-old with no history of psychiatric troubles. Kristin, he said, stole drugs from her lab at the Medical Examiner's Office and used them to kill her husband.

Although Kristin did not look her best, those who saw her in the courtroom, in the newspaper, or on TV still thought she was attractive. Some said she resembled Jennifer Aniston, the television and feature film actress who was married to heartthrob Brad Pitt at the time. Talk of the potential for a TV movie of the week started early.

Ralph Rossum stepped up to the podium and made an impassioned plea to release his daughter from jail on bail. Kristin stood with her hands clasped, her expression changing every few seconds as she stared down at the floor and then up at the judge, the corners of her mouth turned down, like a child about to cry.

"She is a Phi Beta Kappa, *summa cum laude* graduate from San Diego State University," Ralph said. "She would not jeopardize our love or financial future by [fleeing]."

He pointed out that during the eight months she'd been under investigation, she'd never tried to run.

"At no time during that period did she indicate the slightest interest in fleeing," he said. "Mexico is very close. She could've left at any time."

But the judge wanted to ensure that Kristin couldn't go anywhere.

"She certainly would have incentive to run," he said. "No bail."

The judge appointed the county Public Defender's Office to represent Kristin since her parents said they couldn't afford to continue to pay for private counsel. After the hearing, a flock of reporters followed Ralph out of the courtroom and down the hallway, holding television microphones in his face as they walked.

"The cost of this case is beyond our financial means," Ralph told them.

Goldstein had a sound bite on the evening news as well: "This is a compelling case that leaves us with no choice but to charge the defendant, Kristin Rossum, with the murder of her husband," he said.

Von Helms spoke with the prosecutor in the hallway, asking what it would take to get the charges against Kristin reduced. Goldstein said he'd be interested in Kristin's cooperation so he could charge Michael Robertson and get her to testify against him.

Later, von Helms recalled that she discussed this option with Kristin, but she wouldn't give specifics about their conversation, citing attorney-client privilege. Goldstein recalled talking to von Helms, but said she had no authority to negotiate a deal because she wasn't really Kristin's attorney.

The Rossums still hadn't quite decided whether to go with a public defender or stick with private counsel. Von Helms continued to work with them over the next few weeks, handling media inquiries, serving as a liaison for delivering photos for publication, and going through Kristin's belongings to see what she could find that might support her case at trial.

The Rossums interviewed a number of reputable criminal defense attorneys in town. A good attorney could charge more than $250,000 to represent a defendant in such a high-profile case, and the Rossums didn't want their daughter to lose a year of her life in jail, waiting for trial. So, ultimately, they decided to go with the Public Defender's Office and save their money for bail.

* * *

The case initially went to Superior Court Judge Kenneth So, the presiding judge. On July 9, he assigned it to Judge John Thompson, whose reputation for disliking the media was widely known. Thompson had never allowed cameras of any kind in his courtroom as a Superior Court judge.

The preliminary hearing, originally scheduled to begin at the end of July, was delayed until October after Kristin's attorneys said they needed more time to review the thousands of pages of discovery material they'd just received from the prosecution.

Alex Loebig was in charge of a group of three attorneys in the county Public Defender's Office, known as the Profile Homicide Team, which handled most of the county's high-profile murder cases from an office several blocks from the downtown courthouse.

Based on the large number of television cameras and reporters at Kristin's arraignment, not to mention the sexy and unusual details about her and her case, it soon became obvious that Loebig's team should handle it. Loebig decided he needed two attorneys on it, a common approach on a complicated or death penalty case. Typically, one attorney handles the closing argument during the trial, and the other gives the closing in the subsequent death-penalty phase, in case the first attorney had biased the jury in any way.

Loebig, a polite, carefully groomed, and sometimes inscrutable professional, decided to work the case himself. He asked Vic Eriksen, a solid attorney he could rely on, to help him. Each of them already had two or three cases pending. Both attorneys had the reputation of being very reasonable, believable, and honest, all tough characteristics for a prosecutor to overshadow.

This was Loebig's first poisoning case. Eriksen had handled several in which people had been accused of poisoning others, usually by giving them too much heroin, but this was his first involving a death. It was a unique case, but not uniquely difficult.

Loebig had thirty years' experience defending people accused of murder, the last twenty of those with the Public Defender's Office. He started his career in 1971 in private practice with Casa Maravilla, a church-oriented legal assistance group in Los Angeles. From there, he worked for three years with the federal Public Defender's Office and then moved to Guam, where he spent three years as head of its Public Defender's Office.

In 1999 Loebig won an acquittal for a Hawaiian surfer who worked as a sound technician for musicians and had been charged with voluntary manslaughter for shooting two men at a party in his backyard. Loebig had argued that his client acted in self-defense against two threatening members of a white supremacist gang.

Eriksen, a somewhat soft-spoken redhead with freckles and an open, friendly manner, had been an attorney for twenty-four years. He spent twelve of those handling felony cases for the San Diego public defender. He'd been assigned to Loebig's high-profile unit seven months earlier.

Before he became a deputy public defender, Eriksen had his own criminal defense practice for ten years and had developed a methamphetamine addiction. He never crashed and burned enough to lose his license, but when he realized that his daily use was affecting his job and screwing up his life, he knew he needed to stop. He closed up shop in 1988, went through rehab, and then worked construction jobs.

He ended up going to work for a former law associate of his brother in Tustin, doing civil law and some business cases, and decided to apply for a job with the public defender in San Diego. He enjoyed the work. Not just because it was intellectually challenging, but also because he felt he was doing something good for his clients and society at large.

But looking back, he realized that getting that job was the best thing he could've done to help him stay off the stuff, because he got "daily reminders of the waste that methamphetamine could cause."

"I know what it does to your mind," he said, specifically referring to the initial euphoria and then the paranoia and denial that meth causes. Kristin was unusual, he said, because she used meth alone. Most users like to be around other people, to party and enjoy meth's effects in a social atmosphere. But then again, Kristin was different from his average clients in other ways as well. She was prettier, smarter, and more complicated.

His past drug experience gave him insight into many of his clients, including Kristin, whom he told about his past. It also helped him understand her parents, who he felt had an extra dose of denial compared to most addicts' parents, probably because they were so image conscious.

"They're such enablers," he said later.

With Loebig as lead counsel on the case, the two attorneys agreed on a division of labor. Loebig would question the defense and prosecution witnesses in the Rossum and de Villers families. He also would coordinate most of the media, focusing primarily on the high-profile, New York-based national television programs, which were calling him and the Rossums in the weeks after Kristin's arrest. Constance and Ralph were adamant about getting Kristin's story out—or their version of it—on a broad scale. Loebig went along with them, thinking it might help soften the minds of potential jurors. Dealing with national media was a task Eriksen was happy to avoid.

"It's tough to be working a case and trying to figure out what you can and can't say outside of the courtroom," he said.

In turn, Eriksen took on the nuts and bolts of the discovery process, which was no small feat. He was responsible for combing through at least twenty-five thousand pages of evidence, highlighting key points, and deciding which leads were worth sending an investigator out to pursue and which areas he needed to question Kristin about. He found more than forty such leads, such as a local fentanyl dealer from whom Greg could have bought the fentanyl that killed him. Later in the case, Eriksen also prepared to question many of the defense witnesses and to cross-examine the majority of the prosecution's. All told, Loebig estimated that Eriksen logged in twice as many hours as he did.

Initially, Loebig and Eriksen each met separately with Kristin for about an hour at Las Colinas so she could become comfortable with them and understand the legal process she faced. Loebig knew nothing about the case before their first meeting other than what he'd read in the *Union-Tribune,* which had been running stories almost daily since Kristin's arrest.

Early on, Loebig spent more time with Kristin than Eriksen did, because she was feeling distraught and threatened by her new surroundings. She wanted to get out of jail as soon as possible. As time went on, Eriksen and Loebig met with her at least once a week, sometimes together, sometimes separately.

Constance and Ralph urged the attorneys to do whatever they could to get bail set for Kristin. But with a possible death sentence hanging over her head, Kristin's attorneys told them that freeing her on bail would be virtually impossible. Even if the district attorney decided not to seek a death sentence, Loebig and Eriksen thought Thompson would set bail so high as to be prohibitive. They were figuring on anywhere from $2 million to $5 million.

As financially comfortable as the Rossums might have been—they had purchased a 4,000-square-foot home with a pool in Claremont for $692,000 in 1999, after selling two smaller ones for $202,000 and $350,000 earlier that year—

they said they weren't wealthy enough to put up that kind of money.

On July 11, Ralph faxed out a press release with this headline: "Friends and Coworkers Rally to Defense of Kristin Rossum, Two Legal Defense Funds Merge." The release described efforts by Claremont residents and two female faculty members from Claremont McKenna College, who had opened a bank account to help raise money for Kristin. "We have known Kristin and the family for years and know she could not have committed this crime," the release quoted the women as saying.

It also said that Richard Hogrefe, Kristin's boss at TriLink, was cosponsoring the fund. "We want her back at TriLink as soon as possible," he said in the release.

The release went on to say: "While Kristin's case is being handled by the Public Defender's Office in San Diego County, friends were concerned about the additional funds that would be needed as Kristin faces a lengthy and arduous trial. The family remains hopeful of bail at a future date."

"We are blessed to have the support of such fine people who believe in Kristin's innocence," the release said, quoting the Rossum family, saying they'd "learned of the two independent efforts last week. Any funds remaining will be donated to nonprofits that work with inmates and their families."

The fund-raising campaign surprised some Claremont locals, especially given that Constance and Ralph Rossum both earned good salaries.

"We didn't understand how they expected the public to pay for it," said Martin Weinberger, editor and publisher of the weekly *Claremont Courier.*

Some, like Hogrefe, didn't mind contributing financially to Kristin's cause because they believed in her innocence. He visited her once a month in jail, wrote her letters, and defended her character to the media. After placing her on unpaid leave, he later asked her to help him write a scientific paper on some work she'd started in the lab. He said she was doing the work gratis to keep her mind occupied with something other than the murder case.

"It is a shockingly sad story, but there is another side," he told the *Union-Tribune*. "From our side it doesn't fit. None of us believe [these charges have merit]."

Hogrefe said Kristin's job was safe as long she wasn't convicted of any crime.

"She was an excellent employee. In fact, she was a rising star," he said. "She was the kind of person that when something needed to be done, she volunteered. She worked weekends. She would volunteer to do whatever is necessary to help the team."

He described her as an extremely social person who had recently joined the company softball team and was getting better and better. During one game, she got hit in the nose and fell to the ground. He went over to make sure she was okay, and she said to him softly, "It really hurts, Rick. I want to cry but I'm not going to." Five minutes later, he said, she'd sucked it up, not wanting the team to know she was hurt.

Hogrefe said he never saw any signs that Kristin was on drugs, but he seemed forgiving of her problem, of which he'd learned by reading the newspaper stories.

"If she was having a drug problem, you do stupid things," he said.

At the same time the criminal investigators were putting their case together against Kristin and possibly Michael, Marie and Yves de Villers hired the San Diego law firm of McClellan & Associates to file a wrongful death claim against the County of San Diego in Greg's death.

The claim, which is a necessary precursor to a civil lawsuit, was required to be filed against the county within six months of the date the claimant knew or should have known that the county did something wrong. If the county rejected the claim as having no merit, as it did in this case, the claimant had to file a lawsuit within six months of the date the county rejected the claim.

The de Villers family's claim, filed July 18, or eight and a half months after Greg's death, stated that the filing was delayed based on "late discovery of the cause of injury." The family didn't know the "facts demonstrating the negligence and intentional conduct of the Office of the Medical Examiner and its employees in the death of Gregory de Villers" until after the search warrant affidavit for Kristin's arrest on June 25 was released.

The claim also said county officials and police denied numerous requests from the de Villers family for information and documents that were sealed because of the pending investigation. Meanwhile, prosecutor Dan Goldstein, who'd received a detailed letter from Jerome on February 21, outlining the findings of his own investigation, told Jerome he couldn't discuss the case with him.

Essentially, the de Villerses were accusing the county of hiring Kristin, a known drug abuser, without doing a background investigation and then putting her in charge of dangerous and illegal drugs, which she stole to get high and then to kill her husband. They said she also had "illicit sexual intercourse with her boss," a relationship of which their superiors were well aware, and then Michael Robertson "failed, neglected and refused to supervise her, giving her free rein to the office and drug locker."

The county, they said, was also negligent in paying for the lovers to attend a conference where they learned about cases in which fentanyl overdoses resulted in unintentional death or suicide. They said Michael knew his lab did not routinely check for fentanyl in cases involving suspected drug overdoses. He and other employees were trained in the effects of narcotics and should have realized that Kristin was high on crystal methamphetamine.

On or before November 6, 2000, they said, Kristin took fentanyl from the office with Michael's knowledge, consent, and participation, and "during her working hours, she administered fatal doses to her unconscious, unknowing, and unsuspecting husband." Then, "anticipating de Villers's death, [she and Michael] spent several intimate hours together."

The de Villers family alleged that the Medical Examiner's Office was further negligent, first, by allowing Kristin to donate Greg's bones and tissues—"crucial evidentiary parts" that were needed to assess which drugs were ingested and the location of needle marks—and second, by doing a rushed autopsy. The office went along with the story that Greg's death was a suicide and had intended to release the body to Kristin for immediate cremation. It was only due to a court order that the de Villerses were able to "put an end to what would have been a near-perfect crime," the claim stated.

After the county rejected the de Villers family's claim, McClellan & Associates filed a civil complaint in Superior Court on November 14, 2001. The lawsuit made the same negligence and wrongful death allegations against the county, and named Kristin and Michael as codefendants.

Senior Deputy County Counsel Deborah McCarthy later tried to argue that the de Villers family missed the filing deadline for the claim, so the lawsuit should not go to trial.

When Vic Eriksen first met with Kristin, she had the "deer frozen in headlights" syndrome and cried a lot. He didn't see what some others did—that Kristin used her tears to engender sympathy or to manipulate people into helping her—only a young woman who seemed, in many aspects, to be the same little girl her parents still saw when they looked at her.

Eriksen was the one to confront her when they got new evidence. But from the way she whispered to Eriksen during court appearances, her face reflecting an intensity and a high level of trust, she seemed to have bonded more with him than with Loebig.

Once Kristin was able to get past her emotions, she became an active participant in her own defense, giving her attorneys leads to pursue as they went through the stacks of discovery materials turned over by the prosecution. In the beginning, she spoke mostly in generalities. Only later, Loebig said, after the incriminating evidence continued to pile up and she'd had many discussions with her parents, trying to come up with consensus explanations, did Kristin start offering more specific ideas. Among the most important was a notion of where Greg could have obtained the fentanyl on his own.

Because they saw no direct evidence that proved Kristin poisoned Greg with fentanyl, the defense strategy was to provide innocent explanations for the mounting circumstantial evidence. Loebig was hoping for an acquittal, or at least a hung jury, because some or all of the jurors had believed her story.

Eriksen talked to one or both of Kristin's parents at least three times a week during the fifteen months leading up to the trial, which started with jury selection on October 4, 2002. He and Loebig also met personally with them most every weekend, usually on a Saturday, before they visited Kristin in jail. Constance and Ralph wanted to play an integral part in shaping Kristin's defense, so they, too, went through the evidence and suggested possible avenues for investigation.

"The Rossums, being loving parents, did have an answer to almost every piece of incriminating evidence," Eriksen recalled later. "Sometimes those answers were plausible, and some weren't. I think it's fair to say they were desperate, and they had to have answers for Kristin."

As time went on, however, Loebig became increasingly frustrated with Kristin's parents. They were looking so hard for answers that they began disseminating information to the media that oftentimes didn't ring true, and in some cases turned out to be downright false.

In the weeks after Kristin's arrest, Constance and Ralph Rossum contended they spent hours every day fielding calls from all types of print and broadcast reporters and producers, who wanted interviews with them and with Kristin.

During this time, Constance and Ralph Rossum each gave lengthy telephone interviews to a reporter for *The San Diego Union-Tribune,* outlining their version of the events that led up to Greg's death, based on their own observations and what Kristin had told them. They were convinced that Greg committed suicide.

When they first met Greg, they said, they were delighted that he'd helped Kristin get off drugs. Their approach apparently hadn't worked, and they were pleased that Greg's methods, whatever they were, were more successful. So, to them, he was their "saving angel." Greg promised them he would let them know if Kristin started using meth again, and he never said a word, so Constance was sure she was clean.

"Kristin does not have a drug problem," Ralph said, adding that they hadn't seen symptoms of one for years.

Even though Kristin wrote on her sheriff's job application that she'd been arrested, they said, it wasn't true. When she was in high school, Ralph said, Constance called the police to try to "put the fear of God" in Kristin. The cop confiscated meth paraphernalia, but Kristin only thought she'd been arrested. She was being "overly truthful" on her application.

Together, Constance and Ralph painted a picture of Kristin as the innocent victim, wrongly accused, and Greg as a man who was destroying their daughter's life posthumously. They said they'd watched Greg become increasingly possessive and obsessed with controlling her, and they saw sure signs that he was "spiraling down" into a deep depression as he watched his marriage crumble. He obviously didn't want to go through the same kind of breakup as his parents.

They said Kristin started complaining to them about feeling trapped and suffocated as early as January 2000. She told them Greg was clocking how long she'd take to drive home and would say things like "If you loved me, you'd want to be with me every minute." He'd tell Kristin he couldn't go to sleep unless she was lying next to him, and he wouldn't eat lunch unless she made it for him. He also had an anger problem and was volatile, they said, just like his father and his brother Jerome.

"We'd call regularly, and she'd be crying," Constance said. "We'd say, 'What is it?' and she'd say, 'It's Greg.' "

"Mom," she'd tell Constance, "I'm his whole life."

The complaints continued through the spring, when Constance told Kristin she had three choices: one, she could accept Greg's personality, do her best, and maybe seek counseling; two, she could say she wanted a divorce and just leave; or three, she could ask for a trial separation and try to work it out by learning how to be two separate people with two separate identities. Kristin told Constance the trial separation sounded best.

About a week or so after the couple's one-year anniversary in June, the Rossums took Greg and Kristin to dinner. When Constance asked her how they'd celebrated the special day, Kristin got teary-eyed and said, "Greg wasn't feeling well, so we'll probably go out in a week or so for a nice dinner."

Greg had a weird grin on his face as Kristin spoke, Constance recalled, describing it as a "Cheshire cat" grin. Not happy, just strange. She remembered Greg saying, "Being romantic costs money," and Kristin replying, "You could have gotten me a single rose."

In the late summer of 2000, the Rossums went for another visit to San Diego, and this time Kristin was more insistent.

"Mom, I just have to end this," Kristin told Constance.

By this point, Constance said, she was becoming afraid for her daughter's safety. She offered to be there with Ralph when Kristin broke the news to Greg that she was leaving. Constance was worried that Greg might jump off the balcony and take Kristin with him. At the very least, she said, he might start breaking all the china and crystal.

But Kristin was convinced that Greg wouldn't hurt her.

"Mom, I can handle it," she said.

Still, Constance cautioned Kristin that if she was going to leave, she ought to do it before the holidays.

Constance and Ralph both recounted similar recollections of the last night they saw Greg, when they all had dinner in San Diego on Friday, November 3, to celebrate Greg and Kristin's respective birthdays.

The Rossums were running late, so they didn't have time to drink much of the gin martinis that Kristin made for them at the apartment. But before they left for the restaurant, Constance and Ralph said they all talked about the one red rose that was standing in a vase on the table.

"It was a very pretty, still tightly formed rose," Ralph said. "It wasn't opening too much, and we commented, Constance and I, on the beautiful rose. Greg waxed eloquently, said he'd purchased a dozen red roses and this was the only one that survived."

The evening continued to be surreal, the Rossums said, as Greg drank more than usual at the Prado in Balboa Park and raised his voice several times as he ranted about a guy he'd hired as a fund-raising consultant who had ripped off Orbigen. They had to shush him, he was talking so loud.

Constance kicked Kristin under the table so they could go to the ladies' room and she could ask her daughter why Greg was acting so strange. Kristin told her that things had gotten really bad. Constance repeated her offer to go back to the apartment and help Kristin move, but Kristin said no, she wanted to leave amicably. She loved Marie. Greg had been an important part of her life. And she wanted to try and remain friends.

"I wish I said, 'Stop it,' " Constance said. "I wish we had just yanked her out of the way."

On Saturday, November 4, Constance said she and Ralph were so concerned that they went to a real estate office to look for a condo for Kristin to live in during the trial separation.

The next time they heard from Kristin was when she called, hysterical, from the hospital that Monday night. Ralph drove down to San Diego as fast as he could, and when he arrived at the apartment, he saw the rose petals on the bedroom carpet. He asked Kristin if it was the same rose from Friday night and she said yes.

"This was Greg saying, 'I know this is over. The romance is over. I've lost you,' " Ralph said.

When Kristin pulled back the covers to put him on the floor as the 911 dispatcher directed, she told him, she saw the rose petals all over Greg and their wedding photo clutched in his hands.

Constance and Ralph offered a number of scenarios for why Greg might have killed himself: He didn't want to live without Kristin. Without Kristin, he couldn't have children whom he would keep away from his father as a means of getting back at him. Greg was very concerned about his mother's health, and it became overwhelming for him to think that without Kristin's financial resources, he wouldn't be able to take care of Marie. His act was a cry for help, an accidental overdose. Or maybe, with his knowledge of drugs, Greg set

Kristin up for his murder because if he couldn't have her, then no one would.

"Greg was charming, but he was vindictive," Constance said. "He didn't want to anger you; he wanted you to suffer for eternity type of thing."

Plus, Ralph added, Greg had his own knowledge of, and access to, fentanyl, because the dentist had used it on him the year before when he had his wisdom teeth removed.

Michael Robertson, Ralph said, was irrelevant because Kristin was already talking about getting out of the marriage in early 2000.

"Kristin had no motive to do [Greg] in," Ralph said. "One, there was no insurance. She wasn't committed to staying at the Medical Examiner's Office."

Why, he asked, would Kristin kill Greg, then divulge to police that Greg had threatened to report her drug use and infidelity? And why would she tell police that the drugs Greg took were those she'd gotten from Mexico to help get her off methamphetamine?

"If you're going to kill to keep a story quiet, you don't admit it in the first interview, especially when it's a wholly voluntary interview," Ralph said. "Kristin is too darn smart to be so darn stupid. If you're a toxicologist, would you do somebody in in a way that so directly points the finger at you? That's her area. That's what she knows better than anyone. She knows how to do it so no one can detect it."

In subsequent media interviews, the Rossums complained that they were never interviewed by police. They said paramedics and doctors had accounted for every needle puncture wound on Greg's body. They repeated their claim that Kristin had never been arrested—even emphasizing their point by using all capital letters in written answers to questions from

MSNBC.com in September 2001. The Rossums distributed these responses to other media organizations.

The Rossums also told the media that Greg's autopsy showed he had hepatitis B. They went on to say that hepatitis B is generally contracted through sexual contact or contaminated drug needles, insinuating that he'd had an affair or, more importantly, that he was an intravenous drug user and could've injected the fentanyl with a dirty needle he shared with an infected friend.

"Greg couldn't have gotten [hepatitis] from Kristin because she was inoculated against it for her job at the Medical Examiner's Office. We don't know what to make of it, but it does explain why Greg had become so sickly and tired," Constance told *Good Housekeeping* magazine in an interview published in March 2002.

Greg's autopsy didn't mention hepatitis B. However, some of Greg's tissues were rejected by the agency that handled the donation, which saw test results that indicated he could have been exposed to hepatitis B. After some investigation, Eriksen and Loebig decided this was merely a false-positive and let the matter drop. The prosecution asked to have Greg's liver tissue tested for hepatitis, and it came back negative.

The Rossums told the media that Kristin said Greg had access to fentanyl in the storage locker containing items from his father's now-defunct medical practice in Ventura County. When Ralph heard from a reporter that Yves de Villers said he'd never used fentanyl in his practice, Ralph replied, "Charitably, I think he forgot."

Asked by MSNBC.com to explain how fentanyl got into Greg's body, the Rossums said this: "Greg had knowledge of, past use of, and his own independent access to fentanyl. It is unfortunate that the police and prosecutor never talked to Kristin after the drug he used to commit suicide was identified in the toxicology report. If they had, she would have been able to present this information to them, and she would never have been arrested."

They didn't mention to MSNBC.com that Kristin declined Agnew's request for a second interview, in which the detective was planning to do just that. They also didn't mention that they, too, had declined the police's offer to interview them after Kristin was arrested.

Asked by MSNBC.com if the fentanyl was removed from the Medical Examiner's Office, and if so, how and by whom, the Rossums referred the news outlet back to the previous answer.

MSNBC.com asked if the defense would argue that Michael was involved in Greg's death, to which the Rossums replied, "No, it was a suicide. . . . Kristin would have left Greg even if there were no Michael Robertson. He was not a factor."

The Rossums blamed Kristin's drug relapse on Greg, saying she "reverted to a very small amount of drug use two weeks prior to Greg's suicide as a result of his psychological abuse and refusal to consider counseling. She came 'full-circle' after six years of his insistence that he 'was her savior.' "

She got the drugs, the Rossums said, "on the street. During her voluntary interview with the police, she was on the verge of volunteering to them her source when they asked her not to do so."

The validity of the claim that she was about to volunteer her source is debatable. During her interview, Detective Jimmy Valle asked Kristin if she had a current drug habit. When she said yes, he asked what she was taking. She told him it was meth.

"Where are you getting your supply?" he asked. "Don't give me a name. Don't give me a name."

"I'm not," Kristin said.

"Because I think you would if I ask, but I'm not going to ask you."

"No, I don't know him," she said.

During the trial, the prosecution pulled quotes from the Rossums' various media interviews to try to impeach their credibility in court.

The Rossums, Loebig said later, "remained steadfastly pompous, defensive, and aggressive in their public address that their daughter was innocent, without ever coming forward with much specific evidence that helped the case." But Loebig said he didn't blame the Rossums for telling the media what they did, "particularly with a daughter they didn't want to give up on and give every benefit of the doubt to. There was no overt hostility between us. It was just an inherently stressful situation."

Loebig never got personally involved in the case. It didn't really grab him the way some others had. He kept waiting for evidence to be delivered that would exonerate his client, but it never came. So he did his best with the evidence he had.

Eriksen, on the other hand, had more trouble than usual this time around, primarily because of the family dynamics involved. He tried to keep his usual professional distance, but as a father to two boys, he came to feel tremendous sympathy and empathy for Ralph and Constance. He couldn't imagine what it must be like for them to be going through this, believing so strongly in their daughter, but knowing a jury could send her to prison for the rest of her life.

In the months before the trial, Constance had more and more difficulty dealing with people, especially the reporters who didn't accept the Rossums' explanations at face value.

"She felt that she placed trust in some people, and then they double-crossed her," Eriksen recalled later.

Constance and Ralph both developed stress-related conditions as they dealt with the frustration and anger stemming from the prosecution's allegations about their daughter. Ralph's hands started to shake. Constance became anemic, and her cholesterol and blood pressure shot up. Eriksen could see the anxiety in their faces as he watched them age from the experience.

"We're in the fight of our lives," Constance told *Good Housekeeping*. ". . . We have to remember to eat, to sleep, to exercise. . . . Mentally it is very hard. You think about it all the time, and yet you have to go on. You have to get up, do your work, take care of your other children, and be there for Kristin."

Constance Rossum's professional marketing experience and her academic training in journalism prepared her for the most important public relations campaign of her life—convincing anyone and everyone that Kristin had nothing to do with Greg's death. And she set upon her task with a fierce determination.

While Kristin was in jail, Loebig acted as the liaison to the three major news networks, while the Rossums tried to evaluate which one would be the best advocate for their daughter.

"Everyone wanted the story," Loebig said.

Each of the networks sent out producers from New York, all sharp women who were trying to win the exclusive right for their reporter to do Kristin's story. The Rossums wanted a commitment that the reporter would fight for Kristin's innocence, Loebig said, which became more difficult once the evidence started to unravel.

"They wanted agents," Loebig said. "They didn't want impartiality."

Ultimately, the Rossums decided to go with CBS and its national evening news magazine show, *48 Hours*.

In mid-July, Michael agreed to be interviewed about the case by an Australian reporter for the *Melbourne Herald Sun*. For some reason, he seemed to feel safer talking to the Australian media than to American reporters. But in the days of the Internet, not to mention the fact that reporters often share or trade information, that didn't prevent his comments from reaching readers in San Diego, where he was under criminal investigation. Parts of his interview were republished in the *Union-Tribune* on July 15.

Michael told the *Herald Sun* that he did not flee San Diego to escape scrutiny by the police. Rather, his mother was ill, and he wanted to return home to Melbourne to be with her. In addition, his work visa was tied to his job at the Medical Examiner's Office.

"I stayed there for many months after this happened in order to facilitate the investigation as much as I could," he said.

He also said he was shocked to hear that police had named him as a possible suspect in their investigation.

Dr. Harry Bonnell, the pathologist who went to the college basketball game earlier in the year with Kristin and her mentor, Frank Barnhart, was fired from the Medical Examiner's Office on August 7, after a decade with the office. At the time he was fired, Bonnell told the *Union-Tribune* that the chief medical examiner, Dr. Brian Blackbourne, had called him into his office and said, "I'm terminating you because I don't feel confident in you being able to fulfill the responsibilities of chief deputy medical examiner." Blackbourne would not comment on Bonnell's termination.

Bonnell was forced to stop doing autopsies during a state investigation in 1999, when he was accused of negligence and incompetence in connection with two 1995 autopsies. He was cleared in 2000. But Bonnell said he thought the firing had "to do more with administrative conflicts and priorities than professional responsibilities."

Three years later, he said he was fired because he told county officials he would fully answer questions posed by attorneys in the de Villers family's civil case against the county. Loebig and Eriksen subsequently retained Bonnell's services as a consultant to help them with Kristin's defense.

On September 17, 2001, Goldstein made a formal request to Judge Thompson to televise Kristin's preliminary hearing, which was scheduled for October 9. The request wouldn't have been unusual if it had come from a news outlet, but it appeared to be an unprecedented move by a prosecutor, at least in San Diego.

Goldstein said he wanted an opportunity to balance the erroneous information the potential jury pool had been receiving through the media from Constance and Ralph Rossum. He was worried that the one-sided news accounts he'd heard on the radio and seen on TV and in print could interfere with witness testimony. Goldstein was particularly incensed by remarks Ralph made on a conservative radio commentator's show, alleging that Goldstein's motivation in going after him and his daughter was that the prosecutor was running for a judge's seat.

Goldstein was, frankly, fed up with Ralph Rossum. He said he'd rather see the judge put a gag order on the attorneys but allow cameras in the courtroom, because without cameras, the media would interview outside pontificators who often present inaccurate interpretations of the facts.

"I'm willing to rest my case on the evidence," Goldstein told the *Union-Tribune*. "This is a compelling case, and it points to the guilt of the defendant."

After learning about the sexy elements of Kristin's case, Court TV also requested to film Kristin's court proceedings. But Judge Thompson refused to grant either request.

If cameras had been allowed in the courtroom, Thompson said later, the perky, photogenic, blond defendant probably would have drawn just as much, if not more, media than the David Westerfield trial, a child kidnapping and murder case that involved a seven-year-old girl whose parents were sexually adventurous swingers. The Westerfield trial, which ended about a month and a half before Kristin's started, brought more television cameras to San Diego than any other trial in the city's history. The only memorable exceptions were the trial and retrial of Betty Broderick, a former society matron from La Jolla, who was discarded by her ex-husband for a younger version. Broderick, who shot her ex and his second wife in their beds in 1989, was convicted of second-degree murder and is serving a thirty-two-year term. Hers was the first case Court TV ever broadcasted from a San Diego courtroom.

"The presence of cameras changes the game, skews it in a way that, in my opinion, is inappropriate," Thompson said later. "People forget to do their jobs. They do a different job. They're playing to the cameras."

That goes for judges, too, he said. "It's really not fair to the defendant, to anybody associated with the case. We sacrifice justice to ensure good theater, and it's just not right."

Judge John Thompson came from a long line of judges. Every morning when he entered his courtroom, he faced a paneled wall of photos featuring four of his judicial ancestors, who joined the bench in San Diego starting in the early 1900s—his great-grandfather and grandfather, who were dead, and his father and uncle, who were still alive.

His great-grandfather, Adam Thompson, was a volunteer pro tem judge, but his grandfather, father, and uncle made sitting on the bench their full-time job. They were all featured in black-and-white or sepia tones, looking a little stern, but distinguished and, well, judgelike. They were not labeled as such, so their meaning was not apparent to visitors, but to Thompson, they represented tradition, a certain dignity, and an accomplished lineage that kept him on his toes. They also served as a constant reminder of his job's importance.

Thompson never had an epiphany about wanting to become an attorney or judge. It was just in his blood. In fact, it was expected of him.

"I thought everyone's dad was a judge, lawyer, or bad guy," he said. "I thought everyone did these things."

Starting when he was in the eighth grade, the young John Thompson and two friends who'd lost their fathers came to the courthouse over the summer and during the winter holidays to take in juicy trials like most boys watch cartoons. If Thompson's father wasn't trying an interesting case, he would call around and find one for the boys in another courtroom. The boys remained enthralled there for four and five days at a time.

Thompson's father got calls in the middle of the night, prompting him to take a shower and put on a suit.

"Daddy, what are you doing?" young John would ask.

"I'm going to the jail to talk to a new client," his father would tell him.

Former California Governor George Deukmejian appointed Thompson in 1988 to the Municipal Court bench. He served there until 1992, when then-Governor Pete Wilson—who was San Diego's mayor from 1971 to 1983, before becoming a U.S. senator and then governor—elevated him to the Superior Court bench. Thompson assumed that position fifty-six years and a day after his grandfather, Gordon Thompson, Sr., had done the same. Gordon Thompson, Jr., Thompson's father, served as a chief U.S. district court judge in the 1980s.

Thompson saw himself as a much better judge than trial attorney, and the bigger the trial the better—particularly the high-profile cases, the ones some other judges found distasteful because they had a large number of bodies and involved families in ruin and the most violent crimes. But they were the ones that drew the public's attention. It's not that he thrived on tragedy, but a case like Kristin Rossum's was simply more interesting. It was meaty and full of sexy elements: drugs, adultery, and an attractive, complex defendant.

Thompson could sometimes appear gruff, even a little irritated. Other times, though, he joked with the attorneys, slipping in a good-natured expletive or two. It generally wasn't out of anger; it seemed more that he felt comfortable being in his own courtroom with the attorneys, out of public view.

Depending on his mood, he might speak in a quiet monotone, but he was firm, respectful, and polite to defendants. Before sending a handcuffed defendant back to jail, he might say, "Good luck to you, sir." But other times, he could be abrupt, cutting off attorneys who tried to talk out of turn. His one-time desire to become an umpire came through in his own brand of legal slang, a combination of baseball and jurisprudence. In one hearing, he barked at an attorney for a CBS news outlet to "Grab some pine," referring to a bench in the dugout. In other words, "Sit down."

Outbursts like that only contributed to his reputation among reporters for disliking the media. He never allowed cameras, tape recorders, cell phones, or pagers in his courtroom, and he threatened to fine anyone who disobeyed his decree. Unlike his close friend, Judge William Mudd, who presided over the Westerfield trial, Thompson felt that cameras in the courtroom were disruptive and dangerous. The Westerfield trial drew prime-time attention, partly because Mudd allowed cameras to air the proceedings live, but also because the victims' parents were swingers.

But the perception that Thompson didn't like the press, he said, wasn't accurate. "I've never kept the press out of the courtroom. The press isn't the issue."

Thompson suggested that the media's perception that he didn't like them stemmed from his move to hold a reporter in contempt in June 2000 for refusing to turn over his notes from an interview with a defendant in a murder case. After exhausting all appeals, J. Harry Jones, a legal affairs reporter for the *Union-Tribune,* had to make a decision. Thompson gave him a choice.

"You've got to deliver up the notes," Thompson told him. "You bring your notes or you bring your toothbrush."

The toothbrush comment referred to the possibility that Jones would have to go to jail for up to two years if he didn't produce the notes. So, rather than leave his wife and daughter while he proved a journalistic point, Jones worked out a deal with Thompson. Jones was allowed to summarize the contents of his notes in an affidavit.

At the same time Thompson was dealing with Jones, he was the target of an assassination plot by a murderer in another case, a gang member who'd been convicted in his courtroom and was serving a term of life without the possibility of parole for killing a clerk in a liquor store.

At 11:30 one night, Thompson got a call from an investigator with the District Attorney's Office. "When you look outside and see two vans," the investigator said, "they're our guys. We think there's a contract out on you."

The shooters had an address for the prosecutor in the case, an address for the lead detective, and an AK-47 assault rifle, unaccounted for—all reasons to be concerned. For the

next eight weeks, Thompson had as many as ten law enforcement officers around him at all times and two patrol cars to
protect him.

What was not evident from Thompson's courtroom demeanor or his conservative appearance was how truly playful he could be. Literally.

Thompson had performed in bands for forty years—since
he was twelve—and still played guitar and keyboards in a
group called Night Shift. He was most likely the only rock-
and-roll judge in San Diego, a well-known fact only in the
legal community. Performing old favorites such as "Mustang
Sally" and newer ones like Pink's "Get The Party Started,"
Thompson, who wore a black robe over a shirt and tie by
day, traded in his judicial uniform by night for a straw hat,
black pants, and shirt and the shadows of a dimly lit stage.
Part of the reason Thompson got such rock star security
treatment during the hunt for the assassin was because the
shooters also had the schedule for his band.

Chapter 14

On the morning of Kristin's preliminary hearing, October 9, 2001, Constance and Ralph Rossum waited anxiously outside Thompson's courtroom, situated along a hallway known among the judges as Murderers' Row. Although Thompson wouldn't allow cameras in the courtroom, he did nothing to limit their presence in the third-floor hallway.

Television and newspaper reporters approached the Rossums, the bright light of the TV cameras shining down on them. The Rossums seemed quite willing to answer questions, even to welcome the attention. Such a gathering of reporters and their cameras was not an everyday occurrence in the downtown courthouse, so people began to congregate, watching the news story as it developed.

"We should not be here," Constance declared.

Ralph said he and his wife were trying to keep a calm demeanor, but "inside, we are very indignant." Their daughter's life was "in front of the whole world," he said, and she was dependent on her parents for support.

"This is a vibrant, alive woman who should be outside

pursuing her career in chemistry, not defending herself against what is a suicide," Ralph said.

The Rossums huddled with Alex Loebig, who advised reporters he wouldn't be countering any facts the prosecution presented that day.

"It's more effectively done at trial," he said.

After changing out of her jail blues into a loose-fitting plum dress, Kristin was brought into the courtroom. Her eyes were red from crying, just as they were at her arraignment. Her bangs were pulled back from her face with a white elastic band. A woman who was Kristin's boss at TriLink came in and joined the Rossums.

Goldstein called UCSD Detective Sergeant Bob Jones as his first witness. And, with the caveat that he responded to a call of "a possible suicide," Jones relayed the story Kristin told him the night Greg died.

"She said that she found the rose petals on Greg and that they were everywhere," he said. They all fell to the floor, she told him, when she pulled Greg off the bed.

Kristin took notes during Jones's testimony and stared at him, frowning, while a sketch artist sat in the gallery, scribbling a picture of the proceedings for one of the television stations.

On cross-examination by Eriksen, Jones explained that he'd put on rubber gloves to go through the contents of two foot-tall trash bins in the house but found nothing of note. The next morning, when he came back to the apartment with the investigator, he said, he "briefly" examined the two thirty-gallon cans, which were full of trash, on the balcony.

"Actually, what I was looking for was a can of soup," he said.

After he found it near the top of one of the bins, he said, no, he didn't dig any further.

The basis for the defense's case was beginning to emerge.

No, Jones told Eriksen, he didn't inventory the contents of the trash cans on the balcony, nor did he look for syringes, patches, or any other drug-related items in them. And, no, he also didn't collect the soup can or any other items he found there.

He said he noticed some red streaks on the middle third of the fitted bed sheet, which looked like they'd been caused by the rose petals, but he also didn't impound the twenty-five or thirty petals he saw on the floor or the liquid contents of the two plastic cups in the bedroom.

He said he considered calling in the SDPD from the "get-go" but didn't have enough information and saw no obvious signs of foul play. Russ Lowe's call about the affair on November 8 provided him with "the motive for something other than suicide."

On redirect, Goldstein tried to salvage the findings and credibility of the campus police sergeant, whose investigative inadequacies had been underscored by the defense. Jones said he hadn't searched the trash cans on the balcony more carefully because he'd been going on the information that the defendant had provided. He didn't know that fentanyl was involved at the time, he said, because Kristin never mentioned it. Nor did she mention that she'd been having an affair with her boss, the man standing outside on the landing the entire time Jones was in the apartment. Jones also said he had no idea that she was a meth user. She was shaking and crying, and he could hardly understand what she was saying, but at the time he thought she was in shock and that her emotions were genuine. He said the drug most commonly used by students during his twenty-one years at UCSD was marijuana.

* * *

Paramedic Sean Jordan testified that he started an intravenous line in Greg's left arm above the elbow, leaving one or two needle marks.

"I didn't do three," he said.

Since he thought Greg had overdosed on something, he said, he looked for preexisting needle marks on Greg's body but saw none. When he rolled Greg onto the backboard to take him to the hospital, he said, he saw no rose petals under Greg's body.

April Butler, the emergency medical technician who assisted Jordan that night, said she thought "it was kind of weird" that Kristin stayed mostly in the kitchen and living room, talking on the phone, while they were working to revive Greg in the bedroom. Most family members want to help out in any way they can, she said.

She said the wedding photo was propped up on the floor against a chest of drawers, maybe three feet from Greg's head, when she arrived. And as Jones testified, she saw no rose petals in the bed, either, only on the floor.

When Goldstein called Jerome de Villers to the stand, he was expecting him to be one of his strongest and most important witnesses. But Jerome didn't seem like himself. The usually articulate young man who could recite any obscure detail about the case off the top of his head was having problems remembering most everything. He sounded strange and he mumbled. It was almost as if he were uninterested in being there. Goldstein was getting so frustrated that he was about to ask the judge to declare Jerome a hostile witness when they recessed for lunch.

Goldstein took Jerome out into the hall and was asking what was wrong with him when Jerome's family gathered around to explain. Jerome had been attacked from behind in a bar in Costa Mesa two weeks earlier and suffered a bad head injury. He'd only just gotten out of the hospital. Goldstein had known about the assault, which his investigator, Frank Eaton, had checked out with the Costa Mesa Police Department. But Goldstein hadn't understood the extent of Jerome's injuries, so the prosecutor eased up on his witness and cut Jerome's testimony short.

Jerome testified that the last time he saw Greg was at Aaron Wallo's wedding in Palm Springs. Although Greg said he was tired from working hard at his new job, he seemed happy and healthy. They talked about going on a snowboarding trip to Mammoth for his birthday, and Greg was starting to think about having kids. Greg said nothing about feeling depressed or having marital problems with Kristin.

Jerome recounted his investigative efforts in the days after Greg's death.

"I felt something went wrong," he said. "I didn't understand what happened to my brother. . . . I did not believe that Greg [killed] himself."

Goldstein played the tape that Jerome made of his conversation in Kristin's apartment two days after Greg died. Much of it was hard to hear—because of a scratching sound from Jerome's nervous leg rubbing the tape recorder against the inside of his jacket pocket—so Thompson and the attorneys followed along on a transcript.

On cross-examination, Loebig tried to paint Greg as a man trying to steamroll ahead with his relationship with Kristin. While Greg was talking about buying a house, Kristin was sending a clear message that she wasn't ready, for children or any other major step forward.

Loebig asked Jerome if he thought his brother was obsessed with Kristin.

"Obsessed? I don't think that's fair," Jerome said. " 'Obsessed' is a strong word."

To him, Greg's behavior reflected only that he was in love with his wife. But based on the affair she was having, he said, maybe it was more than that. Maybe Greg didn't want her to be alone with other men.

Goldstein then called Bertrand de Villers and Christian Colantoni, the friend Greg and Kristin stayed with in Palm Springs for the wedding, and both testified that they never saw Greg acting depressed or using drugs.

"He did not like to be around chemicals," Bertrand said. "He told me that."

During the breaks between sessions, Kristin was led out of the courtroom to a holding area by a bailiff. She wore handcuffs that were hooked to a chain around her waist, keeping her face to the wall as she walked back and forth along the hallway. She behaved and followed the rules.

Back in court, Kristin cried and wiped her eyes with a tissue as toxicologist Donald "Russ" Lowe testified about handing over the reins to the lab to his new boss, Michael Robertson.

Lowe explained the system for storing drugs collected at death scenes and described a locked box that sometimes overflowed with evidence envelopes through an open slot in the top. Those envelopes were then moved in plastic trash bags to the Balance Room, he said, and all the toxicologists knew where the keys were kept. From there, the envelopes were moved into lockers, and eventually, their contents were destroyed.

After Greg's death, he said, he did an audit of all the drugs involved in the case that were kept in the office. He discovered that fifteen fentanyl patches from three different case envelopes were missing, and the 10-milligram yellow screwtop vial of fentanyl citrate that Kristin had entered in the log in October 1997 was empty. The 100-milligram vial of amphetamine she'd entered in the log in September 1997 was also empty, and the 100-milligram vial of methamphetamine she put in the log in August 1997 was missing entirely.

"The drug standard log should show what had happened to those . . . standards, and there were no entries," Lowe said.

Also, he said, drugs or the entire evidence envelopes containing white powder or paraphernalia were missing from a number of cases in which people died from overdoses involving methamphetamine or cocaine. He did not specifically testify to this, but the audit also showed that twenty Soma pills were missing from one case, clonazepam was missing from two cases, and sixteen OxyContin pills (a time-release form of oxycodone) were missing from another. In addition, half a vial of oxycodone was unaccounted for.

On cross-examination by Eriksen, Lowe acknowledged that theoretically, any toxicologist and just about any Medical Examiner's employee could have had access to the drugs in the Balance Room. In fact, Lowe said, no drug audit had ever been done during the thirty-two years he'd worked at the Medical Examiner's Office.

"So the checks and balances were relatively weak," Eriksen asked.

"Yes," Lowe said.

A story in the *Union-Tribune* that weekend expanded on Lowe's testimony, calling the Medical Examiner's Office "a virtual candy store for any employee tempted by drugs," and noting that no county employee would comment outside of court about the lax security over drugs there. The nickname stuck, and some employees would refer to the office as "the candy store" for years to come.

Goldstein didn't ask Blackbourne to offer any theories or conjecture about the autopsy results or cause of death. Essentially, all he wanted to hear from the chief medical examiner was essentially "dead guy died from fentanyl." So, Blackbourne didn't speculate how long it had been since Greg had gotten up to urinate, and he wouldn't give a more specific estimate for the time of death.

Goldstein asked a number of questions to which Blackbourne replied, "I don't know." Blackbourne said he didn't bring his notes with him to court, and he didn't apologize for it.

Perhaps his most significant testimony was that he found a total of three needle punctures on the victim's left arm, a point emphasized by the prosecution to show there was one extra needle puncture for which paramedics could not account.

Blackbourne also said there was a large bruise on the front of the victim's right arm, with a large needle puncture mark in the middle of the bruise. He found one more needle puncture in the right groin area, where the emergency room doctor had drawn blood.

Greg's liver was normal, he said, and, no, he did not have hepatitis.

Asked by Eriksen to explain why several different labs came up with varying levels of fentanyl in the blood, stomach contents, and urine, Blackbourne said it could have been because some tests were done later than others, so the samples could have evaporated or degraded. Also, he said, different testing techniques may have been used.

But Blackbourne said he could not explain how or when the fentanyl got into Greg's body, or how much was administered. Only that it was a fatal dose.

"The blood levels are all extremely high," he said.

On redirect by Goldstein, Blackbourne confirmed that the Medical Examiner's Office had no set policy that private toxicology testing would be done on cases involving the deaths of employees or their spouses. Testing in the case of investigator Stan Berdan, for example, was done in-house after he died suddenly in 1999. And yes, Blackbourne said, Kristin was working in the toxicology lab when those tests were done.

Thomas Horn, who was a student worker with Kristin back in August 2000, testified that Michael asked him to pull the evidence envelope for case #1591 and bring it to him. Kristin had done the toxicology tests in that case, screening for "drugs of abuse." Michael gave him the key to the Balance Room, where, after some searching, Horn said he found the manila envelope in a large plastic bag.

A few days later, Horn said, he was asked to get that file again and couldn't find it in the bag. That's how he remembered the last time he'd seen it—in Michael's office. He went back and found it there.

On August 31, Michael sent a blood sample from that case to the National Medical Services lab in Pennsylvania, his former employer, for analysis to see if it contained fentanyl. The results came back in early October.

After Greg's death, Horn said, Lowe asked him to find the file again. By that time, Horn had boxed—in numerical order—all the envelopes that had been in the black bags. But the evidence envelope for case #1591, which had contained eight fentanyl patches, wasn't in the box where it should have been. Those eight patches were among the fifteen that Lowe counted as missing in his audit.

Toxicologist Ray Gary testified that he'd seen yellow flowers that looked like roses in Michael's gym bag in his office one day. The next day the same flowers showed up on Kristin's desk.

Gary said he also saw a little wooden box on Kristin's desk, and after noticing at least one flower-giving incident, figured the box was a gift from Michael. He opened it up when neither one of them was around and found at least twenty IOUs, with promises such as "a night out," "a day of lovemaking," and "a walk in the park." There also was a key in the box. He saw the box on Kristin's desk that Tuesday morning, right after Michael informed them of Greg's death. It was gone the next day.

Frank Barnhart smiled at Kristin from the witness stand and referred to her as "my friend Kristin." His answers often seemed evasive, as if he didn't want to implicate the young woman he'd nicknamed "Lil Bandit."

"You would agree, wouldn't you, that she understands the workings of fentanyl?" Goldstein asked.

"She's smart. Her major is chemistry or biochemistry," Barnhart said. "I don't really know what her experience was with fentanyl when she and I worked together at the Medical Examiner's Office."

Goldstein tried to pin Barnhart down, asking him whether he recalled telling an investigator that she "would have had full understanding of fentanyl." But Barnhart would not be pinned. So, Goldstein made a point of questioning his credibility by implying that Barnhart had a conflict of interest and had neglected to disclose his ongoing friendship with Kristin to the prosecution. Goldstein noted that Barnhart had gone to a basketball game with Kristin and discussed fentanyl in connection with the case. He also got Barnhart to confirm that he'd had dinner with Kristin and her parents.

"Do you recall if this was before or after you had been requested by me to examine the gastric contents of Gregory de Villers?"

Barnhart said he didn't remember. "I'm not trying to be evasive," he said.

"No further questions," Goldstein said dismissively.

* * *

Finally, Goldstein called his last witness, Ralph Rossum, to the stand.

Goldstein's approach was far more confrontational and his voice much louder with Ralph than with any other witness. The prosecutor intentionally yelled at the professor to try to get him off his game. Ralph often responded in a manner that sounded as if he were trying to taunt Goldstein, implying that he had information that he was purposely withholding. And so, the feud, which had started with Ralph's attacks against Goldstein in the media, continued.

Ralph started his testimony with a description of the Rossums' last supper with Greg and Kristin in Balboa Park, saying that he and Constance observed "repeated instances of atypical behavior" from Greg, starting with the way he was "waxing eloquently" about the last surviving red rose in the apartment.

"It put us a bit on edge," Ralph said.

Ralph's testimony was generally parallel to what he said in media interviews, including his complaint that he'd never been interviewed by police about any of this.

That's when Goldstein went on the attack. He was not going to let Ralph come into his courtroom and lie. "He's not any better than us," Goldstein thought.

Didn't Ralph remember Jones's call to his house in Claremont on the morning of November 7? Goldstein asked.

"I did not consider that an interview," Ralph declared.

Goldstein read aloud portions of a transcript from Ralph's recorded conversation with Jones to prove that Ralph's recollections had changed dramatically, since he had initially described that Friday to Jones as "a very pleasant evening."

Ralph countered haughtily that he'd assumed Jones was just a "campus security guard . . . a basic rent-a-cop." He said he would have given a fuller version of the events if he'd known he was being formally interviewed and taped by a sworn peace officer.

Upon further questioning by Goldstein, Ralph acknowledged that he'd also turned down an interview with Agnew's boss, Sergeant Howard Williams, in July.

"On the advice of counsel, I had been recommended not to respond," Ralph said.

"On the advice of counsel?" Goldstein asked.

"Yes," Ralph said.

"Did your counsel also advise you to talk to the press about—" Goldstein said.

Thompson jumped in. "Hold it, hold it," he said.

The judge explained to Ralph that he didn't have to discuss privileged discussions with his attorney and told Goldstein to ask him another question.

Goldstein asked whether Frank Eaton, his investigator, had asked Ralph a week ago for any information that "might shed light on this case." "Yes," Ralph said, "and that, interestingly, occurred only one hour prior to a scheduled interview that you had with CBS News where you knew you were going to be asked that question."

Goldstein asked if Ralph had given Eaton all the information Ralph had been disseminating to the media.

"No. I said we would save it for the appropriate time," Ralph said. "Apparently, this is it."

After the lunch break, Ralph testified that Kristin told him Greg obtained the fentanyl from boxes in his father's medical storage area in Ventura County, which they visited in September 2000. Kristin told him that Greg said he was going to dispose of the fentanyl "and that was the last she saw of it." Ralph said he had photos from the unit taken during that trip, though he acknowledged that none specifically showed any fentanyl.

Goldstein asked if Ralph had mentioned any of this to the police sergeant or to the DA's investigator. No, Ralph said.

"I told [Eaton] there was information about fentanyl that would come out at the appropriate time," Ralph said.

Goldstein had had enough of Ralph's snappy retorts.

"Do you think this is a game?" he snarled.

"No," Ralph replied.

At the end of the hearing, Judge Thompson took up the defense's request to throw out Kristin's videotaped police interview.

Eriksen argued that Kristin was considered a suspect at that time and was being interrogated by two detectives who had not read her Miranda rights to her. At some point during the interview, Eriksen said, Agnew adopted a more accusatory tone, and to him, that amounted to Kristin being in a "custodial situation," where she didn't feel she could get up and leave.

Goldstein countered that the detectives' initial questions were extremely open-ended. He acknowledged that Kristin became more upset as the interview progressed, but that didn't stop her from answering the questions. She was never placed under arrest, he said, and she was told at least twice that she was free to go, which she finally chose to do.

"Clearly, there is nothing to indicate the statement was anything but voluntary," Goldstein said.

Thompson agreed and overruled the defense's objection to the interview. He ruled there were sufficient facts to hold Kristin over for trial.

The Rossums, followed by reporters, filed out of the courtroom and cast their own spin on the proceedings.

"We're very disappointed but not in any way surprised," Ralph said. He explained that all the prosecutors had to do was establish probable cause that a crime had been committed and put their "cards on the table." He summed up the four-day hearing as "heavy-handed prosecutorial action" and predicted that the prosecutor's house of cards was going to fall.

Constance chimed in, offering a new reason for why Kristin stayed so long in the apartment even when she was so unhappy: She was scared of Greg's temper. He was acting so obsessively with Kristin that it had risen to the level of emotional abuse.

"It's a cycle of abuse," she said, referring to the domestic violence that Greg's mother described in her divorce papers. "Women stay too long."

Ralph said they'd asked Kristin if Greg was beating her, and she'd said no. Nonetheless, Constance said, "We were afraid he would go berserk."

Asked whether their daughter could be lying to them, Constance was quick to respond. "No," she declared.

Ralph agreed, describing how upset Kristin was when she called him from the hospital on the night of Greg's death, how she sobbed uncontrollably all the way home that night. Anyone could hear the anguish in her voice on the 911 tape, he said.

"Kristin's ability was as a ballet dancer, not as an actress," he said.

Chapter 15

Chris Elliott, Kristin's friend who had finished medical school in New York by the time the preliminary hearing had ended, felt bad for Kristin and her family. He'd written the Rossums a letter sympathizing with their situation. He just couldn't see Kristin as a killer.

"Obviously, something weird happened, but if you ask me, 'Do I think Kristin could be capable of murder?' the answer is no," he said, even with factors such as methamphetamine in the picture. "Could it push her over the edge? No, I don't think so."

When he first heard that Greg had died, he sent Kristin a letter saying he was sorry for her loss. Later, when he learned Kristin had been accused of murder, his first thought was, "Are you kidding me?"

He remembered how nurturing she was to her little brothers, the people she cared about. He wondered if maybe she used drugs because she was insecure or wanted to be a part of something. Maybe to lose weight. A lot of things could have happened to her in the five years since he'd last seen her.

Kristin wrote him back from jail, describing how unreal

her life was and how grateful she was for support from her family and friends. Elliott sent her several books from Amazon.com: *The Road Less Traveled,* because the first sentence reads, "Life is difficult"; *The Artist's Way,* because he saw it as a primer for regaining creativity through adversity; and *Naked,* because it made him laugh out loud.

"I can't really promise you that she's innocent, but I'm not afraid of her. I'd still hang out with her," he said. "A lot of people do drugs, and they're not murderers."

District Attorney Paul Pfingst, who was running for reelection in the March 2002 primary, announced on November 9, 2001 that he would not seek the death penalty against Kristin. Instead, he decided to go for the lesser sentence of life in prison without the possibility of parole. Pfingst would not explain his reasoning, which only encouraged speculation by Kristin's attorneys and the legal community, which was watching the high-profile case closely.

Loebig and Eriksen speculated that Pfingst's decision stemmed from three factors: Kristin was a young woman with no record; this was a circumstantial case; and the alleged act was not nearly as heinous as those in previous local death penalty cases.

"I think it was a deliberate and fair consideration," Loebig said. "For all parties concerned, they made the right choice."

Ralph and Constance said this decision would help the defense attorneys focus all their attention on the murder trial without the distraction of a subsequent trial on whether Kristin should get a death sentence.

"It's also good because it means that jurors who may be riding the fence can't split the difference by saying I'll vote to convict, but not on the [death penalty]," Ralph said.

Rick Hogrefe, the head of TriLink, was delighted and relieved.

"Thank God," Hogrefe said. "I fully expected this from the beginning. This case is already, in my eyes, so weak. If they went for the death penalty, I think no jury would even consider it."

Others in the legal community speculated privately that it could be difficult to obtain a conviction and a death sentence in San Diego against such a pretty, young, educated white woman from a relatively affluent family. Some suggested that Pfingst did not want to take a risk on such a big case during an election year.

Goldstein explained later that he had recommended Pfingst go with the lesser sentence because Kristin didn't have a criminal record, and "the murder, though terrible, [wa]sn't egregious in the sense of maiming, torture," or multiple killings. Plus, he said, her meth use would be viewed as a mitigating factor, and juries had a more difficult time putting women to death. After all, he said, life without parole was a "pretty severe punishment." Goldstein, who was also running in the March primary for a judge's seat, said Pfingst had never used the death penalty as a political tool. Plus, he said, Pfingst never would have overruled him, because that would have forced his removal as prosecutor.

Pfingst, a Republican who had been in office for eight years, had unseated an incumbent of twenty-four years after winning a nationally recognized murder case he prosecuted against California Highway Patrol Officer Craig Peyer. But his honeymoon was long over, and he was in a tough race against three challengers, including an openly gay judge named Bonnie Dumanis, a Democrat who went on to win the seat in November 2002.

San Diego was not the conservative military town it used to be. The electorate—and jury pool—had evolved, although the city still had its share of conservative thinkers who weren't giving up their small-town mindset without a fight.

San Diego County, which had a population of 2.8 million, had grown up since the days when its economy depended largely on the defense and tourism industries. Although the military remained a major presence in the region, the burgeoning biotech and high-tech industries had helped to diversify it economically and politically. Meanwhile, the region's racial makeup shifted as the minority communities continued to grow. Changes in urban areas of the region were mirrored in the makeup of the San Diego City Council, where politically conservative Republicans no longer represented a majority. The suburban and rural unincorporated areas, however, were still voting for a full slate of white Republicans on the county Board of Supervisors.

At the time that Pfingst announced his decision in Kristin's case, he was under fire from many of his own prosecutors, who had registered a no-confidence vote in his leadership. During his tenure, one of his top prosecutors was convicted of fraud for conducting a real-estate business out of the DA's Office. An internal investigation was sparked after a jailhouse informant and his wife said a DA investigator allowed them to have late-night sex—and take nude photos—for two years in the office in exchange for the informant's testimony against gang members accused of killing a police officer. Pfingst's office was also accused of botching a high-profile murder case involving the stabbing of a twelve-year-old girl, and Pfingst himself was accused of being anti-Semitic and of being unethical for failing to prosecute political corruption more aggressively. Pfingst denied all the allegations, saying he'd fallen victim to "the most sleazy and vile" campaign in the county's history.

The Rossums weren't able to pull together the bond package before Christmas as they'd hoped. It wasn't until the afternoon of January 4, 2002, that Constance, Ralph, and their youngest son, Pierce, came to Las Colinas to take Kristin home in their silver Mercedes.

While the media was waiting for Kristin to emerge on that sunny but breezy winter day, a man carried out a large brown paper bag that looked to be full of books and gave it to Pierce to put in the car. Ralph and Pierce brought out two more bags.

The Rossums tried to downplay their affluence and touted their humble beginnings to the media. But they were able to put up a $1.25 million bail bond, which meant they were out a nonrefundable deposit, which constituted up to 10 percent of the total amount paid to the bail bondsman.

They explained that the bond had been backed by cash, stocks, bonds, and three homes—theirs and both of Kristin's grandmothers'—as well as by their sons' investment accounts. They said seventeen friends also pledged money market funds, stocks, and bonds. Because the bail was so high, Loebig said the Rossums were able to work out a lower deposit fee, something closer to $80,000 than $125,000.

Ralph told reporters that the family didn't think Kristin was a flight risk but said, "If she were to flee, it would ruin Constance and me financially."

Kristin's boss, Rick Hogrefe, was by far the most generous contributor to the defense fund. "Without Hogrefe, we wouldn't be here today," Ralph said.

Putting a good face on Kristin's future, Ralph said she'd already asked to order graduate exams in chemistry and physics because she wanted to get a Ph.D. and run a lab. But until the trial was resolved and she was acquitted, those plans would have to be placed on hold.

Ralph said his daughter was a victim of malicious prosecution, something that would never happen in Los Angeles. But in San Diego, he said, the Police Department and District Attorney's Office seemed prone to glom on to facts, even when faced with information to the contrary, picking and choosing from among the evidence.

"We think it's outrageous," he said, characterizing Agnew as inexperienced, with only a few weeks on the homicide team.

"We are deeply troubled to see that the San Diego police and District Attorney's Office have failed to heed the warning offered by the USC Annenberg School of Communication to its aspiring journalists about accepting a story, or in this instance, a case, that is too good to check," the Rossums said in a news release. "We are convinced that had we and others who knew Greg's mental state the weeks before his suicide been contacted, Kristin never would have been arrested."

Ralph said the defense attorneys had advised him and Constance to keep Kristin on edge so she didn't accept her fate. They wanted someone on the witness stand who was alive, not defeatist. That night, he said, the family planned to take Kristin out to dinner at a sushi bar in Claremont.

"It's bittersweet because obviously the battle isn't over, but it's wonderful to know we're going to be able to bring her home," he said.

Constance brought a black sweater, dress pants, and a string of pearls for Kristin to change into before she spoke at her first press conference. Through the glass doors of the jail, Constance could be seen primping Kristin, stroking her hair and hugging her, before she stepped outside.

Kristin was all smiles, practically breathless with emotion as she told reporters she felt overwhelmed. She said she was just so grateful to all the friends and family who helped her get out of jail. She looked a little fuller in the face than before she went to jail.

"I look forward to proving my innocence in court this summer," Kristin declared. The charges are "without truth . . . I did not harm my husband in any way."

Kristin started crying, laid her head on Ralph's shoulder,

and told him she loved him. Then, holding her parents' hands, Kristin walked with them through the parking lot to the car, a mob of cameras following behind.

Still answering reporters' questions, Kristin said, "It's hard not to be bitter, but six months has been taken out of my life. I had no doubt throughout this ordeal that there would be a day that I would go home."

Kristin and her family let *48 Hours* film them drinking champagne that night at their home in Claremont.

After reviewing tapes of interviews Ralph had given to broadcast media, Judge John Thompson decided to put an end to what he saw as a media circus. He'd been particularly irritated by Ralph's recent comments on a local conservative radio commentator's show.

"I'm going to do now what I should have done when this case came to me," Thompson said at a hearing on January 15.

He issued a gag order that covered Kristin, her attorneys, the prosecutors, and all police and investigative personnel.

"You are to have absolutely no contact with anyone from the media," Thompson declared.

Directing his comments specifically at Ralph, Thompson said he certainly would have included him in the order if he could. But at the time, Ralph had not yet been declared an official witness, which would have given the judge the legal jurisdiction to gag him as well.

"You, I can control," Thompson said to the attorneys. "Mr. Rossum, I cannot."

Over the past few months, Thompson said, he had no doubt that Ralph had been trying to "potentially poison the jury pool in this case." And he wanted all of that to stop. If it didn't, Thompson threatened to take action that was in his power and move the trial to another county, possibly north of

San Francisco. He said Kristin's attorneys could request such a move, although he would not agree to hold the trial in neighboring Orange or Riverside Counties. He would, however, approve of taking it to Imperial County, the next jurisdiction to the east.

"We're not going to try the case in the paper," he said.

Although Goldstein liked having the media spotlight on the court process for public education purposes, he didn't mind this particular gag order. It was much less distracting not to have to worry about inadvertently saying something outside the courtroom that he shouldn't or about how his comments would play in the press.

The defense attorneys felt the same way, but they also weren't thrilled that the prosecution had already released details of its case to the media before Thompson imposed the order.

Later, Thompson said he wished he'd handled Ralph Rossum and the gag order differently. He hadn't realized that he did have the authority to gag Ralph because he was going to be called as a witness. But Thompson hadn't been sure of that at the time.

"I rued the day I didn't gag him in the beginning, right out of the chute," Thompson said.

Goldstein was elected in the March primary, though he wasn't scheduled to take his seat on the Superior Court bench until the following January. He and Pfingst discussed whether he should continue on the case, and they decided that he was the best one to follow it through, even if he had to postpone the start of his judgeship. Kristin's trial was supposed to begin in early June, but trials had a way of being delayed.

Goldstein also decided that for the first and last time in his prosecutorial career, he wanted to bring on an attorney as second chair. He picked Dave Hendren, with whom he'd worked for the past eight or ten years, and whom he had supervised for the past two. Goldstein wanted to give Hendren, a very thorough, efficient, and hardworking prosecutor, a shot in the limelight. An oversized Boy Scout wearing a suit and sometimes a big grin, Hendren and his courtroom manner made him a good foil for Goldstein. But Hendren was a capable prosecutor in his own right, with a cross-examining style that could impeach a witness. He'd won his share of cases, though none as high profile as Goldstein's. This case would put his name in the news.

Shortly after the election, Kristin's attorneys filed a motion seeking to remove Goldstein from the case, arguing that letting a judge-elect continue as prosecutor would lead to an unfair trial for their client. Because of the gag order, none of the attorneys could tell the media about the motion, which was filed under seal. Thompson said the media seemed to have an "insatiable appetite" for the case.

When the *Union-Tribune* found out he'd sealed this motion and possibly others, Thompson wouldn't even disclose its topic when questioned informally by the newspaper's attorney, Guylyn Cummins. So, Cummins asked for an immediate hearing.

"We don't have to shield every high-profile case from public scrutiny," she wrote in her motion seeking to unseal the documents.

Thompson held a hearing the next day but wouldn't budge on his decision, so Cummins took it to the Fourth District Court of Appeal. On April 24, the day before Thompson was scheduled to hear the motion, the appeals court overturned his decision to keep this or any other pretrial motion sealed.

Kelli Sager, a First Amendment attorney in Los Angeles, said the law could not be more clear in prohibiting what Thompson tried to do.

"A blanket sealing order like the kind entered in this case is flatly unconstitutional," she told the *Union-Tribune*.

* * *

When Hendren was assigned to the case, he had less than two months to prepare for the June 3 trial date. It was quite a daunting task. His first thought was, "Oh my gosh, twenty-some thousand pages [of discovery] to go through. How am I ever going to get up to speed on this?"

The father of two spent virtually every waking hour reading. And that included a lot of late nights and weekends, constantly analyzing, researching, and doing follow-up, as he tried to catch up with Goldstein's knowledge. As he read through the drug audits, he thought that too many drugs relevant to the case were missing to be a coincidence. He wondered why, when the paramedics arrived, the wedding photo was propped up against the chest next to the bed when Kristin said it had been tucked under Greg's pillow.

Luckily, Hendren's wife was very understanding when he was in trial mode. In fact, because she was about Kristin's size and his tall, lean build was pretty similar to Greg's, she even helped him reenact Kristin's story about how she pulled Greg off the bed and onto the floor to start CPR. Hendren's wife had to pull him by the arms to get him off, and it wasn't easy.

It was somewhat unusual to have two prosecutors working a homicide case, but this one was complicated and high profile, and the records were still coming in. In mid-May, because of the tremendous volume of evidence, both sides agreed it would be better to delay the trial for several months. A new date of October 4 was set.

Goldstein and Hendren divvied up the witnesses and evidence by subject matter, but in such a way that each prosecutor's role would be clear to the jury. Hendren got the computer documentation, the character witnesses, and issues related to the Medical Examiner's Office, such as the drug inventories. Because of his medical background, Goldstein took the paramedics and the expert drug witnesses. They split up the

Rossums, with Hendren taking Constance and Goldstein taking Ralph, his old nemesis. They figured the jury wouldn't like it if Goldstein attacked both parents on cross-examination.

Kristin maintained her innocence during her first televised jailhouse interview, which was featured on *48 Hours* when it first aired in April 2002. It was updated and re-aired after the trial in February 2003.

"I ask myself every day, how did I go from the happy little girl to being in here, facing murder charges?" Kristin said in a childlike voice through tears to reporter Bill Lagattuta, who was on the other side of the glass, talking to her by phone. "I want to shout at the top of my lungs, 'I didn't do it. I didn't do it.' "

Her worst fear, she said, was that she would spend the rest of her life in prison for a crime she didn't commit.

As Kristin characterized her life with Greg, she repeated many of the same images and phrases her parents had been disseminating since her arrest. Not long into the marriage, she said, Greg became "very, very clingy" as she tried to pull away from him and find herself as an individual.

"He always wanted to keep tabs on me and stop me from having any independent life outside our marriage," she said.

Kristin's friend Melissa Prager was interviewed to back up her story.

"Kristin and Greg's relationship was very unhealthy in that he was very controlling; he was very obsessed with her," Prager said. "Kristin was becoming Greg's project and less Kristin Rossum."

The happiest Prager had ever seen Kristin was after she'd fallen for Michael. "It was an entirely different love, a love that was true and sincere and that she was discovering on her own," Prager said.

Bill Leger spoke up in Greg's memory, disputing the

Rossums' claim that his close friend had been a dark, moody person.

"He was just a straightforward, upfront, no-nonsense kind of guy, hardworking guy. Greg was very happy. He was looking forward to possibly purchasing a home."

Asked about the rose petals, Kristin echoed her parents' claim that Greg "had given me a dozen beautiful long-stemmed roses for my birthday a few weeks earlier. He was making a big deal of the last rose standing." Greg may have scattered the petals over his chest, she said, to make a statement that he knew their relationship was over.

Kristin looked and sounded like she was crying, but her eyes were dry. "I don't know if it was a cry for help or, or an intended suicide," she said. "I, I really don't know."

Kristin dismissed what prosecutors cited as her motive—that she wanted to prevent Greg from carrying out his threat to report her affair and her drug use to her superiors.

"That's just ridiculous," she said. "Those certainly aren't motives."

She acknowledged that she hadn't wanted her coworkers to know about her drug problem, but it wouldn't have been "the end of the world." Surely, her bosses would have worked with her on her drug problem and put her into counseling. She also acknowledged that she had access to fentanyl at the Medical Examiner's Office, but so did everyone else who worked there.

"I certainly did not take any of it," she said. "I'm not a murderer. I did not harm my husband."

Goldstein was featured saying he didn't think Kristin had told the truth in ten years and that the evidence against her was "immaculate."

Loebig countered that it wasn't such a stretch of the imagination that Greg committed suicide because he couldn't live without Kristin. All he had to do, Loebig said, was empty an ampule of fentanyl into a water glass, throw away the ampule in one of the trash cans on the balcony, then get into bed and drink the contents of the glass.

48 Hours traveled to Australia to interview Michael Robertson. This was apparently the only time he spoke to the American media.

Before Greg died, Michael said, Greg called him and told him to stay away from Kristin. But, Michael said, "Emotions sometimes rule . . . your better judgment."

Michael said he didn't have anything to do with Greg's death, and he didn't think Kristin was capable of murder.

"It was never an issue of homicide in my mind," he said. "I don't believe Kristin is the type of person that would even consider anything like this."

Lagattuta quoted experts as saying that if Greg had injected the fentanyl into himself, he wouldn't have had time to throw away the syringe because he would have been dead before he got to the bathroom.

Michael didn't disagree.

"So it looks suspicious," Lagattuta said.

Again, as uncomfortable as the comment appeared to make him, Michael had to concur.

"It can look suspicious, absolutely," he said.

In his recusal motion, Loebig brought up Goldstein's "immaculate" evidence comment as an example of "loaded" statements that could prejudice potential jurors, coming from a judge-elect. It was inevitable, he argued, that the public would learn of Goldstein's new position because the "extremely newsworthy" case continued to hold the media's attention. The jury pool would no longer view Goldstein as "an ordinary person," but as someone with exceptional judgment.

Deputy District Attorney Jim Atkins countered that Goldstein's status did not meet the legal standard to have him removed. The defense had to show reasonable doubt that

Goldstein wouldn't conduct himself in an "evenhanded manner."

"It's like trying to ram a square peg into a round hole," Atkins said. "Being elected a judge is not a conflict of interest."

Atkins noted that Goldstein got 178,694 votes, which represented only 8.5 percent of the pool of prospective jurors. That meant 1.9 million potential jurors did not vote for him, plenty to seat an objective panel.

Judge Julie Conger, from the Alameda County Superior Court, wrote an opinion for the Ethics Committee of the California Judges Association, stating that Goldstein had no conflict in this case.

"He has a duty to ensure continued competent representation of his clients, and while he is still licensed as an attorney, that duty is satisfied by uninterrupted and undelayed resolution of his pending cases," she wrote.

Thompson denied the defense's motion, saying he saw no evidence that Kristin wouldn't get a fair trial.

The prosecutors wanted Bob Petrachek, the computer forensic examiner, to have "everything done yesterday." So, he ended up working some weekends, when he also took calls from Hendren to answer questions. The prosecutors' enthusiasm and dedication were contagious.

About midway through his work on the case, Petrachek came across a PowerPoint presentation on Michael's laptop that had some very interesting similarities to Kristin's case. The presentation, called "The Case of the Crooked Criminalist," was based on a study published in the *Journal of Forensic Sciences* in July 1995 by four toxicologists and criminalists who worked at Michael's former employer, National Medical Services. The case involved a state crime lab director who discovered that four fentanyl patches in foil pouches were missing from an evidence bag in the vault. Shortly after two chemists with access to the vault volunteered to be drug-tested using hair samples, one of them got his hair cut shorter than ever before. (The drug is fast acting and clears quickly from the body, so it wouldn't necessarily turn up in blood or urine.) Hair tests revealed that the short-haired chemist was a chronic fentanyl abuser. Initially, he denied breaking into the evidence bag. Rather, he contended, he'd ingested 10 milligrams of fentanyl from a drug standard vial. According to the case study, that amount of fentanyl equated to two thousand fatal doses—one dose being 5 micrograms—over the course of about three months. This, his bosses decided, was "a highly improbable scenario." Ultimately, the chemist pleaded no contest to larceny and possession of a regulated drug.

For Petrachek, finding this case on Michael's laptop "was a hell of a coincidence. The parallel on it was just amazing." Hendren and Goldstein thought so, too. Especially given the thirty-seven articles on fentanyl that police found in a large manila envelope in Michael's office.

Since the Public Defender's Office is part of the county government umbrella, Petrachek also assisted Kristin's defense attorneys. Specifically, he searched three computers seized from a man in San Bernardino County who'd been arrested and jailed for selling fentanyl. Loebig and Eriksen were hoping to find a link between Greg and the man, who'd once lived near the Regents Road apartment. However, they were never able to find one.

As the trial was approaching, Petrachek finished organizing the most important e-mails by sender and recipient, that is, all but the ones that the county's computer contractor could not seem to retrieve. Much to the chagrin of the prosecution, the company that handled the county's information technology business tried but could not produce e-mails from Michael and some from Kristin at the most crucial period—right before and after Greg's death.

Petrachek also made a timeline of Kristin's, Greg's, and Michael's computer activities—such as which Web sites they visited, particularly between November 3 and 6—as well as of Kristin's and Michael's activities after Greg's death.

Petrachek got a few surprises as he searched through the Medical Examiner's records. For one, Petrachek learned that the death of Stan Berdan, a reserve police officer who'd worked at the Medical Examiner's Office, wasn't natural after all.

Goldstein had brought up Berdan's case during the preliminary hearing because it had some rather interesting parallels with Kristin's. There was, however, one important distinction, which Goldstein tied in to Kristin's case: Dr. Harry Bonnell did the autopsy on Berdan's body at the UCSD Medical Center because Berdan was an employee of the Medical Examiner's Office, but his toxicology tests were done in-house by Russ Lowe. Goldstein said Kristin, who was a student worker at the time, had reason to believe that Greg's toxicology tests would be handled the same way.

Berdan's wife, Barbara, said she came home on the evening of February 8, 1999, to find her forty-five-year-old husband playing with their children. He said he'd already eaten some potato soup and didn't need his wife to make dinner for him. He fell asleep, sitting up on the couch, and Barbara raised his feet so he was lying down. He didn't wake up, but that wasn't unusual, and he was snoring loudly. She checked on him at 2 A.M. and again at 5 A.M., and he was still snoring. She returned to bed to read, checking on him again before she took a shower. When she got out, she didn't hear him snoring and found he wasn't breathing. She called her son to help her, but they couldn't rouse him. They pulled him to the floor and started doing CPR. He was turning blue. She was unaware that Stan had called the doctor from work the day before because he was still suffering from a migraine headache he'd had for three days.

His coworkers reported that he'd been acting and talking

so strangely throughout the day that they relieved him of duty at a death scene and a colleague dropped him off at his parents' house. His mother fixed him some soup, then his parents drove him home, where he arrived about ninety minutes before his wife came back. Berdan, who'd been to urgent care over the weekend because of the migraine, had been given a prescription for butalbital, a nonnarcotic sedative, and an injection of Demerol, a narcotic painkiller. His wife was unsure when he'd last taken any medication before he died.

Curiously, the lab did send a blood sample to the Pacific Toxicology Laboratories to test for fentanyl. It came up negative. So Bonnell ruled Berdan's death an accident caused by the ingestion of two pain medications: butalbital and methadone, a narcotic.

Roger Meadows, one of Kristin's attorneys in the civil case, filed court papers in February 2002, arguing that the one-year statute of limitations had expired by the time the de Villers family filed their wrongful death lawsuit.

The de Villerses' lead attorney, Craig McClellan, repeated his previous explanation for the delay—that Kristin had initially termed Greg's death a suicide, and the family had no tangible evidence that it was a murder until Kristin's arrest on June 25, 2001. McClellan argued that the court had "impliedly" agreed by overruling Meadows's objection to the lawsuit.

Meanwhile, Michael Robertson's attorney attempted to stop McClellan from gathering information on Michael in the civil case. The attorney, Michael Gardiner, filed papers saying that his client had never been criminally charged in Greg's death, yet "he lives every day under the threat that such a charge could be made at any time."

On May 17, Superior Court Judge John S. Meyer granted

Kristin's request to temporarily block McClellan from gathering information against her—until the end of her criminal trial or until she waived her Fifth Amendment right against self-incrimination, whichever came first.

Constance and Ralph argued that they were too busy with their daughter's criminal defense to be deposed in the civil trial. The judge granted a delay, but their depositions were rescheduled for July.

On July 16, just days before those deposition dates, Kristin filed for bankruptcy in Los Angeles, contending she had $30,862 in unsecured debt to twelve creditors, mostly credit card companies. The largest bill was $10,542 in American Express card purchases made after Greg's death and up until she was arrested. The de Villers family's wrongful death claim was listed as an "unknown" amount. The filing immediately halted the civil case and moved it from state court in San Diego to federal court in Los Angeles.

McClellan argued that this was a legal ploy to unfairly manipulate state law and block his clients from moving ahead with their $2.1 million claim against Kristin, her lover, and the county of San Diego. Kristin filed Chapter 13 bankruptcy, which is intended for people who are temporarily unable to pay their debts but would like to do so in installments within three to five years. She was proposing to pay $330 a month for three years. In September a bankruptcy judge ordered the civil proceedings to resume against Kristin. The bankruptcy claim was dismissed in December, after Kristin's criminal trial was over.

Kristin's attorneys, still attempting to ensure their client got a fair trial, filed a motion in late August, asking to move the proceedings to another county because of unfair media coverage.

By this time, Kristin's case had been nicknamed the "American Beauty Murder" on national television shows such as *48 Hours, Inside Edition,* and *Good Morning America.* In addition to blanket coverage in *The San Diego Union-Tribune,* which had a Sunday circulation of nearly 450,000 at the time, her case also had received national attention in *People, Cosmopolitan, Good Housekeeping, Reader's Digest,* and the *Star,* as well as in the *Los Angeles Times,* which is among the nation's largest metropolitan newspapers.

The defense commissioned a survey and polled 303 people living in San Diego County by phone in late April. Fifty-seven percent said they were aware of the case, and of those, 20 percent said they believed Kristin poisoned her husband. Only about 4 percent believed she didn't poison him. Nearly 75 percent said they needed more information to form an opinion, and 2 percent refused to answer. The margin of error was 5.6 percent.

Kristin's attorneys also asked the judge to dismiss the special circumstances allegation that she used poison to murder Greg. Although the district attorney decided not to seek the death penalty against Kristin, he did not drop the poison allegation that made her eligible for it.

Eriksen argued that the term "poison" was too vague and was not defined in state law. He also argued that fentanyl was not a "recognized poison." Citing *Webster's Dictionary,* Eriksen wrote that poison was defined as " 'a substance that through its chemical action . . . kills, injures or impairs an organism.' This definition would not cover or include fentanyl or any other narcotic drug used as a painkiller or anesthetic, because such drugs are primarily used as medicine and for their therapeutic value, and they do not usually kill, injure, or impair people."

Goldstein and Hendren countered that poison was defined in California criminal jury instructions as "any substance introduced into the body by any means, which, by its chemical action, is capable of causing death." When mixed with clonazepam and oxycodone, they said, fentanyl "surely may cause substantial injury or illness and fall within the definition of poison."

Thompson sided with the prosecution and denied the poison motion. He said he'd defer ruling on the change of venue motion until after the jury selection process, when he could determine whether he'd been able to seat a fair and impartial panel.

Chapter 16

Goldstein was ready for trial by the original start date in June, so he was able to take some time off and then review the case again closer to the new date in October. It had taken him months to carefully craft his opening and closing statements, while also compiling questions for potential jurors during voir dire and for defense witnesses on cross-examination. He planned to use preliminary hearing testimony and numerous statements the Rossums made to the media to impeach them at trial. Their responses to MSNBC.com's questions were among the most fruitful, because he felt the Rossums "went too far" and, as a bonus for him, they did it in writing.

Kristin had lived a chaotic life. In his opening statement, Goldstein's challenge was to make sense of her behavior for the jury when the conduct itself didn't make sense. The details were complicated but interesting, and he worked long and hard to make them fluid.

When he cross-examined Kristin, his strategy was to stay organized and keep control of her testimony, jumping around somewhat so that she couldn't tell the story the way she wanted, in a linear fashion. He planned to keep her off guard, force her to admit she'd lied, make her concede to incriminating evidence, and stay in her face until she ran out of answers. He needed to persuade the jury that she was guilty and be entertaining in the process.

A month before jury selection started, Alex Loebig held a mini mock trial for several hours in the library of the Public Defender's Office. Six people—a witness expert and her husband, who was a prosecutor and former criminal defense attorney; two investigators; and two others who worked in the office—listened to Kristin practice answering Loebig's questions on direct examination and Eriksen's on cross.

Both attorneys thought she did fine on direct but thought her answers on cross were not convincing enough. Loebig and Eriksen knew the success of their case rested primarily on whether the jury believed her version of events.

"I told her a lot of her answers were very weak and I didn't think the jury would accept them," Eriksen said.

She insisted, for example, that everyone knew people were supposed to separate pills from their vials in case they fell into the wrong hands, such as a child who doesn't know what he's taking. So, she said, Greg must've thrown away the vials but not the pills. Loebig thought the story was simply ludicrous. Eriksen tried to persuade her that it was far-fetched, but she held fast.

"I don't think anything we could have asked would have made it more likely that she would have made a better witness at trial," Loebig said later.

Constance and Ralph held fast to their explanations for the evidence as well. Loebig and Eriksen kept hoping that they could find evidence to support some of them, such as the many theories about how Greg could have obtained the fentanyl on his own, but that didn't happen. In the end, the defense attorneys had nothing more than Kristin's word to back her claim that Greg had accompanied her to the lab and could have nabbed some fentanyl when she wasn't looking. No witnesses had seen him there, other than when Kristin first started as a student worker.

Kristin continued to deny every adulterous relationship the prosecution alleged, including those with the two men she'd e-mailed, Dan Dewall and Joe Rizzo. Both men denied during phone interviews with the prosecution that they'd engaged in sexual encounters with Kristin. But Loebig and Eriksen decided not to call them to the stand because they thought it would only make the two men sound like liars and hurt the defense's case.

"Those e-mails, in my view, were fairly explicit," Eriksen said.

The prosecution felt the same way.

Right up to the trial, Loebig continued to try to persuade Kristin to agree to a plea bargain with the prosecution. Loebig and Goldstein had discussed whether Kristin could provide compelling details about her lover's involvement in Greg's death and whether she would be willing to testify against him. Goldstein later said he "made no offers," though he was "always willing to discuss what the defense has."

But Kristin wouldn't budge.

"She just wasn't interested," Loebig said. "She denied her own guilt or his. . . . She loved her boyfriend and didn't want him to go to prison and thought she would be acquitted."

On October 2, two days before jury selection was to begin, Loebig and Eriksen met with the two prosecutors in Goldstein's office. Loebig asked if there was anything else he should know. Goldstein broke into a smile and said, yes, in fact, there was.

In combing through mounds of subpoenaed documents, their thorough paralegal, Meredith Dent, had found something very interesting. She'd carefully examined records for nearly a year's worth of Kristin's purchases, before and after Greg's death, and hit pay dirt with the supermarket in the strip mall next door to La Jolla Del Sol.

At 12:41 P.M. on the day Greg died, Kristin used her Vons discount card to buy a bottle of nighttime cold medicine, four cans of soup, a Bic cigarette lighter—and a single rose with baby's breath.

After hearing this, Eriksen looked like he'd just been run over by a truck. He and Loebig knew the rose receipt, especially at the eleventh hour, was going to be devastating to their case. They immediately went back to Loebig's office and called Kristin at her hotel. Here they were, two days before trial, with this potentially damning bombshell dumped in their laps. How could she have kept this from them?

Despite the concern in their voices, Kristin sounded somewhat nonplussed by the news. She was having trouble remembering the Vons purchases and didn't offer any explanation. She and her attorneys arranged to speak face to face about the new evidence. But before they could get together, Kristin had a breakdown.

Paramedics responded to a 911 call from Kristin's hotel room and found her lying facedown on her bed, hugging a teddy bear. They took her to the hospital, where she was admitted and treated with something to quell the anxiety. During the trial, she would deny that the episode was sparked by news of the Vons receipt. She testified that she was having muscle spasms and panic attacks because jury selection was only two days away.

"I was scared to death," she said.

Dent also found that Kristin used her Washington Mutual Visa check card on November 6, 2000, to withdraw $240 from the ATM in Vons. Greg's wallet contained cards from a different bank and supermarket—Wells Fargo and Ralph's. That same day, Kristin's credit card records showed she did some other shopping and filled up on gas—twice, which led Goldstein to assume she drove to Tijuana to buy drugs. She spent $80.61 at Cost Plus, $69.88 at Crate & Barrel, and $16.15 at Sears.

And finally, while her husband lay in bed, drugged and dying, she spent $111.50 on lingerie at Victoria's Secret.

The morning of Friday, October 4, finally arrived, and the four attorneys talked jocularly about sports in Thompson's courtroom as they waited to begin the tedious but important process of jury selection. Goldstein, his hair freshly cut, paced around the prosecution table, handed one of the hefty jury questionnaires to Loebig, and popped a mint into his mouth.

Goldstein had been preparing for this trial for nearly two years. Simultaneously nervous, excited, angry, and ready for battle, he lived for moments like these. He felt like the master of the universe and, at the same time, lucky to have such an important case. He tried to freeze time, just long enough to appreciate where he was and what he was about to do. He hadn't come there to lose.

Kristin sat at the defense table wearing a dark gray suit, the highlights in her hair even blonder than before.

At 9 A.M., Judge Thompson read an order that prohibited recording devices and any kind of cameras not just in his courtroom, but on the entire third floor of the downtown courthouse. He said he would aggressively enforce his verbal warning that no reporter was to speak to the jurors or he would "throw his ass in jail."

Seating during jury selection would be limited, he said, so much so that the media probably would be excluded from the afternoon sessions. Thompson decided, however, that he would reserve the first two rows of the small courtroom for the media during the actual trial and would also ensure that seats were always available for Kristin's parents and the de Villers family.

The judge, Kristin, and her attorneys moved to another courtroom for a closed hearing, where jurors were assigned numbers so they could remain anonymous. Each juror was asked to fill out a twenty-eight-page survey with 105 questions and to read a list of 135 potential witnesses to see if they had a conflict of interest with any of them. When the attorneys initially met to discuss what to include in this questionnaire, Thompson told them they were "going to know more about this group of people than generally you will know in any other trial."

After the hearing, the 150 potential jurors spread out on wooden benches in the hallway and scribbled responses during the lunch hour. They were asked personal questions, such as whether they'd had affairs, petitioned the court for a restraining order, or attended a twelve-step program for an addiction to drugs or alcohol. They were asked whether they voted in the most recent election or watched Court TV, *Law and Order,* or *Crime and Punishment*—all of which involve trials and the legal system. And they were asked whether they had had any bad experiences with law enforcement, had been treated by a psychiatrist or marriage counselor, or had knowledge of the specific drugs that would be discussed during the trial. A number of questions pertained to media coverage of the case and whether they'd formed any opinion about Kristin's guilt or innocence based on what they'd read in the newspaper or watched on television.

After the jurors completed the questionnaires, the attorneys for both sides made copies they would study over the weekend, identifying which people they wanted as jurors and which ones they didn't.

Thompson said he had no objection to the *Union-Tribune*'s request for a copy of the witness list and a blank survey, but he left it up to the attorneys to decide. Both sides said no.

The newspaper's attorney filed a motion requesting an immediate hearing to obtain the documents and to gain full access to the jury selection process.

"This trial is of tremendous public importance," attorney Guylyn Cummins wrote in her motion. "It involves serious allegations of murder, drug use, and spousal abuse. . . . The public is interested in this case and entitled to see how the critical issues it raises are resolved through the judicial process."

At a hearing on Tuesday, Thompson agreed to release the documents. He also agreed to make courtroom seats available to the media during voir dire. However, he said he'd changed his mind about reserving the first two rows of seats for reporters, saying the newspaper's attorney had persuaded him that he shouldn't grant preferential treatment to the media over the general public. This was not the decision Cummins had been working toward.

In what the media saw as a punitive measure, Thompson decided that all reporters would have to compete with every other court watcher for one of the fifty seats in his courtroom. Thompson also reiterated his threat to punish reporters who violated his order about interviewing jurors, saying he'd been told that two reporters and a television photographer had already tried to do so.

Over the next three days, Goldstein and Loebig queried the jurors whose written answers elicited more questions. Both sides mutually agreed to dismiss a number of jurors because they'd formed an opinion after reading about the case in the newspaper or had drug use in their family.

The defense attorneys, who hired a consultant to advise them during the jury selection process, were looking for panelists who would be skeptical of a circumstantial case that had, in their view, little or no direct evidence tying Kristin to Greg's death. They were also looking for a cross section of the community, with as big a spread of ages and backgrounds as possible, hoping that a diverse panel would give rise to more questions in the jury room.

The prosecutors were looking for commonsense people who could process all the complicated circumstantial evidence and connect the dots. They also wanted jurors who could work as a group, knew how to listen, could communicate without offending others, and had a stake in the community. They tried to stay away from choosing young men who might not be capable of being objective about the pretty young woman's guilt.

Goldstein repeatedly reminded jurors that they should assess witnesses' credibility, often an important factor in deciding circumstantial cases. He asked one woman, who appeared to be in her thirties, if she had an image in her mind of what a murderer looked like.

"No, not really," she said.

"Have you ever heard the phrase, 'You can't judge a book by its cover?' " Goldstein asked. "Is there anything about the way the defendant looks that would prevent you from convicting her for murder?"

"No," one woman promised. "I wouldn't judge a murder case by the way she looks."

The attorneys went through more than 120 potential jurors before they were able to agree on a panel of twelve, most of whom were white professionals whose ages appeared to range from their twenties to their sixties. The jury was made up of five women and seven men. No juror seemed to have strong opinions about anything—all of those who seemed to have too much interest in this or any other court case were rejected along with those who said they leaned toward the prosecution or expressed frustrations with the criminal justice system. The attorneys also picked four alternates, two men and two women.

The jurors included:

A cryptologist, a white man who had worked primarily

with classified information for twenty-two years; who had fathered three children, ages eight to sixteen; and who had volunteered for a Catholic service agency.

A woman who appeared to be of mixed race and in her early forties, and wrote on her questionnaire that the criminal justice system was designed to give the defendant a fair trial. She told Goldstein that yes, she'd agree that the people, represented by the district attorney, were also entitled to a fair trial.

A white woman who was a software engineer and looked close to Kristin's age.

A Neighborhood Watch captain, a married white man in his early fifties who was a supervisor at his job.

A public relations manager, a white woman in her thirties, who said she heard the charges, looked at Kristin, and thought, "Whoa, this is serious."

A high school umpire, a white man whose son was a fire medic, who said he'd been on a jury in a personal injury trial and learned that "some people will actually take an oath and not tell the truth."

A retired travel agent, a white man with white hair, who said he'd read about the case, but nothing had really stuck with him.

A military housing manager who had served nine years in the Navy and said he had a fairly small staff at work and would prefer not to be chosen.

A black man who said his brother used crystal meth, pot, and PCP back in the 1970s, when he'd been a gang member and drug dealer until law enforcement got involved. "We kept him in line around the house," he said. "I think he learned from his mistake. He's a much better person now."

Once the jury was sworn in, Thompson told the panelists to keep an open mind. He said they shouldn't consider the content of questions as evidence, independently research facts presented at trial, visit the scene for more information, or watch or read any news stories on the case.

"You will in essence be the judges of the facts . . . [and] believability of the witnesses," he said.

Then, as promised, Thompson considered the defense's motion for a change of venue. Eriksen pointed out that the jury included people who had "read, seen or heard something about the case," and this still concerned the defense. But Thompson denied the motion.

Chapter 17

The line outside Judge Thompson's courtroom was trailing down the hall long before the bailiff opened the doors on October 15, when Goldstein would give his opening statement.

Some local reporters got to the courthouse as soon as it opened at 7 A.M.—nearly two hours early—to ensure they got a seat. With such a high-profile case, there would be hell to pay if they missed any of this story. Friends of the Rossums and of the de Villers family had to wait in line like everybody else, including the de Villerses' civil attorneys, Craig McClellan and Cindy Lane. This was the first time anyone could remember that even paralegals for the DA's office had no guaranteed seats.

But what no one understood until the first break, midway through the morning session, was that the bailiffs were going to empty the courtroom at every break, forcing people to wait in line four times a day to get a seat. If they didn't get out of the courtroom fast enough to get a spot near the front of the line, they could miss the next session.

This made for excruciatingly long and stressful days for

the reporters, who had to rush to the bathroom or call in updates before the line started moving again, and then produce a story on deadline that night. Most of the news organizations hired someone or sent over an intern or second reporter to hold the main reporter's place in line, but writers from out of town had to rough it, leaving a jacket or briefcase as a placeholder.

Alliances were formed to save the prime seats in the front row of the gallery behind the prosecution table. The two closest to the aisle had small fold-up desktops that made it easier to take notes and also provided the best view for monitoring Kristin's reactions at the defense table. TV reporters sent updates from the courtroom by handheld computer or scribbled sound bites to dictate during the next break.

Thompson's no-camera rule meant that news photographers generally had to hang around on the sidewalk outside the courthouse, waiting for Kristin, her parents, and her attorneys to walk in and out. Kristin usually wore dark glasses, her head held high, chest out, and ponytail bobbing. People told Loebig his client looked arrogant.

Thompson's bailiff, Frank Cordle, would allow the Rossums and the de Villers family into the courtroom to take their seats a few minutes before the public. The Rossums always sat on the left side of the gallery a couple of rows behind the defense table. The de Villers family sat on the opposite side, behind the prosecution table, usually a row further back and out of the Rossums' line of sight. The families that used to share Thanksgiving dinners did not speak to each other during the trial, even the several times they ended up in the same restaurant.

Young men who'd met Kristin or had seen her picture in the newspaper came alone to the trial, hoping to catch her eye or perhaps just a glimpse of the local celebrity. Some of them e-mailed reporters, asking, "Do you think she did it?"

Meanwhile, the "Trial of Kristin Rossum" forum on the

Union-Tribune's Web site was full of spirited debate as readers weighed in on the latest evidence. One defender called Kristin a "notorious hottie" and, like many others, joked about wanting to date her. The forum, which was initiated just before jury selection began and continued long after trial was over, had drawn more than sixty-seven thousand hits by the summer of 2004.

As it had from the beginning, the case provided ample fodder for cocktail and water-cooler conversation.

Goldstein took four weeks to write his opening statement. He delivered it to the jury in a jam-packed four hours, previewing the case he would roll out over the next two weeks. The dynamic prosecutor was entertaining to watch as he unveiled new evidence and tied it all together for the jury, reading intimate e-mails, playing incriminating audiotapes, showing photos, and using other props to capture and hold the panel's attention.

Goldstein painted Kristin as a young woman who used lies and drama to manipulate the people in her life, had a history of stealing to feed her drug habit, and exhibited a constant need for attention, love, and approval. Image was everything to her and her family. Time after time, he used Kristin's parents' own words against her, illustrating how she wreaked havoc on their quiet, suburban lives.

Essentially, he said, Kristin killed Greg to protect two relationships: her long-standing affair with methamphetamine and her more recent affair with her boss, Michael Robertson. But the power the drugs had over her was stronger than any romantic love, and it poisoned every other part of her life—past, present, and future.

"Robertson will never be in this courtroom, but he will be an integral part of this homicide," Goldstein said. "He's part of the motive. He's part of who protected Rossum. He protected her methamphetamine abuse. He protected the way she stole methamphetamine from the Medical Examiner's Office. He protected her in every way, including trying to cover up this homicide. He was with Rossum throughout the day of the murder. . . . His involvement is inextricably wound into this case."

As their affair intensified, Goldstein said, Michael increased the pressure on Kristin to leave Greg. He wrote her a letter the night after the Yankees won the World Series on October 26, 2000, saying it was getting increasingly difficult to spend so many long nights waiting for her.

"Not many to go now," Goldstein said, quoting Michael's letter. Goldstein said the relationship "reached critical mass," and two weeks later, Kristin's psyche buckled under all the stress. She used the "tools of her trade" to kill Greg, stealing her weapon of choice from "a veritable candy store of drugs" at the Medical Examiner's Office. Then she lied and staged a suicide scene to try to cover up her crime.

The irony of this case, he said, was that Greg didn't use drugs. He hated drugs. In fact, Greg was the one that helped Kristin kick her meth habit and threw away her old prescriptions. Kristin killed Greg, he said, because he found out she was using again and threatened to report her renewed habit to her superiors if she didn't quit her job. As a result, he became the victim of a fatal love triangle. He left no evidence that he committed suicide, no note or pill containers, no syringes or any other sign to explain how the cocktail of narcotics got into his body. Drugs were a part of Kristin's life, not his.

Like a drumbeat that would sound throughout the trial, Goldstein repeatedly flashed on a screen the shadowy booking photo from Kristin's drug arrest two months after Greg's death—lest the panel forget that the clean and healthy-looking blond woman sitting at the defense table was once a gaunt tweaker, her face covered with sores. That she was a drug addict with the state of mind to kill her husband. And that she, without a reasonable doubt, could have easily poisoned Gregory de Villers while he lay in bed, unable to answer his concerned coworkers' calls on the princess phone nearby.

"Greg is in a state of near coma," Goldstein said. "He's unable to get to a phone, unable to call in sick for himself. His lungs are filling up with fluids, his bladder is no longer working, and he's dying."

Greg must have already been out of it early that morning, he said, because for the first time ever, Kristin used her home phone to call Armando Ruelas Garcia, her drug dealer in Tijuana. Not once, but four times in quick succession, from 7:16 to 7:33 A.M. With Greg unconscious, he said, she felt it was finally safe to call the man whose business card she kept in her desk at work. Over the next two months, Kristin's phone records showed that she called Garcia thirty-two times. These calls were followed within a day or two by ATM withdrawals of $300 to $400—eleven of them—starting the day Greg died and ending just days before she was arrested for drug possession.

Goldstein said Kristin and Michael were infatuated with roses. They exchanged them and wrote to each other on cards embossed with them. And it was a rose that did her in.

Goldstein held up a gray Vons card for the jury and showed a blown-up version of the receipt from purchases she made at her neighborhood supermarket on November 6. Kristin told Jerome that she and Michael had gone to Vons to buy some soup between 3 and 5 P.M. that day. But this receipt proved she was lying.

"The defendant, on the day Greg was dying, at about 12:41 P.M., went to Vons. How do we know that? She was trying to get her discount," he said. She swiped her Vons card just as she always did, and it recorded her purchases on the Vons central computer.

"Rose, single, with baby's breath bouquet," he said, reading the receipt.

"She bought a rose," he said as he held up a long-stemmed red rose, turned dramatically, and pointed at Kristin. "What was on scene was one stem, and there were rose petals all over Greg's body, on the floor, not in the bed."

Moving on to the shredded letter, Goldstein told the jury that Kristin told different stories to Jerome and the police about how Greg found the love note. She told police that Greg caught her reading it when he came home, wrestled her to the ground, and got it away from her. She told Jerome that Greg found it after searching her and her purse. Goldstein explained that a police officer spent six weeks at the computer, reconstructing the note, which was written on a notepad taken from the Westin Rio Mar Beach Golf Resort & Spa in Puerto Rico.

Goldstein read from Kristin's diary to show that she'd even lied in her own writings, fabricating thoughts that were written purposely for Greg to read. There she was, ten days before the SOFT conference in Milwaukee, complaining that she was exasperated with Greg for being obsessed with whether Michael was going to go, too.

" 'As far as I knew, he's not,' " Goldstein said, reading from the journal. " 'I'm not going to change my plans if he goes. . . . Regardless of who ends up attending the conference, if [Greg] doesn't believe in me . . . then what do we have?' "

But Kristin, Goldstein said, knew very well that Michael was going to the conference. Their e-mails proved that they'd been planning to go away together since June.

"The whole crime scene, the journal, the shredded note, it was a staged scene to mislead authorities," Goldstein said.

"She had motive to kill Greg de Villers. She was out of control, using dangerous drugs. She had an affair that had reached an apocalypse. [Greg] was going to turn her in for an affair and using meth. She knew that she would lose her job, and she knew that Michael Robertson would lose his work visa and he would be out of the country, and he is. The numerous lies that the defendant went through in the staging . . . [of] her husband's death, her drug use, her affair . . . are tantamount to a confession. The defendant is guilty of murdering Greg de Villers. We are going to prove that in about the next month."

Goldstein finished around 2:30 P.M., leaving only a couple of hours in the afternoon session, but Loebig said he didn't need nearly as long as the prosecution to make his opening statement. He took only ninety minutes to outline his case for the jury in a laid-back manner that posed a stark contrast to Goldstein's aggressive delivery.

Loebig spoke slowly, deliberately, and calmly as he reminded jurors of their promise to keep an open mind and reserve judgment of his client, who he promised would testify. He came across as the more compassionate attorney, attempting to establish a connection with the jury through empathy. He said, for example, that he felt saddened by the number of potential jurors who wrote in their questionnaires that they'd suffered a suicide in their family.

"Sitting here today, for the first time it dawned on me that almost any suicide is a surprise, otherwise any of us would intervene," he said. "We'd help. Get counseling. We might change the way we are living our lives. We might abandon an old relationship or even a new one that we have taken up. We'd probably do about anything we could do, even for a friend, let alone a lover or husband or wife."

He characterized Kristin and her parents in a far more

sympathetic light than Goldstein had. They weren't the rich family that the prosecution made them out to be, he said. Constance and Ralph had modest, Midwestern roots, and Kristin was just a bright young girl who made some bad choices, disappointed her family, and then tried to make things right.

"This is not a blue blood family with a black sheep in it," he said.

Loebig didn't try to sugarcoat Kristin's moral choices, such as sleeping with Greg the night they met and having an affair with her boss.

"We are all adults here," he told the jury. ". . . We are not here, at least I'm not, as some big moral judge, mortal sin, whatever. We all deal with our set of beliefs and values. It's not too unusual—I think 50 percent of marriages end in divorce. It's not too unusual for somebody to fall out of love, if, in fact, they were in love to begin with."

Loebig ran through Kristin's life with Greg, how he helped her kick the drugs, how they got engaged, and how Kristin had reservations about whether Greg was the right man for her. And, how, when her parents encouraged her to go through with the wedding, she did.

Loebig emphasized that he wasn't going to make disparaging comments about Greg, although he described Greg's family life, his parents' divorce, and the emotional baggage that came with it. He talked about how much Greg adored Kristin and how, when Kristin suggested counseling and a trial separation, Greg went into his typical brooding mode.

When it came time to introduce Michael to the jury, Loebig adopted some of the same heightened rhetoric of passion and drama that was reflected in the love notes Michael and Kristin exchanged. He described Michael as "Sir Lancelot" and "a big hunk of an Australian guy. . . . When she'd look at him, it would be with love, make it lust, if you want."

He said the tone of the e-mails between Kristin and Greg illustrated the contrast in her two relationships. Life with Greg was more comfortable and "matter of fact," Loebig said. To her, Greg was more like a roommate than a husband. There was none of the electricity she felt with Michael.

"When Michael Robertson walked in, he had a Ph.D. He played rugby. He had other girlfriends, too. He was one smooth guy. He was married, but he was separated. He was going to counseling. He, initially, I will suggest to you, probably looked at Kristin and just was mutually attracted. But it grew fast and it grew intensely. And, if you believe a third of the communications between them, they were considering a long-term relationship."

Loebig argued that Kristin had no motive to kill Greg. She and Michael didn't try to hide their affair or keep it a secret, as the prosecution suggested, he said. Everyone in their office knew about it. And, it wasn't surprising, he said, that Greg didn't tell anyone the embarrassing truth that his marriage was in trouble.

"What man . . . wants to go to their family and friends and say, 'I desperately love this person that I have loved since I saw her the very first time, and I know she doesn't love me because she's told me, so I guess we'll split up'? You are going to fight to stay in that house. You are going to ignore it. You are going to sleep through it. You are going to drink a little more. You are going to deal with it however you have to from your gut."

Loebig also argued that the prosecution "overly exaggerated" the claim that Kristin went out of her way to keep her renewed meth use a secret out of fear she'd lose her job. On the night of Greg's death, he noted, she admitted to police that she'd used meth, oxycodone, and clonazepam. And, after she lost her job as a county toxicologist, it didn't take her long to find another one.

"So this drug use, it's serious, it's real serious to her personally. But as far as her career as a toxicologist, maybe not for the county . . . there's plenty of other places to work," he said.

Loebig said he was surprised Goldstein didn't play the 911 tape as part of his opening, but the jury would get to hear it before long and would realize that Kristin's emotions were genuine that night.

"When you hear that tape, you will hear the terror, the excitement, the urgency in Kristin's voice," he said. "It's up to you to listen to it and then listen to her before you arrive at any conclusions."

The authorities never tested the contents of the plastic cups in the bedroom, Loebig said, and no one can say for sure whether that's how the fentanyl got into Greg's body. An expert witness would testify that Greg had to have known he was ingesting fentanyl because it has a bitter taste, and so, he said, the "best evidence" was that Greg purposely ate or drank something with the drug in it.

As for the claim that Kristin stole the drugs from her lab, he said, the office had such lax security that anyone could have taken the missing drugs.

"There was no proof by anybody that it was Kristin that took all this stuff," he said.

Attempting to knock down some of the prosecution's other claims, Loebig said Kristin didn't pursue Greg's organ donation. It was a choice he made before he died. She also didn't push for cremation as a way to "get rid of evidence." As a county toxicologist, she knew that eventually they would find the substance that killed Greg. Kristin had no reason to kill her husband, he said. But Greg had a very real reason to kill himself.

"Greg told Kristin Rossum any number of times, from very close to the beginning of their relationship, that he didn't want to live without her. On November 6, unfortunately, before he could tell anybody else, he showed Kristin that he couldn't live without her."

The first witness for the prosecution was paramedic Sean Jordan, who came dressed in uniform. At the defense table, Kristin dabbed at her eyes with a handkerchief while Jordan talked about her.

When he and April Butler arrived at the apartment, Jordan said, Kristin was in the living room, crying and talking to the 911 dispatcher on a cordless phone—not in the bedroom, doing CPR on Greg.

Jordan said he remembered poking Greg's left arm twice to start an intravenous line.

"Did you do a third attempt?" Goldstein asked.

"I didn't do a third attempt, no," Jordan replied, again confirming Goldstein's premise that there was one extra needle puncture in that arm for which the paramedics could not account.

Jordan said he saw no red marks on Greg's chest as he normally would when someone has been doing compressions for CPR. Also, he said, Greg's pupils were fixed and dilated.

"What's that mean to you?" Goldstein asked.

"That he's pretty dead," Jordan said.

Usually, he said, the pupils of someone who'd overdosed on a narcotic were pinpointed.

Jordan said he couldn't figure out why Greg, an apparently healthy young man, was down. And when he repeatedly asked Kristin questions about what Greg might have taken, she wasn't much help.

"At that point, we were pretty much grasping at straws," he said.

On cross-examination by Eriksen, Jordan admitted that he hadn't looked at Greg's hands to see if there was any residue from the red rose petals.

* * *

The next morning, Russ Lowe, who'd retired six months earlier from the toxicology lab after thirty-two years, took the stand. Kristin wore a dark blue suit with a white shirt.

Lowe said he called the UCSD police on November 8 to tell them Kristin was having an affair with Michael, because he felt it could be important to the investigation.

"I felt that Dr. Robertson had told me things that weren't true in the past, and I didn't trust him," Lowe said. "Specifically, he denied a relationship with Kristin."

Lowe said he was cleaning out Michael's desk to make way for a new lab manager sometime in early February 2001 and was surprised to find thirty-seven articles on fentanyl, which he handed over to Dr. Blackbourne.

Lowe proceeded to go into more detail about the series of drug audits he'd mentioned during the preliminary hearing. On November 28, 2000, he said, Lloyd Amborn came to him with Detective Victor Zavala and asked him to do some confidential research in relation to Greg's death, including an audit of evidence envelopes that contained fentanyl collected at death scenes in 2000. He found that fifteen patches were missing from five cases and that Kristin had done some toxicology work on three of those cases. He also found that eleven drug standard vials were missing, including cocaine and amphetamine, and that four vials were there but had contents missing, including the empty vial of fentanyl citrate.

On December 19, 2000, Lowe said, Amborn gave him a list of thirty-eight cases from 2000 in which methamphetamine was listed as the cause of death. He asked him to check the contents of those evidence envelopes, eight of which should have contained some amount of the drug. In seven of those, the white powder was gone.

Then, in July 2001, he said, he and Cathy Hamm did a broader search of cases from 2000, including the types of paraphernalia and drugs that were relevant to this case. Putting together a sixty-three-page spreadsheet, they found that the drugs predominantly missing from the lab were white powder; Soma, the same drug Kristin bought in Tijuana; hydrocodone, the generic name for Vicodin; oxycodone; and clonazepam.

On cross-examination by Eriksen, Lowe acknowledged that some lethal drugs—such as succinylcholine, potassium chloride, and nitroglycerine—could not be detected by drug screenings used by his lab. Asked whether a vial of succinylcholine had, in fact, gone untouched since Kristin logged it in in 1997, Lowe said that drug was not included in the audit.

Lowe acknowledged that Kristin would not have had to touch the actual drug evidence when she did tests for the cases with the missing fentanyl patches. He also acknowledged that toxicologists did not faithfully log drug standards in and out when they used them to do screenings. Kristin did an inventory for the drug standard log when she was a student worker, Lowe said, but she wasn't responsible for ensuring that her coworkers made proper use of the log.

Eriksen asked if Lowe had ever seen Kristin take any impounded drug evidence or anything else out of the Balance Room without logging it out. No, Lowe replied.

On redirect by Hendren, Lowe confirmed that the HPLC machine, which Kristin used alone in a room for hours at a time, had a hood and a vent that sucked up smoke and fumes. The implication was that Kristin could have been smoking meth in that room without anyone knowing.

Dr. Brian Blackbourne, the county's chief medical examiner, confirmed for Hendren that the autopsy for investigator Stan Berdan was done at UCSD, but Greg's case was the first time the lab had sent all the blood samples to private labs for toxicology testing. But Blackbourne said that even if his toxicology lab had done the drug testing on Greg's case and failed to determine a lethal level of any particular substance, they would've sent out for more specific testing until they figured out what killed him.

Shortly after the hospital called the time of Greg's death, he said, his office gave the go-ahead for the organ and tissue donation to proceed because "at the time we didn't think it was an issue." He conceded that he was unable to do a complete autopsy since many of the tissues, bones, and other body parts had been removed.

Blackbourne went over his findings in more detail than at the preliminary hearing, explaining that Greg's lungs were two to three times heavier with congestion than normal, with some pneumonia and blood—all symptoms that he hadn't been breathing properly for a minimum of six to twelve hours. He said Greg also had 550 milliliters, or 18 ounces, of urine in his bladder, which would have felt "very uncomfortable." This was another sign that he'd been semiconscious or unconscious in the minimum six- to twelve-hour range. And yes, he said, the lividity that the paramedics saw when they put him on the board meant he'd probably been dead for about an hour by the time they arrived, so Greg could have been down for as long as fourteen hours, or since around 7:30 A.M.

The delay in getting the blood, urine, and stomach content samples from the Medical Examiner's Office to the sheriff's crime lab, Blackbourne explained, was because Barnhart wanted to maintain the chain of evidence. And because Barnhart wasn't working until November 9, there was a thirty-six-hour wait before they could make the face-to-face transfer. Barnhart, Kristin's mentor and friend, was noticeably absent from the prosecution's list of witnesses at trial.

Asked how he thought the fentanyl got into Greg's body,

Blackbourne answered a slightly different question, which was how such a large amount could have ended up in Greg's stomach. One way was by ingestion, he said, and another way was directly into the bloodstream and then through secretions into the stomach. But Blackbourne said, no, he hadn't been able "with any degree of reasonable medical certainty" to determine how the fentanyl had gotten into Greg's body.

On the morning of day three, the jurors who glanced over at Kristin as they filed into the courtroom to take their seats saw she was wearing a green pantsuit and a woeful expression.

Under questioning by Goldstein, Dr. Theodore Stanley, a fentanyl expert, gave the jury a detailed lesson on the drug.

Fentanyl, Stanley testified, is a synthetic morphine-like opiate. Morphine comes from plants, but fentanyl is made in the lab and is one hundred to one hundred fifty times more potent. Introduced into the United States in 1968 as an anesthetic to produce unconsciousness and supreme pain relief, fentanyl has one serious side effect: it can cause a person to stop breathing.

Stanley, the board chairman of a company working on a more sophisticated fentanyl skin patch, said this was his second foray into fentanyl products. His first company produced the fentanyl lollipop. Because fentanyl is a Class 2 narcotic, highly regulated by the federal Drug Enforcement Agency, he said, these lollipops are available only in hospitals, and the patches only by prescription.

Stanley said fentanyl is odorless and doesn't have a taste "until you use huge amounts of it," such as more than 10 milligrams. When it's swallowed, he said, 65 percent of the drug gets destroyed, so that only 35 percent is absorbed into the bloodstream. There are ways to "fight off" the effects of a fentanyl overdose—shaking a person, yelling at him, or hitting or exciting him would stimulate the brain and central nervous system enough to counteract the depressant effects. Also, if a person has never had fentanyl, he said, he would need less than a regular user to experience the same effects.

For example, Stanley said, if he gave a dose of 4 nanograms per milliliter to people in the courtroom, half of them would be breathing very slowly or not breathing at all.

"What about somebody that had 57 nanograms per milliliter in their blood?" Goldstein asked, referring to the highest level measured in Greg's body, from his heart blood.

"If they were opiate naïve, there would not be anybody in this room who would be conscious, let alone breathing," Stanley said.

Under the law, both sides were required to ask Stanley questions about Greg's blood levels in theoretical scenarios so they didn't have to argue the facts of the case—especially since no one could prove exactly how the drugs got into Greg's body.

After hearing all the different levels of fentanyl in Greg's blood, urine, and stomach identified by the different labs, Stanley summed them up as "a whole lot of fentanyl." In fact, he said he'd never seen such high amounts in a person. He also noted that with fentanyl, blood levels can go up by 20 percent after death.

Based on the high levels of fentanyl found in the stomach, Stanley said, the drug likely was administered in more than one form, possibly through the stomach but also through the bloodstream or skin. He explained how effects of the different forms of administration vary, with injections being fast acting, ingestion less so, and skin patches even less so. Based on the time that Greg was unconscious, Stanley's testimony indicated that he may have had multiple doses of fentanyl over a long period of time before it killed him. The fentanyl, clonazepam, and oxycodone would have compounded each other.

One fentanyl patch alone can take sixteen hours to reach a peak effect, he said, which compares to about five minutes with an injection into the blood, fifteen to twenty minutes for an injection into muscle tissue, and somewhere in between for eating or drinking something containing fentanyl. Stanley said it would take multiple patches to reach the levels found in Greg's blood.

On cross-examination, Eriksen asked Stanley if he was aware that the *Physicians' Desk Reference* said fentanyl has a bitter taste. Stanley said no, pointing out that volunteers given 10 milligrams in his clinical studies for the lollipop did not taste anything.

Quizzed on the properties of succinylcholine, the doctor said the drug was metabolized by the body in five minutes and then was gone without a trace, rendering it undetectable.

Asked how fentanyl could be extracted from a patch and ingested, Stanley said the gel could be squeezed out of the patch and then dissolved in a cup of alcohol. In a powder form, he said, fentanyl citrate could be dissolved in water. In all but 5 to 10 percent of people, he said, a patch didn't leave a mark on the skin after it was removed. After three days, a patch could leave an irritation or red mark on those 5 to 10 percent.

Dr. Jack Stump, an emergency room doctor from Vancouver, Washington, testified on Friday morning of day four. He had a specialty in pharmacology, methamphetamine abuse in particular, and had done clinical research for the Department of Justice that involved the regular observation of addicts.

Methamphetamine, he explained, is in a group of drugs called amphetamines but has a molecular shape that allows it to cause more psychological and physiological effects than most other drugs in that family. Meth causes the heart rate, breathing, and blood pressure to increase, while decreasing the appetite and making users seem jittery, nervous, and anxious. Large quantities can push blood pressure levels to 250. The drug can also cause malnutrition, resulting in dental and skin problems.

But, he said, "in the first two weeks or so of regular use . . . what methamphetamine does for you is give you what's called supernatural pleasure, a pleasure you could not obtain anywhere else in nature. There aren't enough vacations, aren't enough births of babies, not enough pleasant events in life to get remotely close to what methamphetamine can do for you."

After a few weeks of use, however, people no longer get as high as they did at first. Those who try to attain that feeling by using more of the drug find they need that much more just to feel close to normal again. In fact, if they don't use the drug, they will crash and feel depressed. They will also have problems thinking clearly. Chemically, methamphetamine resembles adrenaline, he said, so it causes the same "fight or flight" symptoms, such as dilated pupils, dry mouth, and bad breath.

Typically, a high will last four to six hours in the one-time recreational user and three to five days in someone who is trying to maintain the high with repetitive use. When heavy users come down, they might sleep for two days while their bodies and minds recover. But unlike drugs such as marijuana, heroin, and cocaine, where the body returns to its usual state, methamphetamine changes the brain chemistry.

"People who use, especially repetitive use, don't always return to the person they were before," Stump said.

He said even light users might have trouble learning, demonstrate poor judgment, or experience extreme paranoia, the latter of which can cause hallucinations. In the 1950s, the military fed methamphetamine to bomber pilots to keep them awake, but they found that even these healthy, bright, mentally stable, and physically fit men became paranoid. Also, Stump said, because of tighter government controls on ingredients used to manufacture methamphetamine, makers of the illegal drug have resorted to more toxic chemicals, such as jet fuel, that are less regulated and more available. That is contributing to worsened physical problems, such as enlarged hearts, liver and kidney failure, and brain damage. Facial sores, a common symptom of meth use, are caused when the user scratches an itchy area until he digs a hole in the skin, a symptom known as "meth bugs." Stump said meth users often use other narcotics, such as sedatives or muscle relaxants, to combat such symptoms.

On cross-examination by Eriksen, Stump said low-level users can go unnoticed by coworkers for years at a time, but once the level increases, they often begin to show up late, make mistakes, and let their appearance go.

"Would it strike you as unusual that a heavy meth user would be able to graduate with a B.S. degree in chemistry at the *summa cum laude* level?" Eriksen asked.

"Yes," Stump said, "it would."

When UCSD police Sergeant Bob Jones took the stand later that morning, Goldstein ran him through the items he found in the apartment to establish the chain of evidence, noting the red swipes on the bedsheet and smudges on the carpet—signs that the rose petals were fresh.

Jones said he returned to the apartment the next morning with two officers to make a videotape because he "had some unanswered questions." As Goldstein played the tape for the jury, an eerie silence fell over the courtroom as the camera panned over the empty apartment where the paramedics had tried to bring life back to the body of a young man the night before.

Despite all of his questions, Jones said it wasn't until after Russ Lowe's phone call on November 8 that he finally decided to call in the SDPD's homicide unit for help.

"At the moment I received the telephone call, it caused me to believe this might be something other than what it had appeared earlier and that San Diego probably [should] be brought into the loop," Jones said.

As he did during the preliminary hearing, Eriksen grilled the sergeant to underscore his investigative failures for the jury. Jones repeatedly said he didn't collect the various items of evidence Eriksen listed, including Kristin's diary, because he didn't think they had any "evidentiary value" at the time. He said he left the apartment thinking the death was "equivocal," or uncertain.

Eriksen went on the offensive. "Normally," he said, "when you are investigating an open-ended question like that as to the death of a human being, wouldn't you consider everything around . . . where that person is found to be potentially relevant as evidence?"

"Potentially, yes," Jones replied.

But, no, Jones acknowledged, he did not check whether the phones worked, did not look through the kitchen cabinets, did not inventory the balcony trash cans' contents, did not collect the contents of the plastic cups in the bedroom, did not do any fingerprint analysis, and did not secure the apartment as a crime scene. Jones said he saw no sign in the apartment or trash cans of any baby's breath or cellophane wrapping that would come with a single rose purchased at the supermarket.

Eriksen also pointed out that Jones had changed his description of Kristin's appearance. In Jones's initial report, he said, the sergeant wrote that she "had no visible injuries," that she was "visibly shaking" and "her display of emotions seemed genuine." Yet, Jones had testified that Kristin looked "haggard, disheveled, did not look well, did not look healthy."

Then, in testimony some described as revisionist history at its best, Jones described his initial impressions of the crime scene.

"The apartment was clearly, at least in my estimation . . . staged to look like suicide," he said. "The fact that Ms. Rossum and Mr. Robertson were having an affair entered into the equation that there might be a motive for something other than just a suicide. That's what prompted the call [to San Diego police]."

But Eriksen wasn't going to let him get away with that. "So, after doing your walk-through, your talking to fellow officers, your talking to the Medical Examiner's investigator on the night of November 6 and the early morning hours of November 7, and having returned seven hours later and having done a videotaping session for approximately an hour, your impression was this was a suicide," Eriksen said. "Is that correct?"

"It was still an equivocal death investigation," Jones said. "I wasn't certain that it was a suicide, no, sir."

On redirect, Goldstein had the detective run through all the reasons why he hadn't taken all the measures that Eriksen suggested. They all boiled down to the same excuse: Kristin Rossum had lied to him. If he'd known Kristin had hidden meth in the kitchen, he said, that she was having an affair with the man standing outside on the landing, and that she'd bought a red rose at Vons that afternoon, his actions would have been completely different.

"That would have been . . . concrete information that I could've shared with San Diego [Homicide] and would've called them immediately that evening," he said.

Following up on Eriksen's question about the cellophane

wrapping, Goldstein called Jones's attention to some plastic wrap in one of the photographs of the balcony trash cans and asked him to describe what he saw. From where the jury was sitting, the plastic looked like it could have been the kind of wrapping a single rose would come in. But on closer inspection, it was not so clear.

"There are cardboard remnants; a plastic bag; a cellophane bag, wrapper, if you will, of opaque color; and then a clear cellophane bag or cellophane substance," Jones said.

Finally, Goldstein asked Jones to confirm that he'd asked—and received—Ralph Rossum's permission to tape their conversation on the morning of November 7. This conflicted with Ralph's testimony during the preliminary hearing that he didn't know they were being taped. The tape clarified that Ralph did, in fact, give his permission.

After only a half day of testimony, Thompson let the jury go home for the weekend.

On Monday morning, October 21, Bertrand de Villers took the stand and characterized his brother as a "very rational, calm, levelheaded" guy who "didn't get into despair over problems" but rather would overcome them. Greg was not one to act rashly or introduce drama into a situation, he said. Greg was very honest and was determined to finish projects he started. He also enjoyed his job tremendously. The only time Bertrand had ever seen him use drugs was the night before his wedding, when he smoked some pot.

"I think he felt he shouldn't have done it," Bertrand said. "He didn't really like it."

During the trip to Mammoth the July before Greg died, Bertrand said he and Kristin stayed behind at the campsite and talked while Greg went on a hike. She didn't mention any marital problems, and Bertrand didn't notice any strain between her and Greg. When they were sitting around the campfire, Kristin said she had gotten interested recently in meth's effect on the brain. Bertrand didn't know about her drug history at the time and thought nothing of her remark until later.

Goldstein asked Bertrand a long series of questions about the conversation he, Jerome, and Kristin had in her apartment two days after Greg's death. Bertrand said she mentioned cough syrup as something Greg might have taken, and that she'd spilled most of the bottle. Kristin also told him that the paramedics took a bottle of Vicodin that had been in the house.

"You didn't ask her about cough syrup, did you?" Goldstein asked.

"No, she brought it up," Bertrand said.

Bertrand said he didn't know Jerome was taping that conversation but learned later that they'd talked longer than the transcript showed because the tape ran out. He said he still didn't know anything then about Kristin's drug problem and felt they should go and leave her be, so he left the apartment, but Jerome stayed another twenty or thirty minutes.

"I was pretty emotional," Bertrand said. "I felt Kristin was having a hard time and it wasn't right to ask her any more questions. . . . I believed everything she told me at that time. I no longer believe what she said."

By day six of the trial, the jurors showed signs of collegiality, smiling and talking to each other in the hallway before the bailiff called them into the courtroom. Kristin was wearing beige slacks with a blue shirt and a camel-hair blazer, her hair pulled back in the usual ponytail.

Goldstein played the tape of Kristin's 911 call after the bailiff distributed a transcript to the jury.

"Is he in bed?" the dispatcher asked.

"Yes," Kristin said.

"Can you take him off the bed and put him on the floor?"

"Oh God!" Kristin said as she followed the dispatcher's instructions.

If there was a thudding sound of Greg's body hitting the floor, as she and her parents had described, it was not audible in the courtroom.

Kristin cried as the jury listened to her breathy and distraught voice, talking to the dispatcher through her tears and counting up to fifteen for the compressions on Greg's chest. Ralph Rossum, who was sitting with his wife in the gallery behind Kristin, put his hand to his face, while Constance gazed off into space with a sad expression. When the tape was over, Kristin, still crying, turned and locked eyes with one of the reporters sitting in the gallery behind the prosecution table.

Just before the lunch break, Diane Bartlett, the emergency room nurse who spoke to Kristin at the hospital that night, took the stand.

They had worked on Greg for ten or fifteen minutes before calling the time of his death, she said, then she went out and talked to Kristin in the reception area. Kristin's male coworker was at her side but didn't say anything during their brief conversation. Before she told Kristin that Greg had died, Bartlett asked her a few questions to see if she could get any more information before Kristin grew too emotional to answer.

Kristin said Greg hadn't been feeling well the day before and she'd taken the day off work. When Bartlett asked why Kristin hadn't called for help sooner, Kristin told her she'd been monitoring his condition. When Bartlett asked again why Kristin hadn't called the paramedics, Kristin said she wasn't in the area, then came back and found him unresponsive.

"I thought it was extremely odd that someone would have a family member that they thought might have . . . overdose[d] and they did not call the medics at the time they thought this occurred," Bartlett said.

The nurse said she asked Kristin if she and her friend wanted to view Greg's body in the hospital room. Kristin said she did, but Michael chose to stay outside. This, too, surprised the nurse.

"Most people who have someone there to support them, truly support them, will go back. Sometimes it's very difficult for loved ones to go back and see their deceased family members by themselves," so usually the friend will go with them so they don't feel alone, she said.

But what surprised her most, she said, was that Kristin's coworker kissed her before she went to view her husband's body. Hendren asked her to describe the kiss.

"The kiss was more of—it was not like my coworker would kiss me," Bartlett said. "It was more of an intimate kiss. . . . I had never seen a coworker kiss a coworker like that before."

When Bartlett asked for Kristin's phone number, she said, Kristin gave her Michael's cell phone number.

Eriksen followed up on the kiss during cross-examination as he tried to show that Michael and Kristin were not trying to hide their affair. He also questioned the nurse's memory.

"When he kissed her, you say intimately, he kissed her on the cheek. Is that right?" Eriksen asked.

"No, sir," she said. "He kissed her on the mouth."

Eriksen asked if she remembered telling a detective that Michael had kissed Kristin on the cheek.

"I don't believe I said that, sir," she said. "I may have said he kissed her and it was not on the cheek. It was definitely a kiss that was lip to lip, sir."

Eriksen asked if she remembered telling the detective that it was more of an embrace than a kiss. No, Bartlett said, she told the detective she saw them kiss and embrace.

"Okay," Eriksen said. "So Detective Rydalch got that wrong then?"

"Yes," she said.

The next witness, Bethany Warren, a social worker for the hospital, testified that she saw Michael touching Kristin supportively in the reception area. He held her hand, put his arm around her, and rubbed her arm while she answered Warren's questions.

Warren said Kristin told her that she and Greg had been fighting throughout that day and that she'd gone out "to cool off for a while." Kristin indicated that another coworker from the Medical Examiner's Office would be coming to the hospital and she wanted to leave before then. Warren collected phone numbers from both of them. When she called Michael a couple of weeks later to check on Kristin's welfare, his wife answered and sounded incensed.

"She used very strong language, indicating that there was an inappropriate relationship between the defendant and this man," Warren said.

"When you say 'very strong language,' what do you mean?" Goldstein asked.

"I don't think I can say the words in here," she said.

"Sure you can," Thompson interjected.

"When I identified myself and said who I was and that I was trying to reach Kristin Rossum, she said, 'You tell that whore not to call here,' and yelled that into the phone. I ex-plained myself quickly to say who I was and why I was trying to reach her and clearly I wasn't privy to the information that she had. She used words like 'whore' and 'bitch,' etc."

On cross-examination, Eriksen asked Warren if she might have confused the day that Kristin said she and Greg had been arguing. Warren said she thought Kristin had said the day of Greg's death, but she didn't have her notes with her.

Warren said Kristin looked visibly shaken and was crying after they informed her that Greg had died. She accompanied Kristin into the room to see Greg's body while Michael stayed outside in the hallway. She said Kristin seemed distraught and was "kind of wailing" as she touched Greg on his chest and then laid her head on his torso.

On redirect, Goldstein had only one poignant question.

"When she put her head on his chest, did she say she was sorry?" he asked.

"Yes, she did," Warren said.

"Nothing further," Goldstein said.

Led by Hendren, Bob Petrachek, the computer forensic examiner, explained to the jury how he gathered, searched, cross-checked, and then organized all the electronic data collected in this case. Petrachek's testimony was so full of technical detail that at times it was difficult to follow. But a number of important points got through.

After reading every single e-mail from Kristin to Greg and Michael, and vice versa, Petrachek said he felt like he knew them all pretty well. And, by tracking their Internet browsing interests and poring through their computer files, he also learned a great deal about their finances, friends, family, and leisure activities.

Greg, he said, never mentioned fentanyl or liking opiates in any of his e-mails. He never did any Internet research on fentanyl, and his e-mails showed no signs of him being depressed, suicidal, or infatuated with flowers or roses. A dozen or more e-mails between Kristin and Michael mentioned meeting at the Willows.

Hendren distributed two big white binders to the jury. One contained computer snapshots of the Web sites Greg, Kristin, and Michael visited. The other contained e-mails considered relevant by the prosecution, printed on different shades of pastel paper and arranged chronologically. The first one in the pink section, which contained e-mails between Michael and Kristin, was dated May 12, 2000, shortly after the CAT conference in Los Angeles. That was the message in which Michael forwarded photos of his sister's wedding to Kristin and said he was thinking of and missing Kristin.

Hendren read aloud a sampling of Kristin's e-mails to illustrate her pattern of lying and seeking the attention of men outside her marriage. Noting that many of her and Michael's work e-mails had been recovered after being deleted, he read enough to give the jury a taste of how the two lovers' emotions intensified as their affair progressed.

Petrachek said he was able to track the whereabouts of Kristin, Greg, and Michael based on when they used the Internet on various computers, sent e-mail, or saved files to the hard drives. When investigators couldn't prove exactly who was using the computer, other evidence helped to identify the user. For example, Petrachek said, someone signed on to Kristin's work computer for about seven minutes around 2 A.M. on Tuesday, November 7, when she was driving back to Claremont with her father. Hendren later said the prosecution had other information that placed Michael in the office at that time, when he believed Michael typed in Kristin's password and attempted to change or delete files on her computer. Amborn also found a file on Michael's computer titled "KR the night," which, dated November 10, contained a chronology of the night Greg died. Petrachek testified that Kristin's work computer was booted up with her password a second time on November 7, around noon, and was used for forty-five minutes while Kristin was still in Claremont. The last time prosecutors believe she used that computer was on November 6 at 9:24 A.M., when a file was saved to her hard drive.

Petrachek said a file containing information on four drug-testing centers was saved on Greg's iMac computer at home on Saturday morning, November 4. And on December 31, 2000, and January 2, 2001, someone accessed Michael's Hotmail account, using the Compaq computer in Kristin's apartment, to read messages Nicole and Michael sent to each other.

Under cross-examination by Eriksen, Petrachek acknowledged that there were gaps in the e-mails because the county hadn't backed up the data properly, so certain e-mails couldn't be recovered. Eriksen asked if Petrachek thought the county contractor's inability to recover the e-mails was accidental or intentional. Petrachek said he couldn't say it was deliberate because such a loss wasn't entirely unusual with backup tape, which wasn't the most reliable medium.

Petrachek said he hadn't seen any e-mails from Kristin asking Michael about fentanyl or that mentioned harming or drugging Greg.

Laurie Shriber, whose kids grew up playing with the de Villers boys in Palm Springs, testified that Bertrand had called her son at 1 A.M. on November 7 to tell him the sad news. Shriber said she was "truly beside" herself and wanted to hear what happened directly from Kristin, so she called her later that day.

"She said he took an overdose of over-the-counter sleeping pills," Shriber recalled.

"Are you sure she said 'over-the-counter sleeping pills'?" Goldstein asked.

"She did not say 'overdose,'" Shriber said, correcting herself. "She said 'over-the-counter sleeping pills.'"

Shriber said she was "uncomfortable with the conversation" because Greg wasn't one to take drugs, not even Tylenol.

John Knowlton, Vons's corporate security manager, confirmed that his company's computer records showed which items Kristin purchased on November 6, including the single rose.

But on cross-examination by Eriksen, Knowlton acknowledged that Vons sold single roses in many different colors and their system didn't identify the color at the register.

"Is there any way possible you can investigate further and determine the color of that rose that was purchased in this transaction?" Eriksen asked.

"No, sir."

Kristin got to spend her twenty-sixth birthday on trial for murder, listening to her first diary being read aloud by Detective Laurie Agnew, who noted that none of the entries mentioned Kristin's drug use or the men she was e-mailing—Joe Rizzo, Dan Dewall and Michael Robertson.

Goldstein asked Agnew to read the entry in which Kristin complained about Greg's lack of support and his obsession with whether Michael was going to the SOFT conference in Milwaukee. Agnew also read the one in which Kristin complained about her mother's guilt trip after Kristin tried to call off the wedding.

The detective identified the torn-up items Michael threw away in the trash after police searched his apartment in Hillcrest, including a photo of him and Kristin's Rottweiler puppy. Agnew read aloud one of the ripped letters, in which Kristin told Michael their souls had "melted together."

As Goldstein played the tape of Kristin's police interview

for the jury, Kristin cried and fidgeted in her chair. Afterward, Eriksen raised the same issues with Agnew that came up when the defense previously tried to get Thompson to throw out the tape. Agnew acknowledged that when she called Kristin to ask her to come down for an interview, she didn't say they were looking at her as a suspect, nor did she tell Kristin that she might want to consider consulting an attorney. Agnew also acknowledged that she didn't tell Kristin she was being videotaped during the interview, though she noticed that Kristin kept looking at the camera, which was in plain sight.

Eriksen asked if Agnew ever thought to have Greg's hands tested for the presence of rose petal residue. No, Agnew said. They did test the empty vial of fentanyl citrate for fingerprints, she said, but were unable to get an identifiable print. She also acknowledged that she found no evidence that Kristin would have benefited financially from Greg's death.

The defense attorney tried to punch through the motive the prosecution gave Kristin for murdering Greg by asking Agnew to confirm that early on Kristin had admitted to police many of the facts being used against her—her past use of clonazepam, oxycodone, and methamphetamine; her love for Michael; and her admission of Greg's ultimatum. But Agnew maintained the prosecution's position—that Kristin told police more half-truths than whole truths and only admitted to the incriminating facts of the case after being confronted with evidence she couldn't deny.

Eriksen and Goldstein used their questions to Agnew to argue the semantics and veracity of Kristin's statements to police, whom she initially told that she had only a "drug history" and was having only an "emotional relationship" with Michael.

* * *

Jerome de Villers was the prosecution's last witness. His memory was better than it had been during the preliminary hearing, but he still seemed to have trouble recalling certain things. Goldstein had to tell him several times to listen to his questions more carefully. Loebig objected, saying the prosecutor was leading the witness.

At the end of the day, after the jury had been excused and the courtroom had mostly cleared out, Goldstein broached a subject with Thompson that had been troubling him for days. The judge didn't realize that a reporter or two were still lingering in the back of the courtroom.

Throughout his opening statement and during witness testimony, Goldstein said, Kristin had been making comments such as "I didn't do that" and "No, I didn't." It irked him, to say the least.

"Your Honor, I have been fairly patient during this trial about the defendant's conduct in this courtroom," he said. "In twelve or thirteen years experience in doing cases, I've had very few defendants chipping at me during opening statement. I think defense counsel noted it. I don't know if Your Honor did."

"I did," Thompson replied.

"It's been going on throughout this trial," Goldstein continued. "This last witness, the defendant became actively engaged with during examination, shaking her head, saying, 'No.' It's audible now. I realize she's going to take the stand. She's entitled to her own defense. I don't object to that. My witnesses have not gone up and directed anything at her personally. They have been instructed not to do it. She's interfering with the court process. She's done this throughout the trial. I ask the court, even though this is our last witness, to tell her to stop, knock it off. This is the victim's brother who is on the stand, who doesn't deserve this type of conduct."

Loebig tried to deflect Goldstein's allegations. "Your

Honor, I'm going to accept that in absolute good faith. But I was sitting next to her. While I was busy writing, I didn't observe much other than her reacting to some degree and trying to communicate with me, so I trust the court's judgment."

"Anything further?" Thompson asked.

"No," Goldstein said.

"All right," Thompson said definitively, looking straight at Kristin. "Don't do it again."

"Yes, Your Honor," Kristin said.

"You are smiling at jurors," Thompson told her. "It's absolute bullshit. I think it's really hurting you. I don't think they're buying it for a second. It's up to you. You are to have no contact with any witnesses one way or the other."

As Thompson started walking toward his chambers, Kristin stood up defiantly, hands on her hips, her mouth agape, and started crying. She turned to Loebig, touched her hands to her chest, and said something like, "I didn't do anything."

Thompson could not believe Kristin would even try to deny the inappropriate behavior. He'd seen her smiling at jurors, and he'd seen her shaking her head or mouthing "No" at them while witnesses were testifying. He'd never seen such a conscious and improper effort to manipulate a jury, but it fit with the testimony about the behaviors Kristin had exhibited throughout much of her life. And now that she'd made him angry by trying to avoid responsibility for her actions, he was going to put a stop to it.

"Don't sit there and tell me you are not doing it," Thompson exclaimed. "I'm not a fucking idiot."

Kristin didn't say another word.

The judge stormed out of the courtroom and was barely in his chambers before he heard his outburst being reported on the radio. It was all over the television news that night and again in the morning. The broadcasters couldn't repeat the expletives, but they made it clear that he'd thrown curse words at the defendant.

The next morning, before the bailiff let the jury back into the courtroom, Thompson apologized for his language, but not for the admonition he felt that Kristin and her parents, who were about to testify, needed to hear.

"Before we get started today, I think it's appropriate for me to address my comments of yesterday," Thompson said. "I want to apologize for the use of the words for those who were present at that time. I will not apologize for the message that was delivered. The activity that was alluded to was taking place, and it needs to stop."

Looking over at the defense table, Thompson said, "I frankly didn't think your client was getting it when I admonished her at the beginning of the trial. I think yesterday she got the point. That was my only intention. To the extent anyone was offended by the language that was used, I apologize. But, as I said, I will not apologize for the message."

With that, he told the bailiff to let the jury in for the morning session.

"Got a count? Roll 'em."

Jerome testified that he went over to Kristin's apartment after Greg's memorial service on November 12 and noticed that all of the photographs of Greg had been taken down. He also didn't see any of Greg's clothing around. But he was most upset by the sight of Greg's sandals in the trash outside. This seemed strange, Jerome said, because Kristin seemed to be in such a hurry to leave her parents' house on November 7 so she could return to the apartment and be close to Greg's things.

On cross-examination, Loebig tried to establish that Kristin looked healthy and drug free when Jerome saw her at

Aaron Wallo's wedding several weeks before Greg's death. He also tried to show that Greg had not been open with his family or friends about his marital problems or how upset he was about them, but rather had been doing his best to pretend everything was fine.

Jerome said he wasn't surprised when Greg said at the wedding that he wanted to buy a house. Kristin had mentioned wanting a dog, and an apartment wasn't the place for one. But Jerome said he was surprised when Greg said he was thinking of having kids.

"And isn't it true that Kristin Rossum, when she was seated at that table and heard Greg say he wanted kids, said, 'I'm not ready now'?" Loebig asked.

"She didn't say it like that," Jerome said. "It was after that. I talked to her. She said, 'I'm not ready to have kids.' "

The first Jerome said he heard of any marital problems was on November 7 at the Rossums' house, when Kristin mentioned that Greg had been upset because she wouldn't stop seeing a "past relationship."

"Greg had never mentioned anything at all about a trial separation or a suggestion by Kristin they separate and live in different residences?" Loebig asked.

"No," Jerome said.

"Do you remember stating at the preliminary hearing, 'My brother was taken by her. He was always defending her. I'm not sure if he was in love—addicted or really in love with her. He stopped hanging out with Chris and I. It was only the two of them'?"

Jerome said he couldn't remember saying that but acknowledged that the transcript said he did.

On redirect, Goldstein steered the focus back to Kristin's efforts to hide her affair and renewed meth use. No, Jerome said, Kristin never admitted to having an affair with Michael Robertson or to using drugs again.

"I actually asked her if she was using drugs because it

was pretty obvious to me that she was using something," Jerome said. "She told me she was skinny because of ephedrine. . . . I think it's a weight loss medication."

Loebig tried to get Jerome to say that Kristin wasn't trying all that hard to hide her drug use. But Jerome didn't bite.

"Did you know, from your study in biology, that ephedrine is a precursor to amphetamine or methamphetamine?"

"No," Jerome said.

Chapter 18

Kristin's defense attorneys started putting on their case on October 29, day eleven of the trial. They led off with Douglas O'Dell, the UCSD police officer who videotaped the apartment with Jones the morning after Greg died and then tried to call Orbigen to retrieve a copy of the voice mail Kristin said she'd left the day before.

By presenting evidence that Greg's number seemed to be the first one the public would try at Orbigen, Eriksen characterized Kristin's call to Greg's voice mail as an innocent mistake, not the sinister act portrayed by the prosecution. Stefan Gruenwald later said that the public would actually reach Terry Huang if they called Orbigen's main number.

Next up was Bob Sutton, the autopsy room supervisor who was in charge of watching over the refrigerated blood, urine, and stomach specimens before they were hand delivered to Frank Barnhart at the sheriff's crime lab to send out for toxicology testing.

Eriksen used Sutton to establish that security over those samples was just as lax during the thirty-six hours they sat in his refrigerator as it had been over the drugs stored in the toxicology lab.

"Who had access to the contents of that refrigerator?" Eriksen asked.

"Anybody that would have a key to the building," Sutton said.

"So virtually anybody that worked there in some capacity above, say, student worker, who were issued keys in connection with their employment, could have gotten into that refrigerator and into the contents. Is that correct?"

"They could have, yes," Sutton said.

Eriksen was implying that anyone—including Kristin or Michael—could have snuck in, possibly at night, and spiked the samples with a lethal amount of drugs other than fentanyl to throw off the toxicology tests, but that no one did.

On cross-examination, Hendren tried to protect his chain of evidence from taint and asked Sutton to run through the steps he'd taken to track the whereabouts of the samples. Sutton described where he'd placed them in the refrigerator and said he saw no indication they'd been moved or opened.

Hendren then switched his focus to Michael's unusual behavior the morning after Greg died. Michael was typically happy-go-lucky and joking around, Sutton said, but that morning he was "very serious and just seemed fidgety." He'd never seen Michael that way before.

"How many times, from the time Mr. Robertson started up until November 7, did you see Michael Robertson present a case?" Hendren asked.

"None," Sutton said.

"So the very first time that you ever saw Mr. Robertson present a case at a meeting was on November 7, the day after Mr. de Villers died, with Mr. de Villers's case?"

"Correct."

* * *

Next, Eriksen called Jean Wilson, a realtor from Del Mar, a small coastal town just north of La Jolla. Eriksen called Wilson to back up Ralph and Constance's story that they were so worried about Greg's bizarre behavior during dinner at the Prado that they went out the next morning to look for a condominium for Kristin. But Wilson's testimony seemed to help the prosecution's case more than Kristin's.

Wilson testified that the Rossums walked into her office and "said that they were looking for a property, probably a town house . . . perhaps a semiretirement home for them." They asked what coastal properties were available, and she gave them listings for several small cities to the north.

Eriksen asked Wilson whether the Rossums told her they were looking for a place for their daughter or that she would live there until they retired. No, she said, they didn't.

On cross-examination, Goldstein asked what kind of mood the Rossums were in that day.

They seemed to be "very relaxed" and enjoying themselves in Del Mar, she said. "[It] seemed like life was very pleasant for them."

"One of the reasons why they said they wanted to move down here was to be closer to their daughter. Is that correct?" Goldstein asked.

"Their daughter and son-in-law," Wilson said.

"They specifically said *and* their son-in-law, is that correct?"

"Yes, they did."

On redirect, Eriksen asked Wilson whether she showed the Rossums any properties. No, she said, they took the listings, and she assumed they would drive around and look at them on their own. She left them a message the following week but didn't get a response until a week after that. Constance called to say she was sorry, but they'd decided not to

relocate after all because their "son-in-law had died unex-
pectedly."

Kelly Christianson, Kristin's supervisor in the Oligo group
lab at TriLink, had attended the preliminary hearing and sat
with the Rossums. Now, called as a witness for the defense,
she smiled when Eriksen asked if she knew Kristin, whom
she described in glowing terms.

Christianson said she was among those who interviewed
the young toxicologist and decided that based on her resume
and their first impressions, they would hire her right away to
run the HPLC machine and do other lab work. Kristin, she
said, was friendly to everyone and always upbeat. When
Kristin's coworkers talked about getting rid of a particularly
annoying colleague, Kristin was the one who urged them to
give him another chance.

Eriksen asked Christianson the same series of questions
he would ask most, if not all, the character witnesses who
would testify in Kristin's defense. Had she seen Kristin lose
her temper, act violently, or talk about hurting anybody? No,
Christianson replied.

On cross-examination, Christianson acknowledged that
Kristin didn't mention during her interview that she was
fired from the Medical Examiner's Office.

"She indicated to you or suggested to you that she quit
the Medical Examiner's Office?" Hendren asked.

"I guess so, yeah. I don't know."

"Did she put on her resume that she had been fired from
the Medical Examiner's Office?"

"I doubt it, but I don't recall."

"How did you know that she wasn't telling you the
truth . . . ?"

"Because I now know why she left," she said.

"How do you know?"

"What the newspapers say."

"Is that how you found out?"

"I think so first, yeah."

Hendren then ran her through a long series of questions concerning all the other things Kristin had neglected to tell her or had lied about during the six months they worked together and later, when Christianson visited her in jail. The cumulative effect of the questions and answers was an impression that Christianson knew very little about the true Kristin Rossum. Hendren and Goldstein would use the same tactic with the other character witnesses.

Hendren whittled away some more at Christianson's credibility in his closing questions, creating the inference that she and Kristin had talked about what she should or would say on the stand.

"When was the last time you saw her before court?" Hendren asked.

"Last Thursday."

"Where was that at?"

"We had dinner."

"Who else was present?"

"Just the two of us."

"And you knew at that time that you were going to be a witness here today, right?"

"No, I didn't."

Pressed further, Christianson admitted that, yes, she had filled out a form for the defense attorneys and knew she might be called as a witness.

"Okay," Hendren said. "So you knew it was a possibility."

"Uh-huh."

"Is that a yes?"

"Yes."

* * *

Kathy Vanella, whose daughter, Jessica, knew Kristin from TriLink, testified in her gravelly voice that Kristin lived with them after she was released on bail. Kristin smiled at her while Vanella testified, explaining that she first met Kristin at a softball game soon after Jessica started working at the biotech company.

"This little voice in the crowd asked everybody to please not swear, and it was Kristin," she said.

Vanella said Jessica met Kristin several months before she went to jail, where Jessica visited her every other Sunday. After Kristin got out, she was working at TriLink only a few days a week, so she'd stay two nights at the Vanellas' house and then drive home to Claremont. This went on for about four months. Vanella said she never asked Kristin about the case, nor did she read anything about it in the newspaper because she considered it Kristin's personal business. She wanted Kristin to feel safe with her and free from the judgment of others. Kristin, in turn, never volunteered any information.

On Thursday nights, Vanella said, a bunch of friends raced cars around a track on her forty-acre property. Everyone liked Kristin.

"She's always gracious and pleasant and friendly and eager to talk to everybody," Vanella said.

Like Christianson, Vanella expressed her very firm belief that Kristin was a peaceful, good, and honest person who would never hurt anyone. On cross-examination, Hendren tried to chip away at this perception, asking whether Vanella's position would change if she knew Kristin had repeatedly lied.

"Would it affect your opinion of her truthfulness if the defendant had lied to homicide detectives from the San Diego Police Department during an interview regarding what her relationship was with a man named Michael Robertson?"

"No," Vanella said.

But no matter what example he offered, Vanella would

not be moved. The same went for a series of questions about Kristin's methamphetamine use. Hendren asked if her perception would change if she knew Kristin had been hiding methamphetamine in her apartment or had been smoking it at the Medical Examiner's Office. No, no, and no, Vanella said. When he was finished, Hendren left the impression that Vanella would cling to that mindset, regardless of any evidence presented to her.

On redirect, Eriksen tried to maintain his witness's credibility by asking her to recall a recent conversation they'd had in his office.

"Did I tell you some of the lies or supposed lies that have been attributed to Ms. Rossum?"

"Yes," she said.

"Did we tell you that all of those supposed lies that are attributed to Ms. Rossum are disputed in this case?"

Hendren objected. "Hearsay," he said.

"Sustained," Thompson said.

"Nothing else," Eriksen said.

Hendren attempted several times to follow up with questions to show that Vanella would stick to her beliefs even in the face of proof—such as Kristin's videotaped interview and e-mails—but Eriksen continued to object. Finally, Thompson let the question go, and Vanella said, no, her position would not waver.

"I'm not her judge," Vanella said.

"That's why your opinion is—you are not going to judge her, right?" Hendren asked.

"I have opinions about that, and I'm sure that you don't necessarily want to hear them," she said.

"Thank you," Hendren said.

Not all of Kristin's loyal followers were men.

* * *

When Jessica Vanella took the stand, Kristin smiled up at her as well. If Thompson noticed Kristin's interaction with the defense witnesses, he did nothing about it.

Jessica said Kristin stayed with her and her mom Wednesday, Thursday, and sometimes Friday nights, too. During their evenings out together, whether they played company softball, or went bowling, dancing, to a movie, or for a picnic at the beach, Jessica saw no mean streak in Kristin.

On cross-examination by Hendren, Jessica said the only time she knew Kristin had lied concerned her termination from the Medical Examiner's Office. Hendren asked Jessica to recall a form she filled out for the defense, which included a section about Kristin's honesty and truthfulness.

"What you said was, 'The majority of people I have talked to have doubts about her honesty and truthfulness'?" Hendren asked.

"Yes, I did say that," she said.

When it came to Kristin's methamphetamine use, Jessica echoed her mother's sentiment.

"Have you talked to her about her methamphetamine use?" Hendren asked.

"No, it's none of my business," she said.

Hendren asked Jessica a similar series of questions, such as whether knowing that Kristin was hiding meth in her apartment on the day Greg died would change her opinion about Kristin being peaceful.

"Taking drugs has nothing to do with being peaceful or not peaceful," she said. Jessica acknowledged that some drugs could make a person paranoid or violent but said, "I think that you have to be violent for the drugs to bring out violence in you."

Like her mother, Jessica said she wouldn't change her opinion of Kristin, even if she knew Kristin had tested positive for meth the day she was arrested on suspicion of murdering Greg.

Finally, Hendren asked Jessica about her contact with Kristin and Michael and Kristin's comments about their perfect relationship. Yes, Jessica said, Kristin told her they were going to be together once Michael got divorced. Jessica also said that more recently, Kristin had started seeing a man "other than Michael Robertson."

The next character witness was Professor William Tong, who characterized Kristin as "one of the best undergraduate students [he'd] ever met." He said she was a team player who worked well with others and never missed any classes or appeared to be under the influence of drugs.

On cross-examination, Hendren introduced an ethical issue that would become a focus during his questioning of Constance Rossum: the basis of Kristin's cumulative grade point average, which led to her graduating *summa cum laude,* and the fact that her very poor grades from Redlands were not included on her application to SDSU. After a few rounds of objections by Eriksen, Hendren was finally able to get his question in.

"Would you consider it dishonest if somebody completed [their college] application and did not list their prior educational institution attended?" Hendren asked.

"Yes," Tong said.

Eriksen led Melissa Prager through the chronology of her friendship with Kristin, whom she described as "my dear friend." She stated as fact the story about how Kristin met Greg and about how he had "kind of taken her out of her misery that she was in in Mexico."

Prager said that when she first met Greg, he seemed con-

trolling and possessive of Kristin. Then, later, after he and
Kristin were married, she recounted how Kristin confided
that she'd fallen in love with Michael, and she wanted to
move out of her apartment and leave Greg.

On cross-examination, Goldstein pounded on the fact
that Kristin never did leave Greg, not in August, September,
October, or November.

"The relationship ended because Greg had died, correct?"
he asked.

"Correct," she said.

"There wasn't anything physically preventing her from
leaving, was there?"

"Not that I know of," Prager said.

Prager also talked about watching Kristin's appearance
go from better than she'd ever seen her to the other end of the
spectrum—very thin, with black circles under her eyes—all
within the five months leading up to January 2001.

Goldstein had Prager answer a number of questions that
revealed that she, who'd known Kristin much longer than the
other character witnesses, wasn't all that close to Kristin, either. He underscored that point by noting that Kristin never
tried to call Prager before she ran away from school in Redlands.

"She didn't pick up the phone and call you and say, 'Listen
I'm having a lot of trouble; I'm out of here'?" Goldstein
asked.

No, Prager admitted, she and Kristin didn't have the type
of relationship where Kristin shared very personal things
with her.

Goldstein reinforced the point by showing that Prager
had accepted on its face the story she'd heard from her own
parents, through the Rossums, that Kristin had disappeared
into Mexico for some length of time.

"How long was she in Mexico for?" Goldstein asked.

"It was a long enough period of time where—I think it

was a few months. Might have been a—sometime between three and six months, I think, from what I understand."

"Was she going to school down there?"

"I have no idea," Prager said. "It was during the time—she was gone. I didn't know where she was."

Goldstein pointed out that Prager had testified earlier that she couldn't think of an instance where Kristin had lied to her. So Goldstein reminded her that she'd also testified that she'd tried to confront Kristin about her apparent drug use.

"So, when you had confronted the defendant and said, 'Are you doing drugs?' and she said, 'No,' that was her response, correct?"

"Right."

"You didn't believe her, did you?"

"I didn't know," Prager said. ". . . I could never tell when she was using drugs."

Loebig walked Constance Rossum through Kristin's childhood and how it all started going bad when Kristin began using drugs. Constance admitted that initially, she wouldn't have known a drug if she "fell over one," but over time she became more aware of what was going on and realized she needed to intervene. The problem was, she said, there "wasn't much help available," so she talked to a counselor and took Kristin to her pediatrician for a physical.

"At some point did you contact the Betty Ford Center in the Palm Springs area?" Loebig asked.

"Yes, I did," she said. "That was later."

But Constance said she never enrolled Kristin in that program or took her to a drug counselor. Instead, she and Ralph decided to have Kristin graduate high school early and enroll at the University of Redlands. Things were fine until "the same people who had given her problems at Claremont revisited her at Redlands," she said.

"By 'revisited,' what do you mean?" Loebig asked.

"I meant tried to sell her drugs—sold her drugs," Constance said.

"Let's not blame everybody else here," Loebig said.

Again, Loebig asked Constance if she and her husband tried to do something to help Kristin. Constance didn't answer the question directly, saying they only suspected Kristin was using again but had no hard evidence.

As Constance described Kristin's first call home after running away, she started crying and wiped her eyes with a tissue. Her voice broke again as she talked about the family's reunion with Kristin in January 1995. She paused and apologized before continuing. When the afternoon session ended a few minutes later and Thompson excused the jury, Constance asked if she could stay in the witness box to compose herself. Thompson agreed.

The next morning Loebig picked up where he left off, with Kristin trying to get her life back together.

Constance said Kristin moved into an apartment in Point Loma with a female coworker she'd met at California Pizza Kitchen, one of three jobs she held over the summer before enrolling at SDSU that fall. In May 1995, Constance said, she called the apartment complex where Greg lived, La Jolla Del Sol, and got Kristin a lease for an apartment she moved into in June. Greg moved in with Kristin in October, she said, and the lease was switched over to his name.

Constance said she and Ralph decided they wanted to help the couple financially because Kristin loved Greg. Loebig submitted as evidence three pages detailing the estimated $74,425 worth of rent, tuition, furniture, and gifts, including wedding presents, the Rossums spent on the couple over the years.

"Did Greg or Kristin come to you and ask you specifically for each of these monies, or were they given on your and Ralph's initiative?" Loebig asked.

"It was our initiative," Constance said. "They would remind us if the rent check was late."

Meanwhile, Constance said, Greg explored different job options, looking to Ralph for advice as a "surrogate father." She noted that Greg failed his entrance exam for a job with the state Department of Fish and Game before he finally got a job with Pharmingen.

To back up her claim that Greg had a bad temper, Constance described an argument over wedding invitations that broke out between him and his mother one Thanksgiving at the Rossums.

"She wanted to be listed as Dr. and Mrs. Yves R. Tremolet de Villers. Greg started shouting at us," she said. "He didn't want his father at the wedding. He wanted nothing to do with him." She said they told him it was Marie's decision and asked him "to at least be civil" to Yves.

Then, a month before the wedding, Kristin came home crying and said she wanted to cancel it.

"I gave her the wrong counsel, I'm afraid. I thought it was best at the time," Constance said. "I thought she had wedding jitters because for five years, we'd been saying, 'Kristin, is this wise?' "

Two days before the ceremony, Constance said, Greg threw a fit when he heard that his father was planning to attend the rehearsal dinner and wedding.

"He went into a rage and started shouting at me, saying, 'Let's call the whole thing off,' " she said.

Constance said she tried to calm him down. "I just said, 'I'm so sorry. I should've been more sensitive.' "

Constance gushed as she talked about Kristin's graduation and her being honored as most outstanding chemistry student. Greg was there, too, and so proud of his wife, although she recalled that he seemed a little sad and mentioned that Kristin was "so much smarter" than him.

Just after New Year's Day in 2000, Constance said, Kristin

reiterated the same old concerns about her relationship with Greg and said she thought she'd made a mistake by marrying him.

Soon after Kristin returned from a camping trip to the Grand Canyon with Greg, Kristin told her that she'd applied for a job with the Sheriff's Department. Constance noted that Kristin had done this without talking to her and Ralph. As a result, she said, Kristin wrote on the application that she'd been arrested. Kristin "went overboard in her honesty," because she'd never actually been arrested, Constance said.

"So the incident that you had back in high school where the police were called didn't result in Kristin being formally arrested?" Loebig asked.

"Not at all," Constance said.

In September, she said, Kristin's marital problems came up again when the two of them were having lunch in La Jolla.

"She was definitely leaving Greg, though she described how hard it was given the problems he was having with his family—his mother's eviction, her ill health, and all these other things—and wanted to do it in a way that would not hurt him," Constance said, recalling that she told Kristin, " 'You can't stay with a man simply because you don't want to hurt his mother's feelings. That's very kind of you.' "

Constance said she was concerned about how Greg would react to Kristin moving out, but she wanted Kristin to leave, nonetheless.

"We said, 'We can move you out today'," Constance said, but Kristin wouldn't have it. Quoting Kristin, she said, " 'Mom, I'm his whole life. I've been with him five years. I can't say, "Goodbye, have a nice life".' "

Constance described the last Friday night when she, Ralph, Greg, and Kristin had dinner together, saying Greg's voice quavered as he talked about the single red rose in the apartment.

Greg's demeanor "was strange and scary," she said. "He was facing me. He said, 'Of all the roses, that single rose survived.' Ralph and I looked at each other. We thought, 'Wow, you are waxing poetic there.' "

"Was Greg animated when he said that, like you just demonstrated?" Loebig asked.

"Oh, yes. Greg was very proud of a B+ he had in acting class at UCSD," Constance said.

During dinner at the Prado, she said, Greg shouted at them as he complained that his mother still had not received copies of the wedding photos and that he wanted a consultant he'd hired at Orbigen "to burn in Hell." She said she had to "shush" him to keep his voice down and then kicked Kristin under the table so they could talk about Greg's odd behavior in the ladies' room.

"It's really bad," she recalled Kristin telling her. "I'm going to be leaving him next week."

Constance said she offered to take Kristin away with her and Ralph that night. "Please let us be there when you leave," she told Kristin. She then asked Kristin if she had any objection to them looking for a place she could rent from them, and Kristin said no. She said they ended the evening with a walk in Balboa Park because they didn't want Greg "to feel abandoned."

The day after Greg died, she said, the de Villers family came to their house to discuss arrangements for his body. Asked if a consensus decision was made at the breakfast table about whether to bury or cremate Greg's remains, Constance said, "Marie asked that he be cremated because of the ashes going to heaven."

Finally, Loebig asked Constance about Greg's resume. He noted that there was no mention of his two years in junior college and asked Constance, as a college professor, whether it was a common practice to omit "a subpar year" in school.

Hendren objected. "Speculation, relevance," he said.

Thompson sustained the objection.

Loebig continued, asking Constance whether in her experience on various academic acceptance committees such omissions were common.

"You want to put your best foot forward," Constance said.

"And maybe leave out some of the weaker things?" Loebig asked.

"Like grade point average, for example," Constance said.

On cross-examination, Hendren pointed out for the jury that Constance made a career of marketing, advertising, and promotions. He also got her to acknowledge that, yes, she understood the importance of giving accurate information to the national media, because it was disseminated to millions of people.

Hendren walked Constance through the argument she and Ralph had with Kristin in 1993 over the drugs in her backpack. Constance reluctantly admitted that her daughter was not honest or trustworthy when she was on drugs. For example, when Constance found a plastic bag of white powder in their mailbox, she said Kristin told her she didn't know where it came from.

"So she lied to you again?" Hendren asked.

Loebig objected, and Thompson told Hendren to restate the question. Constance acknowledged that no one else in the house but Kristin was using drugs at the time.

Constance also acknowledged that she and her husband "got physical" with Kristin that day in 1993.

"[Ralph] hit her on the upper arm about four or five times, correct?" Hendren asked.

"You will have to ask him that question," Constance replied.

"You know that he hit her, correct?"

"He grabbed her arm as she was attempting to run away," she said.

"At the time the police came, she had pronounced bruising to her upper arm, right?"

"Yes, as he tried to restrain her."

Constance admitted that she slapped Kristin in the face but said it was only because Kristin had tried to hit her first. Yes, Constance said, she was very angry with her daughter and worried. She said she didn't "go around generally slapping people."

"That's because your daughter was out of control at that time, right?"

"She did things we could not handle," Constance said.

"She lied to you, right?"

"About the meth."

"She deceived you, correct?"

"About the use of meth."

"About where she was going, who she was hanging out with, what kind of things were in her containers like her backpack, right?"

"Yes."

"You were so upset with your daughter, Mrs. Rossum, that you actually called her a slut and said she was worthless, correct?"

Constance said she didn't recall saying that, regardless of what was stated in the police report that Hendren showed her. It made no sense, she said, because she didn't equate meth use with the word "slut."

"So you didn't call her a slut?"

"No."

"You didn't say she was worthless?"

"I don't believe so. Doesn't make sense."

Then, further contradicting the police report, Constance said Kristin did not try to cut herself with a knife in the kitchen. Kristin ran upstairs and locked herself in the bathroom, she said, "called herself worthless and [said] how sorry she was and that we'd be better off without her."

"Did she try to do anything in the bathroom?"

"I understand that she said, 'Perhaps I'll slit my wrists,' but she didn't. . . . There were no marks."

Hendren showed Constance her own statement to Officer Larry Horowitz in April 1993, which again contradicted her testimony.

"It says, 'I don't know if Kristin told you, but she tried to cut her wrists with the knife first,' " Hendren said.

"No, I didn't say that," Constance said.

"The sentence goes on . . . 'then some razor blades,' " Hendren said. "Did you say that part, that she tried to cut herself with a razor blade?"

"I understood when she went to the bathroom that she had some razor blades there. But she didn't do it. You can look at her wrists, hold them up to the light. There's nothing there."

If Kristin's cuts had been bad enough, she said, she would have taken her daughter to the hospital.

"The officer is wrong with that as well?"

"It could be."

Constance said she didn't recall making one other statement quoted in the police report: "I was afraid of what would happen if we had taken her to a hospital. We don't know who to go to or what to do." She said the statement didn't make sense.

Hendren asked if it was fair to say that Constance knew that if she took Kristin to the hospital for an attempted suicide, that it "wouldn't look good, would have a bad appearance."

"Appearance means diddly if you have a child who is hurt," Constance said. "That's why I called the police in the first place."

Hendren moved on to Kristin's other misdeeds, such as stealing her mother's credit cards and personal checks, to establish a pattern of thievery to support her drug habit.

Asked whether she ever checked Kristin into a residential drug rehabilitation facility, Constance restated her efforts to call the Betty Ford Center and counselors but acknowledged that she never enrolled Kristin in any formal program. Instead, she said, Ralph took Kristin to a twelve-step family group.

When they discussed Kristin's second brush with Officer Larry Horowitz in 1994, Constance again denied that Horowitz arrested Kristin that afternoon, even after being shown the police report that contradicted her testimony.

If Kristin wasn't under arrest, Hendren asked, under what authority could Horowitz handcuff her and take her to the police department?

"I don't know," Constance replied.

Moving on to Kristin's grades at Redlands before she ran away, Constance admitted that her daughter had a bad fall semester, earning a 1.67 grade point average. Although she said Greg's resume was incomplete because it didn't include his junior college years, she said Kristin's low grades at Redlands didn't have to be factored into her cumulative grade point average at SDSU because her credits weren't transferred. So, that's why she didn't list them on Kristin's SDSU application.

Until then, Goldstein had not known it was Constance who'd filled out Kristin's application, purposely omitting the previous coursework, which the form said was required, even if the courses weren't completed. He was shocked and befuddled at how arrogant the Rossums were, that they felt that they could "just do anything."

After discovering that Kristin had run away from Redlands, Constance said she never told police that she and Ralph were worried that Kristin was depressed and might try to kill herself. But again, Hendren had a police report that indicated otherwise.

Constance acknowledged that Kristin had problems with her and their relationship while she was using drugs. Kristin wanted to make her own decisions, do things her way, while Constance felt she knew better, especially when it came to the friends Kristin chose for herself.

"And she thought you were controlling and manipulative, right?" Hendren asked.

"You will have to ask her," Constance said. "I don't know."

Hendren went over Constance's earlier testimony about Kristin's false claims, including the one that she was living with a girl in Point Loma when she was truly living with Greg.

"Now, as far as your daughter's honesty and when she tells you the truth, if you don't approve, she doesn't like to tell you the truth, isn't that fair to say?"

"No," Constance said.

Asked if Kristin ever told her about the affair with Michael in the eight months before she was arrested for drugs in January 2001, Constance said no.

"I wouldn't tell my mother if I were having an affair," she said.

Moving on to Constance's various comments to the media, Hendren asked about her interview with *Good Housekeeping*. Constance admitted telling the national women's magazine that Greg "realized he was going to be buried in debt, because the money from us wasn't going to be there." Asked if she knew how much Kristin spent on drugs in 2000, Constance said no.

Constance also admitted telling the magazine that Greg had hepatitis B, "because his eyes and things were rejected." But, no, she said, she didn't recall hearing Dr. Blackbourne testify during the preliminary hearing that Greg didn't have hepatitis B, and, no, she didn't try to verify that Greg had the disease before she mentioned it to the magazine.

Loebig objected, saying Hendren was badgering the witness. Thompson overruled the objection, so Hendren continued, getting Constance to admit that she also suggested to the magazine that Greg had either used infected needles or slept with someone else to contract the disease.

"It wasn't true, was it?" Hendren asked.

"I thought so at the time or I would not have said it," she said.

Hendren showed Constance a series of photos from the last supper they had with Greg the Friday night before his death and noted that she, Kristin, and Ralph were all smiling. Asked to explain the discrepancy between the mood reflected in the photos and her testimony about that night, Constance responded that they had tried to make it a pleasant evening.

Asked to respond to the real estate agent's description of her and Ralph's mood the next day, Constance said she would have described it as more subdued. And no, she admitted, she wasn't so concerned about Greg's behavior that she needed to call Kristin to check on her in the days after the dinner. Nor did she try to insist that Kristin stay in a hotel for her safety.

On redirect, Loebig asked Constance where she got the information that Greg had hepatitis B. Initially, she said, from the discovery papers. But she admitted that she'd learned in the last few days that she was wrong.

Brent Rossum, who was twenty-three, testified that Kristin's e-mails, starting in May 2000, were the first he heard about unhappiness in his sister's new marriage. He said he kept those e-mails to himself until after Greg's death.

When the de Villers family came to the Rossums' house after Greg died, he said, it was Greg's family who wanted Greg cremated.

"Our family's position was it's going to be Kristin's decision and the de Villerses' decision. I think the general consensus after that meeting was that he would be cremated."

Under cross-examination by Goldstein, Brent said he drove Kristin back to her apartment that night and stayed with her while she called Greg's friends to let them know he'd died.

"I was on the couch and heard every phone call," he said. "It was awful."

In the months before Greg died, he said, he remembered Greg acting more insecure about his relationship with Kristin. But he said Kristin never mentioned her affair until January 2001.

"We were all in the kitchen," he said. "She told my family about it. We were very displeased with her."

Marguerite Zandstra, Constance's sister and Kristin's godmother, flew in from Crown Point, Indiana, and was dead set on testifying. But, overcome with nerves, her performance proved far less effective than the defense had hoped.

Zandstra said she babysat Kristin when Constance's family lived in the Chicago area and saw them on holidays regularly after that. Zandstra and her mother went to California right around Kristin's twentieth birthday, when coincidentally, they learned Kristin had just gotten engaged.

Zandra said she was excited to meet Greg, but he ended up getting sick, taking something, and going to sleep. So, she didn't meet him until the day before the wedding, when he told her that if his father showed up at the reception, he'd "kill him."

The next time she saw him was in August 2000 at the Rossums' twenty-eighth wedding anniversary party, where Greg played a videotape of Kristin dancing *The Nutcracker* over and over, probably for a good half hour.

On cross-examination, Zandstra acknowledged that she knew Greg only from meeting him on three separate days. She admitted telling a defense investigator that Greg had "a very wimpy handshake," was immature, and "didn't act like a man." She said it was odd that Greg, "being a man," didn't know how to shoot a gun better. And she also confirmed that she'd told the investigator "it was strange that Greg acted like it was his wedding day rather than Kristin's."

"You've talked to your sister extensively about your niece's situation here and the things that have happened, right?" Hendren asked.

"Correct," Zandra said.

The next day Eriksen called Dr. Mark Wallace, a pain management expert who had treated patients with fentanyl, to try to show that Greg must have known he was drinking the fentanyl because it has a bitter taste.

Wallace explained that he prescribed fentanyl in patches or in a newer form, which came packed in 2 grams of sugar and was placed between the teeth and cheek so it dissolved. Some of the drug flowed into the bloodstream through the cheek, and some was swallowed, he said, a method that allowed twice as much of the drug to be absorbed than other forms of ingestion. Contradicting the testimony by prosecution witness Dr. Stanley, Wallace said the fentanyl comes in this sugary form because it is "very bad tasting" and bitter on its own.

"Have you ever read or heard from any source at all that fentanyl does not have a bitter taste?" Eriksen asked.

"No, I have not," Wallace said.

On cross-examination, Goldstein said that "obviously, 'bitter' is a subjective word. Let me ask you, how bitter is fentanyl?" Wallace said he didn't know.

Goldstein asked if the taste could be masked by alcohol, a salty soup, cough syrup, or cold medicine. Wallace said he didn't know about alcohol, but he thought the bitterness "probably could" be masked by soup or cough syrup.

Goldstein tried to get Wallace to agree with Stanley that

the amount of fentanyl in Greg's body was so high that it must have been taken in more forms than just orally, because it isn't absorbed effectively in the stomach. But Wallace said he couldn't comment on that because it wasn't his area of specialty.

"All I can say is that the blood levels are very, very high. Very high. The stomach contents, I'm a little confused. With the concentrations in the stomach, I would expect them to be higher if it was ingested."

But Wallace did agree with Stanley on one point. He'd never seen a level as high as in Greg's blood.

Kristin's youngest brother, Pierce, testified that besides Kristin, he'd spent more time with Greg than anyone else in his family. They'd gone golfing several times a year, and sometimes Pierce had gone hiking and camping with Greg and Kristin. He'd also seen them at least once a month during visits in Claremont or San Diego.

Pierce said Greg used to play video games with him and let Kristin "do her own thing." But about five months after the wedding, he said, Greg's behavior changed.

"He stopped playing video games, stopped . . . talking with the family," he said. "Just became overprotective of Kristin and very clingy."

He said Greg would follow Kristin from room to room, "wouldn't let her have her own space," and wouldn't play with Pierce unless Kristin was included. He said he, too, saw Greg repeatedly watch *The Nutcracker* videotape during the Rossums' anniversary party. As Greg acted more and more like this, he said, Kristin would get annoyed, and she and Greg would argue.

"Did she ever talk to you about that?"

"No, she didn't," Pierce said. "But you could notice. You could tell."

The last time he saw Greg was in Claremont two weeks before he died.

"I tried to get in a bit of conversation with him, and he would kind of turn away. Kind of made me feel bad, I guess. He plays with me all this time before, and then he doesn't."

On cross-examination by Goldstein, Pierce acknowledged that Greg was not the only one who wanted to watch Kristin dance *The Nutcracker.* The Rossums liked to watch the videotape at Christmastime, too.

Ralph took the stand next. He appeared tired, with dark circles under his eyes, and was thin in the face. His jacket hung loosely on him, as if he had lost weight since he'd purchased it.

Ralph and Constance testified almost as if they were the same person, often using the very same words and phrases, the same observations and points of detail.

More so during this trial than most others in his courtroom, Thompson tried to put himself in the shoes of the defendant's parents, empathizing with what they must be going through. He thought it must be very difficult for the Rossums to watch their pretty, bright, and talented daughter on trial for murder, wondering what they might have done wrong or differently to avoid such an outcome. To him, this was a classic example of how meth use could destroy a person's life.

Questioned by Loebig, Ralph explained that after he and Constance realized Kristin had a drug problem, a woman from the Betty Ford Center came to their house to discuss doing an intervention, but they decided against that option because Kristin was no longer denying her drug use. So, that's why they picked the eight-week family group program Ralph took her to in Chino.

After Kristin met up with Greg, Ralph said, he and Constance moved Kristin and some furniture into the apartment in Point Loma. They were dismayed to find out some time later that Kristin was still living with Greg.

"I consider myself a devout Episcopalian, and I don't approve of premarital sex," Ralph said.

But since Greg had helped her get off drugs, he said, he and Constance figured this was a better alternative than Kristin's life before she met Greg. They were able to persuade the young couple to delay getting married until they'd finished school, and then Kristin expressed reservations to him right before the wedding.

"I told her, 'Look, if you want out, it's going to be complicated to tell Greg that you don't want to marry him when you are actually already living with him. If you want, I'll come down with a truck, and we'll move you out right now to just make it easy,' " he recalled saying.

But, he said, Kristin decided to come to Claremont and talk to her parents instead. To his surprise, she brought Greg. She talked with her mother while Ralph had his own conversation with Greg. Ralph said he'd also had some discussions with Greg about trying to reconcile with Yves, at the doctor's request.

Loebig asked if Greg ever shouted or acted out during these conversations about his father.

"Yes, yes," Ralph said. ". . . It was one issue that I really saw sort of passion and flaring anger."

In the spring of 2000, Ralph said, Constance told him Kristin's marital doubts had resurfaced. Kristin was complaining that Greg was telling her "she should quit her job. She should not pursue a professional life." Meanwhile, Ralph said he was giving his son-in-law career advice. Greg had a chance to be a manager at Rush Legal, but Ralph told him he should take advantage of his college degree in biology and go for the Fish and Game job. When Greg ended up at the biotech firm, Ralph thought it was a "good fit."

Asked about their last supper Friday night with Greg,

Ralph repeated the same story about the last surviving red rose, this time inserting the word "melodrama" as he described Greg's behavior. Twice during dinner, Ralph said, they had to tell Greg to "keep it down, he was making a scene" as he talked angrily about the fund-raiser he'd known since high school who had defaulted on his contract with Orbigen. Ralph said it was "not characteristic" for Greg to say the things he did, such as he was "going to ruin his life forever."

Later in the car, after they dropped off Greg and Kristin, Ralph said Constance told him about her chat with Kristin in the ladies' room. Greg's behavior made them so nervous that they agreed they should go look for a condo for their daughter the next day. He said they met with the agent and then drove around for about three hours looking at condos in the $200,000 range from a list she'd given them.

Two nights later, Ralph said, they got the call from Kristin at the hospital, and he jumped in the car right away. On the drive back that night to Claremont, where they arrived around 4:15 A.M., he said, Kristin seemed to be sincerely mourning the loss of her husband, lapsing into "periods of just wailing and grief."

"It was the most unpleasant car trip I have ever had," he recalled.

Ralph said he got up around 7 A.M. to get his son to school and that's when Sergeant Jones called.

Goldstein started off his cross-examination with some light questions that seemed innocuous on their face, but it soon became obvious that he was trying to lead Ralph down the path of impeachment. As with the other defense witnesses, Goldstein's strategy was to take a fact and build around it, forcing Ralph to come around to his premise, and getting him to concede to certain facts that he couldn't deny. Goldstein also employed the same tactics that he had during the preliminary hearing—intentionally yelling at the professor and questioning him from behind, so that Ralph had to twist around in the witness stand to see his attacker. Goldstein wasn't sure the jury liked his approach much, but he felt that his plan to undermine Ralph was working.

Yes, Ralph replied, he had a very close relationship with his daughter, and it caused the family emotional turmoil to hear about Kristin's drug use in 2000 and her affair with her boss. Yes, it was difficult to see her on trial for murder.

Ralph wanted to protect his daughter, right? Goldstein asked.

"Depends on what it means to protect my daughter," Ralph answered carefully. "For example, I did participate in calling the police on her when we knew that there was this meth problem. So protecting her, in one sense, could be just to hide it. Protecting her in another way would be to do the right thing."

Goldstein moved on to Ralph's earlier testimony about Greg's description of the rose at Kristin's apartment before dinner at the Prado, as he segued into one of the trial's most crucial exchanges with a defense witness and trapped Ralph into contradicting himself.

"In essence, anybody who came into the courtroom and had a different interpretation about Friday night, November 3rd, would be lying," Goldstein said. "Isn't that correct?"

Loebig objected, saying the question was vague and irrelevant. Thompson sustained the objection only because Ralph had already essentially answered the question in the affirmative.

Goldstein had blown up the transcript from Ralph's 7 A.M. conversation with Jones, when the sergeant asked Ralph if he'd learned anything new from Kristin on the drive home. Goldstein put up the exhibit behind Ralph, where the jury could read it, and said he'd play the audiotape as well. He addressed his questions to Ralph using the title "doctor," a title of respect used in academic circles for those who have earned a Ph.D. But his tone was anything but respectful.

Starting with the way Ralph described that last Friday night, Goldstein asked, "Did you not utter the words, 'We had a very pleasant evening'?"

Yes, Ralph admitted.

Goldstein read aloud Ralph's response to Jones's question about whether he'd seen the rose petals on the bedroom floor. Goldstein noted that Ralph had said yes, and explained that Greg bought Kristin a dozen roses for her birthday, which they'd talked about when they were in the apartment Friday night.

"You said, 'At this point, I think there were—I think two roses still on the kitchen table.' Did you say that there were two roses still on the kitchen table?"

"I said that," Ralph said.

"And you stated that 'My wife commented on how beautiful the roses were.' Is that true? Did you say that statement?"

"Yes."

"And the remark was, 'Yeah. And he bought them for my birthday, and here it's a week later and they are still—they remain in such good shape.' Did you say that?"

"Yes."

"The person that said that, 'And he bought them for my birthday, and it's a week later, and they are still in such good shape,' was your daughter Kristin Rossum, correct?"

Ralph's face went blank. He asked Goldstein to repeat the question.

Essentially, Goldstein was showing Ralph that he'd told Jones something quite different from what he'd been telling the media and had just testified to the jury—that, in fact, it was Kristin, not Greg, who made the comment about the last surviving red rose.

But Ralph didn't seem to be getting it, so Goldstein approached the same point in different ways. Loebig objected, saying Goldstein was being argumentative. Goldstein went over the transcript with Ralph several times, hammering the point home for the jury.

"You did not tell the detective that Greg de Villers had waxed poetically about a rose. Is that correct?"

"No."

"When the detective was talking to you, you never said that Greg was acting bizarre on Friday night?"

"No, I did not."

"And you knew that you were talking to a police officer who was asking you questions about your son-in-law's death, correct?"

"I thought this was a follow-up call where he was asking me what I had learned in the drive up the night before," Ralph said. "That's how he opened the interview."

Goldstein pointed out that Ralph had testified at the preliminary hearing that he thought he'd been talking to campus security, and that was why there was some "confusion about the statement." He asked what difference it would have made to Ralph if he'd been talking to a San Diego police officer instead.

Ralph said he "would have given much more fulsome and expansive responses. If the officer really wanted to interview me and get all that I knew, he wouldn't have begun the interview knowing I had to leave to bring my son to school."

"So the officer did a poor interview of you?"

Ralph retorted that the officer could have called back. But, no, he admitted, he didn't call Jones back, either.

"We thought that Greg had died of—of a combination of medications. It might have been intentional. It may have been a cry for help, inadvertent. I was fatigued. I had about an hour's sleep. I had to bring my son to school. I assumed that this was a quick follow-up conversation because he's saying that really what he wants to do is then get access to Kristin's apartment. . . . I had no idea that this was anything more than an unfortunate death, and there was no need at that point to try to besmirch Greg's reputation. He's hardly dead, and I'm going to start speaking ill of him and how he's behaved to somebody that I . . ."

Goldstein continued along the same lines, finally asking if part of the reason Ralph gave a truncated answer was because he didn't realize he was talking "to real police officers," as Goldstein put it.

Yes, Ralph said, that was true.

To illustrate his point, Goldstein raised the level of drama in the courtroom to new heights. He asked the judge if he could be excused for ten seconds to get an exhibit. He went into the hallway outside the courtroom, and when he came back, he had a live one.

He walked back in with Jones, dressed in a suit and tie, and two of the uniformed officers who had responded to Kristin's 911 call. Officers McIntyre and Garcia, who wore badges on their shoulders that read "police" in capital letters, stood at attention in front of the partition between the gallery and the area where the defense attorneys and prosecutors sat. Goldstein reminded Ralph that he'd met these men in Kristin's apartment the night Greg died.

"They were in uniform, correct?"

"Yes. I recall that."

"You saw the uniform," Goldstein said. "They have guns on their belts. They have badges and patches. They looked like police officers, didn't they?"

"Lots of campus security people are armed and wear badges," Ralph quipped.

"When you saw them, they weren't merely just fixtures in the apartment? They were doing things, correct?"

"I cannot attest to what they were doing," Ralph said. "That they were doing something, that makes sense."

When Goldstein asked Ralph about his conversation with Kristin about the rose petals that night, Ralph admitted that he asked Kristin in the car if the petals on the bedroom floor were the same ones from the rose they saw on Friday night. He said she replied, "I don't know. I threw the roses away Sunday night. But they could have—I put them in the trash on Sunday night, but they could have been retrieved."

Ralph admitted he didn't tell Jones any of this because he didn't think it was relevant. Again, he said, he was half asleep when Jones called. Goldstein said the jury could make up its own mind when they heard his taped interview with Jones after the lunch break.

Later in his testimony, Ralph admitted that he and Constance didn't tell the real estate agent about any perceived problem between Greg and Kristin, only that they wanted to buy a place to be "near [their] daughter and son-in-law," because that seemed like "an appropriate response" at the time.

"You were saying you wanted to buy a second home, but that wasn't true," Goldstein said. "Is that correct?"

"I saw no need to tell the real estate agent why we wanted a second home," Ralph said.

Ralph admitted that it was Kristin's attorney, not Kristin herself, who told him after her arrest in January 2001 that she'd been using meth again.

Goldstein asked Ralph about the comment he made to the *Los Angeles Times* that Kristin had not had a drug problem since high school. Ralph said he hesitated to say that newspapers always print the truth.

"I may have said that, but I'm not certain. . . . It would have been put behind her until we knew that she had that problem in January. I think I was referencing at the time of Greg's death."

Later, when Goldstein asked him about the article again, Ralph conceded that he made the statement even though he knew she'd used drugs in college.

"People involved in meth do some dangerous things at times, correct?" Goldstein asked.

Loebig objected. "Calls for speculation," he said.

Thompson said Ralph could answer the question as to his knowledge or opinion.

"We have heard testimony in the trial concerning meth," Ralph said. "I learned a lot about it sitting through this case. I never saw violent conduct by Kristin. I saw agitated and resistant conduct, but never aggression or violence toward anyone save herself."

Asked about the incident when Kristin grabbed a knife and then slashed at her wrists with razor blades, Ralph said they were superficial cuts, "superficial enough that it seemed not real suicide as much as melodramatic."

"Melodramatic and maybe a cry for help?" Goldstein asked.

"Things were desperately wrong at that time," Ralph said. "She did not go through with the act of suicide, did she, obviously?"

"No," Goldstein said. "So it's fair to say it was a feigned attempt at suicide, correct?"

"I would put it more an attempt at a feigned suicide," Ralph said. "It didn't strike me that it was a failed genuine effort. It was melodramatic."

Ralph admitted that yes, Kristin could be self-destructive while on drugs. Deceitful and uncontrollable, too. He also grudgingly conceded that threatening suicide with a knife or razor blades were violent acts by Kristin, but only against herself.

On redirect, Loebig asked Ralph if he believed that Jones had been conducting a criminal investigation when they spoke on the morning after Greg's death. No, Ralph said.

"Have you made statements to various media interviewers that you thought were true that turned out later to be mistaken?" Loebig asked.

"Absolutely," Ralph said. "If I were to draft this document now, I would be in a better position."

After Constance and Ralph finished testifying, they appeared rattled, battered, and just plain tired. Eriksen attributed their reaction to anger and frustration from being grilled so mercilessly by the prosecution, particularly Goldstein. Loebig had no idea the two of them would get "so crossed-up on cross-examination." If he'd known how they were going to fare, he would have advised them not to testify. But they had been determined to do so.

The problem, Loebig said later, was that "they thought they were smarter than everyone else they were dealing with, including the DA. . . . They would not accept the significance of the evidence against her [Kristin]."

Chapter 19

Word had leaked out that Kristin was about to testify, so not knowing exactly how long her father would be on the stand, the reporters pulled in extra bodies to hold places in line outside the courtroom, which was as long, if not longer, than at the start of the trial.

Finally, at 3 P.M. on Thursday, October 31, Loebig called Kristin to the stand. She took three deep breaths and stared imploringly into the row of reporters in the gallery behind the prosecution. Her eyes were already red and brimming with tears, her lips pulled tight with anxiety.

Loebig, employing his calm and low-key demeanor, eased into his direct examination with simple questions about Kristin's early memories. Kristin was so nervous, her voice shook as she spoke, but she soon began to relax and her tone evened out.

Kristin cast her childhood and adolescence in a golden yellow light of happiness and success, repeatedly saying she "loved" this or that and characterizing various parts of her life as "wonderful." Her tone changed and she started to cry, however, as she described the confrontation with her parents over her drug use in 1993. After they found the drugs in her backpack, she said, she remembered grabbing a knife in the kitchen and then a razor blade upstairs.

"I felt devastated that my parents had known this," she said. ". . . I didn't know how to deal with the situation. I just—I wanted them to see how sorry I was."

Loebig asked if she'd made up her mind to get off drugs at the time, or if she was planning to ignore her parents and keep using meth. Kristin said she wanted to stop and did so for at least a few months, maybe four or five, until just before her senior year started that fall.

"I mean, you never want to get back into that kind of despair, hopelessness, helplessness," she said.

Loebig asked for more details about her relapses, though he skipped over the incident in 1994, when her mother called the police and Kristin was arrested. Instead, he had her describe the twelve-step program in Chino, how she started college at Redlands, and then how she began using meth again at a party during the fall semester.

"At that party, did you buy meth, or were you offered it and you took it?" Loebig asked.

"I was offered it, and I took it," Kristin said.

Asked how often she used meth after that, she said, "It might have been half a week, a week, a few days before I went to this person the next time. And before a big exam, I thought I could study harder, work better, not realizing my limitations and how quickly that would snowball into more regular use. . . . Probably by midsemester I was using every day."

Loebig asked her why she ran away from Redlands when she knew it would cause her parents "immediate concern." Kristin started crying again. Goldstein objected, saying Loebig was leading the witness. Thompson overruled his objection.

Kristin's voice rose to a high pitch as she answered Loebig's questions. Stopping to blow her nose, she said she had a friend call her parents around Christmastime to tell them she was okay.

"But you didn't talk to your parents over Christmas?" Loebig asked.

"I didn't," she said.

Kristin said she took the train down to San Diego to get her "act together," checked into a motel in Chula Vista, then took a two-minute trolley ride to the Mexican border, where she met Greg and his brothers. She said she and Greg spoke French to each other and "kind of hit it off from there." When Greg offered to let her stay with him that night, she accepted.

"We were both very interested in one another, and it felt safe," she said. "I didn't want to feel alone."

About a week later, she said, Greg told her he loved her. Loebig asked if she said she loved him, too.

"I believe I reciprocated," she said. "I don't know. I don't remember specifically. But it's hard not to say 'I love you, too' when someone says, 'I love you.' "

When she told Greg about her meth problem about a week later, she said, he told her he wanted to help her get off the drugs. She acknowledged that she took the checks from Greg's roommate, Chris Wren, but said she didn't try to use them.

"You can't use someone else's check, anyway," she said.

As the trial broke for the day, Kristin remained in the witness box, blowing her nose. The next morning was a Friday, so everyone was prepared for a half day in court.

Loebig started off by asking Kristin about her drug use, the three jobs she worked that summer, and the apartment in Point Loma her parents thought she was living in. Kristin admitted she never stopped living with Greg. She said she got clean for a while but started using again after she was hired at California Pizza Kitchen.

"Did you have some problem in that job that resulted in your being fired or let go?" Loebig asked.

Yes, Kristin said, she was late several times and "made errors in a lot of my billing transactions. It resulted in my termination. . . . I made a lot of mistakes in that job in terms of the credit card billing especially. But I didn't take the money to buy meth. I used my tips to."

Greg was angry that she had relapsed, she said, but he stuck by her and helped her get clean again. They were best friends and spent all their time together.

"When we first met, the circumstances were so intense and tumultuous, I really needed the steady support that he was able to offer me," she said.

But over time, she said, the dynamics of their relationship changed, and she wondered whether she would be with him if she hadn't been on drugs when they met. She said she loved Greg very much, but she didn't know if she was *in* love with him. She was also concerned about his estrangement from his father and how it would affect children they might have down the road.

"He had told me the history of his family," Kristin said, "and how he resented his father for what he had done to his mother, the domestic violence and—"

Goldstein interrupted with an objection. "Lack of foundation, unresponsive," he said.

Thompson sustained the objection on the second grounds, saying any such alleged statements by Greg could be used only to establish their effect on Kristin, not to establish whether they were true. So far, no other witness had mentioned anything about domestic violence in Greg's family.

About six weeks before the wedding, Kristin said, she shared her doubts about marrying Greg with her parents and tried to back out. She talked to her father over the phone, then decided to visit her parents in person. She said she wanted to go alone, but Greg insisted on coming with her. Kristin said Constance told her that "relationships do change over time and . . . maybe I was expecting too much in terms of what it's like to be in love." So, in the end, Kristin decided to go through with it.

In the summer of 1997, she got a job as a student worker for the county Medical Examiner's Office and found it fascinating, especially after discovering Patricia Cornwell's novels, in which the protagonist, Dr. Kay Scarpetta, a chief medical examiner in Richmond, Virginia, helps the FBI solve murders.

After graduating from SDSU in December 1999, Kristin said, she'd gained confidence and was thinking about who she was and what was important in life.

"I think that Greg felt very threatened by that," she said.

They'd been happy for the first six months of their marriage, she said, but then Greg became "clingy" and was less willing to give her more time for herself. She felt them withdrawing from each other, and in January she told Greg she needed more personal space.

When she and Michael met, she said, smiling, they "hit it off right off the bat just in terms of how we got along. I think we took to each other very quickly." Initially, they talked about their likes and dislikes, but their conversations soon led to more intimate matters, including their respective marital problems.

"Were you attracted to him?" Loebig asked.

"I sure was. I—I remember distinctly the moment I first saw him," Kristin said.

The first time they were in a social setting together was at a farewell party for a colleague at the 94th Aero Squadron that spring, she recalled, but Greg was there, too. Shortly after that, she and Michael had their first outing alone, when they grabbed a sandwich at lunch. He started sending her personal e-mails in early to mid-May.

Loebig asked when she first slept with Michael, if she could remember. She said she believed it was in June, by which time she was already in love with him.

"It was very romantic, very exciting, very passionate," she said.

Kristin said she told Greg in June or July that she'd developed very strong feelings for her boss. Greg got angry and demanded she give him Michael's phone number. Then, "absolutely irate," Greg called Michael and "told him expressly never to talk to—well, not have any inappropriate contact with his wife, stay away from me."

Loebig asked if Greg demanded to know whether she'd slept with Michael. No, Kristin said, but Greg assumed that she had. He went to bed, devastated, for a couple of days and wouldn't talk to her.

"I was devastated, too," she said, adding that it hurt to see someone she loved feeling so much pain.

Moving on to the SOFT conference, Kristin said she was very excited at the opportunity to give her first professional paper. Michael had some "personal problems" that made him unsure at times whether he would be able to go with her to Milwaukee, but things worked out in the end. She admitted they took the same plane, stayed in the same hotel, and had sex over the course of the six-day conference.

"Were you trying to hide your relationship with Michael Robertson at that conference?" Loebig asked.

No, Kristin said, but she was trying to be discreet so as not to embarrass her husband. Once the conference was over, she said, her feelings for Michael were even stronger, and she knew her marriage would be ending soon.

"I couldn't put up a false front any longer, much longer," she said, correcting herself.

Then, in testimony that conflicted with e-mails Greg and Kristin sent each other on Thursday, November 2, she said she and Greg decided to meet at home for lunch. She was reading one of Michael's love letters when Greg walked into the apartment.

"As Greg was coming in, I put it in my back pocket," she said. "He became suspicious of me and basically wrestled me to the ground to get the letter. He read the letter and was infuriated by it and was storming around."

Kristin said she took the letter from him and tried put it through the shredder because Greg threatened to show the letter to her superiors as proof of the affair. But since the machine was broken, the letter didn't go all the way through. So, she said, Greg retrieved it with tweezers and spent hours trying to tape it back together.

She said she and Greg called their offices to say they needed to take the rest of the afternoon off for personal reasons and spent that time arguing about the state of their marriage. She said she asked for a trial separation, and Greg accused her of doing drugs again.

"During this argument or, for that matter, during any argument you had had with Greg, he never struck you, did he?" Loebig asked. "He didn't slap you around or anything like that?"

"No, but—" Kristin said.

"But what?"

"But in the moment when he entered the room and wrestled me down to the floor for the letter, he almost struck me, and I was just blown away by that," Kristin said. "And he said the words that 'He didn't want to turn into his father.' "

She said she showed Greg some listings she'd gathered— for apartments for herself and for some counselors they could see as a couple and possibly individually as well, then they went to bed around 9 or 10 P.M.

The next night they'd already planned to go to dinner with Kristin's parents, and so they went to the neighborhood supermarket to buy the ingredients for gin martinis, not knowing that a martini was a "summer drink." When her parents arrived, Kristin said, they didn't feel like having a summer drink after all, so they took only a few sips before they all left for the restaurant.

Despite Goldstein's aggressive cross-examination of her father about the last surviving rose, Kristin repeated the same story her parents had been telling since she was arrested.

"I indicated that Greg had bought me, I think, a dozen and a half—I now know it's two dozen roses—beautiful red roses— for my birthday. This was the last remaining rose. Greg proceeded to comment that of all the roses that were there, this is the lone surviving rose. It was still in beautiful condition," she said.

They all took snapshots of each other that night, she said, because they were supposed to be celebrating each other's birthdays, which were about two weeks apart; she and Greg didn't "want to make the evening unpleasant for my parents. My parents didn't want to make the evening unpleasant for Greg. It ended up being a lovely evening, but it was very strained and kind of strange, too."

The next day, she said, she and Greg argued some more about her plans to move out. It was a stressful day, but they tried to make the best of their Saturday night. They started drinking in the afternoon, they had wine with dinner, and then Kristin made Greg a gin and tonic while they were watching *Fiddler on the Roof.* It was unusual for him to drink that much, she said, and they had to stop the movie halfway through so Greg could go to the bathroom and throw up. He went to bed after that.

On Sunday morning, she said, she went to the lab to update her resume because "Greg had fixated on the idea of exposing the affair. And he also said that he would tell the Medical Examiner's Office of my drug history and that he believed me to be using again."

Loebig asked if she had, in fact, relapsed, and Kristin admitted that she had started using again, "I think around the 27th of October. So it had just been a very short time." Asked how she felt about that, Kristin said she felt "very guilty" and ashamed.

"I had used only sporadically up to that point," she said.

By that Sunday, she said, she hadn't used in three days—since they'd started arguing on Thursday—because she "was cleaning out in case he did say anything." If Greg did carry out his threat and it became too uncomfortable to work at the lab, she planned to look for a new job.

Kristin said she felt sympathetic toward but frustrated with Greg as he tried to piece together the love letter, an act she viewed as a way of venting his emotions. Nonetheless, she said, she really didn't think he would follow through on his ultimatum.

"Let me ask you, was that ultimatum so upsetting to you that you planned to take your husband's life?" Loebig asked.

"Absolutely not," Kristin replied.

"At some point, you ended up losing your job, is that correct?"

"Yes."

"And you ended up in jail for six months, isn't that correct?"

"I think it was closer to nine, but yes," she said.

Loebig asked why she called Michael with her new cell phone that Sunday night. Kristin said she and Greg had been arguing again for several hours before Greg turned in early, around 8:30 P.M. She stepped outside, took a walk around the block, and called Michael "to hear a comforting voice."

Around 10:45 P.M., as she was getting ready for bed, she said, Greg complained that he couldn't sleep and got a drink of "something, water"—she couldn't see what it was—from the kitchen. She went to bed but didn't sleep much, because Greg was snoring and breathing loudly all night.

"I had only seen him do that a few times before," she

said. "But it was keeping me up. I would kind of elbow him, and he'd stop for a little bit."

She said she awoke to the alarm clock the next morning and spoke briefly to Greg. He was slurring his words, so she called in sick for him and then went to the lab. She got there about 8 A.M., and Michael pulled her into his office after his morning meeting. When he confronted her about the bindle of white powder he'd found in her desk the day before, she "broke down sobbing. I was very upset. I was devastated and humiliated, disappointed in myself." So, he suggested she go collect herself.

As she gave a timeline for the day Greg died, she provided new explanations for the numerous discrepancies and allegations posed by the prosecution. She said, for example, that she went home for lunch around 11:45 A.M. or noon but then realized they were out of soup, so she went to Vons.

Loebig asked if she remembered what specific items she'd bought at the store. Kristin said she bought a couple cans of soup, some "over-the-counter sleeping aids and a bottle of Nyquil. I didn't know if Greg was coming down with the flu. We were running low. I bought a rose with—rose bouquet with baby's breath that was wrapped up."

She repeated her story about Greg telling her over soup at lunch that he'd taken some of her old prescriptions. And, yes, she said, she did think "it was weird" and figured he was either crying for help or looking for an escape.

However, she said, since he was moving around and his speech was better, she assumed he was "coming out of it . . . If I didn't think so, I would have called 911 at that time or suggested that he call 911 at that time."

After lunch, she said, she went back to work until about 2:30 P.M., then met up with Michael near the place they called "the Willows." They spent about ninety minutes together, she said, until about 5 P.M., mostly talking about her drug problem.

Loebig backed up to the calls she'd made that morning and asked whom she'd been trying to reach. She explained that Armando Garcia was the Tijuana taxi driver she'd bought drugs from for the first time on October 27, after reading in the newspaper that "if you ever wanted to find anything in Tijuana, all you had to do was ask a taxicab driver." She said she'd intended to buy more diet pills from the same pharmacy she'd visited in September, but when she told Garcia what she was looking for, he offered her something stronger: "Christina" or "crystal," both of which are street names for crystal methamphetamine.

After meeting with Michael on the afternoon of November 6, she said, she returned home for about ninety minutes, went shopping at the mall, then stopped at the lab to make sure she'd turned off the HPLC machine. Asked if she often stopped in at work at night, Kristin said yes, and that on at least ten occasions, Greg came with her.

"I gave him the full tour the first time he was down there," she said. She acknowledged, however, that she'd never seen him take any drugs from the lab.

After running her errands, she said, she went home and gave Greg a kiss on the forehead before going into the bathroom to take a bubble bath, shave her legs, and shower "off all the goop." She said she unscrewed the tub stopper and put it on the ledge to let the water drain out faster. Then she dried off, and read through her sample ballot to figure out how to vote in the election the next day.

Loebig asked what happened next.

"I turned on the light and saw that Greg was cold to the touch and not breathing," she said.

"What did you think at that moment?" Loebig asked.

"I was petrified."

"What did you do?"

"I called 911."

Kristin started crying again, clutching her chest as she recounted how she pulled Greg onto the floor and began doing CPR. After the paramedics took Greg to the hospital, she said, she rode over in a police car, then called her parents and also Michael.

"I believe I was practically hysterical," she said. "I told him that Greg was in the hospital in the emergency room, could he please come down there, and I was very scared."

"Were you worried when you called Michael Robertson and invited him to come down to the hospital that it might expose your affair with him?" Loebig asked.

"That was the farthest thing from my mind," she said.

Loebig asked Kristin a final series of questions that jumped around chronologically but were apparently intended to address the prosecution's allegations of malicious intent.

It was the hospital staff, not she, who initiated the process for organ and tissue donation, Kristin said. She'd been a donor since she was sixteen, and four years earlier, she'd also signed up to be a bone marrow donor.

She'd never done any toxicology testing for fentanyl, she said, and Michael had never shown her any of the fentanyl articles he kept in his office. The only time the subject of such testing came up was at a general lab meeting, in the context of putting fentanyl on the "extended to-do list."

She said she knew it was office policy to do autopsies on employee relatives off-site, and she anticipated toxicology testing would be done on Greg because his death appeared to be drug related.

And she admitted she was in love with Michael the day Greg died but said she'd planned to move out on her own, not into an apartment with him.

"By the time Greg passed away, did you love Michael Robertson so much that you intended to take your husband's life so that you could have Robertson?" Loebig asked.

"Absolutely not," Kristin declared. "That's what divorce is for."

"Did you fear the loss of your job because of drug use or your affair so much that you would have killed your husband?"

"Absolutely not."

Loebig showed Kristin the exhibit photos that depicted the yellow plastic cup of colorless, odorless liquid next to the bed and asked if she drank out of it, touched it, or smelled its contents. No, Kristin said. She said the yellow and blue plastic cups and a mug in the bedroom all went into the dishwasher within a day or two of Greg's death.

Asked about the glass pipe with her DNA on it that was found in the lab, Kristin said she put it in the drawer before lunch on Thursday, November 2.

Loebig ended with a dramatic finish. "Had your relationship with Michael Robertson become so intense, so overwhelming that you agreed with him or took it upon yourself to kill Greg?" he asked.

"Absolutely not," Kristin said.

"As you sit here today and testify, what are your feelings toward Greg?"

"Objection, irrelevant," Goldstein said.

"Overruled," Thompson said. "She can answer that."

"I still love him and miss him a lot," Kristin said.

"Nothing further, Your Honor," Loebig said.

As she had during her practice session, Kristin came off as largely believable, and she held her composure well during direct examination. But there would be no more softball questions for this defendant. Since it was 11:57 A.M., with only three minutes until Thompson would call a recess for the weekend, Goldstein chose not to start questioning Kristin until the following Monday morning.

Skipping the introductory pleasantries he'd extended to other witnesses, Goldstein immediately went on the offensive, firing off a question that would show the jury from the very start that he had insight into Kristin's psyche.

"Have you taken any drugs within the past ninety-six hours?" Goldstein asked antagonistically.

"Yes," Kristin said.

Goldstein asked what drugs she was taking, if they were prescribed medications, and if so, by whom.

"I took last night a sleeping pill to help me sleep," she said, adding that it was called Sonata and was prescribed by her primary care physician, Dr. Gary Bloom.

"What other medications have you taken in the last ninety-six hours?" Goldstein asked.

"This morning I also took a half a Xanax, also prescribed to me by Dr. Gary Bloom," she said.

"Did Dr. Gary Bloom tell you to take a Xanax before you came to court today?" Goldstein demanded.

"No, he said when I was particularly anxious or nervous, that that might help."

"So you have taken medication, Xanax, which is some type of mood elevator, before you testified?" Goldstein asked.

"It's not a mood elevator," Kristin said.

"Something to keep you calm?"

"Yes," she said.

"What other drugs have you taken in the last ninety-six hours?"

"Nothing else besides Ibuprofen."

From there, Goldstein engaged in a duel of semantics with Kristin as he got her to admit that Greg's character was largely good, and that he was a nice, honest person who didn't do drugs. Then, for the next two days, he proceeded to elicit details about her own character that were in extreme contrast to her husband's. He continued to trap her into admitting to bad behavior and a series of lies, large and small, that wove through her personal and professional lives.

Kristin resorted to a number of different responses when

Goldstein was about to catch her in a lie or asked her to explain how she'd gotten into trouble in the past. Sometimes she said she'd been confused, ashamed, or embarrassed. Sometimes she apologized for misstating the facts or telling partial truths. Sometimes she just changed her story and contended that the new version was true. And sometimes she tried to answer a different question entirely, a tactic to which Goldstein repeatedly objected as "nonresponsive."

Asked if Greg was honest, Kristin said, "In many respects, yes."

"Is that a yes?" Goldstein asked.

"There were times when he wasn't, and more times than [not], he was," she said.

No, she said, she never told Detective Agnew that Greg was dishonest, because she didn't feel it was appropriate to say harsh things about the dead, but she had "learned things since that [she] didn't know then."

So, Goldstein asked, was she saying he wasn't an honest person? And didn't she describe Greg's family to Agnew, using the unflattering term "dysfunctional"?

Kristin said he wasn't always honest with her, but yes, she'd said his family was dysfunctional. She also said, yes, Greg was "fairly steady" and, yes, he was "a very good human being."

Kristin acknowledged that when she came to San Diego and stayed the night with Greg, she had not broken up with her boyfriend, Teddy Maya.

"Didn't you tell Teddy Maya you were in a trunk of a car in Mexico being driven around?"

"No," she said. "That misstates what I said."

"So, if Teddy Maya gets on the stand and says that, he's lying, correct?"

"Argumentative, Your Honor," Loebig said.

Thompson sustained Loebig's objection.

Goldstein hammered on the point that Greg helped Kristin

get off drugs because he didn't do drugs. Then he asked about her claim that she saw Greg throw away the containers for her oxycodone and clonazepam five and a half years before he died.

She said he got rid of the drugs because "he didn't think it was appropriate for me to ration drugs to myself to kick another drug habit." She added that he also didn't like her using those drugs to get off methamphetamine, and was worried she would merely switch addictions from one substance to another. Greg didn't like her using the diet pills, which she called "fat burners," either, because he thought they were too much like meth and she didn't need to use them, anyway.

She also admitted that when she'd gone to Tijuana in September to buy some diet pills, which she described as a "milder alternative" to meth, that she "was beginning to fall off the wagon and beginning to relapse." When she bought meth from Armando Garcia in Tijuana, she said, she took a long lunch, then smoked it at home one night when Greg was working late.

In one of the trial's more telling moments, Goldstein asked Kristin to explain to the jury how she smoked meth. Kristin showed how she smoked it in a pipe or piece of foil shaped like one, holding a Bic lighter or candle underneath until the meth melted and produced some smoke, which she'd inhale. She said she kept her pipe in a kitchen drawer at home, a location she thought would be "inconspicuous" because she did all the cooking.

She said she never saw the oxycodone or clonazepam after Greg supposedly threw the pills away, not even when they moved to other apartments or when she was looking for a place to hide her meth.

Wasn't she concerned, Goldstein asked, when Greg, "a rookie drug user," told her over lunch that he'd taken the pills? Yes, Kristin said, but "if he wanted to call 911, he could have reached down and dialed it, and they would have showed up regardless if he said anything. I was just trying to protect his image. . . . He told me there weren't any more left. I saw that he was improving. He was up and about."

Later in her testimony, Goldstein prodded her again about why she hadn't called for help after hearing Greg's labored breathing all day.

"I'm sorry I didn't call," she said. "I wish every day that I had . . . I was just thinking, poor thing. This must be really hard on you. . . . It didn't occur to me that he might have taken something else."

Goldstein confronted Kristin about her earlier testimony that she'd stored the glass pipe in the HPLC room on Thursday, November 2. Yes, she said, she'd used meth that morning. But not in the lab. She'd smoked it in a restroom on the way to work.

Goldstein asked if anything stopped her from going to Dr. Blackbourne or Lloyd Amborn and telling them about her drug use or affair with Michael before Greg carried out his threat to do so. No, she said, there wasn't.

"But you went to work Friday and never brought any of that up, did you?"

"No, I didn't. I figured I'd resign from the job before . . ."

Goldstein objected. "That's nonresponsive after 'No,'" he said.

Thompson sustained the objection, striking the last part of her statement.

"He also threatened to expose the affair back in July, and he hadn't gone through with it, so I believed him to be making idle threats. I wanted to be prepared," she said, referring to her attempts to clean up.

Kristin confirmed that, yes, she'd told *48 Hours* that Greg could have taken the drugs to frame her, that he could have wanted to harm and blame her, "and in so doing, destroy [her] life along with his."

She also acknowledged there were no physical barriers preventing her from getting divorced. However, she said, "I cared about Greg a great deal. That alone presents a reason not to consider divorce."

"Is it fair to say that you didn't want to leave Greg because you were aware that Robertson was having affairs also?"

"I didn't know that, actually," she said. ". . . Until I read the e-mails, I had no idea."

She admitted that she'd told Agnew during her interview that she didn't think Greg committed suicide.

"At that point in time," she said, "I wanted to believe it was accidental . . . because I was feeling so guilty."

She also admitted that the book *American Suicide* by Howard I. Kushner, which police found in their apartment, was hers, not Greg's.

Asked about her application to SDSU, Kristin acknowledged that her mother had helped fill it out for her, and they had purposely omitted the information about her poor academic record at Redlands. She also acknowledged that she'd signed a separate document, certifying under penalty of perjury that the answers on her application were accurate and complete.

So, Goldstein asked, if she factored in all the grades from the University of Redlands, she wouldn't have graduated *summa cum laude* or Phi Beta Kappa, would she? No, Kristin said.

"You would have been disciplined for academic dishonesty, wouldn't you?" Goldstein asked.

Kristin said she didn't understand his question, so Goldstein explained that she'd signed the SDSU application, swearing under penalty of perjury that it was complete and accurate. Kristin replied that she "misunderstood the initial application" and assumed she didn't have to disclose the coursework if she wasn't transferring credits.

"What does perjury mean to you?" Goldstein asked.

"That means lying . . . under oath," she said.

Goldstein switched gears and got Kristin to admit that she'd lied to Greg when he'd confronted her on Thursday, November 2, about doing drugs again. Goldstein also forced her to admit that she'd lied to Detective Agnew during her interview about her drug use.

Goldstein asked Kristin why she'd been storing meth at work.

"I had it there because I knew—" she said, pausing.

"Go ahead. Finish your response. You knew Greg was looking for it, didn't you?"

"Yes," she said.

Asked why Michael would have searched her desk on Sunday, November 5, Kristin said he'd noticed that her behavior had changed over the past ten days. Hadn't Michael found a meth pipe three weeks earlier, confronted her, and then broken it? Goldstein asked.

"I know nothing of that," Kristin said.

When Michael flushed the contents of the bindle in her desk that Sunday, Goldstein suggested that he was covering for Kristin.

"I guess you could say that," Kristin said, adding, however, that the bindle was empty. "I think his primary motivation was concern." And yes, she said, Michael used county equipment to test the bindle for methamphetamine.

"You resort to methamphetamine when your life gets stressed out, don't you?" Goldstein asked.

"It has happened before," she said. "It's not my only response to stress."

Goldstein had Kristin read aloud the e-mail she'd written to Greg on the morning of October 9—detailing the different pills she was taking. She said she'd written the e-mail after he'd searched her purse and they'd argued about the diuretic, aspirin, and dietary supplements he found. She said the prescription pills she described in the e-mail "didn't actually exist. I was sending him on a wild goose chase to show how wrong he was."

"So not only are you lying about the drug, but you are lying about the reason why you are taking the drug, correct?" Goldstein asked.

"Yes," she said. "I was upset he was violating my trust."

She said she called Armando Garcia on the morning of November 6 to set up a buy "because it was certainly a stressful situation, leaving Greg," and her home and work supplies were gone or thereabouts.

She said she stayed clean for six months after police arrested her for drugs in January 2001, because she'd been told that she could be arrested for murder any day. Her attorney, who went out of town toward the end of June, told her he had a verbal agreement with police that they wouldn't arrest her in his absence, so she'd bought some meth on June 24, thinking she'd have a week to detox.

"It was one of the most stressful times of my life," she said.

"So you resort to meth when you are stressed out?" Goldstein asked again.

"On that particular instance, I did."

"It's not just that particular instance, is it?"

Goldstein confronted her about hiding the meth pipe in the room where she used the HPLC machine.

"You smoked in that room, didn't you?"

"Never," she said, contending that she just hid the pipe in there. She described a bizarre rationale of hiding love letters, drugs, and pipes in different places at home and at work so that no one, particularly Greg, would find them. When she'd pulled away from him in the past, she said, Greg had searched through her things. But, she said, she did not hide the evidence envelope for case #377, which once contained methamphetamine and was found in the HPLC room after she was fired.

"While you were at the Medical Examiner's Office, did you ever see any other employees smoking meth?"

"No," she said. "Nobody knew about my drug use at the time. I didn't know about anybody else's."

Goldstein asked her to elaborate on the "billing inaccuracies" that led to her firing from California Pizza Kitchen.

"I think I swapped some credit [cards]," she said.

"You were using—running a little scam there, weren't you?" Goldstein asked.

"No," she said.

"Tell us, when you say that there's billing discrepancies, you had pocketed money with these credit cards that people would purchase their meals with, correct?"

"Not intentionally, no."

Goldstein asked if she was claiming to have had trouble adding up people's bills properly.

"No, I mixed up some people's information," she said. ". . . I charged some people's credit cards for two meals instead of one."

"Weren't you stealing from the customers?"

"In a sense, yes," she said, ". . . not intentionally. But it ended up being that."

Goldstein got her to admit that one of her favorite subjects was math, and, yes, she had taken calculus. But, she said, because of her meth use "a lot of errors in both judgment and accuracy, I'm sure, were at play."

Goldstein also got Kristin to admit that she didn't always tell the truth to her parents and refrained from telling them about her relationship with Michael until after police searched her apartment and she was arrested for drugs in January 2001.

"I was embarrassed and ashamed to be having an affair," she said.

"So, when you're embarrassed and ashamed, you lie?" he asked.

When Kristin would not answer the question directly, Goldstein objected to her answer as nonresponsive. Thompson agreed.

When Goldstein confronted her about her false statement to Detective Agnew that she was having only an emotional relationship with Michael, Kristin apologized.

"I'm very sorry I wasn't more forthcoming with that information," she said.

Kristin acknowledged that she lied to Jerome and Bertrand on November 9 and said she must have "misspoken" when she told them she'd gone to Vons with Michael between 3 and 5 P.M. the day Greg died.

"You felt it was necessary to meet Michael Robertson close to the apartment?" Goldstein asked.

No, Kristin said, they always met at the Willows, which happened to be nearby.

She also admitted that she lied to Greg about a raffle at work for Natalie Merchant tickets because she wanted to create an excuse to go to the concert.

When Goldstein tried to pin Kristin down on one of her latest claims—that Greg had accompanied her to the lab numerous times in her off-hours—Kristin admitted that no one from work ever saw them there together. But, she said, Greg had insisted on coming with her five or six times at night and on weekends after she told him about her feelings for Michael, including two visits in October—once before the SOFT conference and once on their way to buy Halloween costumes for the party they went to.

"Greg wouldn't let me go alone, and I had work to do," Kristin said, adding that she didn't know what he was doing while she was in the HPLC room.

Wasn't she worried, Goldstein asked, that Greg might sit

at her desk and find all the cards, letters, rose petals, and
birthday truffles Michael had given her? Kristin said that's
why she tried to remove all the rose petals from her desk, but
apparently she'd left a few.

The next day, November 5, the sixteenth day of the trial,
Goldstein continued to pound on Kristin, getting her to admit
many other instances where she'd lied before the trial. And
now that she'd made certain incriminating statements on the
stand, he could point out to the jurors that she'd lied to them
as well.

Goldstein confronted her about the conflicts between her
diary, her earlier testimony, and the e-mails Michael sent to
her and their colleagues about the SOFT conference—none
of which indicated that he'd ever considered not going.

"Are you telling us that you didn't lie in your journal?"

Kristin explained that the journal had a dual purpose, to
express her feelings and to help Greg understand them if he
happened to read it.

"You wrote this diary, this alleged diary, didn't you, for
Greg to read?" Goldstein asked.

"No, that wasn't the sole purpose," she said.

"Your whole attempt was to deceive Greg de Villers, was
it not?"

"That's not true."

But, asked again about the contents of the October 9 e-mail
she'd already admitted to concocting, she had to acknowledge that she'd written other things to deceive him in the past.

On redirect, Loebig tried to show that Kristin had not disrespected Greg's memory by throwing away his things as
Jerome had testified. Loebig produced a police photo taken

during the search on January 4, 2001, proving that several pictures featuring Greg were still on the mantle. Another police photo showed Greg's clothes were still hanging in the closet. Kristin testified that she didn't give away any of his clothes until she moved to the studio apartment in Golden Hill in April 2001. She also testified that Greg was the one who had thrown away his Nike sandals—because the straps were broken.

She said she'd called Armando Garcia on her home phone because she couldn't make an international call on her new cell phone. She'd tried.

Asked again about the statement she made to Teddy Maya about being driven around in a trunk in Mexico, Kristin admitted that she did, in fact, tell him "some cockamamie story" like that.

"It was an easy way to make me feel less guilty about running out on him, because I had hurt him so badly," she said.

She said she'd never used Greg's iMac computer at home because all of her disks were formatted to use a different type of computer, but he had used her work computer the night before they went shopping for Halloween costumes.

Kristin contended that Greg said he couldn't live without her and went to bed for the weekend after she told him about her feelings for Michael during the summer—the same behavior he'd exhibited the weekend before he died.

Loebig asked Kristin straight out whether she'd made any agreement with Michael to kill Greg.

"Absolutely not," she said.

"Did you, with or without Michael Robertson, kill your husband?"

"I wouldn't hurt Greg," she said.

Goldstein still had more questions. "Have you ever staged a suicide before?" he asked.

When she said no, he brought up the razor-blade incident in 1993, asking her if that didn't fit the description.

"I was acting out as a teenager," she replied. "I was feeling so guilty for what I was putting my parents through that I believe I said something like, 'You would be better off without me.' "

But then, she said, "I realized how stupid I was being. . . . And then I couldn't go through with it even if I wanted to. So call it a feigned attempt; call [it]—I don't know what."

"You knew that you weren't going to kill yourself, correct?"

"I felt like I wanted to."

Goldstein asked if her mother had called her a slut and told her she was worthless. Kristin said she didn't recall her mother's specific words, "just that very hurtful things were said."

On redirect, Loebig revealed the big surprise he'd saved for last: new information about the rose Kristin bought at Vons the day Greg died. The rose that she bought on November 6, he asked, "What color was that?"

"Yellow with peach tipping," Kristin said.

Goldstein followed up, asking her to go over one more time what happened to the rose petals she found on Greg's chest in bed. She said they "came off with him when [she] pulled him off the bed" to the floor, because "they were fresh and had weight to them."

Goldstein asked if she'd ever told Detective Agnew that she'd bought a yellow rose at Vons. No, Kristin said.

In fact, she never told Agnew she'd bought a rose at all, did she? No, Kristin said.

"How do we know it was a yellow rose?" Goldstein asked.

"We don't," Kristin said. ". . . I know that."

Loebig objected, saying Goldstein was being argumentative. Thompson struck both the question and Kristin's answer.

Kristin said she'd bought the rose to give to Michael that afternoon because they'd been arguing all day. In their "little lingo" for roses, she said, yellow stood for friendship.

Chapter 20

With the Rossums' testimony over, the prosecution started calling its rebuttal witnesses to dispute or clarify new points of evidence presented by the defense.

First up was Sergeant Howard Williams, Detective Agnew's boss, to show that the Rossums had, in fact, been given the opportunity to talk to police about information they thought could help their daughter. Williams said he left a message at the Rossums' house in Claremont on July 16, 2001, after Kristin's arraignment, saying he wanted to hear anything they thought might help the investigation. He said Ralph returned his call, but informed him they'd been advised by counsel not to speak to the police.

On cross-examination by Eriksen, Williams admitted that he never tried to contact the Rossums before Kristin was arrested, even after learning they were the last people other than Kristin to see Greg alive.

The next witness was Theodore "Teddy" Maya, who had become an associate at a law firm and looked very uncomfortable testifying as a prosecution witness in his former girlfriend's murder trial.

Maya testified that Kristin didn't look like herself when they met at the motel in Redlands on Christmas night in 1994. She left the next morning without saying good-bye, he said, while he was in the shower. Some weeks later, he said, she called him and "said she had been kidnapped and taken [to Mexico] . . . I believe at gunpoint in the trunk of a car."

On cross-examination, Maya said Kristin admitted to using speed. He said he didn't buy the kidnapping story, and he'd thought they'd been dating each other exclusively.

The next witness was Officer Larry Horowitz, who had since left the police department in Claremont for the one in Arcadia. Since Horowitz was the officer who wrote the police reports about Kristin's brushes with the law as a teenager, Hendren asked Horowitz to recount the events and observations for the record and to repeat the comments that Constance made to him—including the ones about the knife and razor blades that she tried to deny on the stand.

Horowitz also made it clear that Constance was present and watching as he arrested and handcuffed Kristin, put her in his squad car, and drove her away to the station in January 1994. Hendren asked if Horowitz ever told Constance that Kristin was not under arrest or suggested that to her in some way. No, Horowitz said.

On cross, Eriksen asked Horowitz if he had taped his interview with Kristin. No, Horowitz said, he took notes. Had Horowitz explained to the Rossums that Kristin's trip to the station would not represent a formal arrest for future purposes? No, he said. Had he let them know that he wasn't bringing her to Juvenile Hall? Horowitz said that was implied when they picked her up at the police station.

On redirect, Hendren asked Horowitz if Kristin, Constance, and Ralph had all said that Kristin cut her wrists, not that she *tried* to cut them, and also if both Constance and Ralph mentioned that Kristin had used a knife. Horowitz answered yes to both questions.

Next, Hendren called Marie de Villers to the stand for just two questions, one of which was to confirm that Greg was her son. The second one had to do with the claims of domestic violence by Yves against Marie, to which Kristin had referred during her testimony.

"Did your husband—ex-husband—Mr. Yves de Villers, ever in any way, shape, or form hit you or injure you or make domestic violence upon you in any way?" Hendren asked.

"Never," Marie said.

Eriksen said he had no questions for Marie.

After Marie stepped down, Thompson explained to the jurors that they had heard all the evidence in the case. The law required him to meet with the attorneys for an hour or so after lunch to discuss jury instructions, which he would deliver that afternoon. Closing arguments were to begin the next morning, and he expected the case to go to the jury by the end of the week, though he would let the panel decide if it wanted to deliberate on Friday afternoon. Since Monday was a court holiday, deliberations would continue the following Tuesday.

Midway through Kristin's testimony, Eriksen could feel himself getting sick, and there was nothing he could do to stop it. He'd been so busy with the case, he'd forgotten to get a flu shot. And now, with his immune system strained by the long hours and stress of the trial, he'd gone and caught a nasty flu bug.

He and Loebig discussed asking the judge for a delay in their closing argument so Eriksen could give the statement he'd worked so long to prepare, but Loebig wanted to move ahead. He thought Thompson might not allow a delay because there were two defense attorneys. The jurors had been coming every day for a month, and Loebig didn't think it was a good idea to make them wait for the defense's closing;

they might feel irritated or inconvenienced. And finally, he thought the jury might view a delay caused by Eriksen's absence as an indication that he had no confidence in the defense's case.

Eriksen didn't argue. His nose and eyes were running, and he couldn't even think straight. Before going home to collapse, he stayed late at the office to finish typing up the ten single-spaced pages of information he'd been planning to relay to the jury. And he left it up to Loebig to do the rest.

It was pretty unusual for an attorney to call in sick for a closing, and it was also unusual for there to be two attorneys on a case, so it was even more rare for those two phenomena to coincide. Eriksen apologized to the Rossums right before the verdict, but he said later that the fact that Loebig's closing argument was shorter than they would have liked seemed to bother them more than Eriksen's absence.

Once Eriksen recovered, he felt terrible about not being able to be there to finish the job that he'd started.

"I'd put so much into the trial and the case and then was unavailable at the attorney's time to shine," he said.

The jury was excused while Judge Thompson listened to what attorneys from both sides had to say about which instructions the panel should be given. Goldstein did not participate in the discussion so that he could put the finishing touches on his closing argument back in his office. Loebig announced that Eriksen had gone home sick.

Hendren argued that the jury should hear a series of instructions concerning conspiracies.

"It's the people's position that Michael Robertson is an uncharged, unindicted coconspirator in this case," he said. "Theoretically, some of the jurors could conclude that Michael Robertson may have administered the lethal amount of fentanyl to the victim. If he did so, it's the people's contention that he did so in conjunction with Ms. Rossum as part of a conspiracy to kill her husband. They both had the same motive."

Loebig strongly objected, but Thompson said there was "sufficient evidence to suggest that a conspiracy could be presumed."

While the discussion was going on, Hendren spoke to Goldstein on the phone in the courtroom about a matter that had come up over the lunch break. Goldstein was so angry, he was about ready to dismiss the case, and he could be heard yelling on the other end of the phone. Thompson said he'd better come over to the courthouse.

Once Goldstein arrived, Thompson explained for the record that the court had just received a date-stamped copy of Marie de Villers's divorce papers from 1981, which "completely contradicted" her brief testimony that Yves had never physically abused her. Kristin's attorneys wanted a chance to present this information to the jury before the panel got its instructions. Thompson said he'd allow both sides to argue their positions.

Goldstein now regretted that they'd called Marie to testify. He'd made his career out of prosecuting domestic violence cases, and he knew victims often recanted. Now that he was about to leave the District Attorney's Office to become a judge, the irony was not lost on him that the last witness he would ever call to the stand was a woman who claimed abuse and then recanted.

Goldstein told Thompson that Eriksen and Loebig were the most honest defense attorneys he'd ever dealt with, but they'd never turned over Marie's divorce papers as part of discovery.

"He had his chance to cross[-examine] her, and they rested," Goldstein said. "[Loebig]'s been an attorney for twenty-five years. Why give him a chance to reopen?"

Loebig said he was led to believe that Marie wasn't going

to be called as a witness, so he didn't bring the divorce papers with him for the prosecution to examine.

"When she was called, we were surprised," he said. Loebig had reviewed the documents during the lunch hour to confirm that they contradicted her testimony and then notified the court.

"I had no intention of impeaching this poor woman," Loebig said, but he also had no idea she would say what she did. "I have never seen such clear evidence of perjury in such short testimony." He noted that no one wanted the jury to consider such evidence, which he called "poison to the system."

Thompson said it would be "naïve to conclude" that statements made in petitions to obtain restraining orders "are always completely accurate." It was possible, he said, that her attorney typed up the petition, and she, still new to this country and its language, just signed it.

The judge gave the attorneys a choice: the defense could recall Marie and question her about her testimony, both sides could stipulate that she signed court papers stating that the abuse occurred, or they could strike her testimony. The attorneys agreed on the first option.

With Eriksen home sick, Loebig asked Thompson if it would be okay for the court to recess after Goldstein's closing argument on Wednesday, and then if Eriksen was feeling better on Thursday, he could deliver the closing, which the two defense attorneys had intended to split. If Eriksen was still sick, Loebig said he would do the entire closing on Thursday as scheduled.

Goldstein asked Thompson if he could be excused to get back to polishing up his closing, so he could be "artful." Thompson jokingly said that Goldstein had plenty of time to work on it.

"Shit, damn near eighteen hours," Thompson said, laughing.

* * *

After the break, Marie was recalled to the stand, and Loebig showed her the divorce papers she'd filed, with her signature, in 1981. She said she recognized her signature but said she did not remember making the statement about Yves hitting her in the face. And that was that.

Thompson read the jury its instructions, then excused the panel until the morning.

Afterward, Marie told her civil attorney, Craig McClellan, that Yves never hit her and that she never told her divorce attorney that he did.

Goldstein gave his closing argument on November 6, two years to the day after Greg died in the couple's apartment. The prosecutor reviewed the timeline of the events leading up to Greg's death, summarized the prosecution's most incriminating evidence against Kristin, and then tried to punch holes through her explanations, one by one.

First of all, he said, there aren't always two sides to every story, but the truth always makes sense.

"Either Greg de Villers killed himself or he was murdered," he said. "There is no ambiguity, . . . it wasn't a cry for help," and Greg wasn't trying to frame Kristin.

The defense, he said, portrayed Greg's behavior as bizarre and as a motive for suicide, but in reality it was just the opposite. Greg was a regular, steady, nice guy who worked really hard, came home to his wife, and didn't do drugs. Kristin, on the other hand, had a history of doing drugs, lying, stealing, and cheating on the men in her life, behavior the defense used as an explanation for her conduct, when, in fact, it was illegal, immoral, and led to murder.

Kristin Rossum, he said, destroyed two families, the Medical Examiner's Office, and "a great guy" named Greg de Villers.

"Both families have suffered at the hands of the defendant and her narcissism and her self-centered behavior," he said.

Goldstein did not try to describe a specific scenario for how Kristin poisoned Greg, suggesting only that she could have administered the fentanyl by using patches or a syringe or hiding it in something he ate or drank.

"Who knows," he said. "She's the expert. He didn't just die and fade away. . . . The defendant chose to play God."

Flashing Greg's photo up on the screen, the prosecutor described the young man's death as untimely and most unpleasant. On this day two years ago, he said, Greg was breathing shallowly, and his bladder and lungs were filling up with fluid. He was so drugged that he couldn't even reach down to pick up the phone right next to his bed. Meanwhile, in Michael Robertson's office, Kristin was crying and "they're talking about what she's doing to Greg de Villers. . . . She's stressed out of her mind. Her world is collapsing." Kristin and Michael left the office and were unaccounted for for at least two hours that afternoon.

Goldstein spun around and pointed to the empty chair behind Kristin and her attorneys, saying Michael Robertson might as well be sitting there because he and Kristin were working together and they wanted Greg dead.

The truth makes sense, he said, but Kristin's story doesn't. Kristin's motive for killing Greg was to prevent him from exposing her affair and her drug use. And, if that didn't seem like a strong enough motive for murder, he said to the jury, "I'd ask you—when is a motive good enough for murder? . . . There's never a good reason to kill. . . . This is the oldest one in the book—killing for love . . . killing for drugs."

Kristin lied to the police about her drug use and her affair, he said, she and her boyfriend hid evidence, and she used the tools of her trade as a toxicologist to kill Greg. The drugs she used recreationally and to murder her husband were later found missing from the Medical Examiner's Office.

"Coincidence?" he asked. "No, theft."

Goldstein said Kristin's parents were "pretty good people . . . [who] did a lot for their daughter," but at points during the trial, "it would be fair to say they have been untruthful."

Kristin uses stimulants as a crutch when she gets into trouble, he said. She manipulates people and situations, she's deceitful, and she staged her own suicide as a teenager. She picks at her knuckles until they bleed and pulls her own nails off.

"That's the power of methamphetamine," he said.

Don't let the irony of this case escape you, he warned the jury. Greg's "detestation for drugs" is what ended up killing him.

Kristin's journal was staged, too, he said. She left it on the coffee table to send a message, first to Greg, then to police.

"Why would you lie in your own diary?" he asked the jury rhetorically.

Goldstein suggested that Kristin did not bring the love note home on Thursday, November 2, as she'd claimed, but much later, so she could try to make it look like Greg had been trying to piece it back together—a task that a police detective took six weeks to do, even on a computer. What really happened that Thursday, he said, was that Greg came home, "saw that she was tweaking," and told her he would turn her in if she didn't clean up her act. The next night Greg may have been upset about the consultant he hired at work, but otherwise he was fine. Why else would Kristin and her father describe the evening as fun or very pleasant?

Goldstein submitted to the jury that the murder was set in motion with Kristin's cell phone call to Michael, her lover the fentanyl expert, at 9:02 P.M. on Sunday night. Greg was snoring that night. Something was in his system. Clonazepam could have been used to immobilize Greg, which enabled Kristin to administer massive doses of fentanyl. Why else did Kristin feel safe enough to call her drug dealer four times from home for the first time the next morning? Because the threat was gone, Goldstein said. Greg was unconscious, and he was going to die. When she called in sick for him, Goldstein said, she called his own voice mail, even though she had Stefan Gruenwald's and Terry Huang's numbers right there in her address book.

"She had numbers. She could have easily notified people that Greg was sick," Goldstein said. "She didn't want to. . . . Why? Because he was going to die. That's at 7:42 [A.M.]"

Kristin went to Vons, he said. Why? To buy soups, cold medicine, and a rose. But, of course, she wasn't going to admit that the rose was red.

"They know we can't prove what color it is by the receipt," he said.

She is the one obsessed with roses, and whose favorite movie is *American Beauty,* he added.

"That's not Greg de Villers's gig," he said. "She bought a rose. She bought a red rose."

Goldstein told the jurors that they couldn't really believe anything Kristin said. "I'd submit she's been impeached to a degree that it would be very difficult to trust anything this defendant had to say about any subject."

She also didn't take a bath that night, he said, because she was busy staging a suicide scene. On the 911 tape, she did sound hysterical, because it must have been very hard for her to try to pretend to do CPR on Greg and talk on the phone at the same time.

"How was she doing all that and doing real CPR at the same time? You can't," he said.

Why was the wedding photo propped up at the base of the chest? That photo didn't just fall off the bed and stand up by itself, he said. Kristin wasn't expecting the dispatcher to tell her to put Greg on the floor, so she had to sweep all the petals off the bed and move the photo from under the pillow to the floor, where the paramedics found it.

"She had to reset the crime scene," he said. "She didn't do a very good job of it."

Goldstein dismissed the defense's theory that Greg drank fentanyl from one of the cups in the bedroom that went untested, calling it "a red herring."

"She's very good. She's very manipulative.... I don't know if there was fentanyl in there.... I don't care, because there's no container for fentanyl."

The notion that Greg threw the fentanyl container away is ridiculous, he said. If he wanted to frame her, why didn't he just type a message on the computer: 'Kristin Rossum did this to me'?"

Greg had been dead sixty to ninety minutes by the time the paramedics arrived, Goldstein said. "He didn't have lunch with the defendant. He was out . . . and the medical testimony shows it." The opiate had to be in his system since at least 10:30 A.M., he said, and there had to be multiple applications of fentanyl to get it there.

"Ten milligrams of fentanyl would probably wipe out everybody in this room," he said, holding the vial up for the jury to see once again.

The only reason Kristin can say she stopped using drugs between January and June 2001 is because no one tested her, he said.

"She is a methamphetamine addict. That's what she is and she always will be."

Kristin's "numerous lies" about Greg's death, her affairs, the staging of the crime scene, and her drug use are "tantamount to a confession," he said. "The defendant is guilty of murder."

Eriksen was nowhere to be seen the next morning, so Loebig had to do both portions of the closing argument,

using notes he made from the points Eriksen had typed up.
Loebig let the jurors know that Eriksen was home with the
flu, and lest they think his partner didn't have faith in the defense's case, Loebig pointed out that Eriksen was "desperately missing this experience, having lived through this case
for over a year."

Loebig started by telling the jury that he had a different
take than Goldstein about the notion that truth always make
sense.

"I suggest to you, in many, many instances, that things
aren't that black and white," he said. "They aren't that simple."

He said they'd all heard about young people who do
something to the point of obsession, such as playing video
games, or more commonly, engaging in romance, and end
up committing suicide.

"These children, these adolescents, these adults that do
these things usually do it by surprise," he said.

As the prosecutor mentioned, he said, why didn't Kristin
walk out the door? Loebig urged the jury to look again at the
evidence and see that she had been working toward it, certainly. He cited the computer evidence showing she'd sub-
scribed to a rental service in August 2000 as well as the
comments she made to her parents, Melissa Prager, and Tom
Horn that she was looking for a new place to live.

"It's not so easy to say good-bye, even when there are no
children," he said.

Loebig said he wasn't asking the jury to give Kristin extra
credit for being "decent looking," nor was he going to downplay her drug use.

"We all know what addiction means in some form or
fashion," he said. ". . . Once addicted, there's always an addiction. . . . You are never over it."

But, Loebig said, the prosecution overplayed the concerns

expressed by Kristin's parents during her teenage years that she was out of control. There was nothing staged about the confrontation she had with her parents, he said.

"What's the play there? . . . She's not conniving at sixteen; she's not honing her skills. She's desperate. . . . Then she starts using again. That's addiction. She isn't going out and acting violently towards people. . . . She was going to hurt herself. Her MO, if you want to call it that, and reaction to [drug] use and being confronted with it, is to run away, not run at you and do something to you."

When Kristin met Greg, it started off "as a modern-day fairytale," close to love at first sight—at least for Greg. Yes, they slept together on the first night, but, Loebig reminded the jury, they weren't there "to judge her sex life against ours or anyone else's."

Did she ever really love Greg romantically? Who knows, he said, but even if she only loved him as a friend, "You don't harm somebody you love."

With Kristin and Michael's relationship, he said, "There's a bond. There's an enthusiasm. This is a quest for destiny" that started as early as May 2000. And it was no secret to their coworkers, he said, no matter what the prosecution argued.

"So this idea of a secret relationship that was reiterated over and over and over, which doesn't surface, if you believe the prosecution, until after the conspiracy, is malarkey," he said.

Loebig dismissed Kristin's alleged motive—Greg's ultimatum—reminding the jury that Kristin admitted it to police right away.

"So Kristin herself is creating the so-called motive that the prosecution is trying to suggest to you," he said.

Likewise, he said, the prosecution made too much of Kristin's initial denials during her police interview that she was using drugs and having a sexual affair. By the end of the interview, he said, "she basically owned up. . . . I suggest to you that when a woman is describing her relationship with a man, that an emotional relationship easily includes a sexual relationship."

At that point in the closing, Loebig switched to a yellow notepad, from which he read notes for the rest of his statement, the portion Eriksen had intended to deliver.

If this were a conspiracy between Kristin and Michael, Loebig said, they could've used drugs such as succinylcholine that were far less detectable than fentanyl. Or they could've spiked the stomach, blood, and urine samples, left unguarded overnight at the Medical Examiner's Office, with higher levels of oxycodone and clonazepam. But they didn't. He also cautioned the jury not to get sidetracked by the Stan Berdan case.

Kristin's e-mails to Greg were routine, he said, just like the events of their last weekend together. And even though Kristin's e-mails to Michael reflect their passion, he said, "Passion does not translate into violence. It can, but in this case, it didn't."

If Kristin had been planning to kill Greg on Monday, she would not have been expecting to lose her job. So why was she working on her resume on Sunday?

"It's fairly routine," he said. "It's optimistic."

Loebig said Dr. Blackbourne's findings that Greg would have been semicomatose for six to twelve hours were not inconsistent with Kristin's story about seeing him at noon and then finding him cold and not breathing around 9 P.M. In fact, he said, " It's pretty much right on."

Loebig attributed the lack of red marks on Greg's chest from CPR to the fact that Kristin is a "small, petite person . . . not a big, burly EMT person."

If Kristin were trying to hide her relationship with Michael, why would she invite him to the hospital? Why wouldn't she have told him to wait in the bedroom when Jerome and Bertrand came to talk to her the night of November 9?

Because, Loebig said, "there was no secret relationship." She lied to Greg about the affair only because she didn't want to hurt him.

Loebig took one last jab at the lax security over drugs at the Medical Examiner's Office and another at the UCSD police's initial investigation, reiterating that investigators should've collected samples of the liquid in those plastic cups.

"This becomes fairly critically important because we have testimony from very expert doctors that fentanyl was, in all medical certainty, ingested. . . . Greg drank some of it. There was no testimony it was poured down his throat. It didn't go down and into his lungs."

The investigators, he said, also should've inventoried the trash on the balcony. And they should've tested the cups for fingerprints to see if they were handled by the "unindicted coconspirator."

"We're never going to know," he said. "That's a big piece of evidence."

Kristin was an episodic meth user, he said, "but that's not violent."

Jerome's testimony about Kristin throwing away Greg's belongings was disproved by the photos, and Marie de Villers's testimony about her husband's domestic violence was contradicted by her 1981 divorce filing, he said.

"Not everybody has perfect recollection," he said, adding that people may have an interest that "may make them testify less than truthfully."

Fentanyl can be purchased on the street, where it's known as China White, he said. "Fentanyl is around. People use it and abuse it." And while fentanyl patches were missing from the Medical Examiner's Office, no residual patch marks were found on Greg's skin, "so don't just wildly speculate," he told the jury.

The tissue donation was also a red herring floated by the prosecution, Loebig said. Kristin did not initiate the donation at the hospital, and it didn't stop the toxicology tests that found Greg died of a fentanyl overdose.

Kristin did lie to Teddy Maya, he said, but only because she didn't want to hurt him.

He dismissed the prosecution's claim that the murder started with Kristin's short cell phone call to Michael at 9:02 P.M. Sunday, noting that even TV murder plots aren't hatched in a two-minute call.

"There was no conspiracy," he said. ". . . I suggest to you that in this case, not only is there not a motive to commit murder, it's quite the opposite. There's lack of motive. . . . There's reasonable doubt from beginning to end in this case."

When the jurors considered the prosecution's conspiracy theory, Loebig said, they needed to ask this question: Why didn't Kristin leave town between the day Greg died and the day she was arrested, go to Australia, and hook up with Michael Robertson?

"It didn't happen, because she didn't kill her husband to be with this person," he said. "She's not with him no matter what her feelings were then."

In the final portion of the trial, Hendren spent two and a half hours presenting a rebuttal argument, which Thompson thought was one of the best he'd heard in his sixteen years of hearing cases.

Hendren highlighted the many instances where Kristin admitted she'd lied. He also underscored all the instances where Kristin changed her testimony to either agree with or contradict the testimony of other witnesses, meaning she'd also lied to the jury. But perhaps the most powerful portion of his argument was a list of coincidences and conjecture that the jury would have to believe to find Kristin not guilty.

First, that she was a credible witness.

That Greg held on to the oxycodone and clonazepam for five years, even after moving to various apartments.

That he was suicidal and would use drugs to kill himself, contrary to what all his friends and family believed.

That Greg also knew about fentanyl, a highly regulated substance that most people had never heard of before the trial. That he figured out how to get it without ever mentioning it to anyone, only a few days before he decided to kill himself. And that he found a way to get the oxycodone and clonazepam, too.

That someone other than Kristin took the fentanyl vial and the patches that were missing from her lab.

That since Kristin insists she wasn't using or stealing any meth from the office, that someone else with a key and the knowledge of where the meth was kept took all the missing meth. And that someone else stole the missing Soma, oxycodone, clonazepam, and amphetamine.

"Remember, she's got a meth problem that's so bad she's willing to risk her job, felony conviction, respect of her peers, husband, everything else," Hendren said. "It's so bad, she has a meth pipe in the office and meth in the office. That's how bold she was. She has this candy store, drugs missing. But it wasn't her. She's not like somebody that hasn't stolen before."

That it was a coincidence that the drug Greg used to kill himself "was odorless, colorless, soluble in water, lethal in small doses, and difficult to detect," and that it was synergistic with another drug in his system.

That it was a coincidence that Michael Robertson "is an expert, a genius, on fentanyl."

That Greg hid the packaging, container, syringe, or whatever he used to take the fentanyl. "People committing suicide don't hide that stuff," Hendren said. ". . . There's no reason to. They are going to be dead. . . . She didn't think they were going to [detect the] . . . fentanyl, and [she] wouldn't have to explain it."

That Greg was also able to spread the rose petals over himself in bed, tuck the photo under his pillow, and pull the comforter up to his neck, all before he took enough fentanyl to kill himself.

That Kristin was too frail to leave red marks on Greg's chest from CPR, but not so frail that she couldn't pull his 160-pound body off the bed and onto the floor.

That her father was wrong when he said Kristin told him Greg was clutching the wedding photo in his hands.

"You can see how much dad . . . wants to protect her," Hendren said. "That's understandable. . . . Gee, but she says, 'No, that's not what I said.' . . . In any event, it's behind his head, according to her, or [in] the crook of the neck. Somehow in the course of this, that photograph magically flies off when she pulls him off, lands down, and a little three-by-five photograph that's very thin props itself right up next to the head of the victim. That's beyond comprehension."

That it was a series of coincidences that she "loves roses, is infatuated with roses . . . sends them to her boyfriend, keeps cards that have roses in them, and that she bought a single rose at 12:41 P.M. on the day of her husband's death."

And that she "just happened to be mistaken" when she told Jerome and Bertrand that she went to Vons between 3 and 5 P.M. on the day Greg died.

"The evidence is compelling," he said.

Greg was gone, he said, but his "remnants" could still speak to the jury. His tissue, his blood, his urine, all the parts that "have those massive doses of fentanyl. And the remnants of his body are crying out for justice in this case."

Judge Thompson was watching Kristin while Hendren

delivered his argument. Up until then, he sensed that Kristin thought she was going to get off, because the jury would believe her story.

"It was clear that no matter how overwhelming the evidence became, she truly thought throughout the case that she could carry the day," Thompson recalled later. "She thought she was an equal match to Goldstein and would be able to convince one or more of the jurors that she had nothing to do with the case."

But as Hendren was talking, Thompson saw an expression on Kristin's face that, for the first time during the trial, reflected a realization that the prosecution had won.

"It was like the air going out of the balloon," he recalled. "You could just see it coming out of her. At that point in time, she knew the game was up."

Chapter 21

After Hendren finished his rebuttal on Thursday afternoon, the jury deliberated for one hour, then for three more on Friday, before leaving for a three-day weekend. They resumed at 9 A.M. on Tuesday, November 12.

At 2:40 P.M., word came down that the jury had reached a verdict, which would be announced at 3:30. A line formed quickly in the hallway, with more people than there were seats. Granted, it was over a three-day period with a weekend in between, but the jury had deliberated for only eight hours before reaching a verdict.

Constance and Ralph gripped their daughter's hands protectively as they walked as a block of Rossum solidarity toward the courtroom. This was the family's last-ditch effort to shield Kristin from the consequences of her addiction to methamphetamine, the relationship she ultimately chose over her parents, her husband, her lover, and her own future. Despite the hand-holding, Kristin looked frantic. The Rossums, including Brent and Pierce, entered the courtroom around 3:25 P.M. The de Villers family showed up shortly thereafter.

Marguerite Zandstra, Kristin's aunt, reached over the wooden railing of the gallery to embrace her frightened niece and rubbed Kristin's back to try to ease the obvious tension that wracked her body. Constance, too, hugged her daughter, and Ralph put his arm around her before they sat down to await the jury's decision.

Kristin stood up as Thompson emerged from his chambers. Shaky and unsteady on her feet, she rested her hands on the table to support her weight. The jurors filed in to the courtroom wearing a collectively somber expression, a marked contrast to the jovial camaraderie they'd displayed earlier in the trial, when they shared a chocolate cake.

As Thompson read the jury's verdict—that Kristin Rossum was found guilty of murder in the first degree, intentionally killing Gregory de Villers with poison—Kristin shook her head and began to gasp and cry. Ralph stared at the floor and brought his shaking hand to his forehead. Constance looked spent.

Thompson polled the jurors individually to confirm their decision.

"Yes," Juror #1 said softly. The other jurors concurred, speaking loudly and firmly. Yes. Yes. Yes. By then, Kristin was crying so hard, she appeared to be having trouble breathing.

Thompson announced that the sentencing hearing would be on December 12 at 2:30 P.M., until which time Kristin would be sent to the county jail without the ability to post bail. Frank Cordle, the bailiff, put handcuffs on Kristin's wrists and attached them to a chain around her waist. As he was leading her out of the courtroom through a secure rear exit, Kristin turned to look over her shoulder and locked eyes with her parents, pleadingly.

Thompson told the jurors they were under no obligation to discuss the case with anyone, but offered them an opportunity to meet with all the attorneys in a closed session after the hearing. None of them wanted to be interviewed by the group of reporters waiting in the hallway, so they snuck out of the courthouse through a back door. The de Villers and Rossum families declined interviews as well. To the continued chagrin of the media, Thompson announced that the gag order would remain in place until sentencing.

"The gag order is going to live longer than us," Loebig joked as he walked past the reporters in the hallway.

Some speculated that there was significance to the day the jury chose to announce its verdict. November 12 was Greg's birthday. He would have been twenty-nine.

Kristin was led out of the courthouse to a sheriff's cruiser waiting outside to take her back to Las Colinas. Inmates who had court appearances for lower-profile crimes that day were shuttled separately, by bus. Back at the jail, the inmates were expecting Kristin because they'd been watching her on the TV news. Kristin spent some time in protective custody in the A-2 housing unit again, where she cried for a day straight.

A week before her sentencing, a probation officer came to interview Kristin, a routine part of the process even though she was ineligible for parole. The officer's report illustrates that Kristin was still trying to elicit sympathy and offer new details about the events leading up to Greg's death.

Kristin said she told Greg on Thursday, November 2, about her plans to move out, which they continued to discuss over the weekend. Getting teary-eyed, Kristin told the probation officer that Greg went to bed early that Sunday night.

"That's the last time we talked," she said, pausing, "about moving out."

Kristin said she didn't know where Greg got the fentanyl or how he took it, but she theorized that he might have stolen some during one of their nighttime trips to her lab. Police found no evidence at the apartment that proved how he took the drugs, she said, because "there were two trash cans on the balcony that were not searched. There was a tumbler with clear liquid on the nightstand. They assumed it was water and did not test it."

She said that the Medical Examiner's Office hadn't audited its drug inventory in thirty-five years and that while fentanyl and some methamphetamine were missing, so were "lots of things." The lab had no "checks and balances," she said. "It was not secure."

Kristin acknowledged that she'd purchased a rose the day of her husband's death, but she came up with yet another story about its origins. She said it had been a custom for her and her husband to exchange roses when the other partner was feeling badly, but the rose she purchased that day was not red.

She said she'd relapsed about two weeks before Greg's death, but didn't know why.

"Looking back, I had no reason," she said. "I was planning to leave him. I was under stress. It was a bad habit."

"I still can't believe the jury convicted me," she told the probation officer, vowing to pursue every avenue available to appeal and exonerate herself. "We're going to keep fighting this."

If she did win an appeal, she said, she planned to earn a graduate degree in analytical chemistry so she could continue to work in the biotech industry.

"I want to have a family," she said. "That's it."

In an interview with the *Melbourne Herald Sun,* Michael told a reporter that his "roller-coaster ride" of fear and uncertainty had grown even bumpier since Kristin was convicted. He said he'd been living under the specter of possibility that

American authorities would charge him and attempt to extradite him for trial in the murder of Greg de Villers, a crime he said he did not commit. Michael's comments were republished in the *Union-Tribune*.

"For the past two years, every time my phone rings, I wonder what it might be, who it might be," he said. ". . . There were days when I planned just to get to the next weekend. I feel more uncertain now than I did a few months ago."

He expressed mixed emotions about the verdict in Kristin's trial, saying he hoped she wasn't wrongly convicted. "Having said that, I believe in fair punishment for a crime," he said. "If she did do it, then she should be punished."

He said he still couldn't believe that the Kristin he knew could have killed her husband, but he "had no knowledge or participation in the very sad events that led up to Greg's death. . . . I was not there. I don't know what happened over that weekend or that Monday to know if it was an accident, a suicide, or, as the court has found, a homicide."

Michael dismissed questions about the thirty-seven fentanyl articles found in his desk and the half dozen PowerPoint presentations on the drug found on his laptop, saying it was part of his job to collect such things.

"I probably had a hundred PowerPoint presentations on my computer and a thousand or more articles on every drug from A-Z, of which fentanyl would be one," he said.

Michael said prosecutors had had a "free run" with their conspiracy theory, and it hurt knowing he had no chance to defend himself. If prosecutors charged him and sought to extradite him, he said, he would urge Australian authorities to be objective and fair in evaluating the Americans' petition. He said the heavy media attention the case had drawn would make it "quite difficult" for him to receive a fair trial in San Diego.

* * *

Kristin's body language conveyed exhaustion and defeat as she was led into the courtroom on December 12, wearing a black pin-striped dress. She seemed far less put together than usual, with her hair pulled back loosely and little, if any, makeup. Her eyes were red, as if she'd been crying, and she dabbed at them with a tissue while the attorneys met in the judge's chambers.

The defense attorneys had filed a motion asking for a new trial, restating many of the reasons they outlined in the pre-trial motions that Thompson had rejected, including the request to move the trial out of San Diego County and to have Goldstein recused as prosecutor. They also said the judge failed to give instructions to the jury pointing out that Kristin didn't flee while she was out on bail.

Eriksen argued that by referring to Michael as Kristin's "unindicted coconspirator," the prosecution effectively precluded him from testifying for the defense by scaring him into thinking he'd be arrested if he returned to San Diego.

Goldstein noted that the government did not deport Michael, saying that it gave his passport back to him when he asked to return to Australia to care for his dying mother, and it never initiated extradition proceedings to bring him back as a material witness.

Eriksen pointed out that the U.S. extradition treaty with Australia has no mechanism to bring anyone back as a material witness; it only has one to extradite a suspect charged with a crime.

Thompson announced that his previous rulings would stand and rejected the request for a new trial. He said he didn't deny any of the defense's challenges to jurors they thought were biased by pretrial publicity, and he had no doubt that "a fair and impartial panel" had been seated.

Based on the verdict, Loebig said, there was only one

sentence the judge could order—life without the possibility of parole. Constance and Ralph Rossum did not want to speak, he said, but asked him to read a short statement: "We are horrified by the verdict and the sentence. Our innocent daughter has been wrongly convicted. We know Kristin did not murder Greg. We understand there are solid grounds for appeal and intend to pursue them vigorously. Please keep us all in your prayers."

Kristin, too, chose to remain silent rather than, as some defendants have been known to do, apologize or ask the court for mercy.

"Kristin doesn't feel that she is physically or emotionally able to say anything more," Loebig said.

Kristin cried while each member of the de Villers family stood up to read a gut-wrenching statement. Although Jerome, Bertrand, and Marie all testified during the trial, this was their first opportunity to freely express their thoughts and emotions. Because Yves was unable to come to the hearing, he'd asked Bertrand to deliver his remarks.

"You show no remorse and ask for no repentance, for any of your actions. You cried fake tears for Greg and real tears only for yourself. On the outside, you are a smart, beautiful young woman. On the inside, you are a lying, calculating, manipulating person that cares only about herself," Bertrand said, reading his father's words into the record.

Yves said Kristin, either alone or with someone else's help, killed his firstborn son, whom he had delivered himself. Greg had always been good to her and he tried to get her off drugs. But in return for Greg's love, Yves said, Kristin repaid him "in the worst imaginable way." She killed him. And then she lied about it.

Yves went on to say that Greg's death had deeply wounded Marie, tragically scarred Bertrand and Jerome, and prevented Yves from sleeping for three months. In fact, it still gave him nightmares. Yves closed by quoting from the Bible, saying he prayed God would pardon Kristin as "he shows generous patience, since he wants none to be lost but all to come to repentance."

Bertrand went on to read a lengthy heartfelt speech of his own, describing how his oldest brother had helped guide him through life. Greg was his compass, he said, and without him, he was having trouble "finding a direction."

"I feel alone and I feel scared and many times I actually don't know how to feel at all," he said.

Speaking directly to Kristin, Bertrand said it was senseless to try to describe what Greg meant to him, because she already knew what good he could do.

"You have your own personal proof of his abilities, for he saved you from the deepest valley of despair and lifted you to the highest peak of success that you will ever attain. When you reached the top, your reward for him was to push him off the cliff when he wasn't looking. . . . Greg's example to you was to love and trust you with all that he was and you used that against him."

While Greg chose hardship and sacrifice as the means to an end, Bertrand said, Kristin chose cowardice.

"Your betrayal was the most despicable act imaginable. Like Medea, you wielded your black magic to poison your husband. . . . Each day, I feel a void in my spirit like a black hole whose emptiness pulls and sucks at me from the inside. I hate that you have done this to me, and I hate that you have given me this unrelenting sadness to battle against all the time. I pray that God has mercy on you because I cannot. . . . Kristin, you are the only person in the world that I hate, and I do so with all of the strength and all of the feeling that I possess within me."

Jerome followed his brother by talking about his childhood and teenage memories, how much Greg had taught him about riding a bike and how to adjust and change his brakes. Greg was his adviser, he said, a friendly competitor, but all in all, a good person who enriched his life.

Then, in very open and honest terms, Jerome described the "huge emotional and psychological effects" of Greg's death, which affected him for months.

"I was angry and obsessed with finding the truth, so much so that I stayed up at night thinking and questioning everything over and over again. For months . . . I could not sleep or I would wake up in the middle the night. . . . I missed several weeks of work in lost productivity. . . . I became reclusive and tended toward social avoidance. . . . I shut people out. I became paranoid that the Rossums were plotting against my family. I was worried that someone might harm me, Bert, my mom, and girlfriend. At times I felt like I was being watched or followed. I even worried about my phones being tapped. My entire perspective on life changed. It became hard to trust anyone."

Jerome said he felt some closure to see Kristin going to prison, but it wouldn't bring back his brother.

"My family is still struggling and hurt. I don't understand why this happened to us. I do not want this to happen to anyone else. I want justice for Greg, and I want Kristin behind bars for the rest of her life. She is a danger to society."

Finally, in a thick French accent, Marie described the pain of her loss by drawing parallels between Greg's death and the September 11 terrorist attacks on the World Trade Center.

"By an act of terrorism so brutal and unthinkable, [Kristin] caused damage that cannot be rebuilt. Our beliefs were shattered; our hopes have been torn apart," she said.

"[Greg] treated life as a gift . . . always caring for people he loved. Greg paid the ultimate price for his goodness, because Kristin Rossum's poor choices and irresponsible judgments led to his murder. He could not save someone drowning

in turbulent waters mainly because this person was only thinking about surviving herself. As in most cases, the spouse is
the last one to know his spouse was cheating on him, and
often parents, who think they know their children, are the
last to recognize the truth about their children's involvement
with drugs."

The de Villers family would never be able to forget the
image of Greg dying in bed, she said, and would be "forever
shaken by [Kristin's] cold disrespect of life. She played a
dangerous game with feelings and perpetually tried to cover
up her secrets."

Marie said she wanted Kristin to receive the maximum
penalty, because only then would "human justice . . . be
levied."

As expected, Judge Thompson sentenced Kristin to life in
prison without the possibility of parole. He denied Kristin's
request to go free on $1.25 million bail while her appeals
were pending, saying she'd exhibited tendencies to run away
and remain incommunicado for periods of time. And, at long
last, he lifted the gag order.

Immediately following the sentencing, Eriksen walked
down the hallway to file papers to start the appeal process.

Goldstein, Hendren, and Agnew held a brief press conference in the Hall of Justice next door, which was attended by
at least one Australian journalist, whose focus was the future
for Michael Robertson and his possible extradition.

Agnew, Hendren, and Goldstein confirmed that Michael
was still under investigation in the murder of Greg de Villers,
but they said they couldn't comment further.

"We're happy to see that justice was done in this case,"
Goldstein said. "[A life sentence] is the next best thing in the
justice system that we can do. We can't bring Greg de Villers
back."

Goldstein said they were pleased that Kristin took the

stand because they knew they'd "get incriminating evidence that way." He also credited Jerome for his role in the case.

"Jerome de Villers is a good human being," he said. "He knew his brother better than anybody else. . . . He got the ball rolling."

As for the Rossums, he said, he didn't blame them for not seeking a more aggressive drug treatment program for Kristin.

"There's no other blame to allocate other than to the defendant," he said.

During the investigation and trial, he said, the Rossums were just trying to protect their daughter. There was nothing unique about a murderer's parents distorting the truth, he said, because "no one ever wants to believe their child is guilty."

"I see them also as victims of the defendant's narcissism," Goldstein said. "She was lying to them, too."

As Loebig walked back to his office after the hearing, he said Kristin was fearful of going to prison. After the verdict, her mood was "emotional but not irrational." She'd turned out to be more resilient than he would have anticipated.

"Her life is pretty much turned upside down," he said.

Loebig said he told her to "keep the faith" because convictions do get overturned. Personally, though, he said he would've liked to see Michael Robertson charged and the two of them tried together. In fact, he said, he'd still like to see Michael indicted.

In talking with jurors after the verdict, Loebig said he got the impression that they came to a guilty verdict because they simply didn't believe Kristin was telling the truth. A couple of them said that if Michael had also been on trial, they would have found him guilty as well.

Asked if he thought Kristin had lied to him, Loebig said, "Who knows?"

He said he didn't think Kristin would try to hurt herself in prison.

"She's intelligent enough to look at the half-full glass," he said, and the first thing she planned to do once she got to state prison was to explore the educational programs.

San Diego CityBEAT, a local alternative weekly paper, described the outcome of Kristin's sentencing hearing as follows: "Convicted killer-tweaker-hottie Kristin Rossum, who's just twenty-six, learned that she'll be spending the rest of her life in prison alongside all manner of scary, nasty women."

After Kristin's notoriety had died down at Las Colinas, she was moved out of protective custody in the A-2 housing unit and into the B unit, where three inmates shared each cell and slept in a triple-bunk bed. Because Kristin was about to be moved to the state prison system, jail officials saw no point in providing special protection to her anymore.

Inmates in the B unit, where she spent six days before being transferred to the women's prison in Chowchilla, were woken up at 4:30 each morning by a deputy's voice over a loudspeaker and ate their meals in a large dining room of picnic tables. Here, those in for the most serious crimes received the most respect—and Kristin certainly got her share. Corporal Erika Frierson heard that inmates were asking Kristin for her autograph.

"Here they brag about their charges and their case," Frierson said.

Kristin volunteered to do cleaning, sweeping, and mopping, which gave her special privileges to shower alone between the three regular shifts—8 to 10 A.M., 1 to 4 P.M., and 7 to 9 P.M. Frierson said some inmates—and she thought this was Rossum's motivation—sought these privileges to get attention. The shower areas, which are hung with partial curtains, are visible to the deputies who monitor the B unit from their station in a centrally located glass room, and also to the inmates, who can watch through their cell door windows.

"Long showers for some inmates are a big thing," Frierson said.

Central California Women's Facility in Chowchilla, one of the largest women's prisons in the United States, is about four miles off the freeway on a two-lane road surrounded by almond groves. CCWF, as it's called within the prison system, is also right across the street from another women's prison, Valley State Prison for Women. CCWF was built in 1990 to house about two thousand inmates. But by 2004 the prison's population had grown by nearly sixteen hundred inmates, and it housed more than it was designed to hold. All the women on California's death row, of which there were fourteen when Kristin arrived, were housed separately from the rest of the population.

Kristin was first taken to the reception center at CCWF, where she was held and evaluated for a couple of months.

Unless her conviction was overturned, Kristin would spend the rest of her life being identified by a series of numbers. As inmate W97094, she slept in the upper bunk of Bed #3 in Room 2 of a one-story cinder-block building called 516.

She shared her cell—a room 18 by 19.4 feet—with seven other high-security prisoners who had committed similar crimes. The dormlike room had two sinks, a toilet, and a shower, where inmates' feet, necks, and heads were always visible to guards watching over them.

The CCWF staff members were well aware that Kristin was coming. "We knew when we received her that she was high notoriety," prison spokesman Greg Schoonard said soon after she arrived. "We have not had any problems with Ms. Rossum."

With no chance for parole, Kristin was placed in a highly restrictive unit and would be confined there for the next five years. The only educational or vocational training she could receive in that time would be through the mail because she wasn't allowed to leave the unit, even to attend classes.

"It's going to be difficult for Kristin Rossum. She's obviously a very intelligent person," Schoonard said. "I mean, what kind of education program can a prison offer someone who already has a bachelor's of science degree?"

It isn't common for women to come to prison with such degrees, he said, but Kristin could certainly pursue a second one through the prison's Education Department. She, like the other inmates, had access to a full law library as well as a general library of books and magazines; any new books had to be sent directly from the vendor. The same went for television sets, which had to be made of clear plastic so the inmate couldn't hide any drugs in them. Kristin was not allowed access to the Internet, and she would never be allowed conjugal visits—even if she got married.

An inmate with a sentence of "life without [parole] is considered an escape risk," Schoonard said. "That's the reason we establish a very high custody level for them."

Kristin was initially assigned to a job as a porter—a prison term for janitor.

"It gives her something to do, although it's probably not what she's used to doing," Schoonard said. ". . . They really have to come up with a way to look at their life and find something positive to do with it, despite their circumstances."

Someday, he said, she might get a clerical or secretarial position, though there weren't as many of those available.

She also could be assigned to do kitchen cleanup, serve food, or join the yard crew, which maintained the grounds.

"We're not going to have her working in the lab here, that's for sure," he said.

By May 2004 Kristin had been assigned to yard crew. Her disciplinary history included what one prison spokeswoman characterized as "a list of small-time infractions." Because of privacy laws, prison officials said they were unable to discuss anything more about Kristin's behavior, health, or other activities—including whether she was attending Narcotics Anonymous meetings, which are held twice a week in California prisons.

Nearly three months after the sentencing, the investigation into Michael's possible involvement in Greg's murder was in high gear, so Hendren and Agnew flew to Melbourne with the hopes of interviewing Michael, his friends, and colleagues.

They met up with Detective Inspector Chris Enright of the Victoria state police's homicide unit, who was helping them try to gather enough evidence to charge Michael and start extradition proceedings. Hendren and Agnew interviewed a dozen of Michael's friends, family members, and former coworkers and also explored his training as a toxicologist at various local institutions.

But Michael wouldn't talk to Hendren and Agnew, referring them to his attorney. He also put out the word that he'd rather his friends remain tight-lipped, so the investigators weren't able to get enough information to charge him.

At the time, Agnew and Hendren would not comment on the pending investigation, but Enright said Michael was working in Rowville, a suburb of Melbourne "for some food company or company that analyzes chemical components or testing for food or consumables . . . nothing to do with toxicology or medical issues."

By the fall of 2004, Agnew said Michael and Nicole had divorced in 2001. When she and Hendren went to Australia, she said, Michael was working in a lab, but not in a director's position. She speculated that no reputable lab would hire him with the allegations still hanging over his head. Neither she nor Hendren would comment further.

In April 2003, Jerome de Villers was recognized at the Citizens of Courage luncheon, which the San Diego County District Attorney's Office put on at the U.S. Grant Hotel for about two hundred people. Originally billed as a luncheon for crime victims, the event had been renamed by the new district attorney, Bonnie Dumanis.

Listed first among the seven recipients on the program, Jerome was given an award for seeking justice for his brother's murder.

"Trying to figure out what happened to Greg consumed my life for a long time," Jerome said as he accepted the award. "It still does."

While Kristin was getting used to her new accommodations and the de Villers family was trying to move on with their lives, the case took an unexpected twist.

John Varnell was talking to his friends at Sunny's Donuts in Chula Vista one morning, when Kristin's case came up in conversation. Varnell is the first to admit that his memory for dates and times isn't so great, but when he retold the story in early 2004, he initially said he thought the conversation had occurred right after Kristin was sentenced. After several attempts to remember a more exact date, he couldn't really say for sure.

The *Union-Tribune* ran a foot-tall photo of Kristin on the front of the local section the day after her sentencing, with a headline that read "Rossum Gets Life" in big, black capital letters. The photo featured Kristin with her wrists handcuffed in front and linked to a thick silver chain around her waist, being led to the sheriff's cruiser by Thompson's bailiff, Frank Cordle. She looked pale, her eyes cast down at the sidewalk. Part of Yves's statement from the sentencing was quoted in big letters above the headline: "You show no remorse and asked no repentance for any of your actions."

Varnell hadn't been following the case in the newspaper or on TV, but he said he probably saw Kristin's picture that day. He remembered talking with his friends about the case one morning and then walking out of the donut shop behind a young blond woman who resembled Kristin. The woman was about twenty-six, slender, and cute and wore a ponytail, just as Kristin had during the trial. He told her she looked like the young woman in the paper. She said she'd heard that before.

"That little gal isn't guilty," he said.

The woman asked him to explain, and he told her about a series of phone calls he'd gotten from a man whose wife was having an affair with someone at work. After hearing his friends discuss the case, Varnell said he'd become convinced that the caller had been Greg de Villers and that Kristin Rossum was innocent.

"I talked him out of shooting that guy who was messing with his wife," Varnell told her.

Varnell's wife, Betty, was a Pentecostal minister with the Country Church in Chula Vista. The two of them joined the church more than forty years earlier, when Varnell was in the Navy. After leaving the military, Varnell drove an eighteen-wheeler for twenty-two years, until he retired about twenty-five years ago.

The Country Church was small, with fewer than one hundred members in the congregation, and the Varnells' home phone number is posted on the church sign, in case somebody needs guidance. Varnell often talked to callers when his wife was out.

The man called three days in a row, twice just before noon. The first time, Betty was at the store, so Varnell talked to him for about ten minutes. From the background noise, it sounded like the man was calling from a pay phone in a bar or restaurant.

"Are you the pastor?" the man asked.

"No, but my wife is," Varnell said.

The man asked if Varnell knew the Bible well, and after Varnell assured him he did, the man said his wife was messing around with some guy at work. The man said he had a gun, and he was going to "shoot the son of a bitch."

"Don't shoot him," Varnell recalled saying. "He's not worth shooting. You'll just go to jail, and he'll still have your woman."

Varnell told him a lot of marriages don't work. "You can't make people stay with you," he said.

Career women don't make good wives, the man said. The man seemed anxious to talk, but he didn't want to give Varnell his name. He wanted to know what the Bible said about killing somebody and about people who commit suicide, whether they could still go to heaven.

The man called again the next day and asked some of the same questions. This time, Varnell told him about how Judas betrayed Christ, how he threw down his money and hung himself. The man wanted to know what happened to Judas then.

"There's no guarantee Judas is in heaven," Varnell recalled saying.

"What if I just throw up a handful of rose petals and do myself in?" the man asked.

"I told you yesterday that won't cut it," Varnell said. "Taking your own life is an unpardonable sin. Thou shalt not kill. It's one of the Ten Commandments."

Varnell knew the man was crying out for help. Varnell could feel his pain.

The third time the man called, Varnell wasn't home, but he left a message on the answering machine. He said he appreciated Varnell's efforts to help him out, but he'd decided what he was going to do. Varnell didn't remember hearing any background noise on the message that last time. Just quiet.

Sometime later, Varnell mentioned to his wife that the man had never called back. But he said he didn't put the pieces together until he heard about Kristin's case at the donut shop. Varnell remembered that the man sounded like he was in his thirties, and the details—especially the rose petals—seemed to fit this case to a tee. He was sure the man was Greg de Villers and felt guilty that he hadn't been able to stop him from killing himself. He felt that he "kind of let him down."

"I really believe in my heart she didn't kill him," Varnell said. "She didn't have no reason to kill him."

The young woman from the donut shop, whose name he couldn't remember, told Varnell he ought to talk to Kristin's attorneys.

Eventually, two women came to his mobile home to take statements from him and his wife, and their statements became the basis of a writ of habeas corpus that Kristin's appellate attorney, Lynda Romero, filed in October 2003, asking for a new trial.

Romero wrote in the writ that in addition to this new evidence, Kristin also deserved a new trial because she had "ineffective assistance of counsel." She faulted Kristin's attorneys for a number of things, including failure to object to the prosecution's introduction of "false and misleading evidence" from Kristin's past. She also said the defense opened the door to "massive impeachment evidence" by calling Kristin's parents to the stand, where the prosecution trounced them on cross-examination.

"The defense called Mr. and Mrs. Rossum as witnesses, and they were thereafter literally converted into prosecution witnesses," Romero wrote. ". . . It is painfully clear that they struggled to avoid portraying [Kristin] as a liar, thief, and drug user capable of committing acts of violence. However, the prosecution was relentless and later told the jury the parents, too, were liars. . . . Even trial counsel attacked the parents' testimony when he said they were biased. . . . By the time [Kristin] took the stand, her credibility was completely demolished."

Romero also faulted the defense for failing to request a continuance when Eriksen got sick, which resulted in a closing argument by Loebig that "failed to discuss critical evidence and which contained statements that contained inferences [Kristin] was guilty," she wrote.

The court ruled that the writ would be consolidated with the criminal appeal, which was filed separately the same day.

Although Varnell signed an affidavit saying the caller told him he planned to use poison to commit suicide, Varnell later said the man never said that. Varnell also noted that his affidavit erroneously said the man called only twice, when it was actually three times.

Asked to use personal details from his life to better identify when the man called, Varnell tried but still couldn't remember exactly when it was. Nonetheless, Varnell was absolutely convinced that the caller was Greg de Villers. Sometimes, he said, he just knew things.

"I have no idea when it was, but I know it was him," Varnell said. "There's no doubt in my mind."

* * *

According to the writ, Varnell ran into the young blond woman at the donut shop on March 27, 2003, more than three months after the sentencing. And the woman's name was Kathleen Spratt.

The way Spratt told the story in the writ, she was leaving the shop when Varnell told her she looked just like a young woman who'd been convicted of murder. Because other people had told her she looked like Kristin Rossum, Spratt mentioned her name, and Varnell confirmed that Kristin was whom he was talking about. Spratt told a slightly different version than Varnell about his conversations with the caller.

"He was considering staging his suicide, poisoning himself, and throwing rose petals around his bed," Spratt said in the writ.

Later that morning Spratt felt compelled to e-mail Ralph Rossum at Claremont McKenna College.

"Mr. Rossum: I am sorry to track you down like this; I don't mean to invade your privacy. However, I had a very strange conversation this morning, and for reasons you will soon understand, I thought I should relate it to you," she wrote.

She explained that Varnell had received several calls from a man "who may have been Greg." She gave Ralph the particulars, saying Greg had died two days after the calls. If she hadn't known Varnell's wife from church, she told him, she would have "dismissed it as just a story."

"It is probably way too late for this to come out, but I wanted to try," she wrote, offering to help Ralph get in touch with Varnell.

In her signed statement, dated April 26, 2003, Spratt said

she was subsequently contacted by Romero but had never met or spoken to the Rossums.

Kristin's appeal asked for a reversal of her criminal conviction, contending that her due process rights had been violated.

Romero argued that the jury was given certain instructions it shouldn't have been, and not given others it should have been. For example, she said the jury should have been given a cautionary instruction that the extremely prejudicial evidence of Kristin's "prior drug use, possible thefts, and alleged extramarital affairs" had limited relevance.

She said the jury also shouldn't have been allowed to hear the prosecution present its conspiracy theory or call Michael "an uncharged, unindicted coconspirator" because there was no evidence that Kristin and Michael conspired to kill Greg, only that they were having an affair. The prosecution's claim that Kristin and Michael hatched their murder plan during a two-minute cell phone call the night before Greg died was "rank speculation" by the prosecution and "strains credibility," Romero wrote. Michael's denials about the affair to Lloyd Amborn "are not abnormal, do not constitute criminal behavior, and do not support a conspiracy." No one heard Kristin and Michael plotting or planning at any time before Greg's death, and all the notes, cards, and e-mails they wrote to each other reflected only their "heartfelt desires on the part of each other to be together."

On the updated *48 Hours* show that aired in February 2003, the Rossums complained that Kristin's defense attorneys had been disorganized and careless in presenting the case at trial.

"The prosecution went on for a total of seven and a half hours of closing arguments," Ralph said. "That was offset on the defense side by a meager one and a half-hour presentation."

After the trial, Kristin's friend and mentor, Frank Barnhart, communicated with Constance and Ralph Rossum by e-mail and wrote a number of letters to Kristin in prison.

He encouraged Kristin's parents not to rush through the appeal process simply because their daughter was behind bars. He suggested they take their time and do it right, proceeding with great caution.

"It's not like you get a lot of chances," he recalled saying while he was being deposed in February 2003 in the de Villers family's wrongful death lawsuit.

The Rossums told Barnhart in no uncertain terms that they believed the verdict was wrong, he said. They still firmly believed that Kristin was innocent, the victim of her husband's suicide.

In his letters to Kristin, Barnhart shared parts of the Bible with her, primarily Romans, chapters 1–12. Even though she was in prison, he still considered her a friend.

Part of Barnhart believed that if Kristin was guilty, Michael must have been involved as well. Sometimes the whole scenario looked to him as if it had been really well thought out, and other times, the exact opposite. But if it was a premeditated crime, he figured the best way to try to ensure they got away with it would be to try to control the toxicology testing.

"And when that gets taken away from you, you lose that trump card," Barnhart said.

If he could go back in time, Barnhart said, he wouldn't have agreed to get involved in the testing of Greg's remains. In fact, he wished he'd said he "wouldn't touch that with a ten-foot cattle prod."

In the end, Barnhart said, this case was a summation of so

many tragedies. A young man who had a good future was dead. An incredibly brilliant young lady took drugs, he said, went down "some wrong roads," and sacrificed her own future. Both families were victims, too. The de Villers family had lost a son and a brother, and Kristin's family had lost a daughter and a sister.

Chapter 22

On April 7, 2003, attorney John Gomez flew into the airport at Fresno, spent the night, and then drove the next morning to the women's prison in Chowchilla, about forty-five minutes north, to take Kristin's deposition in the civil case. Gomez worked for McClellan & Associates, which represented the de Villers family. Deborah McCarthy, the county's attorney, arrived separately, to ask her own questions.

Gomez was familiar with prisons. When he was in his early thirties and right out of Yale Law School, he'd mentored a male inmate in the California Youth Authority's Volunteers in the parole program at the coed facility in Camarillo. Later, in his career as an assistant U.S. attorney, he frequented federal prisons to interview witnesses.

Gomez spent less than an hour in the video arraignment room with Kristin, her attorney Walter Tribbey, McCarthy, a court reporter, and two prison guards.

Kristin wore her hair in a ponytail, a shirt with long blue sleeves and a white torso, a pair of jeans, and dark blue, prison-issued tennis shoes with no laces. She'd even put on a little lipstick for the occasion. Gomez figured it was a rare pleasure for her these days to be the center of attention. She seemed happy to have visitors, including Gomez, a tall man in his late thirties with dark hair and a kind face. He noticed that her hands were small, like a child's, and her waist seemed tiny. She was "five-foot nothing," and definitely not physically threatening. The skin on her face looked like it would be soft and warm if he touched it. She had a sweet way about her, a contradiction that struck him as odd given the circumstances. He felt puzzled by it, but even if he weren't married, he knew he'd be scared to be in a relationship with her. He wondered what had happened in her life to make her do something like poison her husband. She was so intelligent, so animated, and so attractive. She was an enchantress. What a waste, he thought.

Gomez was prepared for Kristin to take the Fifth Amendment on every question he and McCarthy asked. And he was right. Kristin's voice was composed, and she used dramatic pauses for effect. She knew what she was doing. Nonetheless, he felt compassionate toward her and wondered if she would stay and eat with the lawyers. He knew that any kind of diversion was a big deal for a prisoner. He thought she would even try to come to the civil trial if she could, just to get out the confined space for a while.

McCarthy went first. "Have you taken any medications or is there any reason that you can't give me your best testimony here this morning?" she asked.

"No," Kristin replied.

"What I want to talk about first is the extent of your knowledge of Gregory's relationship with his father, okay?"

"All right," Kristin said.

"Now, I've—there's been some testimony in this case that the relationship between Gregory and his father was a poor one, so what I want to ask you about this morning is what firsthand knowledge you have of that relationship."

Kristin's attorney began his first of many interjections. "I'm going to advise her not to answer that on the grounds of self-incrimination," Tribbey said.

Tribbey and McCarthy debated the extent to which Kristin could assert her Fifth Amendment privilege. McCarthy felt Kristin should answer because she'd already testified about these topics during the criminal trial.

Tribbey disagreed, saying he didn't want to open the door to incriminating areas, so he was going to continue to advise Kristin not to answer McCarthy's questions. McCarthy asked them, anyway, to put them on the record.

"Are you going to follow your attorney's instruction?" she asked Kristin.

"I am," Kristin said.

McCarthy asked about Greg's salary at Orbigen, contending that financial questions were relevant because they would affect the amount the jury might decide to award in damages. Kristin took the Fifth again.

Tribbey did allow Kristin to answer a couple of questions about Greg's education and his job and salary history before Orbigen.

"Do you have any knowledge that Gregory intended to pursue a degree beyond a bachelor's of science?" McCarthy asked.

"Yes," Kristin replied. "He was considering an advanced degree of some sort. Nothing concrete, just thinking toward the future. He was considering that as a possibility."

Kristin also asserted her Fifth Amendment privilege when asked about Greg's possible plans for supporting his mother, why Yves didn't attend the wedding, whether Yves was in Claremont the day of the wedding, how many times Kristin met with Yves during her relationship with Greg, her duties as a student worker at the Medical Examiner's Office, and the disclosure of her drug history on her job application to the Sheriff's Department.

"Having disclosed that information to the San Diego County Sheriff's Department, did you have any concern in, I believe, August of '99, that that information would, in turn, be conveyed to the Medical Examiner's Office?"

Tribbey told Kristin not to answer that, and not to discuss her relationship with Michael Robertson or her denial of it to Lloyd Amborn.

McCarthy warned that she might be back to ask more questions if the judge ruled that Kristin could not assert the privilege. Then, it was Gomez's turn.

"Is it true that you were told that among the conditions for your employment were that you would be subject to a preemployment drug test?" Gomez asked.

Tribbey told Kristin not to answer that, so she took the Fifth again. But like McCarthy, Gomez proceeded to ask his questions for the record.

"At that time in March 2000, were you using methamphetamines such that a drug screen would have shown?" he asked.

Tribbey pointed out that it's improper to call a witness, knowing she is going to assert the privilege, "just for purposes of making them do that in front of the jury or in front of a judge."

Gomez asked a number of other questions, all of which Kristin refused to answer. Had she communicated with Michael Robertson since she'd been in prison? Before Greg's death, had she and Michael discussed giving Greg fentanyl? Was Michael aware that she had given Greg fentanyl? Had he assisted her in any way in administering fentanyl to Greg?

Tribbey instructed Kristin not to answer questions about

ter assets, including potential book, movie, or other deals
that might come out of the case.

The deposition was over after Kristin refused to answer
McCarthy's last few questions about Yves's medical practice
in Thousand Oaks, her knowledge of Greg's drug use, and
his access to fentanyl.

The next day Gomez felt a bit sad as he thought about
Kristin spending the rest of her life in that place. But he
couldn't forget what Marie de Villers had told him. Greg had
been the rock of the family, and the pain of losing him was
never going to go away. It was like losing a finger, she said.
She had to learn to live without it.

Marie de Villers died on August 16, 2003, at the Los
Robles Hospital & Medical Center in Thousand Oaks, finally succumbing to the respiratory ailments she'd lived with
her entire life.

Her health had been getting progressively worse in recent
years. One night in 1998, Jerome came home after being out
with his buddies and didn't check his answering machine
messages until the next morning. After discovering that Marie
had called to tell him she wasn't well and wanted him to take
her to the hospital, Jerome immediately called her line, but it
was busy. He rushed over to her house, but she wasn't there.
She was in the hospital. The doctor said they'd found Marie
unconscious in her car in the hospital parking lot, with her
head on the horn. Knowing she was about to pass out, she'd
figured out a way to call for help. She was never the same
after that and had to remain on medication so that she could
breathe. After Greg's death, she seemed even weaker.

"Marie was a strong person emotionally; she was a frail
person physically," said Craig McClellan, her lead civil attorney. "She had definite beliefs, and she worried to death

about her kids. I mean they were the main thing in her life."

Originally, the civil lawsuit had been filed on behalf of Greg's parents and his estate. Because of some legal technicalities, Greg's brothers had to decide whether they wanted to continue to pursue the lawsuit after their mother's death. They did, and in forging ahead, they stepped into her shoes as the representative of Greg's estate so they would be able to collect punitive damages from the "survival action" portion of the lawsuit. That portion covers the period of time that Greg was being harmed up until he died.

The standard to win a conviction in criminal court is "beyond a reasonable doubt." In civil court, the standard is lower: all that is required is a "preponderance of evidence, which boils down to more likely than not," McClellan said. He said he wasn't sure why the District Attorney's Office had not charged Michael in Greg's death but acknowledged that perhaps the evidence wasn't strong enough to win a criminal conviction.

Since McClellan opened his private practice in 1987, he and his firm had won more than sixty-eight verdicts and settlements of $1 million or more in personal injury and product liability cases against companies such as Honda, Ford, and Porsche. McClellan, a snappy dresser with bright blue eyes, exuded a deep calm that reflected confidence and experience. He and his easygoing style were a contrast to Gomez, who emanated an ambitious energy and a desire to win. Gomez joined the firm in 2000, after working four years as a federal prosecutor. Together, they billed themselves as trial attorneys who would rather fight than settle a case. The firm was renamed McClellan & Gomez after the departure of Cindy Lane, the attorney who had worked intently on the forensic details of the de Villers case when the trial was scheduled to begin in October 2003. The civil trial was delayed indefinitely until Kristin's criminal appeal could be decided. If her conviction was overturned, McClellan would have to reprove her guilt.

Based on Michael's statements to police and evidence presented during Kristin's criminal trial, McClellan offered his theories on the events leading up to Greg's murder. Essentially, he contended that the county failed to take certain measures, which made it possible for Michael and Kristin to kill Greg.

First, McClellan said, the county allowed one of its managers to have an affair with a subordinate.

"They had a relationship that was mixed with sex and drugs," which resulted in a lack of supervision and drugs being stolen from the office, he said. Kristin stole the drugs, he said, but Michael probably helped her to "keep her happy. . . . to keep the love machine going. . . . He encouraged her to leave her husband and spend the holidays with [him]." Greg wasn't going anywhere, he said, so with Michael's expert knowledge and Kristin's own research, "they decide to get rid of him, and no one will notice the difference."

McClellan believed that Michael had to know that Kristin was smoking meth in the HPLC room and that all those drugs were missing, especially the fentanyl patches. Michael found meth in her desk, and surely, being an expert in illicit drugs, he would have recognized its effects on her.

McClellan also believed that Kristin began putting drugs in Greg's food or drinks a few days before he died. He said Michael and Kristin were probably discussing "how to do someone in," at least in general terms, while they were at the SOFT conference in early October 2000. And when Kristin called Michael at 9:02 P.M. Sunday night, November 5, he said, it was to tell him that she'd given Greg enough of the drug mixture to knock him out. It's possible, he said, that Kristin, with or without Michael's help, put fentanyl patches all over Greg and removed them before she called 911. But he believed that it was Michael, the more experienced toxicologist of the two, who administered the fatal dose of fentanyl by injection, taking the drug paraphernalia—vials, wrappers, syringes, or whatever—with him.

Kristin never mentioned fentanyl to the authorities, he said, because she knew the Medical Examiner's Office didn't test for the drug, and she didn't think they'd detect it in Greg's body. Michael gave interviews to police and hung around San Diego until May 2001 because he didn't think the authorities had enough evidence to prove he was involved. Plus, Michael thought they would believe his story.

McClellan said the county was at fault for allowing the love affair to continue even after Amborn confronted Michael about the rumors several times; failing to follow federal laws that regulate the safekeeping, inventory, and security of controlled substances by agencies or individuals to protect the public from the risk of injury; not doing background checks on its employees; failing to impose a policy requiring sister agencies to share personnel information—such as Kristin's self-admitted drug history and arrest; neglecting to keep track of illicit drugs and to ensure they were locked away properly; and putting a known drug user in charge of the log of drug standard vials used in toxicology testing.

"The county knew or should have known what was going on," McClellan said.

McClellan predicted that Kristin would attend the civil trial to try to convince the new jury that the previous jury was wrong. As for Michael, he said, he didn't have to come back for the trial and probably wouldn't, especially if he was scared he could be arrested.

Michael Robertson's civil attorney in San Diego said Kristin's criminal case and the allegations made against his client during her trial had effectively prevented Michael from returning to the United States to pursue his former career in forensic toxicology or even to take a vacation. In the summer of 2004, the attorney, Michael Gardiner, said his client was working in a related field in Australia, but he would not be more specific.

"I wouldn't want to come to a country that has told me they were going to arrest me," Gardiner said. "They've gone down to Australia to continue to investigate him. . . . [Goldstein] has said that prosecuting Michael was a priority. . . . They've put him in a legal limbo. They won't clear him. They won't say they're not going to prosecute him, but they don't do it, prosecute him or clear him. I think they should clear him."

The case "has forever changed his life, and it's made it impossible to pursue the livelihood, the dreams, and the career that he built during his entire professional life," Gardiner said. "He's been punished all right."

In September 2004, nearly two years after Kristin's conviction, District Attorney Bonnie Dumanis "respectfully declined" to be interviewed about Gardiner's claims. However, a Dumanis spokesman said the San Diego Police Department still had the case and had not officially asked the DA's office to begin the prosecution process against Michael Robertson.

"That just proves what I've said all along, they're keeping him in legal limbo," Gardiner responded when he heard the news. "They refuse to make a decision, in order to punish him without trying him."

Gardiner dismissed McClellan's theory outlining Michael's involvement in Greg's death as "an absolutely remarkable, preposterous work of fiction. I don't think it passes the smell test. I have a lot of trouble imagining that a jury will buy that Michael was involved in this."

Asked to explain why Michael Robertson would try to protect Kristin after Greg died, Gardiner said, "I think that the relationship itself is enough to explain frankly anything that needs explaining. If he's guilty of anything, he's guilty of having an affair with Kristin Rossum, and I think that's as far as it goes."

Gardiner declined to discuss specific aspects of McClellan's theory, saying, "I don't want to give credence to the theory by delving into the what-ifs on a lengthy chain in which every link is tenuous, and by the time you get to the end of it, it's crumbling."

As of late 2004, Senior Deputy County Counsel Deborah McCarthy had tried and failed to get the civil lawsuit dismissed against the county of San Diego.

"One young man is dead, a young woman will spend the rest of her life in prison, and two sets of parents have lost their children," McCarthy wrote in her request for summary judgment in 2003, which the judge rejected. "These are tragic facts. But the county of San Diego did not kill Greg de Villers and certainly had no idea he was in harm's way. To hold a public entity liable for the deliberate criminal act of an employee, that all parties agree was activity outside the course and scope of employment . . . would require this court to stretch current law beyond all recognition."

McCarthy, like Gardiner, had argued that the de Villers family did not meet the statute of limitations on injury claims. Within days of Greg's death, she said, Yves and Jerome de Villers suspected "something was not right," and within a month, they "suspected that Kristin and Michael were responsible and that the county, to some degree, was at fault."

She and Gardiner interpreted the judge's ruling in 2003 to mean that there was a factual dispute on this point and a jury should decide it. McClellan and Gomez contended that the judge had already done so.

McCarthy had also argued that the federal laws McClellan

said the county failed to follow could not serve as the basis for a civil lawsuit. In response to his other allegations, McCarthy said the county could not prohibit managers from getting involved with their subordinates, only from giving them performance evaluations. When Amborn learned of the rumored affair from Michael and Kristin's coworkers, she said, he had no actual proof, so he followed county policy by investigating and then counseling Michael and Kristin against such a relationship.

The only existing evidence that Michael knew of Kristin's drug use, she said, came from statements he made to police and Lloyd Amborn: Michael told police he'd learned from Kristin on the day Greg died that she was currently using drugs, and he told Amborn he'd known about her past drug use since June 2000. However, McCarthy added, none of Kristin's coworkers ever saw any signs of impaired performance.

As for McClellan's claim that sister agencies of the county should share information, she said, that is against the law.

"We can't change that and decide to do it differently," she said.

The Sheriff's Department promised confidentiality on its background checks because it wanted full disclosure, she said. But even if the Medical Examiner's Office had done a check on Kristin before hiring her as a student worker in 1997, her drug arrest from 1994 would not have been revealed, because all juvenile records are sealed. The DA's office was allowed access to Kristin's only because it was doing a criminal investigation.

Dan Anderson, Michael's forensic toxicologist friend from Los Angeles, said he had no idea whether Michael had anything to do with Greg de Villers's death.

"I can't even tell you," Anderson said in early 2004. "In my heart I want to say no way, but I just don't know."

But what he did know, he said, was that it was common for a toxicologist to have drugs on his desk and dozens of articles on drugs such as fentanyl in his filing cabinet. The community of forensic toxicologists was tightly knit, and Kristin, to his knowledge, was the first drug addict among them.

The last Anderson had heard from Michael, he was working as a scientist at a drug company in Australia.

"He said his life has been difficult to put back on track," Anderson said. "He's trying to get past this, but the DA's office isn't letting it happen."

To Anderson, the fact that Kristin didn't "roll on" Michael showed one of two things, either she was stupid and wanted to take the full rap because she was trying to protect him, or Michael didn't have anything to do with Greg's death.

Michael's former boss, Fredric Rieders, said he hadn't been following the case, but he still supported Michael, especially since he hadn't been charged with a crime.

"In my world we presume them to be innocent even when we are testifying for the convicting side of a case," Rieders said. "My own personal presumption is innocence until proven guilty. Suspicion very often is not much more than calumny."

Rieders said it would be much more difficult for a toxicologist to get away with murder by poison than a layperson because a toxicologist would be a more likely suspect.

"You never know what a person will do," he said, but from what he knew of Michael, he was "an honorable, decent person who is kind, who is a good colleague and a gentleman. I would never suspect him of [committing murder] . . . I certainly would never think of him as being a person who does evil things."

* * *

Soon after Kristin went to CCWF, Constance Rossum applied for an appointment to the prison's Inmate Family Council, where she became an inmate advocate. The ten-member panel met with the warden and her executive staff every other month to air grievances and foster communication between inmates' friends, family, and the institution. Other California prisons have similar panels.

This particular council was originally formed to deal with issues such as visiting hours, which were reduced from four to two days in January 2004 because of the state budget crisis. In some cases, visits were cut short so that other family members could have time with the inmates as well.

"That's one of the major complaints from the [council]," prison spokesman Kevin Kostecky said. "They tried to fight that, but this was direction we received from headquarters, and there's nothing that we can do about it."

Under Constance's leadership, he said, the council expanded its scope to deal with other issues, such as medical care. Constance had alleged that the prison doctors were inefficient, were not seeing to the inmates' needs, and were not giving inmates the same medications they had been prescribed on the outside.

At Christmas in 2003, the council was allowed to buy candy canes from an independent contractor and distributed them to the inmates. The council also donated used books, complained about delays in mail delivery, and asked for a vacant supervisor position to be reinstated for the hobby craft program.

The council tried to start a garden-planting project, but prison officials said they didn't have the space, a secure area, enough staff to oversee it, or the ability to monitor whether the vegetables had developed any health-related problems.

"We could be adding to our health problems here at the institution unknowingly and innocently," Kostecky said.

* * *

Eriksen predicted that Kristin's chances of appealing based on allegations of incompetent counsel were "slim to none." Such allegations had to be "pretty bad" to be upheld, he said, unless the defense's legal strategy was "completely out of bounds and substandard work." He said he respected Kristin's new attorney for raising the issue but did not agree with her position.

Loebig said he, too, saw the chance of Kristin's appeal being granted as "marginal."

"Almost anything in the case is going to be found harmless error, because none of it affects the importance and weight of evidence of fentanyl missing from where she worked and found in her husband where they lived," Loebig said. "And it's a straight line."

"Had she been believable, she wouldn't have been convicted," he said. To fare any better, he added, she should have had better answers for the hundreds of questions she was asked on cross-examination.

Eriksen said he saw no problem with the prosecution's pursuit of a conspiracy theory because there was enough evidence to at least suggest that such a conspiracy existed.

"My feeling is that if Kristin did poison Greg, then Michael could've been anything from an unwitting dupe who aided and abetted her, up to a full-fledged conspirator who assisted her and may have even administered the fatal dose," Eriksen said. "That's apparently how close the DA can get to Michael Robertson, or they would've charged him."

Unless police turned up new evidence that "suggests his participation in a murder," he said, then Michael should be safe.

But Loebig wasn't so sure, reiterating his belief that Michael should have been charged and tried as a codefendant.

"He was with her that morning. He was with her that after-noon, at the hospital, and soon after, when [Greg's] brothers arrived at the door," he said. He was the one who knew the most about fentanyl, and he, too, had access to those missing evidence envelopes. He and Kristin had "joint motive, op-portunity, and expertise."

Loebig acknowledged, however, that time was on Michael's side because it weakened the evidence, and with every pass-ing day, the likelihood of his being convicted diminished.

Even if the District Attorney were to decide to put Michael on trial, Loebig said, the jurors would see that "the defen-dant with the most access to the victim has [already] been convicted, and that [Kristin] would testify on Michael's be-half, so why go ahead with a lengthy, expensive trial that is not likely to end up with a unanimous guilty conviction?"

It was too late for Kristin to broker a deal to lessen her prison sentence by agreeing to testify against Michael, he said. The only way she could get out of prison would be if her ap-peal was granted and she was acquitted after a second trial, or if new evidence that exonerated her came to light.

But he still didn't think Michael should relax. Yet.

"He should be worried . . . particularly with Dumanis in office," he said. "She's very aggressive."

As of October 2004, the deadline had passed for Romero to ask to present an oral argument in Kristin's criminal ap-peal to the 4th District Court of Appeal, and the court had not asked Deputy Attorney General Niki Shaffer to respond to the writ. In Shaffer's response to Kristin's appeal, she argued that the jury was given proper instructions, including those related to the prosecution's conspiracy theory. But even if the court rejected that argument, she wrote, there was "ample evidence supporting the jury's probable conclusion that

[Kristin] was the direct and sole perpetrator of Greg's murder." She argued that any alleged errors made by Kristin's attorneys were "harmless."

Kristin and her family have maintained close contact through visits and letters.

"Mom, Dad, I love you so much," Kristin wrote in a letter her mother read on *48 Hours.*

"I'm able to tolerate this injustice because I know we have truth on our side, and I know that each day that passes is one closer to the day I can return home. Mom, Dad, there is not a moment that goes by that I don't miss you. You are always in my heart."

Constance and Ralph have written an article based on their knowledge of prison life, a piece titled "Rehabilitating Rehabilitation," which was published in *The World & I* in December 2003. The article closes with an argument for prison officials to establish a "culture of respect and civility" within institutions, noting that family members who "seek to intervene" on inmates' behalf "have reportedly been told to 'back off.'" Their bios in the article say they both serve on the Statewide Inmate Family Council of California, but nowhere do the Rossums mention that their daughter is in prison for murder.

Four years after his oldest brother's death, Bertrand de Villers was still dreaming about him once a week. In his dreams, Greg was still alive, and they were doing things together, things they used to do, things they might do now.

His mother was a different person after Greg's murder, he said, and he believed it contributed to her passing.

"You can imagine what it's like for a mother to lose a son," he said. "I think she did a remarkable job of getting through that, but ultimately it wore her out. I'm [glad] she doesn't have to struggle with it anymore."

Because Greg was murdered and the case became so high profile, Bertrand said, he and his family were never able to go through the normal grieving process. And, with books being written, TV documentaries being made, talk show hosts calling, and Kristin's appeal and the civil case pending, he said, "It's still not over."

"It made me a different person," he said. "I was naively trusting of people. I don't think I'm still like that anymore. I don't think things happen for a reason anymore."

Acknowledgments

As my first published book, this project has been a journey into new territory for me. I've learned a tremendous amount along the way, and I couldn't have done it without the help of the people who gave me information, advice, and emotional support.

First and foremost, I'd like to express my appreciation to all the people who spent time answering my endless questions and providing me with documents and other materials over the past three and a half years.

In particular, I send my deep gratitude to Craig McClellan, Cindy Lane, John Gomez, and their staff, who were always polite and helpful no matter how many times I called.

I give special thanks to Dan Goldstein, Laurie Agnew, and Dave Hendren for going over details of the investigation with me—after the gag order was lifted, of course. The same goes for Vic Eriksen, Alex Loebig, and Bob Petrachek.

I especially want to thank Jerome and Bertrand de Villers for undergoing gruelingly long interviews about painful and personal memories. Also thanks go to their father, Yves de Villers, for his recollections. You all helped me and readers of this book better understand Greg's memory.

My thanks go to Judge John Thompson for the interview and to his clerk, Sherry Blevins, and to Tom Murray for assisting me with the court order. I am also indebted to Sergeant Larry Horowitz and Dan Anderson for their lengthy interviews, and to Karen Maya, Bill Leger, Cathy Hamm, Sergeant Bob Jones, Niki Shaffer, Greg Schoonard, Erika Frierson, Mike Barletta, Harry Bonnell, and John Varnell for helping to fill in various parts of the story.

I owe much to John McCutchen for all the hours he spent helping me with photos, as well as for his other rat-killing and paint-stripping contributions.

A big thank-you also goes to Lorie Hearn and other editors at *The San Diego Union-Tribune* who gave me the opportunity to cover this story from beginning to end and then granted my leave, and to J. Harry Jones for stepping aside on his beat to let me step up. To my humble readers, Susan White, Kathy Glass, Jon Sidener, and Anne Dierickx, who, along with Hal Fuson, also helped me with much appreciated legal advice. To Gene Cubbison for the arraignment footage and for saving me that nice seat in the courtroom. To Joe Schneider for his searching efforts. And to all the family and friends who supported me through the summer of 2004—you know who you are even if your name doesn't show up on this page.

Finally, I wish to express my gratitude to my agent, Stephany Evans, for her patience and perseverance, and to the folks at Kensington for helping me to achieve a lifelong dream.

Author's Note

This book has been in the making since Kristin Rossum was arrested on June 25, 2001, the day I got a hold of the story and wouldn't let go. Because Kristin and her lover Michael Robertson had been fired by the county Medical Examiner's Office, my sources told me the story behind her arrest, and it immediately grabbed my attention. This was not only a story about a pretty and bright young woman who seemed to have everything going for her, but it also opened a door into a secretive county department that had been plagued by allegations of mismanagement. The more stories I wrote about the case, the more fascinated I became.

My aim in writing this complex tale was to make it come alive without taking sides, presenting evidence gathered by the defense and prosecution teams as well as details I uncovered myself. I tried to be as thorough as I could, cross-checking my research with as many sources as possible, so any errors are unintentional. I interviewed dozens of people involved in the case, many of them repeatedly, for as long as seven hours at a time. I also sat through virtually every one of Kristin's court appearances, read every document I could get my hands on, and combed through every box of evidence, reading every e-mail, card, letter, and journal entry, and inspecting all personal effects seized by the police.

In recreating scenes with dialogue, I tried to quote from as many official sources as I could, such as transcripts from the trial, police interviews, or taped conversations; police reports; sworn depositions; or other public documents, all of which I had to condense and edit to make the story flow. Frank Barnhart, for example, did not want to be interviewed, so I quoted the thoughts and statements he recalled during his deposition in the civil case. When I pulled statements from the interviews I started doing the day of Kristin's arrest, I generally tried to quote only the person who remembered saying the words, paraphrasing most if not all of the other people's comments. I relaxed that rule when I wrote about conversations between Kristin and her parents, which they relayed to me in interviews early on and then generally backed up in their court testimony. In rare situations where I felt dialogue was necessary to tell the story but couldn't check with other participants in the conversation, such as Kristin or the anonymous man who called John Varnell, the statements I recounted are based on at least one person's memory.

I interviewed Constance and Ralph Rossum a number of times before Judge Thompson instituted the gag order, but they chose not to cooperate with this book. I also interviewed Melissa Prager early on, but she, too, did not want to talk further for this book. I wrote Kristin twice asking for interviews but was rebuffed. I also asked Michael Robertson for interviews through his attorneys, and although he initially said he would cooperate, he later changed his mind. His criminal attorney, Chuck Goldberg, also decided not to respond to the outstanding allegations against his client. I was unable to interview Marie de Villers, who died in August 2003, but I was able to learn about her and her marriage from her sons and through her deposition from the civil case and her divorce filings. Yves de Villers, who lives in Monte Carlo, did not want to be interviewed but did answer some questions by e-mail.

Finally, for purposes of full disclosure, I want to tell readers why I have had such a strong interest in this story and why I believe I was able to bring a unique insight to it. First, I know what it's like to grow up in a family of academics, with all the pressures that entails. Like Kristin, I consider myself a perfectionist. Both of my parents have Ph.D.s and worked at San Diego State University while I was growing up, my father as an English professor and my mother as an administrator, eventually rising to dean of undergraduate affairs.

But perhaps more importantly, I was married to an alcoholic. My late husband, who died in April 1999, was a talented pension fund investment executive who, like Kristin, worked for the County of San Diego. He was an ambitious and emotional man, who, again like Kristin, seemed to have a bright future ahead of him. He managed to keep his alcoholism hidden from me and many other people before we got married. But his lies and his addiction, coupled with depression and the shame he felt about it all, cost him at least two jobs, three marriages, and ultimately, his own life. He committed suicide in a hotel room in Mexico a few days after I told him our relationship was over. I was scared of him and his demons when he drank, and I didn't want to become one of those murder-suicide statistics I'd read about so often in my own newspaper. Still, when I tried to help get him back into treatment one last time, he refused and ran away. He'd threatened to kill himself in the past and told me at least once that I'd helped stop him with stories I'd written about others' suicides, one of which earned me a Pulitzer Prize nomination. I was not surprised to learn that he'd finally carried out his threat. In fact, I was expecting the call, but that didn't make it any less traumatic when it finally came.

Yes, this book is a sexy story about a fatal love triangle, illicit drugs, adultery, addiction, and murder. But I hope people will also see it as a cautionary tale about how drugs can destroy not just one life, but many others in the process.

BOOK YOUR PLACE ON OUR WEBSITE AND MAKE THE READING CONNECTION!

We've created a customized website just for our very special readers, where you can get the inside scoop on everything that's going on with Zebra, Pinnacle and Kensington books.

When you come online, you'll have the exciting opportunity to:

- View covers of upcoming books
- Read sample chapters
- Learn about our future publishing schedule (listed by publication month *and author*)
- Find out when your favorite authors will be visiting a city near you
- Search for and order backlist books from our online catalog
- Check out author bios and background information
- Send e-mail to your favorite authors
- Meet the Kensington staff online
- Join us in weekly chats with authors, readers and other guests
- Get writing guidelines
- AND MUCH MORE!

Visit our website at
http://www.kensingtonbooks.com